Doug McAdam

Political Process and the Development of Black Insurgency 1930–1970

The University of Chicago Press
Chicago and London

Doug McAdam is an assistant professor in
the Sociology Department of the University
of Arizona. He is coauthor (with James Rule,
Linda Stearns, and David Uglow) of *The
Politics of Privacy*.

The University of Chicago Press, Chicago 60637
The University of Chicago Press, Ltd., London

Library of Congress Cataloging in Publication Data

McAdam, Doug.
   Political process and the development of Black
insurgency, 1930–1970

   Bibliography: p.
   Includes index
   1. Afro-Americans—Politics and suffrage.   2. Afro-
Americans—Civil rights.   3.   United States—Race rela-
tions.   I. Title.
E185.61.M475   305.8'96073   82-2712
ISBN 0-226-55551-8   AACR2

To Deidre, Don and Pat

Contents

Preface

Superficially this book can be traced to my involvement, while a graduate student at Stony Brook, in a larger study of social insurgency directed by Charles Perrow. After joining that project, I chose as my specific research interest the black movement. Therein lies another story. Why the black movement? At a more basic level, both this book and my choice of the black movement have their origins in the dramatic images of racial conflict that played across the television screen as I was growing up in California in the late 1950s and early 1960s. The fear, courage, exhilaration, eloquence, high moral purpose, and soaring oratory of the participants captivated me. The drama that was developing against the backdrop of such exotic—even foreign-sounding—locales as Plaquemine, Tuscaloosa, and Tuskegee engaged my attention far more than any Hollywood-manufactured story ever could.

That my image of the conflict was filtered through the medium of television insured wholesale misconceptions and misinformation on my part about the movement. Yet it also must be credited with instilling in me a fascination—more accurately, a fixation—for the movement that has only grown stronger in the course of this research. This project truly has been a labor of love. And through it all, the shadowy images—a burning bus, a clenched fist, a line of registrants in the rain—enlivened otherwise tedious research tasks. And if in the process I learned there was calculation behind the "soaring oratory" and an instrumental logic to the "high moral purpose" of the demonstrators, all the better. This knowledge fleshed out and deepened my appreciation for some of the great American heroes of our generation: the Fred Shuttlesworths, Ella Bakers, Lawrence Guyots, Bob Zellners, and Charles Sherrods.

Perhaps my only regret is that the elemental drama of those shadowy images and the extraordinary personal qualities of the participants are not adequately captured in a book that is of necessity purely academic in nature. Know, though, that those images inform every line; and those who served as the foot soldiers of the most important insurgent challenge of our times are there on every page. In a very real sense the book is dedicated to them. To them goes the first and most important acknowledgment of all. There are others, however, to whom I owe more specific debts of gratitude.

Singled out first for thanks are four persons who shaped the content of this work to an unusual extent. James Rule was a source of substantive insight and personal encouragement throughout the course of the project. Michael Schwartz offered as thoroughgoing, but ultimately reinforcing, critiques of my efforts as one could ever hope for. The same could be said of Charles Tilly, who contributed that rarest of academic commodities: a truly useful, constructive review. Finally, to Charles Perrow I owe a special debt of gratitude. Over the past seven years he has functioned as intellectual mentor, unsparing critic, and supportive colleague. The book is a tribute to his skill in all of these roles.

In addition to these four, a host of other colleagues have provided invaluable assistance at various stages of the project. At the risk of over-looking someone, I offer my gratitude to: John McCarthy, Gene Weinstein, Lois Horton, Anthony Hickey, Judith Tanur, Craig Jenkins, Kurt Lang, Peter Freitag, Robert Marcus, Gladys Rothbell, Peggy Gay, Arnold Anderson-Sherman, Dave McCaffrey, Victoria Rader, Carolyn Ellis, an anonymous reviewer, and the members of the Washington, D.C., Social Movements Seminar.

I would also like to acknowledge the kindness shown me by several movement scholars who willingly made available certain of their unpub-lished works and, in some cases, data for use in my research. To Neil Fligstein, Jo Freeman, Gary Marx, Paul Burstein, and Adrian F. Aveni go my thanks.

Finally, several thanks of a more personal nature are in order: to Aldon Morris for reinforcing my enthusiasm and deepening my appreciation of the topic; David Uglow for helping me maintain my sanity at various stages of the research; Claire Graham for first stimulating my interest in sociology; Joe Scimecca and the entire Sociology Department at George Mason University for creating the most genuinely warm, supportive, and productive academic environment I've ever been associated with. And finally, to Deidre McAdam for simply making it all worthwhile.

Introduction

In writing this book I was guided by four distinct objectives. For the sake of categorization, two of the objectives could be classified as theoretical, another as empirical, and the fourth as a marriage of theory and empirical analysis.

The principal theoretical goal of this work is to summarize and evaluate the current state of social movement theory within sociology. The 1960s saw a level of social movement activity in the United States unparalleled since the depression decade of the 1930s. Blacks, students, women, farm workers, and a variety of other groups struggled to effect basic changes in the political and economic structures of society as well as to redefine minority status. The political turbulence of the era, however, caught the social scientific community off guard, triggering a renewed interest in the study of social movements. A decade later, however, social movement theory remains a conceptual muddle. The various classical formulations that earlier dominated theorizing in the field—collective behavior, mass society, etc.—remain much in evidence.[1] These formulations, which emphasize the irrationality of movement participants and the discontinuity between "ordinary" political activity and movement behavior, must be seen as ideologically and substantively flawed.

Recent movement analysis has criticized the classical model on both substantive and theoretical grounds. The result of these efforts has been a systematic shift in attention from social-psychological to political and organizational determinants of movement development. The dominant theoretical perspective to emerge from this literature has been the resource mobilization model. In some hands, the perspective reads like little more than an organizer's manual on fund raising. A discernible model of movements, however, does emerge in the work of the model's more sophisticated proponents. Emphasizing the constancy of discontent/strain and the variability of resources, mobilization theorists have sought to account for the emergence and development of insurgency on the basis of this variability. That the model represents a marked improvement over the psychologism of the classical formulations is beyond dispute. At the same time, for reasons to be discussed later, the ultimate utility of the resource mobilization perspective must be questioned. As yet, however, the model has received very little empirical attention or, for that matter, critical comment, in general.

Building on the critiques of these two models, I propose to outline an alternative "political process" model of social movements. This alternative model seeks to explain insurgency on the basis of a favorable confluence of factors internal and external to the movement. Specifically, I will argue that the emergence of widespread protest activity is the result of a combination of expanding political opportunities and indigenous organization, as mediated through a crucial process of collective attribution. Over time, these same factors continue to shape the development of insurgency in consort with one additional factor: the shifting social-control response of other groups to the movement.

The second theoretical objective alluded to above concerns a standard topic for much social scientific—and indeed popular—speculation: power in America. It is my contention that all models of social movements imply adherence to a more general conception of institutionalized political power. Accordingly, one of my intentions will be to link the three models of social insurgency to the more general models of political power implicit in each.

This objective has its roots in my growing sense of dismay over the absence of any real dialogue between political scientists and sociologists working in the field of social movements. All too often sociologists discuss social movements without assessing their relationship to institutionalized political processes. There are, of course, exceptions (Gamson, 1975; Tilly, 1978), but I think it is fair to say that most movement scholars treat their subject matter as a bounded field of inquiry distinct from more general questions of political power.

On the other hand, political scientists have traditionally conceptualized power almost exclusively in institutional terms. Accordingly, they have failed to adequately explain or take account of the impact of social movements on the institutionalized political establishment. Certainly, one can cite exceptions to this rule such as Theodore Lowi's fine book, *The Politics of Disorder* (1971). Yet even here, a sociologist reading Lowi's book would be struck by the author's ignorance of the relevant sociological literature on social movements. This ignorance may result from the traditional conceptualization of social movements as an apolitical form of "collective behavior," a conceptualization that assigned the topic to social psychologists for study, leaving the field of "rational" (read institutionalized) politics to the political scientists. Whatever the origins of this separation, it remains, in my view, both an artificial and an unfortunate one. I agree with Gamson: "In place of the old duality of extremist politics and pluralist politics, there is simply politics. . . . Rebellion, in this view, is simply politics by other means. It is not some kind of irrational expression but is as instrumental in its nature as a lobbyist trying to get special favors for his group or a major political party conducting a presidential campaign'' (1975: 138–39).

It is time the links between institutionalized and insurgent politics were established and the insights from both sociology and political science brought to bear on a complete analysis of the topic of power in America. One aim of this volume, then, is to contribute to this emerging dialogue.

Distinct from these theoretical objectives is the empirical focus of the work. Quite simply, I hope to provide a more comprehensive empirical analysis of the black protest movement than has yet appeared in the literature. Much, of course, has already been written about the movement. That material generally falls into two categories: journalistic or impressionistic accounts of particular phases or campaigns during the movement (Brooks, 1974; Watters, 1971), or scholarly analyses of particular aspects of the movement (organizational structure, tactics, etc.). However, to my knowledge, no systematic scholarly treatment has yet been completed on the movement as a whole.

Besides the comprehensive focus of this analysis one other factor marks the perspective adopted here as distinctive. Virtually all other treatments of the black movement date its beginnings with either the Montgomery bus boycott of 1955–56 or the 1954 Supreme Court decision in the Brown case. Certainly these were landmark events. Nonetheless, to single them out serves, in my view, to obscure the less dramatic but ultimately more significant historical trends that shaped the prospects for later insurgency. Especially critical, I will argue, were several broad historical processes in the period from 1930 to 1954 that rendered the political establishment more vulnerable to black protest activity while also affording blacks the institutional strength to launch such a challenge. Later events such as the 1954 decision and the Montgomery bus boycott merely served as dramatic (though hardly insignificant) capstones to these processes.

While distinct, the theoretical and empirical foci discussed above should not be regarded as unrelated. Indeed, they come together in the fourth and final objective of this work. In the next three chapters I will discuss the aforementioned models of social movements. My intention in doing so is to analyze the existing classical and resource mobilization perspectives and to outline the alternative political process model. Ultimately, however, the analytic utility of these three models will be determined not on their abstract theoretic merits but on the basis of how well each accounts for particular social movements. Thus, my final objective will be, wherever possible, to assess the degree of "fit" between the empirical implications of these three perspectives and the data drawn from the analysis of the black movement.

It should be noted that this exercise in no way amounts to a rigorous "test" of these three models. Given the complexity of the processes under examination and the broad time frame adopted in this study, even a rough approximation to the experimental model of scientific inquiry is impossible. Instead, I am simply presenting evidence that I think allows for a comparative judgment of the empirical merits of these three models as regards the single example of insurgency analyzed here. My claims are modest, indeed. Nonetheless, on the basis of this evidence I will argue that the black movement is more consistent with a political-process than with a classical or resource-mobilization interpretation of insurgency.

The mix of these empirical and theoretical objectives is reflected in the structure of the book. Chapters 1 through 3 contain discussions and critiques of the three models of social movements mentioned earlier. The classical model is critically examined in Chapter 1. Resource mobilization comes in for the same treatment in Chapter 2. In Chapter 3 the political process model is outlined and proposed as an alternative to these two models. In Chapter 4 the empirical implications of all three models are discussed and outlined to afford a basis for the empirical analysis to follow. In Chapters 5 through 8 the focus is largely empirical, with each succeeding period in the development of the movement analyzed in chronological order. The period from 1876 to 1954 is discussed in Chapter 5 as a means of providing the reader with an understanding of the historical context out of which the movement developed. In Chapter 6 the crucial period (1955–60) of movement emergence and white reaction is analyzed. The period popularly conceived of as the heyday of civil rights protest, 1961–65, is the focus of attention in Chapter 7. Finally, in Chapter 8, the complex period from 1966 to 1970 is analyzed in an attempt to shed light on the much-neglected topic of movement decline. Chapter 9 presents a synthesis of the empirical findings and theoretical themes contained in the previous eight chapters. Specifically, the analytic utility of all three models of insurgency will be assessed in light of the study's empirical findings. In turn the practical implications of those findings for insurgency in contemporary America will also be discussed.

1 The Classical Model
of Social Movements
Examined

During the past twenty years the accuracy of the pluralist model as a description of the American political system has been increasingly questioned. Yet pluralism represents more than just a description of institutionalized politics in America. In addition, the model is important for what it implies about organized political activity that takes place *outside* the political system.

The pluralist view of social movements follows logically from the way the model characterizes institutionalized politics. The central tenet of the pluralist model is that, in America, political power is widely distributed between a host of competing groups rather than concentrated in the hands of any particular segment of society. Thus Dahl tells us that, in the United States, "Political power is pluralistic in the sense that there exist many different sets of leaders; each set has somewhat different objectives from the others, each has access to its own political resources, each is relatively independent of the others. There does not exist a single set of all-powerful leaders who are wholly agreed on their major goals and who have enough power to achieve their major goals" (1967: 188–89).

This wide distribution of power has favorable consequences for the political system. The absence of concentrated power is held to ensure the openness and responsiveness of the system and to inhibit the use of force or violence in dealing with political opponents. With regard to the openness of the system, Dahl writes that "whenever a group of people believe that they are adversely affected by national policies or are about to be, they generally have extensive opportunities for presenting their case and for negotiations that may produce a more acceptable alternative. In some cases, they may have enough power to delay, to obstruct, and even to veto the attempt to impose policies on them" (1967: 23). The implication is clear: groups may vary in the amount of power they wield, but no group exercises sufficient power to bar others from entrance into the political arena.

Once inside the arena, groups find that other organized contenders are attentive to their political interests. This responsiveness is again a product of the wide distribution of power characteristic of the pluralist system.

Groups simply lack the power to achieve their political goals without the help of other contenders. Instead, they must be constantly attuned to the goals and interests of other groups if they are to establish the coalitions that are held to be the key to success in a pluralist system.

Efficacious political interaction also requires that groups exercise tactical restraint in their dealings with other contenders. Any attempt to exercise coercive power over other groups is seen as a tactical mistake. Lacking disproportionate power, contenders are dependent on one another for the realization of their political goals. Thus, according to the pluralists, the exercise of force is tantamount to political suicide. A broad distribution of power, then, insures not only the openness and responsiveness of the system but its restrained character as well. "Because one center of power is set against another, power itself will be tamed, civilized, controlled and limited to decent human purposes, while coercion . . . will be reduced to a minimum" (Dahl, 1967: 24). In place of force and coercion, the system will "generate politicians who learn how to deal gently with opponents, who struggle endlessly in building and holding coalitions together . . . who seek compromises" (Dahl, 1967: 329).

If the pluralist portrait is accurate, how are we to explain social movements? Why would any group engaged in rational, self-interested political action ignore the advantages of such an open, responsive, gentlemanly political system? One possible explanation would be that the group in question had simply made a tactical mistake. Yet the regularity with which social movements occur makes it difficult to believe that, as a historical phenomenon, they represent little more than a consistent strategic error made by countless groups.[1] However, pluralist theory implies another logical answer to the question. Movement participants are simply not engaged in "rational, self-interested political action." Accordingly their departure from the "proper channels" is not seen as evidence of tactical stupidity so much as proof that the motives behind their actions are somehow distinct from those leading others to engage in "ordinary" politics. This answer represents the underlying assumption of the "classical" model of social movements.

The Classical Model

As referred to here, the classical theory of social movements is synonymous with a general causal model of social movements rather than with any particular version of that model. For analytic purposes, the following variations of the model have been subsumed under the general designation of classical theory: mass society, collective behavior, status inconsistency, rising expectations, relative deprivation, and Davies' J-curve theory of revolution. No claim is made that these models are interchangeable. Each possesses features that are unique to the model. However, the idiosyncratic components of each are relatively insignificant when compared to the consistency with which a general causal sequence (see fig. 1.1) is relied on in all versions of the model to account for the emergence of social movements. This sequence moves from the specification of some underlying structural weakness in society to a discussion of the disruptive psychological effect that this structural "strain" has on society. The sequence is held to be complete when the attendant psychological disturbance reaches the aggregate threshold required to produce a social movement.

Figure 1.1   Classical Model

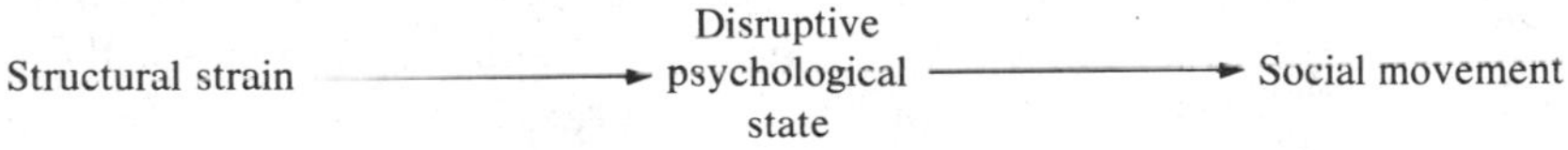

Structural strain ⟶ Disruptive psychological state ⟶ Social movement

The various versions of the classical model agree on this basic sequence and differ only in their conceptualization of the parts of the model. That is, a variety of antecedent structural strains have been held to be casually related to social movements through an equally wide range of disturbed "states of mind." To appreciate the similarities underlying these various formulations, it will help to review briefly a number of them.

Mass Society Theory

According to proponents of this model, the structural condition known as mass society is especially conducive to the rise of social movements.[2] "Mass society" refers to the absence of an extensive structure of intermediate groups through which people can be integrated into the political and social life of society. Social isolation is thus the structural prerequisite for social protest. The *proximate* causes of such activity, however, are the feelings of "alienation and anxiety" that are supposed to stem from social "atomization." Kornhauser tells us that "social atomization engenders strong feelings of alienation and anxiety, and therefore the disposition to engage in extreme behavior to escape from these tensions" (1959: 32). This sequence is diagramed in figure 1.2.

Figure 1.2   Mass Society

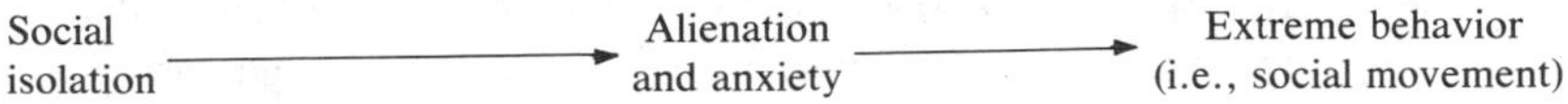

Social isolation ⟶ Alienation and anxiety ⟶ Extreme behavior (i.e., social movement)

Status Inconsistency

Another version of the classical model is status inconsistency (Broom, 1959; Laumann and Segal, 1971; Lenski, 1954).[3] Like "mass society," the term "status inconsistency" has both an objective and subjective referent. Objectively, status inconsistency refers to the discrepancy between a persons's rankings on a variety of status dimensions (e.g., education, income, occupation). If severe, we are told, this discrepancy can produce subjective tensions similar to those presumed to "afflict" the "atomized" individual. For some proponents of the model, these tensions are explainable by reference to the theory of cognitive dissonance. Geschwender, for example, writes: "Dissonance is an upsetting state and will produce tension for the individual. This tension will lead to an attempt to reduce dissonance by altering cognitions . . . or deleting old ones. Attempts to alter reality-based cognitions will involve attempting to change the real world. . . . The set of circumstances described by the 'status inconsistency' hypothesis would produce varying intensities of dissonance and dissonance-reducing behavior according to the degree of discrepancy between relevant status dimensions" (Geschwender, 1971b: 12, 15). As diagrammed in figure 1.3, status inconsistency is thus another variant of the basic causal sequence moving from structural strain, to discontent, to collective protest.

Figure 1.3   Status Inconsistency

Severe and widespread ——————▶ Cognitive ——————————————▶ Social
status inconsistency   dissonance   movements

Collective Behavior

Collective behavior is the most general of all the classical models.[4] As a result, it approximates the causal sequence outlined in figure 1.1 quite closely. The model, as proposed by such theorists as Smelser, Lang and Lang, and Turner and Killian, does not specify a particular condition, such as status inconsistency or atomization, as the presumed structural cause of social movements. Instead, any severe social strain can provide the necessary structural antecedent for movement emergence. Thus, according to Smelser, "some form of strain must be present if an episode of collective behavior is to occur. The more severe the strain, moreover, the more likely is such an episode to appear" (1962: 48). Such strains are the result of a disruption in the normal functioning of society. The precise form this disruption takes is not specified, but frequent mention is made of such processes as industrialization, urbanization, or a rapid rise in unemployment. Indeed, any significant social change is disruptive in nature and therefore facilitative of social insurgency. Joseph Gusfield captures the essence of this argument: "We describe social movements and collective action as responses to social change. To see them in this light emphasizes the disruptive and disturbing quality which new ideas, technologies, procedures, group migration, and intrusions can have for people" (1970: 9).

In this model, then, social change is the source of structural strain. Social change is described as stressful because it disrupts the normative order to which people are accustomed. Subjectively this disruption is experienced as "normative ambiguity," which we are told "excites feelings of anxiety, fantasy, hostility, etc." (Smelser, 1962: 11). Once again, the familiar causal sequence characteristic of the classical model is evident in the theory of collective behavior (see fig. 1.4).

Figure 1.4   Collective Behavior

System strain ─────────→ Normative ambiguity ─────────→ Social movements

These brief descriptions of various classical theories demonstrate that, despite superficial differences, the models are alike in positing a consistent explanation of social movements. Specifically, all versions of the classical model seem to share three points. First, social movements are seen as a collective reaction to some form of disruptive system strain. Such strain creates tensions which, when severe enough—when some aggregate "boiling" point or threshold is reached—trigger social insurgency. Movement emergence is thus analogous to, and as inexorable as, the process by which water boils.

Second, despite the emphasis on system strain, the classical model is more directly concerned with the psychological effect that the strain has on *individuals*. In this view, individual discontent, variously defined as anxiety, alienation, dissonance, etc., represents the immediate cause of movement emergence. Some versions of the model account for discontent on the basis of the personal malintegration of movement participants. Such accounts depict movement participants as anomic social isolates. However, even if one discounts hints of personal pathology, the individual remains, in empirical analysis, the object of research attention. As seen in these formulations the social movement is an emergent group of discontented individuals.

Third, in all versions of the classical model, the motivation for movement participation is held to be based not so much on the desire to attain political goals as on the need to manage the psychological tensions of a stressful social situation. The functions ascribed to movement participation by various classical theorists support this contention. For the mass

society theorist the movement offers the atomized individual the sense
of community he lacks in his everyday life (Arendt, 1951: 316–17; Kornhauser, 1959: 107–13; Selznick, 1970: 263–66). Selznick, for example,
notes that for individuals in mass society:

> The need to belong is unfulfilled; insecurity follows and, with it, anxiety-
> laden efforts to find a way back to status and function and to a sense
> of relationship with society.
>   But these efforts are compulsive: enforced by urgent psychological
> pressures, they result in distorted, pathological responses. There arises
> the phenomenon of the Ersatzgemeinschaft, the "substitute commu-
> nity," in which essentially unsatisfactory types of integration—most
> explicitly revealed in fascism—are leaned upon for sustenance (Selz-
> nick, 1970: 264).

Similarly, proponents of the status inconsistency model describe movement participation as one means by which the individual can reduce the
dissonance produced by his inconsistent statuses (Geschwender, 1971b:
11–16). In a more general sense, the same argument is advanced by collective behavior theorists. The social movement is effective not as political
action but as therapy. To be sure, movements are not unrelated to politics.
Indeed, Smelser explicitly tells us that they frequently represent a pre-
cursor to effective political action (1962: 73). Nonetheless, in themselves,
movements are little more than crude attempts to help the individual cope
with the "normative ambiguity" of a social system under strain. The
"therapeutic" basis of movement participation is implicitly acknowledged
by Smelser in his discussion of the "generalized beliefs" that underlie
collective behavior: "collective behavior is guided by various kinds of
beliefs. . . . These beliefs differ, however, from those which guide many
other types of behavior. They involve a belief in the existence of extraordinary forces—threats, conspiracies, etc.—which are at work in the universe.
They also involve an assessment of the extraordinary consequences which
will follow if the collective attempt to reconstitute social action is successful.
The beliefs on which collective behavior is based (we shall call them *generalized beliefs*) are thus akin to magical beliefs" (Smelser, 1962: 8).
    Movement participation is thus based on a set of unrealistic beliefs that
together function as a reassuring myth of the movement's power to resolve
the stressful situations confronting movement members. Movement participants, we are told, "endow themselves . . . with enormous power. . . .
Because of this exaggerated potency, adherents often see unlimited bliss
in the future if only the reforms are adopted. For if they are adopted, they
argue, the basis for threat, frustration, and discomfort will disappear"
(Smelser, 1962: 117). The message is clear: if the generalized beliefs on
which the movement is based represent an inaccurate assessment of the

political realities confronting the movement, it is only because they function on a *psychological* rather than a *political* level. The same can be said for the movement as a whole.

WEAKNESSES OF THE CLASSICAL MODEL

The classical model has not been without its critics (Aya, 1979; Currie and Skolnick, 1970; Gamson, 1975; Jenkins and Perrow, 1977; McCarthy and Zald, 1973; Oberschall, 1973; Rogin, 1967; Rule and Tilly, 1975; Schwartz, 1976; C. Tilly et al., 1975; Wilson and Orum, 1976). In general, I agree with the wide-ranging criticisms advanced in these works. The critique offered here, however, is limited to a discussion of the three general tenets discussed in the previous section.

Social Movements as a Response to Strain

The first proposition, that social movements are a reaction to system strain, is problematic because of the implicit assertion that there exists a simple one-to-one correspondence between strain and collective protest.[5] We are asked to believe that social movements occur as an inexorable response to a certain level of strain in society. But since widespread social insurgency is only an occasional phenomenon, we must conclude that system strain is also an aberrant social condition. The image is that of a normally stable social system disrupted only on occasion by the level of strain presumed to produce social insurgency. However, as others have argued, this view of society would appear to overstate the extent to which the social world is normally free of strain. The following passage by John Wilson represents an important corrective to the imagery of the classical model. "The lesson to be learned for the purposes of studying social movements is that since societies are rarely stable, in equilibrium, or without strain because change is constant, the forces which have the potential of producing social movements are always present in some degree. No great upheavals are needed to bring about the conditions conducive to the rise of social movements because certain tensions seem to be endemic to society" (Wilson, 1973: 55). If, as Wilson argues, the structural antecedents of social insurgency are "always present in some degree," then it becomes impossible to rely on them to explain the occurrence of what is a highly variable social phenomenon.[6] At best, system strain is a necessary, but insufficient, cause of social movements.

What is missing in the classical model is any discussion of the larger political context in which social insurgency occurs. Movements do not emerge in a vacuum. Rather, they are profoundly shaped by a wide range of environmental factors that condition both the objective possibilities for successful protest as well as the popular perception of insurgent prospects.

Both factors, as we will see, are important in the emergence of organized protest activity. Together they comprise what Leites and Wolf have termed "cost push" factors in the generation of a social movement (1970: 28). By overlooking these factors, classical theorists are guilty of suggesting that the absence of social insurgency is a simple product of low levels of strain and discontent in society. This ignores the distinct possibility that movements may die aborning, or not arise at all, because of repression or rational calculations based on the imbalance of power between insurgents and their opponents. As Schattschneider reminds us, "People are not likely to start a fight if they are certain that they are going to be severely penalized for their effort. In this situation repression may assume the guise of a false unanimity" (1960: 8).

In short, the insistence that strain is the root cause of social movements has resulted in an overly mechanistic model that conceives of social movements as the result of a fixed and linear process rather than as the interplay of both "cost push" and "demand pull" factors. In John Wilson's view, the classical model "is based on the assumption that circumstances establish predispositions in people who are in turn drawn toward certain outcomes—more specifically, that structural conditions 'push' people into protest groups. But social movements are not a simple knee-jerk response to social conditions" (1973: 90). Wilson is right. Social movements are not simply a "knee-jerk response" to system strain. Rather they emerge and develop as a product of the ongoing interaction of organized contenders within a shifting politico-economic environment. In Chapter 3 this theme will be developed more fully. For now, the important point is that social movements are not, as the classical theorists contend, only the product of factors endemic to the aggrieved population (alienation, dissonance, etc.). The characteristics and actions of opponents and allies, as well as those of movement groups, must be taken into consideration in accounting for any specific social movement. Insofar as classical theorists have failed to do so, they have diminished the utility of their model.

Individual Discontent as the Proximate Cause of Social Movements

While system strain, however defined, is seen by classical theorists as the structural cause of social movements, the motive force behind social insurgency remains some form of individual discontent. This atomistic focus is problematic on a number of counts.

Perhaps the most glaring weakness of this second proposition is the assertion that movement participants are distinguished from the average citizen by some abnormal psychological profile. In extreme versions of the model, nothing less than severe pathological traits are ascribed to movement participants (Hoffer, 1951; Lang and Lang, 1961: 275–89; Le Bon, 1960; McCormack, 1957). While perhaps effective as a means of discrediting one's political enemies, such formulations are less convincing as scientific accounts of social insurgency.[7] Maurice Pinard summarizes a number of objections to these models:

> we do not see how such political movements could recruit a disproportionately large number of people characterized by pathological personality traits. For one thing, deep psychological traits are not necessarily translated into political beliefs, and the connections of these two with political action is not as simple as is often implied. Moreover, people affected by these traits are relatively few in the general population. . . . If such a movement were to draw only on such people, it would be small indeed and very marginal (Pinard, 1971: 225).[8]

By other accounts, movement participants are not so much distinguished by personal pathology as social marginality. This is the case with status inconsistents who, by virtue of their discrepant rankings on a number of status dimensions, are held to be poorly integrated into society. Similarly, mass society theorists attribute movement participation to the "uprooted and atomized sections of the population" (Kornhauser, 1959: 47). However, impressive empirical evidence exists that seriously challenges the assumption of individual malintegration. Especially significant are the many studies that have actually found movement participants to be better integrated into their communities than nonparticipants. Two examples will serve to illustrate the point. A study of the personal characteristics of participants in a right wing group in the early 1960s showed members to have higher rates of organizational participation, as well as higher incomes, levels of education, and occupational prestige, than a comparable national sample (Wolfinger et al., 1964: 267–75). In a finding more relevant to this study, Anthony Orum discovered participation in black student-protest activity to be highly correlated with integration into the college community (1972: 48–50).[9]

The lack of supportive evidence is not the only empirical weakness associated with the claim that movement participants are social isolates. Indeed, attempts to document the more general proposition that participation in social insurgency is the product of particular psychological factors have traditionally foundered on a host of empirical/methodological deficiencies. For one thing, classical theorists have frequently inferred the presence of the presumed psychological state (alienation, dissonance, anxiety) from objective, rather than subjective, data. Thus, after comparing income, education, and occupational levels for whites and nonwhites, Geschwender concludes that, as an explanation for the emergence of the civil rights movement, " 'the Status Inconsistency Hypothesis' . . . is consistent with the data examined" (1971c: 40). His conclusion is empirically unwarranted, however. Wilson explains why:

Status inconsistency is intended to describe the processes and product of social interactions in which perceptions, impressions, and responses to these play an important part in influencing attitudes. Underlying the whole model is a motivational scheme in which the perception of certain attitudes helps produce certain outcomes. And yet nowhere is data presented on these motivations. Despite the fact that the model contains crucial social-psychological variables, reliance is made exclusively on objective indexes of inconsistency (John Wilson, 1973: 80).

More damning is the consistent failure of classical theorists to document an aggregate increase in the psychological condition they are attempting to measure. The various versions of the classical model rely for their explanatory power on just such an increase. The claim is that social movements arise *only* when a certain level of psychological strain or discontent is present. This threshold can be conceived either as an increase in the proportion of the aggrieved population "suffering" the specified psychological state, or as an increase in the intensity of the psychological stress associated with the condition. Either way, a demonstrated increase in the presumed causal condition remains a basic requirement of any reasonable test of the model. Unfortunately, this "basic requirement" has been almost universally ignored.[10] In summarizing the findings of relative deprivation studies, a proponent of the model has remarked: "practically all of these studies fail to measure [RD] relative deprivation . . . over a period of time" (Abeles, 1976: 123). Instead, the usual approach has been to measure the degree of relative deprivation (or any of the subjective states deemed significant) in a specified population at a given point in time. On the basis of this analysis, the conclusion is drawn that relative deprivation is causally related to the protest activity of the population in question. But nowhere have we been shown data reporting comparable levels of relative deprivation *over time*.[11] That a certain proportion of the population is judged to be relatively deprived (or alienated, status inconsistent, etc.) at any point in time is hardly surprising. Indeed, it is likely that the incidence of these psychological conditions is relatively constant over time. If so, reliance on them to account for social insurgency is problematic indeed.

Finally, classical theorists have generally been remiss in failing to measure the incidence of these psychological conditions among comparable samples of movement participants *and* nonparticipants. Geschwender, for example, in the study discussed above, based his support for the status inconsistency hypothesis on aggregate data for the entire nonwhite population of the United States. Such data, however, are inadequate to test the theory. Insofar as movement involvement is held to stem from status inconsistency, a comparison of the proportion of status inconsistents among movement participants *and nonparticipants* is required to assess the explanatory worth of the model. If we were provided with such a breakdown, we might very well find that the proportions were not significantly different. This was the case in one study that serves as a significant exception to the methodological weakness under discussion here. In his study of protest activity among black college students, Orum divided his sample into participants and nonparticipants and then compared the two groups on a variety of background variables. On the basis of this analysis, Orum concluded that: the "theory . . . of rising expectations, received no support in our data. Finally, the . . . interpretation, that the civil rights movement arose largely as a means of expressing the discontent of middle-class Negroes, who feel relatively deprived, was not confirmed" (1972: 45).

Orum's findings also illustrate what is perhaps the most serious, yet least acknowledged, weakness associated with the assertion that movements are a product of particular states of mind. While models based on personal pathology or social marginality have come under increasing fire, the same atomistic focus survives intact in less extreme formulations of the classical model. Geschwender illustrates this focus: "He [the Negro in America] is not experiencing as rapid a rate of occupational mobility as he feels he is entitled to. He is not receiving the economic rewards which he feels he has earned. As a result, he is becoming increasingly status inconsistent . . . He feels relatively deprived and unjustly so. Therefore, he revolts in order to correct the situation" (1971c: 42).

Social movements are thus viewed as emergent collections of discontented *individuals*. But to adopt this perspective requires that we ignore a fact that, on the surface, would appear to be obvious: social movements are *collective* phenomena. Obvious or not, classical theorists are guilty of failing to explain the collective basis of social insurgency. They offer no explanation of how individual psychological discontent is transformed into organized collective action. Rule and Tilly make the same point when they criticize Davies' variant of the classical model for treating "as automatic precisely what is most problematic about the development of revolutions: the transition from uncoordinated individual dissatisfactions to collective assaults on the holders of power" (1975: 50).

Quite simply, social movements would appear to be collective phenomena arising first among those segments of the aggrieved population that are sufficiently organized and possessed of the resources needed to sustain a protest campaign. Isolated individuals do not emerge, band together, and form movement groups. Rather, as numerous studies attest, it is within established interactional networks that social movements develop (Cameron, 1974; Freeman, 1973; Morris, 1979; Pinard, 1971; Shorter and

Tilly, 1974; C. Tilly et al., 1975). According to Shorter and Tilly, "individuals are not magically mobilized for participation in some group enterprise, regardless how angry, sullen, hostile or frustrated they may feel. Their aggression may be channeled to collective ends only through the coordinating, directing functions of an organization, be it formal or informal" (1974: 38).

Social Movements Represent a Psychological Rather than a Political Phenomenon

By claiming that the motive force behind movement participation is supplied by the disturbing effect of particular "states of mind," classical theorists are arguing that the proximate cause of social insurgency is psychological rather than political. Indeed, we are really being told that the movement as a whole is properly viewed as a psychological rather than a political phenomenon. Social movements are seen as collective attempts to manage or resolve the psychological tensions produced by system strain. In contrast, "ordinary," or institutionalized politics, is generally interpreted as rational group-action in pursuit of a substantive political goal. The contrast is clearly visible in the relationship that is presumed to exist, in each case, between the problem or strain to be resolved and the means taken to resolve it.

In the case of institutionalized politics, a straightforward relationship between the problem and the means of redress is assumed. If, for example, a government contract vital to the economic well-being of an area were terminated, we would expect the representatives of the affected constituency to initiate efforts to prevent the anticipated recession. Moreover, our interpretation of these efforts would, in most cases, be straightforward. In addition to ensuring their political survival, the elected officials of the region are simply trying to provide their constituents with jobs.

All of this may seem so obvious as to fail to merit such extensive attention. The important point is that classical theorists deny this straightforward link between problem and action when it comes to social movements. In fact, in some versions of the model, there is no logical connection whatsoever. Mass society theory provides us with such an example. According to proponents of the model, widespread isolation is the basic structural problem, or "strain," underlying social insurgency. The social movement is an attempt to resolve this problem, but it is, at best, an indirect attempt. To illustrate the point, let us return to our hypothetical example. Suppose, in addition to the institutionalized efforts of the area's elected officials, a protest movement emerged among workers who had lost their jobs as a result of the contract termination. How should we interpret their actions? Surely the workers are also engaged in instrumental political action designed to insure their means of livelihood. Not so, according to the mass society theorists. Quite apart from the movement's stated politico-economic goals, the primary motivation for participation remains psychological. Kornhauser is explicit on this point: "mass movements appeal to the unemployed on psychological . . . grounds, as ways of overcoming feelings of anxiety and futility, and of finding new solidarity and forms of activity" (1959: 167). Clearly, the functions ascribed to movements by Kornhauser are universal. That is, all movements offer their members a sense of community and an escape from the tensions engendered by social isolation. In this sense, movements are interchangeable. Following Kornhauser, the unemployed workers could as easily have solved their "problems" by joining a fundamentalist religious group as by engaging in political protest. The implication is clear: the political content of the movement is little more than a convenient justification for what is at root a psychological phenomenon.

We have thus come full circle. I began the chapter by raising the issue of the relationship between the pluralist view of the American political system and the classical model of social movements. At the heart of the issue was the puzzling question of how to account for social movements in the face of the open, responsive political system described by the pluralists. Why would any group engaged in rational political action ignore the benefits of this system in favor of noninstitutionalized forms of protest? The classical theorists have provided an answer to this question: movement participants are not engaged in rational political action. Instead, the rewards they seek are primarily psychological in nature. The logic is straightforward. Social movements represent an entirely different behavioral dynamic than ordinary political activity. The pluralist model, with its emphasis on compromise and rational bargaining, provides a convenient explanation for the latter. Social movements, on the other hand, are better left, in Gamson's paraphrase of the classical position, to "the social psychologist whose intellectual tools prepare him to better understand the irrational" (1975: 133).

This distinction, however, raises serious questions about the accuracy of the classical model. It suggests, for example, that we need not take seriously the political goals of the movement. The substantive demands voiced by participants are more accurately viewed as epiphenomenal since the movement is, at root, a vehicle by which members resolve or manage their interpsychic conflicts. According to Kornhauser: "Mass movements are not looking for pragmatic solutions to economic or any other kind of problem. If they were so oriented, their emotional fervor and chiliastic zeal . . . would not characterize the psychological tone of these movements. In order to account for this tone, we must look beyond economic interests to more deep-seated psychological tendencies'' (1959: 163).

And what of the participants in these movements? Are they aware of the "true" motivation behind their involvement? If not, how can we account for these periodic exercises in mass delusion? If, on the other hand, it is argued that they are aware, what explanation is there for their conscious rhetorical distortion of the "true" nature of the movement? Smelser offers the following explanation: "The striking feature of the protest movement is what Freud observed: it permits the expression of impulses that are normally repressed. . . . The efforts—sometimes conscious and sometimes unconscious—of leaders and adherents of a movement to create issues, to provoke authorities . . . would seem to be in part efforts to 'arrange' reality so as to 'justify' the expression of normally forbidden impulses in a setting which makes them appear less reprehensible to the participants'' (Smelser, 1973: 317).

The ideological implication of Smelser's account is none too flattering. At the same time, however, adherence to such a position makes it extremely difficult to explain the substantive impact social movements have had historically. If movement participants are motivated only by the desire to express "normally forbidden impulses," or to manage "feelings of anxiety and futility," then we would hardly expect social movements to be effective as social change vehicles. In fact, however, movements are, and always have been, an important impetus to sociopolitical change. The American colonists defeated the British on the strength of an organized insurgent movement. Mao, Lenin, Khomeini, and Castro all came to power as a result of similar movements. An incumbent president, Lyndon Johnson, was forced from office and this country's policy on Vietnam altered as a result of the antiwar movement. And through the collective protest efforts of blacks, the South's elaborate system of Jim Crow racism was dismantled in a matter of a decade. Are we to conclude that such significant historical processes were simply the unintended byproducts of a collective attempt at tension management? The argument is neither theoretically nor empirically convincing.

In summary, classical theorists posit a distinction between ordinary political behavior and social movements that is here regarded as false. At root, this distinction is based on an implicit acceptance of the pluralist model of the American political system. Michael Rogin has cut to the heart of the matter: "Having denied the importance of a problem of power, pluralists do not treat mass movements as rational forms of organization by constituencies that lack power. . . . since the pluralists stress that power is shared in a pluralist democracy, movements that do not accept the normal political techniques of that society must be dangerous and irrational'' (Rogin, 1967: 272–73). By assuming that all groups are capable of exercising influence through institutionalized means, the pluralists have made of social movements a behavioral phenomenon requiring "special" explanation. The classical theorists have, in turn, obliged with a host of such explanations based on any number of social psychological determinants. If, however, one rejects the pluralist model in favor of either an elite or Marxist view of power in America, the distinction between rational politics and social movements disappears.

2 Resource Mobilization
A Deficient Alternative

Elite theories of the American political system offer an implicit account of social movements considerably different from the one sketched in Chapter 1 (Bachrach and Baratz, 1973: 51–64; Domhoff, 1970; Mills, 1959; Prewitt and Stone, 1973). Such theories rest on the assumption that groups in society differ markedly in the amount of political power they wield. There may exist a political arena in America but it is not the teeming convention hall depicted by the pluralists, but rather a restricted club reserved for the wealthy and powerful. Only those with sufficient political capital need apply. Lacking such capital, most groups in American society have virtually no bargaining power with which to advance their collective interests. Instead, by virtue of their disproportionate control over the political arena, powerful groups are generally able to exclude the powerless with little fear of political reprisal.

Social movements, in this view, are not a form of irrational behavior but rather a tactical response to the harsh realities of a closed and coercive political system. Viewed in this light, the distinction between movement behavior and institutionalized politics disappears. Both should be seen as rational attempts to pursue collective interests. Differences in behavior between movement participants and institutionalized political actors are attributable, not to the cognitive or psychological inadequacies of the former, but to the different strategic problems confronting each.

Given the assumptions of the pluralist model, social psychological theories were required to explain the phenomenon of social movements. By contrast, elite models dictate a more political/organizational view of social movements. Specifically, the dynamic of interest is the process by which powerless groups attempt to mobilize sufficient political strength to bargain successfully with established polity members.

Consistent with this focus is the resource mobilization model. McCarthy and Zald (1973, 1977) were the first to use the term explicitly, but elements of the model are evident in the work of others (Aveni, 1977; Breton and Breton, 1969; Handler, 1978; Jenkins, 1975; Jenkins and Perrow, 1977; Leites and Wolf, 1970; Oberschall, 1973; James Q. Wilson, 1973).[1] Although these authors exhibit considerable theoretical variation, taken collectively, their work seems to embody two key tenets.[2]

First, the aggregate level of strain or discontent, which classical theorists presume to be of ultimate causal significance, is seen by proponents of the resource mobilization model as an insufficient cause of social movements. The claim is that discontent is more or less constant over time and thus inadequate as a full explanation of social movements: "rather than focusing on fluctuations in discontent to account for the emergence of insurgency, it seems more fruitful to assume that grievances are relatively constant and pervasive" (Jenkins and Perrow, 1977: 266).

What varies, "giving rise to insurgency, is the amount of social resources available to unorganized but aggrieved groups, making it possible to launch an organized demand for change" (Jenkins and Perrow, 1977: 250). At the most fundamental level, then, the generation of insurgency develops not from an aggregate rise in discontent but from a significant increase in the level of resources available to support collective protest activity. This basic scenario, however, leaves two crucial questions unanswered. First, what is the source of this "significant increase" in resources, and second, what determines that these resources will necessarily be employed in the service of insurgent aims? The second question will be discussed in more detail later. For now, it is enough simply to make the obvious point that resources do not dictate their use, people do. All too often however, a nonproblematic link between resources and insurgency is implied in the mobilization perspective.

On the source of the increased resources, some proponents of the model are vague, merely asserting that such an increase is essential to the generation of insurgency. The closest thing in the mobilization literature to a specific answer to the "source" question is that variations in the availability of resources are the product of shifting patterns of elite largess.

It is here that the imprint of elite theory on the mobilization perspective is perhaps most evident. Elite theorists depict society as characterized by a marked disparity in power between some societal elite, however defined, and the mass of ordinary citizens. The effect of this disparity is virtually to preclude most segments of society—especially the lower class—from any meaningful role in the exercise of political power. Consistent with this perspective, most proponents of the resource mobilization model reject the classical theorists' exclusive focus on the movement's mass base in favor of an analysis of the crucial role played by segments of the elite in the generation of insurgency. The claim seems to be that the movement's mass base, or "potential beneficiaries," to borrow a phrase from McCarthy and Zald, are too poor or politically powerless to generate a movement on their own: "one must realize that a negatively privileged minority is in a poor position to initiate a social protest movement through its own efforts alone" (Oberschall, 1973: 214). What is required is a healthy input of resources from some external "sponsor." Most frequently mentioned in this regard are church groups, foundations, organized labor, and the federal government. In short, most versions of the model contain an implicit assertion of powerlessness on the part of most segments of the population. Instead, the focus of research attention has been firmly fixed on powerful groups external to the movement's mass base, on the assumption that such groups are the crucial catalyst for social insurgency. Jenkins and Perrow have expressed these final two points nicely: "collective action is rarely a viable option because of lack of resources and the threat of repression. . . . When deprived groups do mobilize, it is due to the interjection of external resources" (1977: 251).

STRENGTHS OF THE MODEL

In general, the resource mobilization perspective can be seen as a reaction to the deficiencies of the classical model. As such, it is hard to overstate the powerful and positive impact that resource mobilization has had on the field of social movements. It has shifted the analytic focus of debate and research in such a way as to stimulate a rebirth of interest in a field that, under the dominance of the classical perspective, had become somewhat of an intellectual dead end.

More specifically, resource mobilization has proven to be a welcome departure from the earlier classical formulations for at least four reasons. First, and perhaps most important, the widespread acceptance of the perspective has served to redefine the basic ontological status of social movements within sociology. As noted earlier, social movements are seen, in the classical model, as psychological phenomena born of the efforts of discontented individuals to manage the interpsychic tensions endemic to their lives. By contrast, resource mobilization theorists describe social movements as collections of political actors dedicated to the advancement of their stated substantive goals. Thus, social movements are explicitly seen as political rather than psychological phenomena. In light of the myriad insurgent movements of the 1960s, as well as of a number of contemporary protest efforts, this shift seems clearly warranted.

Second, in describing social movements as a political phenomenon, resource mobilization theorists have attributed rationality to movement participants. The hints of pathology and irrationality implicit in the classical formulations have been replaced by the explicit assertion that movement behavior is informed by as much rationality as other forms of social action. In short, the resource mobilization perspective relies on no unique behavioral dynamic to explain collective protest. Social movements may be distinct from institutionalized political action, but this distinction owes more to the respective political positions of the groups involved than it does to any characteristic psychological profile of the individuals involved.[3]

Third, resource mobilization theorists have improved on the classical model by broadening the scope of their analysis to take account of the effect of external groups on the development of the movement. This is in contrast to the various classical theories which attribute sole causal importance to the aggregate level of discontent within the aggrieved population. This latter focus betrays a simplistic "demand-pull" view of social movements (Leites and Wolf, 1970). In contrast, Leites and Wolf stress the significance of "cost-push" factors in the generation of social insurgency. They explain the distinction as follows: "the hearts-and-minds analysis [classical model] focuses principal attention on the preferences, attitudes, and sympathies of the populace (demand), to the neglect of the opportunities and costs required to indulge these preferences" (1970: 29). According to most resource mobilization theorists, these "opportunities and costs" are, in large measure, structured by groups external to the movement. Accordingly, these groups command far more research attention in this perspective than in the classical model.

Finally, proponents of the resource mobilization model have alerted researchers to a seemingly obvious fact that has, nonetheless, been virtually ignored by classical theorists. While not necessarily synonymous with organizations, social movements would nonetheless seem to be dependent on some combination of formal and informal groups for their persistence and success. Movement groups, no less than other types of organizations, require a steady input of resources to survive over time. The ignorance of this fact by classical theorists reflects their failure to take seriously the movement as an ongoing political phenomenon. As long as the movement is seen as little more than a cathartic expression of the pent-up tensions of movement participants, no serious analysis of the resource requirements of movement organizations is required. By according legitimacy to a more explicitly organizational view of movements, resource mobilization theorists have redressed the long-standing neglect of this important topic and opened up a crucial area for further study.

The positive contributions of these theorists are as significant as they are numerous. Indeed, the resource mobilization approach provides a solid theoretical point of departure for the alternative model outlined in the next chapter. In the final analysis, however, the approach would seem to raise nearly as many questions as it resolves.

WEAKNESSES OF THE MODEL

To some extent, the weaknesses of the various versions of the mobilization model stem not so much from flaws inherent in the general perspective as from a general deficiency in the movement literature. There is, in fact, no widely accepted typology, within the field, to differentiate the diverse phenomena encountered in the empirical literature. To theorize about social movements, then, is to address activities ranging from peyote cults on the one hand to revolutions on the other, with all manner of variations arrayed in between. Obviously, no theory—save perhaps the most general and therefore least useful—can adequately account for such a diverse range of phenomena. The failure to distinguish between these various be- havioral forms has, in the view of one critic, "produced a field of study loosely joining phenomena so diverse as to defy explanation by any single theoretical framework. The desire for inclusiveness has had a high but hidden cost in theoretical specificity" (Traugott, 1978: 42).

What is needed are several theories specifically tailored to particular categories of action. Resource mobilization is such a theory: defensible when applied to a certain class of collective actions, inadequate as a general explanation of insurgency. The limits of the model's applicability stem from the failure of its proponents adequately to differentiate orga- nized change efforts generated by excluded groups and by established polity members. Tilly (1978) and Gamson (1975) define *members* as groups possessing sufficient politico-economic resources to insure that their in- terests are routinely taken into account in decision-making processes. Excluded groups, or *challengers*, to use Gamson's term, are groups whose interests are routinely "organized out" of institutionalized political de- liberations because of their lack of bargaining leverage. Because of this central difference, organized change efforts on the part of members and challengers are likely to differ in a number of crucial respects. Chief among these are the extensiveness of the changes sought, the change strategies employed, and the relationship of each to elite groups.

Change efforts generated by established polity members are likely to involve only limited reforms pursued exclusively through institutionalized channels. Moreover, because of the considerable bargaining power of the sponsoring group(s), as well as the limited goals sought, such efforts will usually receive considerable support from other polity members. In gen- eral, it is these kinds of "top-down" reform efforts that proponents of the mobilization perspective have used to illustrate their model. McCarthy and Zald illustrate the beneficial effects of elite support by reference to such organizations as The Citizens' Board of Inquiry into Hunger and Malnutrition in the United States, the National Council of Senior Citizens for Health Care through Social Security, Common Cause, and the various organizational offshoots of Ralph Nader's consumer-rights campaign (McCarthy and Zald, 1973: 21–22). In regard to such groups, the McCarthy-Zald version of the resource mobilization model affords a useful framework for analysis. The real question is whether it is defensible to call such groups social movements in the first place. Without discounting the significance of these phenomena, such groups would seem to resemble public interest lobbies (Common Cause) or formal interest groups (Sierra Club) rather than social movements. Certainly, their broad links to the centers of decision-making power and their heavy, if not exclusive, reliance on institutionalized change strategies mark them as different phenomena than social movements popularly conceived. The latter term I would reserve for those organized efforts, on the part of excluded groups, to promote or resist changes in the structure of society that involve recourse to noninstitutional forms of political participation. It is in regard to this class of collective actions that the above version of the resource mobilization model is found wanting. In particular, proponents of the model offer descriptions of (a) the relationship of elite groups to social movements, (b) the insurgent capabilities of excluded groups, (c) resources, and (d) the role of discontent in the generation of social insurgency that are regarded here as problematic when applied to the broad class of movements subsumed under the definition proposed above.

Elite Involvement in Social Movements

Proponents of the resource mobilization model suggest, by implication, that elite institutions provide insurgent groups with resources in the absence of indigenous pressure to do so. The movement's mass base, it will be recalled, is seen as virtually impotent as a result of its overwhelming poverty and political powerlessness. Incapable of exerting pressure on its own behalf, it must await facilitative action on the part of external sponsors. We are left to conclude that elite funding sources (foundations, government agencies, etc.) are willing, even aggressive, sponsors of social insurgency.

Given the examples proponents of the model have relied upon to illustrate the perspective, it is not surprising they have reached this conclusion. We would expect change efforts organized by established polity members often to benefit from elite involvement. In the first place, the traditional political resources mobilized by such efforts are enough to insure the receptivity of elite groups. This is not to say that all components of the elite will aggressively support such efforts, only that the political wherewithall they command grants them routine access to centers of power normally closed to challengers. Second, insofar as these are elite-generated reform efforts, they pose no threat to the established structure of polity membership. Finally, the more enlightened members of the elite are likely to recognize that such efforts function ultimately to strengthen, rather than challenge, the status quo. Not only are they likely to diffuse indigenous discontent by assuring the public that "something is being done" about the problem in question, but they also serve to confine change efforts to institutionalized channels, thus preserving member control of the process. When viewed in this light, top-down reform efforts may be seen by members as necessary societal tinkering to prevent major political disruption. For all these reasons, then, various components of the elite may choose to support member-generated reform activities. When we move, however, to a discussion of insurgent efforts initiated by excluded groups, the accuracy of this version of the mobilization perspective must be increasingly questioned.

As defined earlier, *all* social movements pose a threat to existing institutional arrangements in society. The basis of this threat is only partially a function of the substantive goals of the movement. Indeed, the stated aims of a movement are often no more radical than those embodied in elite-sponsored reform efforts. What marks social movements as inherently threatening is their implicit challenge to the established structure of polity membership and their willingness to bypass institutionalized political channels. Emerging, as they do, among excluded groups, social movements embody an implicit demand for more influence in political decision-making. This raises the spectre of a restructuring of polity membership, a prospect that is anathema to all components of the elite. When this demand is coupled with a departure from "proper channels," the threat is magnified all the more. For it is within such channels that the power disparity between members and challengers is greatest. In effect, "proper channels" afford members the means to monitor and control any substantive threat to their interests. Moreover, they are able to do so without recourse to more costly control strategies (i.e., violence) that might call the legitimacy of their actions into question. Accordingly, deviation from these channels renders the contol of insurgent challenges both costlier and more difficult.

These observations carry with them the implicit conviction that elite involvement in social protest is not as willing as some resource mobilization theorists suggest. In the face of the substantive and strategic threats posed by movements, it is unlikely that polity members would act aggressively to promote insurgent challenges. Rather, elite involvement would seem to occur only as a response to the threat posed by the generation of a mass-based social movement. When faced with such an indigenous challenge, members manifest a wide range of responses depending on the degree to which the movement threatens their interests. If the threat is severe enough, the various components of the elite may well be turned into a unified opposition intent on suppressing the movement by whatever means necessary. However, even in the case of less threatening movements, member response typically consists of a two-pronged strategy that combines attempts to contain the more threatening aspects of the movement with efforts to exploit the emerging conflict in a fashion consistent with the members' own political interests. Given this typical response to insurgency, elite involvement in social movements is not likely to benefit insurgents. Here again, we find ourselves at odds with the central thrust of certain versions of the mobilization perspective.

To judge from the writing of some of the model's proponents, we would be justified in concluding that elite involvement in social protest generally has the effect of facilitating insurgency. McCarthy and Zald, for instance, seek to explain the full flowering of protest activity in the 1960s largely on the basis of an increase in available funding opportunities on the part of external support groups (1973). Similarly, Jenkins and Perrow argue that the key to success in the farm workers movement was the "massive outpouring of support, especially from liberals and organized labor" (1977: 264). That elite involvement may prove beneficial for certain movements, or at various times in the case of others, may well be true. Resource mobilization theorists are not to be faulted for pointing to such instances. They are open to criticism, however, for failing to place these examples in the context of the broader range of possible outcomes of elite/movement interaction.

What is overlooked is the distinct possibility that elite involvement in social protest may more often contribute to the demise of a movement than to its success. Nor is this only true in the case of radical movements that "succeed" in uniting all components of the elite in open opposition to the movement. Even in the case of moderate reform movements, ostensibly supportive elite/movement linkages are likely to prove detrimental to insurgency in the long run. This is so for at least three reasons. The first concerns the control granted elite groups as a result of resources supplied to the movement.

In a provocative article, Adrian Aveni has described support linkages between movement organizations and elite groups as a type of exchange relationship (1977).[4] This view is consistent with the one advanced here. If they are to survive over time, movement organizations, no less than other types of organizations, must routinize resource input as a hedge against the uncertainties of the environment they confront (Allen, 1974). The establishment of elite linkages is one way of doing this.[5] At the same time, however, the establishment of such linkages grants considerable leverage to groups whose interests are clearly distinct from those of insurgents. Like all exchange relationships, then, elite/movement linkages reflect a trade-off between benefits obtained and costs incurred. "Costs," in this case, refer to the efforts that must be expended by insurgents to balance the conflicting demands of movement goals with the interests of their elite benefactors. Should either be overemphasized, the movement organization runs the distinct risk of cooptation on the one hand or dissolution on the other.

Co-optation can occur either in advance of elite support, as the organization seeks to modify its operation in such a way as to make itself "acceptable" to elite sponsors, or after receipt of support, as a condition of continued backing. Perhaps the most damaging outcome of co-optation is the channeling of potentially disruptive protest into institutionalized channels. In such instances, elite support is offered as an inducement to insurgents to pursue movement goals through normal political means. If successful, such efforts usually have the effect of rendering the movement impotent by confining it to the forms of "participation without power" (Alford and Friedland, 1975) that prompted insurgents to abandon "normal" political channels in the first place.

Ultimately, of course, the determination of whether resource benefits outweigh the substantive modifications required for receipt of support depends on the particular circumstances of the exchange as well as on the political bias of the observer. At the very least, it should be obvious that such linkages involve the distinct possibility that movement organizations will cease to be an effective force for social change and instead become little more than an appendage of the sponsoring organization. As Jenkins puts it: "Given the instability of the resources supporting such organizations and their high level of dependence on economic and political elites, such organizations are virtual chameleons, changing tactics and programs to suit the whims of their sponsors and, in many cases, functioning as a cooptative mechanism for siphoning off movement leadership into more moderate, less disruptive reform efforts" (Jenkins, 1981: 135).

If co-optation results from an overemphasis on the cultivation or retention of elite support, neglect of that same goal can have equally disastrous consequences. "Irresponsible actions" (as adjudged by the standards of the sponsoring institution) can readily lead to the disaffection of elite sponsors and the ultimate withdrawal of support. Summarizing the results of his study of a New York-based, government-supported community action organization, Helfgot provides a vivid example of this danger: "From the MFY [Mobilization for Youth] experience it appears that government-sponsored social change efforts may be permitted to exist only as long as they remain ineffectual. Once a potential for change in power relationships becomes manifest, support is quickly revoked" (1974: 490). Donovan's account of the federal government's War on Poverty program includes a similar example of funding cutbacks for a local OEO-sponsored group that came to be seen as too "radical" by program administrators (1973: 85–87). These examples illustrate the special danger inherent in the establishment of elite ties. Cultivation of such links is likely to divert energies from the alternative sources of support that would serve as a hedge against the vagaries of elite sponsorship. Moreover, having established and structured their operation on the basis of those same links, insurgents will be unlikely to feel motivated to seek additional sources of support. Thus, the cultivation of elite linkages frequently results in the development of an exclusive dependence on external support. Dependence, even on the most lucrative and seemingly stable funding source, leaves the organization in a highly vulnerable position should that support be withdrawn. And given the latent conflict of interest that defines challenger/member relations, the withdrawal of elite support must always be counted a distinct possibility.

In light of the twin dangers of co-optation and the withdrawal of elite support, the assessment, by various mobilization theorists, of the effect of elite involvement on the development of social movements must be seen as overly optimistic. That movement organizations require a routinized flow of resources is beyond question. That elite groups may provide a nonproblematic source of such support in rare instances is also acknowledged. At the same time, the cultivation of external support linkages carries with it enormous risks that tend to be underemphasized or ignored by resource mobilization theorists.

The Importance of the Mass Base

A second major weakness of the resource mobilization model concerns the consistent failure by many of its proponents to acknowledge the political capabilities of the movement's mass base. If, in its account of the generation of social insurgency, the model grants too much importance to elite institutions, it grants too little to the aggrieved population. Indeed, these two aspects of the model are clearly linked. The importance of elite support is magnified, in the resource mobilization model, by the political impotence ascribed to the mass base. In effect, we are told, without such support social movements are highly unlikely. In the words of Jenkins and Perrow: "discontent is ever-present for deprived groups, but . . . collective action is rarely a viable option because of lack of resources and the threat of repression. . . . When deprived groups do mobilize, it is due to the interjection of external resources" (1977: 251). Their conclusion is clear: in the case of deprived groups, the aggrieved population is usually incapable of generating a social movement on its own.

The political impotence ascribed to these deprived groups stems, presumably, from two factors. First, as Jenkins and Perrow assert, such groups lack the organizational resources needed to generate and sustain social insurgency. Second, these groups are handicapped by their lack of such traditional political resources as votes, money for campaign contributions, etc. Lacking these conventional political resources, deprived groups are unable to exert the leverage that would enable them to bargain effectively in institutional forums. However, in regard to both these factors, the claims of the resource mobilization theorists are found wanting.

I suggest that, except for the most deprived segments of society, aggrieved groups possess the ability to exert significant political leverage on their own behalf and certain indigenous resources facilitative of organized social protest.

In a bargaining context we can distinguish, following Wilson, between negative and positive inducements (1961). The latter involve the offer of desired rewards—money, votes, etc.—as an inducement to engage in specified political actions. It is only in regard to this class of inducements that many groups find themselves handicapped. This statement is in no way intended to minimize that handicap. Indeed, if, as Gamson notes, "the central difference among political actors is captured by the idea of being inside or outside of the polity," it is the lack of positive inducements that usually serves to exclude groups from the polity (1975: 140).

As significant a handicap as this is, it need not confine a group to the state of political impotence suggested by some mobilization theorists. There is always the matter of negative inducements. Negative inducements entail "the withdrawal of a crucial contribution on which others depend" (Piven and Cloward, 1979: 24). The strike represents the classic example of a negative inducement. Workers seek to compel an employer to grant concessions by refusing to perform some function essential to the employer's business. Similarly, the illegal occupation of nuclear facilities are attempts to compel increased official responsiveness to insurgent demands through the creation of negative inducements. In such cases the "crucial contribution" being withheld by protesters is nothing less than "business as usual" for the site in question.

Negative inducements, then, involve the creation of a situation that is disruptive of the normal functioning of society and antithetical to the interests of the group's opponents. Mass demonstrations, boycotts, riots, selective buying campaigns, sit-ins—all are examples of actions designed, in Wilson's phrase, to "create or assemble resources for bargaining" (1961: 292). In essence, what insurgents are seeking in such instances is the ability to disrupt their opponent's interests to such an extent that the cessation of the offending tactic becomes a sufficient inducement to grant concessions. There are, of course, limits to the effectiveness of the "politics of protest," as Wilson, Lipsky, and Piven and Cloward remind us (Lipsky, 1970 [see especially chap. 7]; Piven and Cloward, 1979: 24–25; Wilson, 1961: 293–302). No doubt the ability of deprived groups to bargain effectively is limited by their necessary reliance on negative inducements. Nonetheless, in characterizing the majority of such groups as politically impotent, resource mobilization theorists are to be faulted for their failure to acknowledge the power inherent in disruptive tactics. Even the most deprived groups possess a greater potential for the successful exercise of political leverage than they have been given credit for in most versions of this perspective. The fact that these groups fail to exercise this potential much of the time is more often attributable to their shared perception of powerlessness than to any inherent impotence on their part.

Proponents of the model have also undervalued the political capabilities of the mass base by overlooking the crucial importance of indigenous resources. In some cases the claim is direct: deprived segments of the population simply lack the resources to generate and sustain social insurgency. The Jenkins/Perrow quotation at the beginning of this section is a representative expression of this point of view. In other formulations, it is not so much the existence as the necessity of indigenous resources that is questioned. McCarthy and Zald champion this latter viewpoint: "in the classical model the membership base provides money, voluntary manpower, and leadership. Modern movements can increasingly find these resources outside of self-interested memberships concerned with personally held grievances" (1973: 17–18). The claim is that external sponsorship of social protest has rendered the traditional contributions of the mass base unnecessary. To accept this claim, however, would be to accept, as well, the proposition rejected earlier in the chapter: that elite institutions actively seek to generate social insurgency, even in the absence of indigenous protest activity. In contrast, I have argued that elite involvement in social protest is generally reactive, occurring only as a response to pressures generated by a mass-based social movement.

This still leaves unanswered the more basic question of whether, in fact, deprived groups possess sufficient resources to generate a social movement in the first place. That there may exist some collective poverty level below which deprived groups are simply incapable of organizing is, of course, a real possibility. However, even the most cursory review of the empirical literature will convince the reader that the practical effect of this hypothetical level is to prohibit only the most deprived of groups from organizing. Indeed, one of my intentions in this book is to document the indigenous origins of an insurgent challenge that developed among a group—the southern black population—that by any standards would have to be adjudged deprived.

What the black movement shares in common with many other insurgent challenges is the existence of an indigenous organizational network in which it developed. The empirical literature does not lack for other examples. In his landmark analysis of Quebec's Social Credit party, Maurice Pinard has demonstrated the mobilizing effects of a wide variety of intermediate groups (1971: see especially chap. 11). Studying "Nationalism in Tropical Africa," Coleman has noted that "in some instances, kinship associations and separatist religious groups have been the antecedents of nationalist organizations; in others they have provided the principal organizational bases of the latter" (1954: 408). Finally, in regard to French strike activity in the period from 1830 to 1968, Shorter and Tilly observe that the scale and intensity of such activity "depend closely on the prior organization of the workers in the setting, on the availability of a structure which identifies, accumulates and communicates grievances on the one hand, and facilitates collective action on the other" (1974: 284).

If many analysts have identified indigenous social networks as the source of much insurgent activity, they have differed in the functions they ascribe to these organizational bases. Some stress the importance of these existent organizations as a communications network; others as a source of leaders; still others as an interactional network out of which an ideology and a plan of action can emerge. As conceived here, the indigenous organizations of an aggrieved population serve all these functions and then some. In effect, these networks function as the organizational locus of a variety of resources supportive of insurgency. In the next chapter these resources will be discussed in greater detail. For now the important point to note is that the existent organizations of all but the most deprived groups represent an important source of resources that, when mobilized for political purposes, has been proven capable of generating organized insurgency.

The Definition of Resources

Another serious deficiency of the mobilization perspective stems from the ways in which proponents of the model have defined the concept of resources. Actually, in some cases, the concept is never defined, leaving the reader to puzzle over the precise criteria for distinguishing what is from what is not a resource. However, even when explicit definitions have been proposed, they have generally proved to be only marginally more useful than no definition at all. Oberschall, for instance, has described resources as "anything from material resources—jobs, income, savings, and the right to material goods and services—to nonmaterial resources—authority, moral commitment, trust, friendship, skills, habits of industry, and so on" (1973: 28). For McCarthy and Zald, resources "can include legitimacy, money, facilities, and labor" (1977: 1220).

No doubt all the aforementioned items facilitate insurgency, but to define resources in such a vague, all-inclusive fashion is to rob the concept of much of its analytic utility. Indeed, the failure to propose an adequate operational definition of the concept has rendered the model's implicit account of movement emergence as untestable and simplistic as many of the classical formulations. It is ironic that mobilization theorists, having rightly criticized earlier models for their vagueness and ambiguity, are themselves open to criticism on the same counts. With regard to the classical model, Aya has expressed the key point nicely: "Not surprisingly . . . a look backward from the accomplished fact of revolution or revolt turns up evidence of discontent among all manner of groups and individuals. But then so does a glance at routine social life in times of political continuity" (1979: 54). That is, by defining the various conceptions of discontent (alienation, normative ambiguity) in such vague fashion, classical theorists have virtually assured confirmation of their models. Who could fail to turn up evidence of "discontent" or "strain" in an analysis of the period preceding any social movement? In similar fashion, it would be exceedingly difficult, given the all-inclusive definitions quoted earlier, to find a social movement that was not preceded by *some* increase in *some* type of "resource." What ultimately casts doubt on such accounts are well-founded suspicions that the "resources" so identified are in no simple sense the cause of the movement and that similar increases in "resources" take place in periods of political quiescence as well as those of turbulence. Ostensibly hardheaded departures from the post-hoc fuzziness of many classical formulations, most versions of resource mobilization would seem to turn on a concept as vague and problematic as those—strain and discontent—underlying the classical theory.

The Collective Definition of Grievances

The final major weakness of the resource mobilization perspective concerns the hypothesized relationship between grievances and insurgency stressed by proponents of the model. In summarizing that relationship, McCarthy and Zald contrast it to the classical view of discontent or grievances:

> The ambiguous evidence of some of the deprivation/relative deprivation/generalized belief research has led us to search for a perspective and set of assumptions that lead to a deemphasis upon grievances. We want to move from a *strong* assumption about the centrality of deprivation and grievances to a *weak* one, which makes them a component, indeed *sometimes* a secondary component in the generation of social movements.
>
> We are willing to assume "that there is always enough discontent in any society to supply the grass-roots support for a movement . . ." (McCarthy and Zald, 1977: 1215).

In effect, proponents of the mobilization perspective are arguing that there is a constancy to grievances that seriously contradicts the causal significance assigned them by classical theorists. Inasmuch as movement activity fluctuates wildly over time, it is problematic to account for the generation of such activity on the basis of an aggregate level of discontent that, presumably, remains fairly constant. What must be questioned in this view is the simple assertion that discontent is an invariant property of social life. The problem would seem to stem from the failure to distinguish *objective* social conditions from their *subjective* perception. The former undoubtedly does supply a constant stimulus to insurgency. That is, there would apppear always to be sufficient inequality in the distribution of valued goods in society as to afford people an objective basis for organized protest activity. But the link between objective conditions and action is seldom straightforward.[6] As Edelman notes, "the same real conditions . . . may or may not be perceived as serious deprivations and may or may not be regarded as grounds for resistance and violence" (1971: 108). In short, what is absent from most versions of the mobilization perspective is any acknowledgment of the enormous potential for variability in the subjective meanings people attach to their "objective" situations.

The important implication of this argument is that segments of society may very well submit to oppressive conditions unless that oppression is collectively defined as both unjust and *subject to change*. In the absence of these necessary attributions, oppressive conditions are likely, even in the face of increased resources, to go unchallenged.

The crucial question, then, is: what set of circumstances is most likely to facilitate the transformation from hopeless submission to oppressive conditions to an aroused readiness to challenge those conditions? This question will be addressed in detail in the next chapter. For now, the less than satisfactory answer offered is that the individual's sophisticated capacity for attributing significance to diverse sets of events makes it possible that a wide variety, rather than a single set, of circumstances, could trigger this process of "cognitive liberation." Obviously, this answer is not without problems. Not the least of these are the methodological difficulties involved in any attempt to measure this transformation of consciousness. The creation of methodological problems, however, is hardly a rationale for ignoring the process. For, indeed, if the process is a slippery and troublesome one to address empirically, it is just as certainly crucial to any complete account of the generation of insurgency. The point is that neither "strain" nor some propitious combination of underlying grievances and newly mobilized resources create a social movement. People do, on the basis of some optimistic assessment of the prospects for successful insurgency weighed against the risks involved in each action. To the extent that resource mobilization theorists have failed to acknowledge this crucial intermediate process, their model is incomplete.

To summarize, I return to a point made earlier in the chapter: resource mobilization affords a useful perspective for analyzing organized reform efforts initiated by established polity members. It is less convincing, however, as an account of social movements. Part of the problem stems from the vagueness with which proponents of the model define the key concept of resources. That vagueness serves to limit the predictive utility of the model, even as it renders it virtually immune to testing.

Issue has also been taken with the claim, advanced by mobilization theorists, that discontent is constant and therefore of little significance in the generation of insurgency. This claim would appear to rest on the confusion of objective condition with subjective perception. Structural inequities may be constant, but the collective perception of the legitimacy *and* mutability of those conditions is likely to vary a great deal over time. By attributing a certain constancy to discontent, the model's proponents have glossed over a crucial process in the generation of insurgency: that of "cognitive liberation."

As important as these deficiencies are, however, the central criticism of the version of the mobilization perspective discussed here concerns the respective roles assigned elite groups and the movement's mass base in the generation of insurgency. In contrast to the implicit thrust of the mobilization argument, the various components of the elite would appear to share an abiding conservatism that does not predispose them to initiate any insurgent activity that might conceivably prove threatening to their interests. Accordingly, their involvement in insurgency is more likely to take the form of reaction to mass-based movements rather than the aggressive sponsorship of same. This latter statement carries with it the important conviction that not all excluded groups are as politically impotent as some resource mobilization accounts imply. That challengers face real disadvantages in their attempts to organize and that many insurgent efforts never surface as visible political phenomena is readily conceded. Nonetheless, the very fact that such attempts are made and, on occasion, carried out with considerable success suggest a greater capacity for insurgent action by excluded groups than is ordinarily acknowledged by proponents of the resource mobilization model. What is required, then, is another model specifically tailored to the class of insurgent challenges under discussion here.

3 The Political
Process Model

The political process model represents an alternative to the classical and resource mobilization perspectives. The term "political process" has been taken from an article by Rule and Tilly entitled "Political Process in Revolutionary France, 1830–1832" (1975: 41–85).[1] It should, however, be emphasized that the model advanced by Rule and Tilly is compatible but not synonymous with the perspective outlined here. The name has been adopted, not because the two models are identical, but because the term "political process" accurately conveys two ideas central to both perspectives. First, in contrast to the various classical formulations, a social movement is held to be above all else a *political* rather than a psychological phenomenon. That is, the factors shaping institutionalized political processes are argued to be of equal analytic utility in accounting for social insurgency. Second, a movement represents a continuous *process* from generation to decline, rather than a discrete series of developmental stages. Accordingly, any complete model of social insurgency should offer the researcher a framework for analyzing the entire process of movement development rather than a particular phase (e.g., the emergence of social protest) of that same process.

THE POLITICAL PROCESS MODEL AND INSTITUTIONALIZED POLITICS

A point stressed repeatedly in this work is that theories of social movements always imply a more general model of institutionalized power. Thus, in Chapter 1, it was argued that the classical view of social movements is best understood as a theoretical extension of the pluralist model. By contrast, it was suggested, in Chapter 2, that the resource mobilization perspective implies adherence to the elite model of the American political system. The political process model is also based on a particular conception of power in America. In many respects this conception is consistent with the elite model. Like the latter, the perspective advanced here rests on the fundamental assumption that wealth and power are concentrated in America in the hands of a few groups, thus depriving most people of any real influence over the major decisions that affect their lives. Accordingly, social movements are seen, in both perspectives, as rational attempts by excluded groups to mobilize sufficient political leverage to advance collective interests through noninstitutionalized means.

Where this perspective diverges from the elite model is in regard to the extent of elite control over the political system and the insurgent capabilities of excluded groups. While elite theorists display a marked diversity of opinion on these issues, there would seem to be a central tendency evident in their writings. That tendency embodies a perception of the power disparity between elite and excluded groups that would seem to grant the former virtually unlimited power in politico-economic matters. Excluded groups, on the other hand, are seen as functionally powerless in the face of the enormous power wielded by the elite. Under such conditions, the chances for successful insurgency would seem to be negligible.

By contrast, on both these counts, the political process model is more compatible with a Marxist interpretation of power. Marxists acknowledge that the power disparity between elite and excluded groups is substantial but hardly regard this state of affairs as inevitable. Indeed, for orthodox Marxists, that which is inevitable is not the retention of power by the elite but the accession to power by the masses. One need not accept the rigidity of this scenario, to conclude that it represents an improvement over elite theory insofar as it embodies a clear understanding of the latent political leverage available to most segments of the population. The insurgent potential of excluded groups comes from the "structural power" that their location in various politico-economic structures affords them. Schwartz explains the basis and significance of this power:

> Since a structure cannot function without the routinized exercise of structural power, any threat to structural power becomes a threat to that system itself. Thus, if employees suddenly began refusing to obey orders, the company in question could not function. Or if tenants simply disobeyed the merchant's order to grow cotton, the tenancy system would collapse. . . . Thus, we see a subtle, but very important, relationship between structural power and those who are subject to it. On the one hand, these power relations define the functioning of any ongoing system; on the other hand, the ability to disrupt these relationships is exactly the sort of leverage which can be used to alter the functioning of the system. . . . *Any system contains within itself the possibility of a power strong enough to alter it* (Schwartz, 1976: 172–73; emphasis in original).

A second Marxist influence on the model outlined here concerns the importance attributed to subjective processes in the generation of insurgency. Marxists, to a much greater extent than elite theorists, recognize that mass political impotence may as frequently stem from shared perceptions of powerlessness as from any objective inability to mobilize significant political leverage. Thus, the subjective transformation of consciousness is appreciated by Marxists as a process crucial to the generation of insurgency. The importance of this transformation is likewise acknowledged in the political process model.

The perspective advanced here, then, combines aspects of both the elite and Marxist models of power in America. Central to the perspective is Gamson's distinction between "members" and "challengers": "the central difference among political actors is captured by the idea of being inside or outside of the polity. Those who are inside are *members* whose interest is vested—that is, recognized as valid by other members. Those who are outside are challengers. They lack the basic prerogative of members—routine access to decisions that affect them" (1975: 140). Gamson's distinction is not unique. Indeed, a similar notion is embodied in all versions of the elite model. What distinguishes this perspective from that advanced by most resource mobilization theorists, is the latter's characterization of the relationship between "challengers" and "members." Proponents of the resource mobilization model depict segments of the elite as being willing, at times even aggressive, sponsors of social insurgency. By contrast, the political process model is based on the notion that political action by established polity members reflects an abiding conservatism. This conservatism, according to Tilly, encourages polity members to "resist changes which would threaten their current realization of their interests even more than they seek changes which would enhance their interests" (1978: 135). He goes on to state that these members also "fight tenaciously against loss of power, and especially against expulsion from the polity. They work against admission to the polity of groups whose interests conflict significantly with their own. Existing members tend to be more exacting in their demands of contenders whose very admission would challenge the system in some serious way" (Tilly, 1978: 135).

Tilly's remarks are reminiscent of Gamson's characterization of what he terms the "competitive establishment" in American politics (1968: 19). Gamson describes the competitive establishment as that "collection of represented groups and authorities" who control to a considerable degree the workings of America's institutionalized political system. According to Gamson, they are motivated by the same desires Tilly ascribes to established polity members. They seek to "keep unrepresented groups from developing solidarity and politically organizing, and . . . discourage their effective entry into the competitive establishment if and as they become organized" (Gamson, 1968: 20).

Tilly and Gamson's statements are instructive in view of the dominant resource mobilization characterization of member/challenger relations as facilitative of social protest activity. Their remarks serve to undermine this characterization by forcefully asserting the contradictory notion that established polity members are ordinarily not enamored of the idea of sponsoring any insurgent political activity that could conceivably threaten their interests. This conservative bias extends not only to those insurgents who advocate goals contrary to member interests but also to those protest groups—regardless of how moderate their goals—who simply pressure for membership in the competitive establishment. For any change in the makeup of the polity is inherently disruptive of the institutionalized status quo and thus something to be resisted. As Gamson asserts, "the competitive establishment is boundary-maintaining" (1968: 20).

Gamson and Tilly's discussion of the characteristic conservatism of established polity members implies an important point that is central to the political process model. If elite groups are unwilling to underwrite insurgency, the very occurrence of social movements indicates that indigenous groups are able to generate and sustain organized mass action. In positing the primacy of environmental factors, most resource mobilization theorists have seemingly rejected this point. This, of course, is not to suggest that such factors are unimportant. The strategic constraints confronting excluded groups should not be underestimated. The Tillys describe the rather unenviable position of the challenger:

> the range of collective actions open to a relatively powerless group is normally very small. Its program, its form of action, its very existence are likely to be illegal, hence subject to violent repression. As a consequence, such a group chooses between taking actions which have a high probability of bringing on a violent response (but which have some chance of reaching the group's goals) and taking no action at all (thereby assuring the defeat of the group's goals) (C. Tilly, L. Tilly, R. Tilly, 1975: 283).

Thus, while excluded groups do possess the latent capacity to exert significant political leverage at any time, the force of environmental constraints is usually sufficient to inhibit mass action. But this force is not constant over time. The calculations on which existing political arrangements are based may, for a variety of reasons, change over time, thus affording certain segments of the population greater leverage with which to advance their interests. The suggestion is that neither environmental factors nor factors internal to the movement are sufficient to account for the generation and development of social insurgency. I agree with Gary Marx that "social movements are not autonomous forces hurling toward their destiny only in response to the . . . intensity of commitment, and skill of activists. Nor are they epiphenomena completely at the mercy of groups in their external environment seeking to block or facilitate them" (Marx, 1976: 1). The political process model rests on the assumption that social movements are an ongoing product of the favorable interplay of *both* sets of factors. The specific mix of factors may change from one phase of the movement to another, but the basic dynamic remains the same. Movements develop in response to an ongoing process of interaction between movement groups and the larger sociopolitical environment they seek to change.

The Generation of Insurgency

The political process model identifies three sets of factors that are believed to be crucial in the generation of social insurgency. The first is the level of organization within the aggrieved population; the second, the collective assessment of the prospects for successful insurgency within that same population; and third, the political alignment of groups within the larger political environment. The first can be conceived of as the degree of organizational "readiness" within the minority community; the second, as the level of "insurgent consciousness" within the movement's mass base; and the third, following Eisinger, as the "structure of political opportunities" available to insurgent groups (Eisinger, 1973: 11). Before the relationships between these factors are outlined, each will be discussed in turn.

Structure of Political Opportunities

Under ordinary circumstances, excluded groups, or challengers, face enormous obstacles in their efforts to advance group interests. Challengers are excluded from routine decision-making processes precisely because their bargaining position, relative to established polity members, is so weak. But the particular set of power relationships that define the political environment at any point in time hardly constitute an immutable structure of political life. As Lipsky points out:

> attention is directed away from system characterizations presumably true for all times and all places, which are basically of little value in understanding the social and political process. We are accustomed to describing communist political systems as "experiencing a thaw" or "going through a process of retrenchment." Should it not at least be an open question as to whether the American political system experiences such stages and fluctuations? Similarly, is it not sensible to assume that the system will be more or less open to specific groups at different times and at different places? (Lipsky, 1970: 14).

The answer offered here to both of Lipsky's questions is an emphatic yes. The opportunities for a challenger to engage in successful collective action do vary greatly over time. And it is these variations that are held to be related to the ebb and flow of movement activity. As Eisinger has remarked, "protest is a sign that the opportunity structure is flexible and vulnerable to the political assaults of excluded groups" (1973: 28).

Still unanswered, however, is the question of what accounts for such shifts in the "structure of political opportunities." A finite list of specific causes would be impossible to compile. However, Eisinger suggests the crucial point about the origin of such shifts: "protest signifies changes not only among previously quiescent or conventionally oriented groups but also *in the political system itself*" (1973: 28; emphasis mine). The point is that *any* event or broad social process that serves to undermine the calculations and assumptions on which the political establishment is structured occasions a shift in political opportunities. Among the events and processes likely to prove disruptive of the political status quo are wars, industrialization, international political realignments, prolonged unemployment, and widespread demographic changes.

It is interesting to note that classical theorists have also described many of these same processes as productive of mass protest. In particular, industrialization and urbanization have been singled out as forces promoting the rise of social movements (Kornhauser, 1959: 143–58). The difference between the two models stems from the fact that classical theorists posit a radically different causal sequence linking these processes to insurgency than is proposed here. For classical theorists the relationship is direct, with industrialization/urbanization generating a level of strain sufficient to trigger social protest.[2]

In contrast, the political process model is based on the idea that social processes such as industrialization promote insurgency only indirectly through a restructuring of existing power relations. This difference also indexes a significant divergence between the two models in terms of the time span during which insurgency is held to develop. The classical sequence of disruption/strain depicts insurgency as a function of dramatic changes in the period immediately preceding movement emergence. By contrast, the perspective advanced here is based on the notion that social insurgency is shaped by broad social processes that usually operate over a longer period of time. As a consequence, the processes shaping insurgency are expected to be of a more cumulative, less dramatic nature than those identified by proponents of the classical model. The Tillys have nicely captured both these differences: "urbanization and industrialization . . . are by no means irrelevant to collective violence. It is just that their effects do not work as . . . [classical] theories say they should. Instead of a short-run generation of strain, followed by protest, we find a long-run transformation of the structures of power and of collective action" (C. Tilly, L. Tilly, R. Tilly, 1975: 254).

Regardless of the causes of expanded "political opportunities," such shifts can facilitate increased political activism on the part of excluded groups either by seriously undermining the stability of the entire political system or by increasing the political leverage of a single insurgent group. The significance of this distinction stems from the fact that the former pattern usually precipitates widespread political crisis while the latter does not.

Generalized political instability destroys any semblance of a political status quo, thus encouraging collective action by *all* groups sufficiently organized to contest the structuring of a new political order. The empirical literature offers numerous examples of this process. Shorter and Tilly, for example, marshall data to show that peaks in French strike activity correspond to periods in which organized contention for national political power is unusually intense. They note that "factory and white-collar workers undertook in 1968 the longest, largest general strike in history as student unrest reopened the question of who were to be the constituent political groups of the Fifth Republic" (Shorter and Tilly, 1974: 344). Similarly, Schwartz argues that a period of political instability preceded the rise of the Southern Farmers Alliance in the post–Civil War South. With the southern planter aristocracy and emerging industrial interests deadlocked in a struggle for political control of the region, a unique opportunity for political advancement was created for any group able to break the stalemate (Schwartz, 1976).

Such situations of generalized political instability can be contrasted to instances in which broad social processes favorably effect the opportunities for insurgent action of particular challengers. In such cases, long-term socioeconomic changes serve simply to elevate the group in question to a position of increased political strength without necessarily undermining the structural basis of the entire political establishment. The Jenkins-Perrow study cited earlier provides a good example of this latter process. In comparing the farm-worker movements of the 1940s and the 1960s, the authors attribute the success of the latter to "the altered political environment within which the challenge operated" (Jenkins and Perrow, 1977: 263). Moreover, this all-important alteration of the political environment originated, they contend, "in economic trends and political realignments that took place quite independent of any 'push' from insurgents" (Jenkins and Perrow, 1977: 266). Successful insurgency, the authors suggest, was born, not of widespread political instability, but of broad social processes that strengthened the political position of the challenging group. In Chapter 5, I will argue that a similar process facilitated the rise of black insurgency in the 1950s.

It remains only to identify the ways in which favorable shifts in the structure of political opportunities increase the likelihood of successful insurgent action. Two major facilitative effects can be distinguished. Most fundamentally, such shifts improve the chances for successful social protest by reducing the power discrepancy between insurgent groups and their opponents. Regardless of whether the broad social processes productive of such shifts serve to undermine the structural basis of the entire political system or simply to enhance the strategic position of a single challenger, the result is the same: a net increase in the political leverage exercised by insurgent groups. The practical effect of this development is to increase the likelihood that insurgent interests will prevail in a confrontation with a group whose goals conflict with those of the insurgents. This does not, of course, mean that insurgent interests will inevitably be realized in all conflict situations. Even in the context of an improved bargaining position, insurgent groups are likely to be at a distinct disadvantage in any confrontation with an established polity member. What it does mean, however, is that the increased political strength of the aggrieved population has improved the bargaining position of insurgent groups and thus created new opportunities for the collective pursuit of group goals.

Second, an improved bargaining position for the aggrieved population raises significantly the costs of repressing insurgent action. Unlike before, when the powerless status of the excluded group meant that it could be repressed with relative impunity, now the increased political leverage exercised by the insurgent group renders it a more formidable opponent. Repression of the group involves a greater risk of political reprisals than before and is thus less likely to be attempted even in the face of an increased threat to member interests. For, as Gamson notes in summarizing the evidence from his survey of challenging groups, insurgents "are attacked not merely because they are regarded as threatening—all challenging groups are threatening to some vested interest. They are threatening *and* vulnerable" (1975: 82). To the extent, then, that shifting political conditions increase the power of insurgent groups, they also render them less vulnerable to attack by raising the costs of repression. Or to state the matter in terms of the insurgent group, increased political power serves to encourage collective action by diminishing the risks associated with movement participation.

Indigenous Organizational Strength

A conducive political environment only affords the aggrieved population the opportunity for successful insurgent action. It is the resources of the minority community that enable insurgent groups to exploit these opportunities. In the absence of those resources the aggrieved population is likely to lack the capacity to act even when granted the opportunity to do so. Here I am asserting the importance of what Katz and Gurin have termed the "conversion potential" of the minority community (1969: 350). To generate a social movement, the aggrieved population must be able to "convert" a favorable "structure of political opportunities" into an organized campaign of social protest.

Conditioning this conversion is the extent of organization within the minority community. That indigenous structures frequently provide the organizational base out of which social movements emerge has been argued by a number of theorists. Oberschall, for instance, has proposed a theory of mobilization in which he assigns paramount importance to the degree of organization in the minority community. If no networks exist, he contends, the aggrieved population is capable of little more than "short-term, localized, ephemeral outbursts and movements of protest such as riots," (Oberschall, 1973: 119). Likewise Freeman (1973, 1977b) stresses the importance of an established associational network in the generation of social insurgency. Echoing Oberschall, she argues convincingly that the ability of insurgents to generate a social movement is ultimately dependent on the presence of an indigenous "infrastructure" that can be used to link members of the aggrieved population into an organized campaign of mass political action.

I agree with the importance attributed to existent networks or organizations in these works. Specifically, the significance of such organizations would appear to be largely a function of four crucial resources they afford insurgents.

Members. If there is anything approximating a consistent finding in the empirical literature, it is that movement participants are recruited along established lines of interaction. This remains true in spite of the numerous attempts to explain participation on the basis of a variety of individual background or psychological variables.[3] The explanation for this consistent finding would appear to be straightforward: the more integrated the person is into the minority community, the more readily he/she can be mobilized for participation in protest activities. The work of Gerlach and Hine supports this interpretation. They conclude, "no matter how a typical participant describes his reasons for joining the movement, or what motives may be suggested by a social scientist on the basis of deprivation, disorganization, or deviancy models, it is clear that the original decision to join required some contact with the movement" (Gerlach and Hine, 1970: 79). The significance of indigenous organizations—informal ones no less than formal—stems from the fact that they render this type of facilitative contact more likely, thus promoting member recruitment. This function can be illustrated by reference to two patterns of recruitment evident in empirical accounts of insurgency.

First, individuals can be recruited into the ranks of movement activists by virtue of their involvement in organizations that serve as the associational network out of which a new movement emerges. This was true, as Melder notes, in the case of the nineteenth-century women's rights movement, with a disproportionate number of the movement's recruits coming from existing abolitionist groups (1964). Curtis and Zurcher have observed a similar phenomenon in connection with the rise of two contempory antipornography groups. In their study, the authors provide convincing data to support their contention that recruits were overwhelmingly drawn from the broad "multi-organizational fields" in which both groups were embedded (Curtis and Zurcher, 1973).

Second, indigenous organizations can serve as the primary source of movement participants through what Oberschall has termed "bloc recruitment" (1973: 125). In this pattern, movements do not so much emerge out of established organizations as they represent a merger of such groups. Hicks, for instance, has described how the Populist party was created through a coalition of established farmers' organizations (1961). The rapid rise of the free-speech movement at Berkeley has been attributed to a similar merger of existing campus organizations (Lipset and Wolin, 1965). Both of these patterns, then, highlight the indigenous organizational basis of much movement recruitment, and they support Oberschall's general conclusion: "mobilization does not occur through recruitment of large numbers of isolated and solitary individuals. It occurs as a result of recruiting blocs of people who are already highly organized and participants" (1973: 125).

Established Structure of Solidary Incentives. A second resource available to insurgents through the indigenous organizations of the minority community are the "established structures of solidary incentives" on which these organizations depend. By "structures of solidary incentives," I am simply referring to the myriad interpersonal rewards that provide the motive force for participation in these groups. It is the salience of these rewards that helps explain why recruitment through established organizations is generally so efficient. In effect, these established "incentive structures" solve the so-called "free-ride problem."

First discussed by Mancur Olson (1965), the "free-rider problem" refers to the difficulties insurgents encounter in trying to convince participants to pursue goals whose benefits they would derive even if they did not participate in the movement. The fact is, when viewed in the light of a narrow economic calculus, movement participation would indeed seem to be irrational. Even if we correct for Olson's overly rationalistic model of the individual, the "free rider" mentality would still seem to pose a formidable barrier to movement recruitment. The solution to this problem is held to stem from the provision of selective incentives to induce the participation that individual calculation would alone seem to preclude (Gamson, 1975: 66–71; Olson, 1965).

In the context of existent organizations, however, the provision of selective incentives would seem unnecessary. These organizations already rest on a solid structure of solidary incentives which insurgents have, in effect, appropriated by defining movement participation as synonymous with organizational membership. Accordingly, the myriad of incentives that have heretofore served as the motive force for participation in the group are now simply transferred to the movement. Thus, insurgents have been spared the difficult task of inducing participation through the provision of new incentives of either a solidary or material nature.

Communication Network. The established organizations of the aggrieved population also constitute a communication network or infrastructure, the strength and breadth of which largely determine the pattern, speed, and extent of movement expansion. Both the failure of a new movement to take hold and the rapid spread of insurgent action have been credited to the presence or absence of such an infrastructure. Freeman has argued that it was the recent development of such a network that enabled women in the 1960s to create a successful feminist movement where they had earlier been unable to do so:

> The development of the women's liberation movement highlights the salience of such a network precisely because the conditions for a movement existed *before* a network came into being, but the movement didn't exist until afterward. Socioeconomic strain did not change for women significantly during a 20-year period. It was as great in 1955 as in 1965. What changed was the organizational situation. It was not until a communications network developed among like-minded people beyond local boundaries that the movement could emerge and develop past the point of occasional, spontaneous uprising (Freeman, 1973: 804).

Conversely, Jackson et al. (1960), document a case in which the absence of a readily co-optable communication network contributed to "The Failure of an Incipient Social Movement." The movement, an attempted property tax revolt in California, failed, according to the authors, because "there was no . . . preestablished network of communication which could be quickly employed to link the suburban residential property owners who constituted the principal base for the movement" (Jackson et al., 1960: 38).[4]

These findings are consistent with the empirical thrust of studies of cultural diffusion, a body of literature that has unfortunately been largely overlooked by movement analysts despite its relevance to the topic.[5] To my knowledge, only Maurice Pinard (1971: 186–87), has explicitly applied the empirical insights of this literature to the study of social movements. He summarizes the central tenet of diffusion theory as follows: "the higher the degree of social integration of potential adopters, the more likely and the sooner they will become actual adopters . . . on the other hand, near-isolates tend to be the last to adopt an innovation" (1971: 187). The applicability of this idea to the study of social insurgency stems from recognition of the fact that a social movement is, after all, a new cultural item subject to the same pattern of diffusion or adoption as other innovations. Indeed, without acknowledging the theoretical basis of his insight, Oberschall has hypothesized for movements the identical pattern of diffusion noted earlier by Pinard: "the greater the number and variety of organizations in a collectivity, and the higher the participation of members in this network, the more rapidly and enduringly does mobilization into conflict groups occur" (Oberschall, 1973: 125).

Oberschall's statement has brought us full circle. Our brief foray into the diffusion literature only serves to amplify the basic argument by placing it in a theoretical context that helps explain the importance of associational networks in the generation of insurgency. The interorganizational linkages characteristic of established groups facilitate movement emergence by providing the means of communication by which the movement, as a new cultural item, can be disseminated throughout the aggrieved population.

Leaders. All manner of movement analysts have asserted the importance of leaders or organizers in the generation of social insurgency. To do so requires not so much a particular theoretical orientation as common sense. For in the context of political opportunity and widespread discontent there still remains a need for the centralized direction and coordination of a recognized leadership.

The existence of established organizations within the movement's mass base insures the presence of recognized leaders who can be called upon to lend their prestige and organizing skills to the incipient movement. Indeed, given the pattern of diffusion discussed in the previous section, it may well be that established leaders are among the first to join a new movement by virtue of their central position within the community. There is, in fact, some empirical evidence to support this. To cite only one example, Lipset, in his study of the Socialist C.C.F. party, reports that "in Saskatchewan it was the local leaders of the Wheat Pool, of the trade-unions, who were the first to join the C.C.F." His interpretation of the finding is that "those who are most thoroughly integrated in the class through formal organizations are the first to change" (1950: 197). Regardless of the timing of their recruitment, the existence of recognized leaders is yet another resource whose availability is conditioned by the degree of organization within the aggrieved population.

Existent organizations of the minority community, then, are the primary source of resources facilitating movement emergence. These groups constitute the organizational context in which insurgency is expected to develop. As such, their presence is as crucial to the process of movement emergence as a conducive political environment. Indeed, in the absence of this supportive organizational context, the aggrieved population is likely to be deprived of the capacity for collective action even when confronted with a favorable structure of political opportunities. If one lacks the capacity to act, it hardly matters that one is afforded the chance to do so.

Cognitive Liberation

While important, expanding political opportunities and indigenous organizations do not, in any simple sense, produce a social movement. In the absence of one other crucial process these two factors remain necessary, but insufficient, causes of insurgency. Together they only offer insurgents a certain objective "structural potential" for collective political action. Mediating between opportunity and action are people and the subjective meanings they attach to their situations. This crucial attribution process has been ignored by proponents of both the classical and resource mobilization perspectives. As Edelman has pointed out: "our explanations of mass political response have radically undervalued the ability of the human mind . . . to take a complex set of . . . cues into account [and] evolve a mutually acceptable form of response" (1971: 133). This process must occur if an organized protest campaign is to take place. One of the central problematics of insurgency, then, is whether favorable shifts in political opportunities will be defined as such by a large enough group of people to facilitate collective protest. This process, however, is not independent of the two factors discussed previously. Indeed, one effect of improved political conditions and existent organizations is to render this process of "cognitive liberation" more likely. I will explore the relationship between this process and each of these factors separately.

As noted earlier, favorable shifts in political opportunities decrease the power disparity between insurgents and their opponents and, in doing so, increase the cost of repressing the movement. These are objective structural changes. However, such shifts have a subjective referent as well. That is, challengers experience shifting political conditions on a day-to-day basis as a set of "meaningful" events communicating much about their prospects for successful collective action.

Sometimes the political significance of events is apparent on their face as when mass migration significantly alters the electoral composition of a region. Thus, as early as the mid-1930s black leaders began to use the fact of rapidly swelling black populations in key northern industrial states as bargaining leverage in their dealings with presidential candidates (Sitkoff, 1978: 283). However, even when evolving political realities are of a less dramatic nature, they will invariably be made "available" to insurgents through subtle cues communicated by other groups. The expectation is that as conditions shift in favor of a particular challenger members will display a certain increased symbolic responsiveness to insurgents. Thus, in a tight labor market we might expect management to be more responsive to workers than they had previously been. Or, as regards the earlier example, should internal migration significantly increase the proportion of a certain population residing in a region, we could expect area politicians to be more symbolically attentive to that group than before.

As subtle and substantively meaningless as these altered responses may be, their significance for the generation of insurgency would be hard to overstate. As Edelman notes, "political actions chiefly arouse or satisfy people not by granting or withholding their stable substantive demands, but rather by changing the demands and the expectations" (1971: 7). In effect, the altered responses of members to a particular challenger serve to transform evolving political conditions into a set of "cognitive cues" signifying to insurgents that the political system is becoming increasingly vulnerable to challenge. Thus, by forcing a change in the symbolic content of member/challenger relations, shifting political conditions supply a crucial impetus to the process of cognitive liberation.

The existent organizations of the minority community also figure prominently in the development of this insurgent consciousness, lending added significance to their role in the generation of insurgency. Earlier the relevance of the diffusion literature for the study of social movements was noted. Based on the main finding derived from that literature, the argument was advanced that the importance of indigenous organizations stemmed, in part, from the fact that they afforded insurgents an established interaction network insuring the rapid and thorough diffusion of social insurgency throughout the minority community. But that insight can now be extended even further. It is not simply the extent and speed with which insurgency is spread but the very cognitions on which it depends that are conditioned by the strength of integrative ties within the movement's mass base. As summarized by Piven and Cloward, these "necessary cognitions" are threefold:

The emergence of a protest movement entails a transformation both of consciousness and of behavior. The change in consciousness has at least three distinct aspects. First, "the system"—or those aspects of the system that people experience and perceive—loses legitimacy.

Large numbers of men and women who ordinarily accept the authority of their rulers and the legitimacy of institutional arrangements come to believe in some measure that these rulers and these arrangements are unjust and wrong. Second, people who are ordinarily fatalistic, who believe that existing arrangements are inevitable, begin to assert "rights" that imply demands for change. Third, there is a new sense of efficacy; people who ordinarily consider themselves helpless come to believe that they have some capacity to alter their lot (Piven and Cloward, 1979: 3–4).

It is important to recognize, however, that these cognitions "are overwhelmingly not based upon observation or empirical evidence available to participants, but rather upon cuings among groups of people who jointly create the meanings they will read into current and anticipated events" (Edelman, 1971: 32). The key phrase here is "groups of people." That is, the process of cognitive liberation is held to be both more likely and of far greater consequence under conditions of strong rather than weak social integration. The latter point should be intuitively apparent. Even in the unlikely event that these necessary cognitions were to develop under conditions of weak social integration, the absence of integrative links would almost surely prevent their spread to the minimum number of people required to afford a reasonable basis for successful collective action. More to the point, perhaps, is the suspicion that under such conditions these cognitions would never arise in the first place. The consistent finding linking feelings of political efficacy to social integration supports this judgment (Neal and Seeman, 1964; Pinard, 1971; Sayre, 1980). In the absence of strong interpersonal links to others, people are likely to feel powerless to change conditions even if they perceive present conditions as favorable to such efforts.

To this finding one might add the educated supposition that what Ross (1977) calls the "fundamental attribution error"—the tendency of people to explain their situation as a function of individual rather than situational factors—is more likely to occur under conditions of personal isolation than under those of integration. Lacking the information and perspective that others afford, isolated individuals would seem especially prone to explain their troubles on the basis of personal rather than "system attributions" (Ferree and Miller, 1977: 33).

The practical significance of this distinction comes from the fact that only system attributions afford the necessary rationale for movement activity. For movement analysts, then, the key question becomes, What social circumstances are productive of "system attributions"? If we follow Ferree and Miller, the likely answer is that the chances "of a system attribution would appear to be greatest among extremely homogeneous people who are in intense regular contact with each other" (1977: 34).

Figure 3.1   A Political Process Model of Movement Emergence

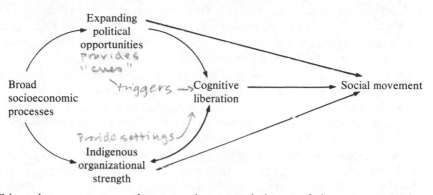

This point serves to underscore the central thrust of the argument: the significance of existent organizations for the process of movement emergence stems from the expectation that cognitive liberation is most likely to take place within established interpersonal networks.

To summarize, movement emergence implies a transformation of consciousness within a significant segment of the aggrieved population. Before collective protest can get under way, people must collectively define their situations as unjust and subject to change through group action. The likelihood of this necessary transformation occurring is conditioned, in large measure, by the two facilitating conditions discussed previously. Shifting political conditions supply the necessary "cognitive cues" capable of triggering the process of cognitive liberation while existent organizations afford insurgents the stable group-settings within which that process is most likely to occur.

It is now possible to outline in broader fashion the alternative model of movement emergence proposed here. That model is shown in figure 3.1. As the figure shows, the generation of insurgency is expected to reflect the favorable confluence of three sets of factors. Expanding political opportunities combine with the indigenous organizations of the minority community to afford insurgents the "structural potential" for successful collective action. That potential is, in turn, transformed into actual insurgency by means of the crucial intervening process of cognitive liberation. All three factors, then, are regarded as necessary, but insufficient, causes of social insurgency.

THE DEVELOPMENT/DECLINE OF SOCIAL INSURGENCY

The generation of social insurgency presupposes the existence of a political environment increasingly vulnerable to pressure from insurgents. Specific events and/or broad social processes enhance the bargaining position of the aggrieved population, even as insurgent groups mobilize to exploit the expanding opportunities for collective action. Over time the survival of a social movement requires that insurgents be able to maintain and successfully utilize their newly acquired political leverage to advance collective interests. If they are able to do so, the movement is likely to survive. If, on the other hand, insurgent groups fail to maintain a favorable bargaining position vis-à-vis other groups in the political arena, the movement faces extinction. In short, the ongoing exercise of significant political leverage remains the key to the successful development of the movement.

What is missing from the above discussion is any acknowledgment of the enormous obstacles insurgents must overcome if they are to succeed in this effort. This is not to say that social movements are doomed from the outset or that they are an ineffective form of political action. History contradicts both notions. Just the same, the fortuitous combination of factors productive of insurgency is expected to be short-lived. Even as insurgents exploit the opportunities this confluence of factors affords them, the movement sets in motion processes that are likely, over time, to create a set of contradictory demands destructive of insurgency. Of principal importance in this regard are two dilemmas on whose horns many movements seem to have been caught. (After a brief review of the factors shaping the ongoing development of insurgency, I will address these dilemmas.)

Conditioning the development of the movement over time is the same mix of internal and external factors that shaped the generation of insurgency. Indeed, with a few important modifications, the general causal model outlined in the previous section affords a useful framework for analyzing the ongoing development of insurgency. These modifications are reflected in figure 3.2.

Perhaps the most significant change evident in figure 3.2 is the emergence of the movement as an independent force shaping its own devel-

Figure 3.2   A Political Process Model of Movement Development/Decline

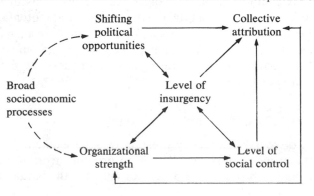

opment. In analyzing the generation of insurgency, one considers the movement only as the end product of a specified causal sequence. Once under way, however, the pace and character of insurgency come to exercise a powerful influence on the development of the movement through the effect they have on the other factors depicted in figure 3.2. For example, the opportunities for insurgency are no longer independent of the actions of insurgent groups. Now the structure of political alignments shifts in response to movement activity, even as those shifts shape the prospects for future insurgency.

Much the same dynamic is evident in regard to the relationship between organizational strength and insurgency, with the pace, character, and outcome of collective protest shaping the availability of those organizational resources on which further movement activity depends. Reciprocal relationships also hold in the case of insurgency and the other two factors shown in figure 3.2. With the outbreak of insurgency, then, the movement itself introduces a new set of causal dynamics into the study of collective protest activity that are discontinuous with the process of movement emergence.

At the same time, however, there is a basic continuity between the generation and ongoing development of insurgency. The reader will note that all three factors discussed earlier in connection with the generation of insurgency are included in figure 3.2 as well. To these three factors I now add a fourth: the shifting control response of other groups to the insurgent challenge posed by the movement.

Little needs to be said about two of the original factors. It is enough simply to note that "the structure of political opportunities" and the process of "collective attribution" are expected to influence the development of the movement in much the same ways as they did in the generation of insurgency. The former conditions the ongoing vulnerability of the political system to pressure from the movement, while the latter determines the extent to which insurgents continue to share the particular mix of cognitions needed to sustain insurgency. As explained earlier, these cognitions involve the perception that conditions are unjust yet subject to change through group efforts.

The remaining two factors require more explanation. Though discussed earlier, the determinants of "organizational strength" are expected to shift, following the generation of insurgency, in accordance with an anticipated transformation of the movement's organizational structure. For that reason, the factor will be discussed anew. Finally, as the only factor set in motion by the emergence of the movement, "level of social control" merits attention if only because it has not been discussed previously. The importance of these remaining factors also results from their relationship to the two critical dilemmas alluded to above. That is, both factors index a set of cross-cutting pressures that must be carefully negotiated if the movement is to survive. In discussing these factors, then, I will not only be analyzing the ongoing process of movement development but also emphasizing the difficulties inherent in sustaining any insurgent challenge.

Sustaining Organizational Strength

Although social insurgency is expected to develop out of the established organizations of the aggrieved population, the movement cannot rely on such groups to sustain an ongoing protest campaign. It must be remembered that these organizations were not intended to serve as insurgent vehicles in the first place. Indeed, more often than not, the actual leadership of the burgeoning movement is supplied by ad hoc committees and loosely structured working coalitions with ill-defined and often indirect connections to these established organizations. The latter may function as sources of support and resources vital to the generation of insurgency but rarely as protest organizations per se.

For the movement to survive, insurgents must be able to create a more enduring organizational structure to sustain insurgency. Efforts to do so usually entail the creation of formally constituted organizations to assume the centralized direction of the movement previously exercised by informal groups. This transfer of power can only occur, however, if the resources needed to fuel the development of the movement's formal organizational structure can be mobilized. Accordingly, insurgent groups must be able to exploit the initial successes of the movement to mobilize those resources needed to facilitate the development of the more permanent organizational structure required to sustain insurgency. Failing this, movements are likely to die aborning as the loosely structured groups previously guiding the protest campaign disband or gradually lapse into inactivity.

This view is obviously at odds with Piven and Cloward's contention that organization is antithetical to movement success (1979: xxi–xxii). The authors base their pessimistic conclusion on a view that equates the development of movement organization with certain processes destructive of insurgency. The problem with their conclusion is in the inevitability they ascribe to these processes.

If Piven and Cloward overstate the negative effects of organization on insurgency, theirs is nonetheless an important thesis that indexes a major dilemma confronting movements. Without the minimal coordination and direction that organizations (informal no less than formal) afford, insurgency is nearly impossible. This is true even in the case of the most disruptive forms of insurgency (riots, strikes, etc.) as the work of the Tillys and others makes clear (Feagin and Hahn, 1973: 48–49; C. Tilly, L. Tilly, R. Tilly, 1975). At the same time, the establishment of formal movement organizations does have the potential to set in motion any one (or some combination) of three processes ultimately destructive of the effectiveness of the movement as a social change vehicle.

The first process is that of oligarchization. One need not accede to the rigidity of the Weber-Michels view of this process to acknowledge the potential danger it poses.[6] Quite simply, the establishment of formal movement organizations *may* create a certain class of individuals who come to value the maintenance of that organization over the realization of movement goals. In such cases, the insurgent potential of the movement is sacrificed to insure the survival of its organizational offshoot.

The creation of formal movement organizations also increases the likelihood of a second danger: co-optation. Having mobilized the resource support needed to create a formal organizational structure, insurgents still face the challenge of sustaining that structure over time. In this effort the resources of the movement's mass base are likely to be found wanting. The more impoverished the aggrieved population, the more likely this will be the case. In such instances, supplementary support must be drawn from outside sources. The establishment of external support linkages, however, grants considerable control over movement affairs to the source from which the resources are obtained. Of course, the control embodied in these support linkages need not be exercised in any particular case. If the movement organization uses the resource(s) in a manner consistent with the interests and goals of its sponsor(s), then support is likely to continue without interruption. Therein lies the dilemma. Owing to the impoverished state of the mass base, insurgents are likely to experience grave difficulties in trying to sustain insurgency solely on the basis of the limited resources of the movement's "beneficiary constituents." On the other hand, the establishment of external support linkages threatens to tame the movement by encouraging insurgents to pursue only those goals acceptable to external sponsors. The latter course of action may insure the survival of the movement—or at least of its organizational offshoots—but only at the cost of reducing its effectiveness as a force for social change.

The final danger inherent in the creation of formal movement organizations is the dissolution of indigenous support. What amounts to a virtually inevitable by-product of the establishment of external support links, this process has been largely ignored by movement analysts. The dynamic is simple. As insurgents increasingly seek to cultivate ties to outside groups, their indigenous links are likely to grow weaker. The potential negative consequences of this process are threefold. First, it may encourage oligarchization as movement leaders are increasingly insulated from the indigenous pressures that would tend to insure their responsiveness to the original goals of the movement. Second, the process increases the movement's dependence on external sources of support, thus rendering co-optation more likely. Third, and most important, the weakening of indigenous ties deprives the movement of the "established structures of solidary incentives" that earlier supplied the motive force for movement participation. Insurgents now face the difficult task of inducing participation through the provision of the sort of selective incentives that have been shown to correlate with movement success (Gamson, 1975: 66–71).

To summarize, sustained insurgency depends, in part, on the level of organizational resources that movement forces are able to maintain over time. Efforts to insure a routinized flow of resources usually lead to the establishment of formal organizations to supplant the indigenous groups out of which the movement emerged. Although necessary, if the movement is to attain a degree of permanence, this transformation is nonetheless likely to set in motion several processes ultimately destructive of insurgency. Specifically, the creation of formal organizations renders the movement increasingly vulnerable to the destructive forces of oligarchization, co-optation, and the dissolution of indigenous support. Should insurgents manage somehow to avoid these dangers while maintaining an adequate flow of resources the movement is likely to endure. However, the long list of movements that have failed to negotiate these obstacles attests to the difficulties inherent in the effort.

The Social Control Response to Insurgency

The identification of this response as a crucial factor affecting movement development only serves to reemphasize the reciprocal relationship that exists between the movement and its external environment. If the likelihood of movement emergence is partly conditioned by shifting political conditions, the movement itself introduces new pressures for change into the political system. Other organized groups are expected to respond to these pressures in a fashion consistent with their own interests. Over time, the development of insurgency is expected to be profoundly affected by these responses.

Two factors are of principal importance in shaping these responses. The first is the strength of insurgent forces. In different ways, both Gamson and Tilly have argued as much in asserting that weakness encourages repression (Gamson, 1975: 81–82; Tilly, 1978: 111–15). When one reflects on it, the proposition, although not completely intuitive, makes sense. Quite simply, both the costs and risks involved in repressing a weak target are minimal when compared with those associated with the repression of a powerful opponent. Quite apart from the degree of threat each poses, the latter must be handled with greater caution because of the potentially graver repercussions associated with an unsuccessful attempt at repres-

sion. In part, then, the strength of insurgent forces conditions the responses of other groups to the movement by determining the costs
associated with various alternative control strategies.

The second factor affecting the response of other parties to insurgency
is the degree to which the movement poses a threat or an opportunity to
other groups in terms of the realization of the latter's interests. In this
regard, most movements confront an elite divided in its reaction to the
insurgent challenge. Some components of the elite usually perceive the
movement as a threat and seek through their actions to neutralize or
destroy it. Others see in it an opportunity to advance their interests and
thus extend cautious support to insurgents. Still others perceive their
interests as little affected by the challenge and remain uninvolved. The
mix of these three responses determines, for any particular movement,
the relative balance of supporting and opposing forces it must confront
at any given point in time. To oversimplify matters a bit, if the movement
is to survive, it must retain (in consort with its allies) sufficient strength
to withstand the control responses of the opposition.

What is absent in the above discussion is the element of time. The point
to be made is that the level of threat or opportunity embodied in a movement is not constant over time. Not only are the interests of elite groups
likely to change, but so are important characteristics of the insurgent
challenge itself. Specifically, it is the goals and tactics of insurgents that
are of crucial importance, since together they largely define the degree
of threat/opportunity posed by the movement.

Tactics. The myriad tactics available to insurgents communicate varying
degrees of threat to other organized groups in the political environment.
The key distinction is between institutionalized and noninstitutionalized
tactics. Even if used to pursue "radical" goals, the former implicitly
convey an acceptance of the established, or "proper," channels of conflict resolution. Such tactics are, thus, viewed as nonthreatening by elite
groups, both because they leave unchallenged the structural underpin-
nings of the political system and because it is within these "proper"
channels that the power disparity between members and challengers is
greatest.

Reliance on noninstitutionalized tactics represents the converse of the
above situation and, as such, poses a distinct challenge to elite groups for
at least two reasons. At a symbolic level, it communicates a fundamental
rejection of the established institutional mechanisms for seeking redress
of group grievances; substantively, it deprives elite groups of their recourse to institutional power. For both these reasons, elite groups are
likely to view noninstitutionalized tactics as a threat to their interests.
Thus, any significant shift in tactics on the part of insurgents will generally

condition a commensurate shift in the response of elite groups to the movement. A greater reliance on noninstitutionalized forms of protest is likely to broaden opposition to the movement while decreased use of such tactics will usually diminish the intensity of movement opposition.

Goals. Much the same dynamic applies to the goals of the movement. That is, substantive shifts in the goals embraced by insurgents profoundly effect the response of elite groups to the movement. The central distinction here is between those goals that embody a fundamental challenge to the existing political and economic structures of society (revolutionary goals) and those that merely call for piecemeal reform of those structures (reform goals). By virtue of their narrow focus, *reform* goals stand to engender the opposition of only those few elite groups whose interests are directly effected by the proposed changes. Moreover, such goals usually facilitate the mobilization of limited support from those components of the elite who stand to benefit either from the reforms themselves or from the defeat they would spell for their opponents. Thus, reform movements are frequently aided in their efforts by their ability to exploit existing divisions among the elite.

Truly *revolutionary* goals, on the other hand, are rarely the object of divided elite response. Rather, movements that emphasize such goals usually mobilize a united elite opposition whose minor conflicts of interest are temporarily tabled in deference to the central threat confronting the system as a whole. In terms of this discussion, then, shifts from reform to revolutionary goals will almost surely be accompanied by an intensification of movement opposition while a change in the reverse direction will usually diminish the strength of opposition forces.[7]

This indicates a second critical dilemma confronting insurgents. Although recourse to institutionalized tactics and moderate goals is likely to diminish opposition to the movement, it will just as surely reduce the overall impact of the movement. Indeed, with respect to tactics, it was their fundamental powerlessness *within* institutionalized channels that led insurgents to abandon "proper channels" in the first place. Accordingly, insurgents must chart a course that avoids crippling repression on the one hand and tactical impotence on the other. Staking out this optimal middle ground is exceedingly difficult. Yet failure to do so almost surely spells the demise of the movement.

SUMMARY

The political process model represents an alternative to both the classical and resource mobilization perspectives. Rather than focusing exclusive attention on factors internal or external to the movement, the model

describes insurgency as a product of both. Specifically, three sets of factors are identified as shaping the generation of insurgency. It is the confluence of expanding political opportunities, indigenous organizational strength, and the presence of certain shared cognitions within the minority community that is held to facilitate movement emergence. Over time these factors continue to shape the development of insurgency in combination with a fourth factor: the shifting control response of other groups to the movement.

4 The Empirical Implications of Various Models of Social Movements

Debating the theoretical merits of models of social behavior is an important—and certainly challenging—exercise, but one whose ultimate relevance could be questioned. For the utility of any theory ultimately depends less on the elegance and logical structure of that model than on how well it predicts or describes concrete empirical phenomena. And so it is with the three models of social movements outlined in the preceding chapters. Accordingly, I turn, in the remainder of the book, to empirical analysis of the origins and development of black insurgency between 1876 and 1970. The purpose of this analysis is twofold. One goal is simply to provide as thorough an analytic history of the black movement as possible. The second aim is to structure the analysis around certain "comparative topics" that will allow for an assessment of the predictive utility of the three models as applied to a single instance of insurgency. In this chapter, seven such comparative topics will be identified and discussed as a means of providing a loose framework for the empirical analysis that is to follow. These topics have been listed under seven headings, each representing a distinct phase or aspect of social insurgency.

THE CHRONOLOGICAL ORIGIN OF INSURGENCY

With respect to this topic the key contrast involves a fundamental disagreement regarding the time span over which insurgency is expected to develop. Both resource mobilization and classical theorists seem to posit a stimulus-response view of the origin of social movements. That is, social movements are seen as emerging as a response to some short-run change in the period immediately preceding the outbreak of protest activity. By contrast, the political process model is based on the assumption that movements only emerge over a long period of time in response to broad social, economic, and political processes that afford insurgents a certain structural potential for collective action.

THE GENERATION OF INSURGENCY

In addition to stressing different time frames during which insurgency is assumed to develop, proponents of the three models also attribute causal significance to very different sets of factors. Of primary importance in the classical model is some form of severe "structural strain" in society that, in effect, propels people into protest activity. The key causal factor identified by mobilization theorists is a significant—and usually rapid— increase in the resources available to support insurgency. Finally, in the political process model, the generation of a social movement is attributed to the confluence of three factors: expanding political opportunities; the mobilization of indigenous organizational resources; and the presence of certain shared cognitions within the minority community.

SOURCE OF MOVEMENT RESOURCES

In the case of this and the next two topics, a comparison can only be drawn between the political process and resource mobilization models (or more accurately a particular version of the resource mobilization model). All three of these topics concern the relationship between the movement and external groups. The classical model is excluded from the discussion simply because its proponents have had little to say on the topic. This is not the case with political process or resource mobilization theorists. On the specific matter of resources, at least some of the latter hold that support for insurgency usually comes from outside the movement's mass base through links to external groups. On the other hand, political process theorists argue that it is usually the mass base, through the existing organizations of the minority community, that furnishes the resources needed to initiate a movement.

THE TIMING OF INVOLVEMENT OF EXTERNAL GROUPS IN THE MOVEMENT

The fundamental contrast between the mobilization and political process positions on this issue follows logically from the divergent views each adopted on the matter of resource support. Having argued that insurgency usually requires a healthy infusion of resources from external groups, mobilization theorists would seem to be ascribing an active, aggressive role to such groups in the generation of insurgency. That is, the involvement of external groups in the movement would seem to precede the outbreak of widespread protest activity. Not surprisingly, political process theorists reject this characterization of the timing of external involvement. Having described the mass base as possessing sufficient resource strength to initiate a movement on its own, they logically view the involvement of external groups in the movement as reactive. The expectation is that external involvement will occur only after the outbreak of protest activity as a response to the perceived threat or opportunity embodied in the movement.

The Consequences of External Involvement in the Movement

With regard to external involvement, the final contrast between the political process and resource mobilization models centers on their different views of the effect of such involvement on the chances for movement success. One implication of the mobilization perspective would seem to be that the fundamental poverty and powerlessness of most excluded groups renders any movement on their behalf virtually dependent on external "sponsorship" for success. Such a view tends to define the consequences of external involvement in favorable terms. By contrast, political process theorists attribute to most member groups a fundamental conservatism that is likely to lead them to oppose any social movement that threatens to disrupt the political status quo. For this reason, it is assumed that elite involvement in insurgency will be motivated more often by a desire to control, exploit, or perhaps even destroy the movement than to assist it. Thus, the expectation is that external involvement is likely to prove detrimental rather than advantageous to the movement.

Characteristics of Movement Participants

Here the contrast involves only the classical and political process models. The stress on resources and external groups in the resource mobilization model has led to a corresponding devaluation of the role of the mass base in social insurgency. Accordingly, little attention has been focused on the characteristics of the rank-and-file participants in a social movement. In fact, in some versions of the model, mass participation is seen as largely irrelevant to the outcome of social protest (McCarthy and Zald, 1973). However, both the classical and political process models emphasize the importance of the mass base as the participatory backbone of social insurgency. Here the similarity ends. In their descriptions of who participates proponents of these two models differ markedly. For their part classical theorists see participants as distinguished from nonparticipants on the basis of some characteristic psychological "profile." Frequently this "profile" serves implicitly to define participants as the marginal or poorly integrated members of society. Proponents of the political process model, on the other hand, emphasize the structural as opposed to psychological roots of movement participation. For them, participants are distinguished from nonparticipants on the basis of their greater integration into the established organizations of the minority community.

THE DECLINE OF INSURGENCY

The last topic concerns the different accounts of movement decline embodied in two of the three models. Once again classical theorists have said very little about this issue. Proponents of the mobilization perspective have also failed to address the topic of movement decline explicitly. However, the causal importance assigned to the growth of resource support in the process of movement emergence would seem to suggest an implicit account of movement decline. That is, it would seem reasonable to assume that movement decline would result from a significant drop in the level of resources available to support insurgency. As for political process theorists, they again deny the exclusive importance attributed to resources by proponents of the mobilization perspective. Instead, they stress the importance of four processes in the decline of insurgency: a significant contraction in political opportunities; the decline of organizational strength within the movement; a decline in the salience of certain cognitions essential to sustained insurgency; increased repression by movement opponents.

So much for an abstract comparison of various aspects of the classical, resource mobilization, and political process perspectives. This exercise will, however, take on empirical significance in the next four chapters as I return to these topics as a means of assessing the relative accuracy of the models as accounts of the history of black insurgency between 1876 and 1970. In the service of this assessment it will at times be necessary to interrupt the flow of the historical narrative so that the empirical implications of these models can be specified and discussed in light of the history of the movement. While less than desirable stylistically, this theoretical stocktaking is essential to insure the minimal degree of continuity between the theory and data required for this assessment.

Finally, the reader should be cautioned against misinterpreting the nature of this comparative analysis. In no way does it amount to a "test" of the models in question. In the first place, the single case of insurgency under analysis hardly affords an adequate basis for such a test. Second, the quality and relevance of data bearing on these models are highly variable. In some cases the fit between data and theory will be reasonably good; at other times it will be merely suggestive. For both these reasons, then, I am clearly not in a position to conduct a rigorous scientific test of competing models. To repeat, all I am endeavoring to do is to present data that will allow for an assessment of the general fit between the three models outlined earlier and the recent history of black insurgency in this country. With these necessary caveats disposed of, I can now turn to the analysis in question.

5 The Historical Context
of Black Insurgency
1876–1954

Both the classical and resource mobilization models suggest that the factors shaping the development of a social movement operate in the short run. For classical theorists the presumption is that some form of severe structural strain in the immediate premovement period is the proximate cause of insurgency. For these theorists the task "is to identify the change in social configurations which preceded and accompanied the growth of the movement. These changes are then identified as sources of strain in the system, as impairments in the normally smooth working of . . . society" (John Wilson, 1973: 37). Informed by much the same logic, resource mobilization theorists search for evidence of increased resource support for insurgent groups in the period immediately preceding the generation of widespread protest activity. The adequacy of both these specific explanations of movement generation will come in for empirical scrutiny in the next chapter. For now the important point is that both models adhere to an implicit stimulus-response view of insurgency, in which social movements are pictured as a direct product of recent changes in the larger environment confronting insurgent groups.

In contrast, the political process model suggests a considerably different historical time frame for the study of movement emergence. In attributing causal significance to the interplay of expanding political opportunities and developing organizational strength, attention is focused on the long-range processes that shape these two sets of factors. Instead of focusing exclusive attention on the period immediately preceding the generation of insurgency, the time frame is broadened to include the entire span of years during which conditions facilitative of insurgency are developing. In the case of the black movement, it is the quarter century preceding the 1954 Supreme Court decision in *Brown* v. *Topeka Board of Education* that is viewed as especially significant. For it was during this period that both the opportunities for successful insurgent action and the organizational strength to exploit those opportunities were developing. However, to provide a context for appreciating the significance of the changes that occurred during this crucial twenty-five-year period, I will begin my

analysis even earlier, with a discussion of conditions as they existed during
the period from 1876 to 1930.

THE STRUCTURE OF POLITICAL OPPORTUNITIES, 1876–1930

In a successful effort to resolve the deadlocked presidential election of
1876, northern Republicans agreed to relax federal reconstruction efforts
in the South in exchange for southern support for their candidate, Rutherford B. Hayes. The practical effect of the compromise was, once again,
to render the "Negro question" a matter of regional rather than federal
purview. In Dahl's phrase, the compromise of 1876 was an important
step in the process by which "the issue of the freed Negro was de-
nationalized (1967: 182). Schattschneider's famous statement is worth
repeating here: "all forms of political organization have a bias in favor
of the exploitation of some kinds of conflict and the suppression of others
because *organization is the mobilization of bias. Some issues are organized into politics while others are organized out*" (1960: 71; emphasis
mine). In this sense, the compromise serves as a convenient historical
referent marking the point in time at which the question of the sociopolitical status of black Americans was consciously "organized out" of national
politics. This arrangement held for better than fifty years, reflecting, over
that period of time, the continuing viability of the politico-economic calculations that had given rise to the compromise. The factors supporting
the arrangement were many.

"King Cotton" and the Confluence of Economic Interests

It has long been a commonplace that national politics was dominated to
an unusual extent by powerful northern economic interests in the last
quarter of the nineteenth century. Though generally affiliated with the
Republican party, this northern industrial elite grew increasingly unwilling
to adhere to the program of racial equality and economic radicalism characteristic of Reconstruction. This despite the fact that, as Barrington
Moore notes, the northern industrial elite had attained its position of
dominance by virtue of the war and Reconstruction and the crushing
defeat inflicted on the class of southern planters with whom northern
industrialists had vied for political-economic dominance in the prewar era
(1966: chap. 3). Continued support for the traditional Republican "war
issues," however, had, in the view of this industrial elite, produced little
but a state of economic chaos antithetical to their interests.

As the linchpin of the South's prewar economy, slavery had insured
the abundant supply of cheap labor that was vital to cotton farming. The
degree of political and economic freedom granted blacks during Reconstruction jeopardized this supply. The attendant disruption of the cotton

economy coupled with the prospect of a real agricultural revolution in the South in turn threatened to disrupt the smooth flow of cheap cotton on which the textile mills of the Northeast and the American export economy had come to depend.

Thus, following a decade of chaos in the South, northern industrialists were willing to abandon the goals of Radical Reconstruction in order to resolve these contradictions and again bring a measure of economic stability to the region. As Buck has written, "Cotton brokers of New York and Philadelphia, and cotton manufacturers of New England . . . knew full well the importance of bringing discipline to the Southern labor force. When theories of Negro equality resulted in race conflict, and conflict in higher prices of raw cotton, manufacturers were inclined to accept the point of view of the Southern planter rather than that of the New England zealot" (1937: 154–55).

On one level, then, the Compromise of 1876 can be seen as an economic rapprochement between northern industrialists and southern planters. In turn, this confluence of economic interests contributed to the relaxation of federal Reconstruction efforts and the gradual establishment of a system of cotton tenancy. The impact of this system on the institutional strength of the black population will be discussed later. Here, the key point is simply that in terms of the material interests of both the southern planters and northern industrialists, the system proved highly successful. Through debt bondage, cotton tenancy (buttressed by the elaborate set of caste restrictions established to support it) bound blacks to the land nearly as effectively as slavery had done.[2] Thus, the system insured the supply of cheap labor that Reconstruction had temporarily interrupted.

With the resolution of this "troublesome" problem, the flow of raw cotton northward increased dramatically. It would be hard to overstate the extent of this expansion or its importance to northern commercial interests. Between 1870 and 1910 the production of raw cotton increased threefold. More significantly, the "consumption of cotton by domestic manufacturers increased . . . from 800,000 bales in 1870 to 4,800,000 bales in 1910" (Baron, 1971: 13). Over the same period of time, cotton emerged as this country's leading export commodity. As late as 1917, cotton exports continued to account for one-fourth of the total value of all American goods shipped abroad. As an economic arrangement, then, the Compromise of 1876 proved a smashing success.[3] That is until 1920 or so when certain socioeconomic processes intervened to disrupt the consistency of material interests on which this arrangement had, in part, been based.

The Populist Threat and Disenfranchisement

Radical Reconstruction was not the only threat to the economic stability of the South to arise during this period. Some ten years after the last of the federal troops were withdrawn from the region, internal political pressures threatened once again to disrupt the politico-economic hegemony enjoyed by the southern planter elite. The threat took the form of the budding Populist movement then gaining strength in the South. Founded on an awareness of the common class-interests of all farmers, Populism threatened a radical restructuring of southern agriculture, provided the incipient coalition of black and white farmers could be forged into the potent electoral coalition envisioned by its architects. Ultimately the effort failed, but only after the movement attained sufficient strength to trigger a period of intense political conflict between the Populists and the planter elite. The result was a stalemate of sorts that introduced considerable uncertainty into the structure of political power in the region. In time, both sides came to regard this state of affairs as unsatisfactory and to attribute it to the presence of a black electorate that neither side had yet been able to "capture." The fear was that, in time, one side or the other would succeed in doing so, thereby reducing the political leverage exercised by the other. In the end both sides concluded it would be "much better to have clear-cut constitutional disenfranchisement of the Negro and to leave the white group to fight elections out among themselves" (Franklin, 1967: 337).

This conclusion was "encouraged" by the planter elite's use of time-honored racist appeals to "white supremacy" and "racial purity." So effective were these appeals that by the mid-1890s the black vote had come to be a liability rather than an asset in southern electoral politics. As Henri points out: "The Democrats played on race hatred and fear of black domination, a fear to which white Populists in the South were no more immune than other white Southerners. White men hastened to disclaim interest in black advancement. By 1896 a southern white man's place in his community and among his friends was threatened if he voted the Populist ticket, which according to Democratic propaganda was a 'nigger' ticket" (1975: 8).

With the black vote so thoroughly discredited, efforts at disenfranchisement, largely informal and covert in the past, took on a highly visible and official character after 1890. Thus, one delegate to Virginia's constitutional convention of 1900 could openly acknowledge that the purpose of the convention was "to discriminate to the very extremity of permissible action under the limitations of the federal Constitution, with a view to the elimination of every Negro voter who can be gotten rid of legally, without materially impairing the numerical strength of the white electorate" (in Lawson, 1976: 12).[4] That these official disenfranchisement efforts were effective is amply demonstrated by a comparison of voter registration numbers pre- and post-1900. The figures for Louisiana serve as a representative case. In 1896, 130,344 blacks were registered to vote. After the revision of Louisiana's constitution in 1898 the number was reduced to some 5,000 in 1900 with an ultimate low of 1,772 reached in 1916 ✳ (Lewinson, 1932: 218–20). Perhaps more significantly, the number of parishes in which blacks represented a majority of the voters declined from twenty-six in 1896 to zero four years later (Woodward, 1966: 85).

Through such efforts the southern planter elite was able to survive the Populist "scare" with the institutional imperatives of its dominant class position intact. By granting a semblance of political power to white farmers, the planters were able to implement a kind of "divide and conquer" strategy that effectively destroyed the Populist movement while preserving the political basis of cotton tenancy. Quite obviously the losers in this process were southern blacks.[5]

Disenfranchisement adversely effected black political prospects in three ways. First, it destroyed their ability to bargain for political and economic gains through the adoption of a "balance of power" strategy vis-à-vis competing segments of the white population. Second, it rendered the exercise of violent control measures against blacks increasingly likely by eliminating any threat of electoral reprisals against the parties responsible. Finally, because of their small numbers outside the South—only 10 percent of all blacks lived in the North and West in 1900—disenfranchisement had the practical effect of eliminating blacks as an electoral force at the national level as well.

The Decline of Black Influence Nationally

Though important, disenfranchisement wasn't the only factor responsible for the waning political fortunes of blacks nationally. Even prior to disenfranchisement, Republican party leaders had sought to broaden their southern electoral appeal by withdrawing support for controversial Reconstruction efforts. This decision reflected a growing devaluation of the so called "radical" Republican vote—including the black vote—in favor of an alliance with what was believed to be a widespread latent conservative political constituency throughout the South.

Following the election of Rutherford B. Hayes in 1876, Republican leaders confidently pursued this policy of political rapprochement, expecting to pick up seats in the off-year congressional elections of 1878. Election returns hardly justified their confidence. Indeed, as Hirshson accurately remarks, in place of an increase in Republican strength in the region "the Southern wing of the party virtually disappeared" (1962: 47–48).

This electoral setback did not, however, lead the Republicans to abandon the premises on which the party's "southern strategy" was based. On the contrary, the search for southern white support remained a consistent component of the party's electoral strategy from 1877 to 1892.

Hirshson explains: "With national political power during this period almost equally divided between the two great parties, Republican officials realized that if they could not carry some areas of the South they would frequently lose control of Congress and the Presidency. . . . Every Republican president between 1877 and 1893, comprehending that only a national party could wrest power away from the Democrats, adopted a scheme which he hoped would attract Southern white men to Republicanism" (Hirshson 1962: 253).

Ultimately, the party's southern strategy was to prove a miserable failure. Despite repeated overtures to white voters in the South, Republicans were never able to establish a strong electoral presence in the region. Faced with another disastrous setback in the presidential election of 1892 and the growing threat that disenfranchisement posed to the one "natural" constituency—blacks—they had been able to retain, Republicans effectively conceded the region to the Democratic party. "Aware that in the past fifteen years all of their plans to build Republicanism in the South had failed, almost all Republicans now conceded that their party was destined to be a Northern, not national, organization" (Hirshson, 1962: 236).

Republican abandonment of the South contributed to a nationwide diminution in competitive party politics that was to last for over a generation. A comparison of presidential election returns before and after 1892 supports this conclusion. Whereas the vote totals in thirty-six states depict a competitive two-party situation in 1896, eight years later the number of competitive states stands at only six, with fully thirty states clearly established as the exclusive electoral province of one or the other of the two major parties (Schattschneider, 1960: 83). Party competition during this period survived only in the border states and on occasion in New York, Indiana, and Ohio. Elsewhere, as Schattschneider notes, contests "were nearly always so one-sided that the voters had no significant choices" (1960: 85).

For blacks, this situation proved disastrous. Outside the South, blacks simply constituted too small a proportion of the electorate to prompt much attention from the Republican party, whose strength was mainly confined to the northern and western portions of the country. On the other hand, in the South, where blacks constituted better than 30 percent of the population, disenfranchisement effectively neutralized their numerical strength and left them powerless in the face of a Democratic party firmly committed to a repressive policy of white supremacy. Thus, in the period from 1896 to 1928, the geographic alignment of political loyalties, coupled with disenfranchisement, destroyed whatever chance blacks might have had of mobilizing any semblance of national electoral leverage.

Increased Volume of Antiblack Federal Action

Reflecting the powerless position of blacks nationally, the volume of discriminatory federal action increased significantly during the period under examination. The significance of this trend was twofold. Substantively, federal action contributed to black powerlessness, even as it was partially a product of it. Second, at a symbolic level, these actions communicated to blacks the virtual impossibility of successful group action to combat discrimination. I will return to this point later in the chapter. For now the key point is that these actions were of substantive as well as symbolic significance. Nowhere was this more apparent than in regard to the decisions handed down by the Supreme Court during this period. Between 1876 and 1930, the thrust of Supreme Court decisions in cases involving blacks had the effect of further limiting the opportunities for black political action by gradually eroding earlier constitutional provisions safeguarding civil rights. Of principal importance was the court's progressively narrow interpretation of the constitutional principles embodied in the Fourteenth Amendment. Originally intended as a basic foundation for the constitutional protection of black rights, the Amendment's three clauses were reinterpreted, through a series of judicial decisions, to afford only a weak safeguard against discrimination. Instead, reflecting the dominance of commercial interests during the period, the amendment was successfully employed as a defense of laissez-faire capitalism against state intervention in economic affairs. For example, one author has found that of the 604 decisions handed down by the Supreme Court between 1868 and 1911 involving the Fourteenth Amendment, only 28 dealt with the protection of black civil rights. Of these, only six upheld the basic principle involved (Collins, 1912: 68). Writing in 1912, the author concluded that "it is not the negro, but accumulated and organized capital, which now looks to the Fourteenth Amendment for protection from state activity" (Collins, 1912: 47). The depressing result of these Fourteenth Amendment cases accurately mirrors the overall judicial record for the period. An analysis of all relevant cases reaching the Supreme Court between 1876 and 1930 shows that only twenty-three of fifty-three (43 percent) were decided in favor of blacks (see fig. 5.2).

Nor was discriminatory federal action confined only to the judiciary during this period. There is also ample evidence of legislative and executive action between 1876 and 1930 that contributed to the erosion of black civil rights. Such action was not constant during these years but seemed to alternate between periods of strict noninvolvement and aggressive opposition to black aims. At the beginning of the 1876–1930 period, there were even occasional reminders of the supportive federal involvement of Reconstruction. But such support gradually waned as the period wore on. Illustrative of this trend is the decline in the number of federal court cases prosecuted in the South under the Enforcement Acts of 1870–71. Berger reports that the number dropped from a high of 1,271 in 1873, to 954 in 1874, 221 in 1875, to only 25 in 1879 (1950: 9). Finally, during Grover Cleveland's second term (1893–97), the very provisions under which these cases had been brought were themselves struck down by Congress. Nonetheless, as Hirshson reminds us, the period spanning the Compromise of 1876 and the election of 1892

> was not the nadir for the Negro. Certainly a span of time marked by the Lodge bill, the Blair bill, numerous Congressional investigations of Southern atrocities, and a steady stream of Republican speeches in favor of equal civil and political rights for the colored race cannot be considered a low point. The bottom was actually reached after 1891, when Republican efforts for the Negro dramatically and suddenly stopped. A student of the period between the Force bill struggle and the First World War will search in vain if he looks for election acts, education bills, and other political measures designed to aid the Negro (Hirshson, 1962: 251–52).

By the turn of the century, then, the federal government was, by virtue of its rigorous adherence to a policy of noninterference, lending its tacit support to white supremacy throughout the South. During the first two decades of this century, however, noninvolvement increasingly gave way to aggressive antiblack legislative and executive action. Ironically, this trend received its fullest expression during an administration generally conceded to have been one of the most progressive in this nation's history—that of Woodrow Wilson. The volume of antiblack legislation during the first Wilson Congress was greater than during any other session in congressional annals. "No less than twenty bills were proposed that would segregate Negroes on public carriers in the District of Columbia, exclude them from commissions in the army and navy, and set up segregated accommodations for white and Negro federal employees" (Lomax, 1962: 223). Still other pieces of proposed legislation called for an end to further black immigration to this country and a ban on intermarriage in the District of Columbia (Kellogg, 1967: 180). That most of these bills failed to obtain the support needed for passage hardly diminishes the significance of the trend. Moreover, in some cases presidential action rendered legislation unnecessary. Shortly after his inauguration, Wilson ordered segregation in a number of federal agencies, including the Department of the Treasury and the Post Office. The prohibition in these cases extended to "race mixing" in work areas, toilet facilities, and food services (Weiss, 1970: 131). While largely symbolic, the number of black federal appointees also showed a significant decline during Wilson's tenure as president (Weiss, 1970: 133).

Cumulatively, the evidence is impressive. In less than forty years the federal government had been transformed from an advocate of black equality into a force buttressing the southern racial status quo. As such, the actions of the federal government strengthened and legitimized the processes discussed earlier even as they represented a response to those same trends.

THE STRUCTURE OF POLITICAL OPPORTUNITIES, 1931–54

The factors reviewed in the previous section severely restricted the opportunities for successful political action by, or on behalf of, blacks for a period of more than fifty years. In combination, these factors constituted a set of political realities upon which a restrictive racial status quo was successfully structured. In effect these factors rendered the black population relatively powerless while elevating the southern politico-economic elite to a position of considerable importance. On the basis of their perception of this gross power disparity, other parties to the conflict constructed lines of action vis-à-vis these two groups that they believed would best serve their interests. Overwhelmingly, these third parties instituted policies of noninvolvement so as not to antagonize the politically powerful opponents of black equality. Thus deprived of allies, and (as will be discussed later) organizationally weak in their own right, blacks were unable, throughout the period, to generate the leverage needed to break the racial stalemate. Indeed, the arrangement held for over fifty years, reflecting, for that span of time, the continuing viability of the calculations that had given rise to it. But, as Myrdal remarked with great foresight in 1944, the arrangement never constituted a "stable power equilibrium" and appeared at last to "be approaching its end" (1970: 34). Specifically, it was a series of broad social processes occurring roughly in the quarter-century from 1930 to 1954 that served to undermine the politico-economic conditions on which the racial status quo had been based. Together, these processes facilitated the development of the black movement by profoundly altering the "shape" of the political environment confronting blacks.

The Decline of "King Cotton"

If one had to identify the factor most responsible for undermining the political conditions that, at the turn of the century, had relegated blacks to a position of political impotence, it would have to be the gradual collapse of cotton as the backbone of the southern economy. So long as cotton remained—despite some lean years—the lucrative cash crop it was during the 1876–1920 period, a certain consistency of interest between southern planters and northern mill owners and cotton brokers was assured. However, as early as 1915, and especially after 1930, several factors combined to undermine the preeminence of cotton and the confluence of material interests on which the racial status quo had depended.

The first note of discord sounded during World War I as the conflict in Europe interrupted the flow of immigrants to northern industrial states just as wartime production pushed the demand for labor to record levels. From a total of some 8 million wage earners in manufacturing in 1914 the number rose to nearly 11 million five years later, more than double the rate of increase during any preceding five-year period (U.S. Bureau of the Census, 1975: 137). At the same time, the flow of European immigration that had swelled America's rapid industrial expansion slowed to a trickle. The decline was precipitous, with the total number of immigrants dropping from 1,218,480 in 1914 to less than one-tenth that figure— 110,618—in 1918 (U.S. Bureau of the Census, 1975: 105). In combination, these trends produced a calamitous labor shortage which northern industry sought to fill by luring southern blacks northward to work in the expanding war industries. The level of black out-migration from the South during the decade suggests just how successful these efforts were. From less than 200,000 black out-migrants in the 1900–1909 period, the number rose to better than half a million in the succeeding ten-year period (Lee et al., 1957).

The reaction of the South to these "raids" on "their" work force attests to the severity of the conflict and, by implication, to the continuing intensity of the region's labor requirements:

> Alarm spread throughout the white South as farm laborers and city menial and domestic help drifted off in twos, twenties, and two hundreds. State laws and city ordinances were passed to oust or curb the agents who were taking most of the workers. . . . In Montgomery, recruiting labor for out-of-state jobs was punishable by a $100 fine and six months at hard labor on a convict gang. Force was not infrequently used to prevent the taking of blacks North. . . . Labor agents were arrested. Trains carrying migrants were stopped, the blacks forced to return and the agents beaten. Blacks might be terrorized or lynched on suspicion of trying to leave the state (Henri, 1975: 62).

For the first time since Reconstruction the material interests of various segments of the nation's economic elite diverged on the "Negro problem." The solid economic alliance between northern industrialists and southern planters was showing signs of strain. "The profit-maximization imperatives of Northern capitalist firms for the first time outweighed the socio-political reasons for leaving the Southern planters' control over black labor undisturbed and without any serious competition" (Baron, 1971: 21).

Nor did the end of European hostilities provide a permanent solution to this conflict. Instead, the postwar growth in nativist and isolationist sentiment in this country coupled with the "Red scares" of the Palmer years, resulted in the passage of restrictive immigration laws that left northern industry increasingly dependent on southern black out-migrants as their principal source of labor. The strength of this "pull" factor is reflected in a rate of black migration from the South in the 1920s even higher than that of the preceding decade.

However, the intensity of the South's efforts to combat this increased northward exodus of blacks declined noticeably after 1920. The explanation for this shifting pattern of response is to be found in a series of internal factors that were simultaneously reducing the South's labor needs by undermining the preeminence of cotton as the region's principal cash crop. The decline of "King Cotton" is shown in figure 5.1, which depicts the fluctuations in cotton acreage and the price of raw cotton between 1911 and 1950. Following a number of bad crop years prior to World War I, demand for cotton increased dramatically during the war years, as the sharp rise in cotton prices attests. It was during this period that the antilabor-recruitment measures were instituted. The boom in cotton farming did not, however, survive the war years. Instead, declining prices and the rapid spread of the boll weevil made for hard times in the immediate postwar period. Prices rebounded somewhat in the mid-1920s, but tumbled again by decade's end as record acreage levels led to a glut of cotton on the market.

If the events of the 1920s reduced the viability of cotton farming, it was the Depression that ended, once and for all, the crop's dominant role in the South's economy. Reflecting the reduced demand for all manner of goods, the price of raw cotton plummeted from a high of 35 cents per pound in 1919 to less than 6 cents in 1931. In the late 1930s the farm policies of the New Deal further diminished the economic importance of the crop by significantly reducing cotton acreage in an effort to stimulate demand (Fligstein, 1980; Sitkoff, 1978).

Such policies were only marginally effective, however. It remained for World War II to trigger a resurgence in cotton prices. By that time total acreage had declined to 40 percent of the record levels set in the 1920s. Following the war, prices remained high, but increased competition from both synthetic fibers and foreign cotton markets combined to reduce overseas demand for American cotton even more. Finally, during the 1950s and early 1960s radical changes in the nature of southern agriculture served to accelerate the dissolution of cotton tenancy. Of principal importance in this regard was the mechanization of southern agriculture and

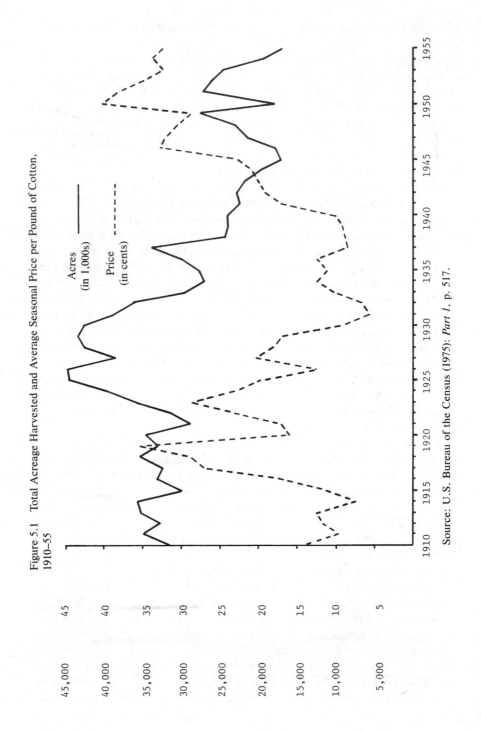

Figure 5.1 Total Acreage Harvested and Average Seasonal Price per Pound of Cotton, 1910–55

Source: U.S. Bureau of the Census (1975): *Part 1*, p. 517.

the less intensive system of farm labor it made possible (Dillingham and Sly, 1966: 344–51).

In little more than a generation, this complex mix of factors had destroyed the economic system on which southern life, and race relations, had previously been structured. In turn, the demise of "King Cotton" improved black political prospects for at least four reasons. First, the declining importance of cotton in the national economy, coupled with increased northern demand for black labor, undermined the economic basis of the powerful southern-northern alliance that had for years precluded any change in the racial status quo. Second, as the need for an abundant supply of cheap labor declined (commensurate with the decreased demand for cotton), so too did the necessity for the elaborate set of oppressive controls needed to insure the system's labor requirements. The practical effect of this relaxation of social control was to make black insurgency more feasible by reducing the risks associated with protest activity. Third, the collapse of cotton tenancy triggered a massive rural-to-urban migration within the South that was to ultimately afford blacks a stronger organizational context within which they could mobilize. Finally, in addition to stimulating movement within the region, the collapse of the cotton market also propelled large numbers of blacks north and westward where they were able to exercise the voting rights denied them in the South. This increased electoral strength contributed to a restructuring of political alignments that was to encourage later insurgency.

The Great Migration and the Black Vote

One of the most massive and significant movements of people in this country's history was the black migration out of the South during the period from 1910 to 1960. The extraordinary magnitude of this demographic transition is indicated in table 5.1. While the total black population of the United States increased by 92 percent between 1910 and 1960, the rate of increase in the non-South was more than six and a half times this figure. In the South the change in the black population was a mere 29 percent during this same period. In these fifty years the South lost nearly 5 million blacks to out-migration (see table 5.2).

Conditioning the migration was the same mix of "push" and "pull" factors discussed in the previous section. The "push" was supplied by the many factors contributing to the decline in cotton farming. Among these were the spread of the boll weevil, the collapse of the cotton market during the Depression, New Deal farm policies, and increased competition from synthetic fibers and overseas cotton production. The "pull" was a function of increased northern demand for labor stimulated by restrictive immigration legislation, two world wars, the Korean "action," and the "baby boom"–fueled prosperity of the 1950s and 1960s. My concern, however, is less with the causes of the migration than with its political consequences.

The political significance of this mass exodus can be seen from an analysis of the departure and destination points of the migrants. With

TABLE 5.1
Black Population by Geographical Region, 1910 and 1960

| | Black Population | | |
	1910	1960	% Change
North	1,027,674	6,474,536	530
New England	66,306	243,363	267
Middle Atlantic	417,870	2,785,136	567
East North Central	300,836	2,884,969	859
West North Central	242,662	561,068	131
West	50,662	1,085,688	2043
Mountain	21,467	123,242	474
Pacific	29,195	962,446	3197
Non-South (combined North and West)	1,078,336	7,560,224	601
South	8,749,427	11,311,607	29
South Atlantic	4,112,488	5,844,565	42
East South Central	2,652,513	2,698,839	2
West South Central	1,984,426	2,768,203	39
U.S. Total	9,827,763	18,871,831	92

Sources: Figures for 1910 from U.S. Bureau of the Census (1935): chap. 3, table 4; for 1960 from idem (1961): table 56.

TABLE 5.2
Net Black Out-Migration from the South by Decade, 1870–1960

Decade	Black Migration from the South
1870–1880	71,000
1880–1890	83,000
1890–1900	195,000
1900–1910	197,000
1910–1920	522,000
1920–1930	872,000
1930–1940	407,000
1940–1950	1,599,000
1950–1960	1,457,000

Sources: Figures for 1870–1940 from Lee et al. (1957); for 1950–60 from U.S. Bureau of the Census (1962b).

regard to the former, table 5.3 shows that the migrants were drawn disproportionately from states with the lowest black-voter registration percentages. The correlation between the percentage of the black voting-age population registered to vote in 1940 and the total number of black out-migrants between 1910 and 1960 is − .61.[6]

Thus, the black migration was not so much a general exodus from the South as a selective move from those areas where the political participation of blacks was most severely limited. This is not to say that the intensity of political restrictions to which various geographic groupings of southern blacks were subjected accounts for differences in migration rates. Rather, it just so happens that the areas in which the force of economic push factors was most severe were also those characterized by the lowest voter registration rates. Thus, as Brooks has accurately observed, "the move was more than a simple migration and change in folkways; for blacks, it was a move, almost literally, from no voting to voting" (Brooks, 1974: 17). That this was the case is clear from a comparison of the rates of increase in the total black population and the black voting population between 1910 and 1960. While the former increased by 92 percent (see table 5.1), the total number of blacks voting in the presidential election showed an eightfold rise over the same period of time (Weiss, 1970: 131; Wilson, 1966: 431).

This simple numerical increase takes on added political significance when informed by an analysis of the states that absorbed the bulk of the net black migration from the South. Table 5.4 shows that 87 percent of the total number of black immigrants from the South in the 1910–60 period settled in seven key northern (or western) industrial states: New York,

TABLE 5.3
1940 Black Voter Registration and 1910–60 Black Out-Migration Figures for All Southern States

State	% of the Black Voting Age Population Registered in 1940	Total Black Out-Migration 1910–60
Mississippi	.3	779,000
Alabama	.4	572,300
South Carolina	.8	713,000
Virginia	4.1	283,000
Georgia	3.4	784,300
Louisiana	.4	265,100
North Carolina	7.1	403,500
Florida	5.7	194,300
Texas	5.6	67,000
Arkansas	8.1	305,300
Tennessee	6.5	125,100
Total	3.5	4,103,300

Sources: For voter registration data, Lawson (1976: 134); for migration data, U.S. Bureau of the Census (1975): *Part 1*, Series C 25–75, p. 95.

TABLE 5.4
Estimated Net Migration of Blacks for Selected States, by Decade, 1910–60

State	1910–20	1920–30	1930–40	1940–50	1950–60[a]	Total
Pennsylvania	82,500	101,700	20,300	89,600	77,000	371,100
New York	63,100	172,800	135,900	243,600	282,000	897,400
Illinois	69,800	119,300	49,400	179,800	189,000	607,300
New Jersey	24,500	67,000	9,500	64,000	112,000	277,000
Michigan	38,700	86,100	28,000	163,300	127,000	443,100
Ohio	69,400	90,700	20,700	106,700	133,000	420,500
California	16,100	36,400	41,200	258,900	354,000	706,600
All other northern and western states	90,500	76,000	43,700	138,900	211,000	560,100
Total	454,600	750,000	348,700	1,244,800	1,485,000	4,283,100

Sources: U.S. Bureau of the Census (1963): Series C 25–75; and idem (1962): Series P–25, no. 247, table 4.

[a] Figures for 1950–60 refer to nonwhites and were estimated by a different procedure from that used for the 1910–50 estimates.

New Jersey, Pennsylvania, Ohio, California, Illinois, and Michigan. Brink and Harris comment on the strategic importance of these seven states; "no candidate for President in modern times has won without taking a substantial share of the votes of the big seven" (1963: 80). Quite simply, the electoral college, with its population-based proportional system of voting and winner-take-all provision, has rendered these states the key to electoral success in presidential contests. Thus, by moving disproportionately to these states blacks greatly enhanced their electoral importance.

By 1930 the political effects of the migration were already apparent. In that year, the NAACP, in what the *Christian Science Monitor* termed "the first national demonstration of the Negro's power since reconstruction days," joined with other groups in successfully blocking Senate confirmation of Herbert Hoover's Supreme Court nominee, John J. Parker.[7] Moreover, two years later, the NAACP followed up the confirmation battle with a coordinated electoral campaign that contributed to the defeat of several senators who had supported Parker (Hughes, 1962: 74–75; Sitkoff, 1978: 86). These demonstrations of political strength, coupled with the continuing flow of migrants northward, had, by 1936, firmly established blacks as an electoral force to be reckoned with. In that year *Time* acknowledged as much when it wrote: "In no national election since 1860 have politicians been so Negro minded as in 1936. In Missouri, Illinois, Indiana, Ohio, Michigan, West Virginia, Pennsylvania, New Jersey, and New York live some 2,500,000 Negroes, of whom over 1,000,000 are prospective voters this year. Moreover, in these same nine states the Roosevelt-Landon battle will be waged especially hard, with the result in each perhaps turning in favor of the party which can bag the largest Black vote" (*Time*, 1936: 10–11).

Nor did that year's election results do anything to dissuade political analysts of the growing electoral significance of the black vote. Deserting the Republican party for the first time in large number, blacks emerged as one of the key components of the new Democratic coalition that swept Roosevelt to a stunning victory in November.

As dramatic as these developments were, in one sense they were but harbingers of things to come. Indeed, the electoral strength of the black population increased at an even faster rate between 1940 and 1960 as black out-migration from the South reached record levels. Table 5.2 shows that the number of black migrants during these two decades far exceeded the combined total for the preceding seventy years. In all, better than three million blacks moved out of the South between 1940 and 1960.

The electoral significance of this stepped-up migration was evident in both the 1944 and 1948 elections. In both instances, had blacks reversed the proportion of votes they gave the two major candidates, the Republican challenger, Thomas Dewey, would have defeated his Democratic opponents, Franklin Roosevelt and Harry Truman (Brooks, 1974: 121).

The crucial importance of the black vote was especially apparent in the 1948 election. Essential to Truman's victory that year were the electoral votes of California, Illinois, and Ohio, three states which had absorbed 42 percent of all black net immigration between 1940 and 1950 (see table 5.4). The fact that Truman's combined 57,000-vote margin of victory in these three states was barely one-tenth the total number of black votes he received in those same states emphasizes the crucial role played by the black electorate in the 1948 election (Glantz, 1960: 999). By 1950, then, the so-called black vote was firmly established as an electoral force of national significance.

The Electoral Shift to the Democratic Party

The electoral powerlessness of blacks in the 1896–1930 period was as much the product of party affiliation and sectional political alignments as it was the result of disenfranchisement. Firmly committed to the Republican party, yet overwhelmingly concentrated in a South controlled by the Democrats, blacks were in a poor position to bring effective pressure to bear on the region's political elite. According to Lubell, "as long as the Negroes voted Republican nationally they could exert little political leverage on the South" (1964: 64). It remained for black electoral strength to grow strong enough to prompt favorable attention from northern Democrats before pressure could develop within the party for a change in racial policy. This process began to happen, albeit haltingly, in the early 1930s as a result of the first great wave of black migration between 1910 and

1930. Democratic politicians in a number of northern cities began actively to court the black vote as one component of what was to become the familiar urban Democratic coalition. Nationally the decisive break came a bit later in 1936 when the black electorate, which had returned Republican majorities in seventeen straight presidential elections, went overwhelmingly for Roosevelt.

If blacks lagged one election behind the other elements of the New Deal coalition in establishing a pattern of Democratic allegiance, the impact of this shift on the party was, nonetheless, profound and immediately felt. While southern states contributed 90 percent of all electoral college votes captured by the Democratic presidential candidates in 1920 and 1924, their proportion declined to just 23 percent in 1936. In effect, the growing significance of the black vote, and that of other elements of Roosevelt's New Deal coalition, served to break the South's veto power over matters of party policy. As Woodward notes, "the strategic location of the Negro minority in the North had made it sometimes more important to the success of the Democratic party in national elections than the disaffected whites in the southern wing of the Democracy" (1966: 129). This fact was registered dramatically in the 1948 campaign when Truman, running on what for the time was a radical civil rights platform, emerged victorious despite the active opposition of much of the southern wing of the party which had broken away to support Strom Thurmond's States' Rights party candidacy. By 1950, then, the sectional political alignment that had earlier confined black political fortunes to a solidly one-party South had been rendered obsolete by the growing strength of the black electorate and its shift from the Republican to Democratic party.

Thus, the expansion of the northern black electorate introduced an element of political conflict into a northern-southern racial alliance already weakened by the economic conflict of interest produced by the growing northern demand for black labor. So long as blacks constituted an insignificant proportion of the nonsouthern electorate, northern and national politicians had no reason to oppose the South on racial matters. Northward migration provided a reason: the black electoral support crucial to the fortunes of all manner of nonsouthern politicians. Thus, while the southern political elite fought bitterly to maintain adherence to a repressive racial status quo, northern and national politicians found it increasingly necessary to support, if only symbolically, proposals for change in that system. Once characterized by a strong consistency of material and political interests, the northern-southern "arrangement" on racial matters was crumbling.

World War II and the End of American Isolationism

If the electoral realignments of the New Deal era served to enhance the political importance of blacks, the Second World War continued this trend.

It did so by effectively terminating the isolationist foreign policy that had long defined America's relationship to the rest of the world. As a result, national political leaders found themselves exposed, in the postwar era, to international political pressures and considerations that their predecessors had been spared. Locked in an intense ideological struggle with the USSR for influence among the emerging third-world nations, American racism suddenly took on international significance as an effective propaganda weapon of the Communists. That this was of concern to the federal government is evidenced by a brief filed in December 1952 by the United States attorney general in connection with the public school desegregation cases then before the Supreme Court. In part the brief read: "It is in the context of the present world struggle between freedom and tyranny that the problem of racial discrimination must be viewed. . . . Racial discrimination furnishes grist for the Communist propaganda mills, and it raises doubt even among friendly nations as to the intensity of our devotion to the democratic faith" (in Woodward, 1966: 132). The statement remains impressive testimony to the shifting political realities of the postwar period and the added strains they placed on the prevailing racial status quo. Writing in 1944, Myrdal had both anticipated these international developments and fully appreciated their significance: "the Negro problem . . . has also acquired tremendous international implications, and this is another and decisive reason why the white North is prevented from compromising with the white South regarding the Negro. . . . Statesmen will have to take cognizance of the changed geopolitical situation of the nation and carry out important adaptations of the American way of life to new necessities. A main adaptation is bound to be a redefinition of the Negro's status in American democracy" (Myrdal, 1970: 35).

Increasingly Favorable Government Action

The processes reviewed above served to redefine the issue of black civil rights as a matter for national as well as regional debate. Just as earlier conditions had made it politically and economically expedient for the national elite to abstain from involvement—save for antiblack involvement—in the "Negro question," the broad changes outlined above made it increasingly difficult for them to adhere to this policy. This "nationalization" of the "Negro question" enhanced the strategic political importance of the black population and forced the federal government to react, at least symbolically, in support of an expansion in black rights. In turn, this supportive federal action accelerated the pace of social change by strengthening and legitimizing the trends already visible in other areas of life.

Fittingly, the reversal of the federal government's discriminatory racial policies saw its earliest expression in the same body that had, in the preceding period, given legal sanction to that policy. Prodded by the

NAACP's aggressive legal assault on Jim Crow, the Supreme Court, in a series of landmark decisions beginning in the early 1930s, invalidated most of its earlier narrow interpretations of the constitutional safeguards embodied in the Fourteenth and Fifteenth Amendments. In so doing, the Court restored to those provisions the formal potency that their framers had originally intended. Having earlier elevated property to a preferred legal position, the Court accorded civil rights much the same treatment after about 1930 (Berger, 1950: 37, 72). An analysis of the Court's decisions between 1876 and 1955 supports this conclusion. Figure 5.2 documents a steady increase after 1930 in both the number of Supreme Court civil rights cases and the proportion of those cases decided in favor of black litigants. A simple comparison of the percentage of favorable decisions before and after 1930 makes the same point even more forcefully. Of the decisions handed down before 1931, only 43 percent (23 of 53) were supportive of black civil rights. The comparable figure for the 1931–55 period is 91 percent (68 of 75).

Over the same span of time, a similar trend is visible with respect to supportive presidential action. Between 1930 and 1940 the executive branch adhered to the policy of inaction on racial matters established by Hayes and perpetuated by all succeeding presidents. However, the growing political leverage exercised by blacks was to render this "hands-off" policy increasingly difficult to maintain. The decisive break came in 1941, with the March on Washington movement. Scheduled for July 1, 1941, the march was intended as an all-black, mass protest against discrimination in the defense industries. Reflecting the increased political strength of blacks and the unique leverage afforded them by the developing wartime crisis, the march itself was never staged, the threat being sufficient to prompt Roosevelt to issue an executive order establishing the Fair Employment Practices Commission to investigate charges of discrimination in wartime employment.[8] That order marked the official termination of the earlier policy of executive inaction, and as such established an important, if largely symbolic, precedent.

Following a lull during the war years, supportive executive action resumed in 1946 with Truman's appointment of a Committee on Civil Rights, charged with investigating the "current state of civil rights in the country and recommending appropriate legislative remedies for deficiencies uncovered." This action was followed in quick order by a series of similar actions first initiated by Truman and then by his successor, Dwight Eisenhower. In 1948, two executive orders were issued, the first establishing a fair employment board within the Civil Service Commission, and the second calling for the gradual desegregation of the armed forces. In February of that same year, Truman became the first president since Grant to present a comprehensive civil rights package to Congress. Three years

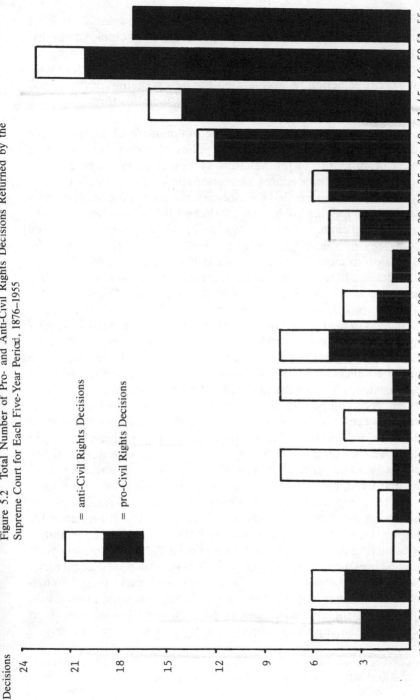

Figure 5.2 Total Number of Pro- and Anti-Civil Rights Decisions Returned by the Supreme Court for Each Five-Year Period, 1876–1955

Source: Berger (1950); Bullock (1967); Hughes (1962); Meier (197?); Miller (1966); Motley (1966); Ploski and Marr (1976); Sitkoff (1978); Waite (1946); Woodward (1966).

later he closed out his term in office by establishing a Committee on Government Contract Compliance, aimed at preventing employment discrimination by private firms holding government contracts. During his first term, Eisenhower continued the trend established by Truman. Through executive action he accelerated the desegregation of the armed forces and pressed for the integration of public facilities throughout the District of Columbia.

During this period only Congress seemed immune from the pressures that prompted major (if only symbolic) policy shifts in the other two branches. Due primarily to the Senate's system of equal representation for states and certain procedures characteristic of the whole Congress (e.g., two-thirds support needed for cloture), the legislative branch failed to pass a single civil rights bill between 1930 and 1954. Even here, though, there were signs of change. Between 1937 and 1950 the number of pro–civil rights measures introduced in Congress rose from thirteen during the 1937–38 session to more than seventy in 1949–50 (Berger, 1950: 30–31).

Taken together, then, the evidence presented in this section provides consistent support for the contention that the evolving politico-economic realities of the postdepression era prompted the federal government to support changes in the racial status quo. This should not be read to suggest a form of aggressive governmental advocacy on behalf of black interests. Instead, this shifting pattern of federal response reflects the emergence of important conflicts in the 1931–54 period that contrast sharply with the marked consistency of interest that defined southern-northern race relations in the preceding period. Federal action during this period was thus overwhelmingly reactive in nature, both in relation to the broad historical trends summarized above and in regard to immediate political pressures (e.g., Roosevelt's executive order in response to the threatened march on Washington). The reactive nature of the government's racial policy, however, hardly diminishes its significance. It symbolized, even as it contributed to, a dramatic shift in the balance of forces in American race relations during the middle decades of this century. Still it remained for forces within the black community to exploit the expanding opportunities for political action this shift afforded them. For, if the federal government could now be pressured to adopt increasingly favorable positions on racial issues, it was nonetheless not about to sponsor a serious insurgent challenge by an excluded minority. Fortunately, during this same period, processes internal to the southern black population were simultaneously at work favorably shaping the prospects for indigenous insurgent action. This was in marked contrast to conditions during the segregation era which deprived southern blacks of the organizational resources needed to generate and sustain a successful social movement.

ORGANIZATIONAL STRENGTH OF THE SOUTHERN BLACK POPULATION, 1876–1930

In Chapter 6 an analysis of the emergence of widespread black protest activity in the 1955–60 period will be presented. For what is to follow in the next section of this chapter, however, it is important to report, in preliminary fashion, one key finding from Chapter 6. The analysis shows that three indigenous institutions dominated protest activity during the emergent phase of the movement. Specifically, the black churches, black colleges, and southern chapters of the NAACP functioned as the organizational base out of which most of the protest activity was to emerge during the initial period of insurgency. The primary purpose of this section, then, is to analyze the growth of these three institutions over the 1876–1954 period. The contention is that, far from remaining constant, the organizational resources available to southern blacks increased simultaneously with the expansion in political opportunities reviewed earlier. Indeed, the two processes are closely linked. Both have their origins in the decline of cotton as the economic basis of southern life. In the context of later black insurgency, the significance of the collapse of "King Cotton" arises as much from the dramatic reorganization of black life it triggered as from any increase in political opportunities it afforded insurgents. However, as long as cotton remained king, the organizational resources available to southern blacks were necessarily limited.

Cotton Tenancy as a System of Social Control

Any discussion of the prospects for black insurgency in the South prior to 1930 must take account of the extraordinary extent to which everyday black life was dominated by the institution of cotton farming. In 1880, 91 percent of all blacks living in the South resided in rural areas. Fifty years later the proportion was still better than two-thirds (68 percent). The majority of these rural dwellers were involved in cotton farming. A reasonable estimate of the proportion so involved can be gained by comparing the ratio of black farm operators in the South to the total southern black population residing in rural areas. In 1910, the southern rural black population stood at about 6,900,000. In that same year, there were approximately 820,000 black farm operators in the South. If we multiply that figure by Henri's estimate of six persons per black farm family, we get a total black farm population of some 4,920,000, or 71 percent of all rural blacks residing in the South (Henri, 1975: 26). This estimate is consistent with available figures for individual states. In 1940, for instance, 76 percent of all rural blacks in South Carolina were engaged in farming. In Tennessee the figure was 68 percent; in Texas 67 percent (Bullock, 1971: 216).

The significance of these figures derives from an awareness of the elaborate set of social controls to which all blacks engaged in southern agriculture were subject. These controls served to inhibit the political organization of the rural black community by raising to prohibitive levels the personal costs associated with such efforts. Two forms of social control proved especially effective during this period in discouraging any but the most innocuous forms of organizational activity within the black community.

The first of these was a pervasive system of debt bondage that rendered blacks extremely vulnerable to economic sanctions by white creditors. The simple fact is that most blacks who were engaged in southern agriculture during this period never attained the status of independent farm owners. The majority were either tenant farmers working a plot of land in exchange for a portion of the crop produced, or sharecroppers working as little more than hired farmhands. In 1920, 76 percent of all black farm operators were in these two categories (U.S. Bureau of the Census, 1962a). Ten years later, the comparable proportion stood at 79 percent. The extreme economic dependence of these two classes is captured in the following description of the dynamics of the tenant system:

> According to the usual arrangement, tenants had to buy their seed and supplies on credit from the plantation owner, paying him back with a quarter to a third of the crop they made. Exorbitant charges for purchases and interest usually ate up any remaining profit, and before the next crop the tenant was deeper in debt than the year before. . . . But generally he had no option about staying or going, because with a debt that grew more mountainous year after year he either stayed bound to the land in a fruitless effort to pay off what he owed or was subject to arrest (Henri, 1975: 27–28).

Du Bois's early study of black farmers in one Georgia county provides evidence consistent with Henri's description. In a year of particularly low cotton prices, Du Bois reports, "of 300 tenant families 175 ended their year's work in debt to the extent of $14,000; 50 cleared nothing; and the remaining 75 made a total profit of $1,600." He goes on to note that "in more prosperous years the situation is far better—but on the average the majority of tenants end the year even or in debt" (in Baron, 1971:13).

Nor was it simply the economic vulnerability embodied in these labor arrangements that restricted indigenous organizing efforts. In addition, violence and physical force were freely employed as a second form of social control to compel adherence to these restrictive economic arrangements and the elaborate set of caste restrictions that propped them up. A measure of the severity of these controls is indicated in table 5.5, which reports the annual number of lynchings for the years 1882–1954. That the

TABLE 5.5
Number of Lynchings by Year, 1882–1954

1882	49	1906	62	1930	20
1883	53	1907	58	1931	12
1884	51	1908	89	1932	6
1885	74	1909	69	1933	24
1886	74	1910	67	1934	15
1887	70	1911	60	1935	18
1888	69	1912	61	1936	8
1889	94	1913	51	1937	8
1890	85	1914	51	1938	6
1891	113	1915	56	1939	2
1892	161	1916	50	1940	4
1893	118	1917	36	1941	4
1894	134	1918	60	1942	6
1895	113	1919	76	1943	3
1896	78	1920	53	1944	2
1897	123	1921	59	1945	1
1898	101	1922	51	1946	6
1899	85	1923	29	1947	1
1900	106	1924	16	1948	1
1901	105	1925	17	1949	3
1902	85	1926	23	1950	1
1903	84	1927	16	1951	1
1904	76	1928	10	1952	0
1905	57	1929	7	1953	0
				1954	0

Source: Ploski and Marr (1976: 275–76).

level of supremacist violence was related to the control requirements of southern agriculture is clearly suggested by the fluctuations in the number of lynchings reported in table 5.5. The number rose sharply in the early 1890s at the peak of the Populist "crisis," remained at high levels during the heyday of "King Cotton," and declined steadily throughout the remainder of the period as the factors reviewed earlier combined to reduce the economic viability of cotton farming. Historical accounts of particular instances of supremacist violence provide additional evidence suggestive of the economic roots of repression. Seligmann describes one such occurrence that took place in 1919. In Phillips County, Arkansas, black farmers organized that year in an effort to effect a legal end to debt peonage. Whites responded with violence. When it was over, more than 200 blacks (and 40 whites) were dead and 79 other blacks were indicted on counts of murder and insurrection (Seligmann, 1969: 225–48).

Finally, there is the consistent finding linking harsher patterns of social control with rural residence. For instance, Davis and Dollard, writing in 1940, report a high correlation between distance from urban areas and harshness of white control measures (1940: 247). Similarly, in *The Tragedy of Lynching*, Raper discusses the disproportionate rural basis of lynch mob violence (1969: 28–29).

Quite apart from the violence and economic controls on which southern agriculture depended, the general characteristics of rural life acted as yet another impediment to organizational development within the black community. The grinding poverty and overwhelming time demands of agricultural labor severely limited the discretionary time and income available to facilitate organizational activity. In addition, the scattered pattern of rural residence restricted people's access to one another, thereby impeding the development of the communication networks so crucial to organizing efforts. The majority of black southerners, then, were simply too poor, too geographically dispersed, and too vulnerable to oppressive controls during this period to render social insurgency very likely.

The retardant effect of these factors on organizational development is further attested to by the weak state of the three institutions identified earlier as the infrastructure out of which the black movement was later to emerge.

The Southern Black Church, 1876–1930

Of these three institutions, only the church was well established in the rural black communities of the South. In fact, in many cases, the church constituted the *only* organization in these communities.[9] However, in the overwhelming majority of cases, the organizational characteristics of the rural church rendered it too weak an institution to serve as an effective base for insurgent activity. Specifically, three organizational deficiencies have been identified by various authors writing on the rural black church of this period.

Perhaps the most basic weakness noted is the small size of church membership. Although his figure is only an impressionistic estimate, Johnson placed the average size of the rural congregations in the "black belt" counties he studied at between 75 and 100 (Johnson, 1941: 145). Mays and Nicholson provided a more rigorous estimate in their landmark study, *The Negro's Church*. The 185 rural black churches surveyed by the authors had a total membership of 26,875, or a mean of 145 per church (Mays and Nicholson, 1969: 15). However, as the authors indicate, the modal category was even lower than this figure. Forty-two percent of all the rural churches surveyed had less than a hundred members.

Another factor contributing to the organizational weakness of the rural black church was the absence of adequate funds to support it. According to the 1926 *Federal Census of Religious Bodies*, the combined expenditures for the 29,603 rural black churches responding to the survey totaled $16,621,723, or a mere $561 per church (Mays and Nicholson, 1969: 259). This comes to an average expenditure of only $6.14 per member per year.

Findings reported by Richardson twenty-one years later indicate that little had happened in the intervening years to alter the depressed financial picture of the rural black church (Richardson, 1947).

In itself a weakness, the lack of adequate resources contributed to a final deficiency characteristic of the rural church of this period. Lacking adequate funds, these churches were generally unable to secure the high-caliber ministerial leadership that was to be the hallmark of later church-based protest efforts. That the salaries paid rural ministers were much lower than those received by their urban counterparts is verified by data gathered by Mays and Nicholson. Ministers of rural black churches averaged only $266 in salary as compared with $1,268 for the southern urban black clergymen in their sample (Mays and Nicholson, 1969: 187, 263). Receiving such low salaries, many of the rural clergy found it economically necessary to hold positions simultaneously with a number of churches. Under such arrangements the minister functioned more as a circuit preacher than a resident pastor. Thus, most rural congregations were not only deprived of resident leadership but were forced to reduce the frequency of church activities to coincide with the schedule of the visiting preacher. Of the 185 rural black churches surveyed by Mays and Nicholson, 72 percent held Sunday services only one or two times per month (Mays and Nicholson, 1969: 252). Obviously, such a limited schedule of church activities could only serve to restrict the frequency of contact so crucial to the development of a strong organizational structure. Limited financial resources and restricted ministerial leadership combined during this period to impede the development of any semblance of the varied and effective church programs characteristic of the urban black churches so crucial in the early civil rights campaigns.

To the three weaknesses discussed above must be added the ideological conservatism of many of the rural black churches of the period. In part, this orientation can be seen as little more than the temporary ascendance of one historically pervasive perspective in black theology over another: a stress on "otherworldly rewards" over an emphasis on the everyday demands of the social gospel. This characteristic conservatism, however, must also be seen as a rational, if regrettable, adaptation to a repressive system of caste restrictions. That is, white social-control efforts during this period also "encouraged" an "acceptable" content in the overt teachings of the black rural church. Mays and Nicholson explain:

> Not many years ago the militant Negro preachers in a certain section of South Carolina were silenced by threats of violence, and in some cases actually run out of the county, because their messages were not considered the kind that would keep Negroes in their "places"; but those who preached about heaven, who told Negroes to be honest and

obedient, and that by and by God would straighten things out, were helped financially in church projects. . . . Economically, it was profitable to the landowners to keep Negroes satisfied and have them honest. The Negro preacher and the Negro church were instruments to this end. And the methods most often employed were to boost and encourage the Negro preacher who taught the Negro the "right" doctrine . . . these Negro preachers could be relied upon to convey to their Negro congregations the advice of the leading whites of the community (Mays and Nicholson, 1969: 7).

Thus, as the dominant institution in the lives of the majority of southern blacks, the rural church was, in most cases, organizationally weak and conservative in orientation. Both factors served to limit the effectiveness of the rural black church as an institutional vehicle of social change. In this regard, Johnson's conclusion seems warranted; "it is an inescapable observation that the rural Negro church is a conservative institution, preserving in large part many values, which, in the general cultural ferment of the Negro group, might well be altered" (1941: 169).[10]

The Black Colleges, 1876–1930

Unlike the black church, the black college has, throughout its history, been a predominantly urban institution. This should not be read merely to mean that black colleges have been overwhelmingly located in urban areas. This has certainly been the case. However, there is a more significant sense in which the black college is properly described as an urban institution. Students enrolled in such institutions have been disproportionately drawn from urban areas. Given the extremely low levels of education and income characteristic of black residents of the rural South during the 1876–1930 period, the explanation for the urban bias in college attendance should be obvious. The socioeconomic correlates of rural black life simply did not afford most blacks the training and financial resources normally required for college attendance. So long as the bulk of the black population remained in rural areas, the growth of black colleges was likely to proceed at a slow pace. Certainly the historic development of the black colleges fits with this assumption.

Within a decade of the end of the Civil War, philanthropic generosity had already resulted in the establishment of thirty black colleges in the South (Bullock, 1967: 159). By 1900, the number of such institutions had risen to ninety-nine, fully 85 percent of the number in existence in 1964 (Clift, 1966: 382). This seemingly rapid growth, however, is illusory. For in the ninety-nine schools operating as of 1900, a total of only 2,624 students were enrolled in college credit courses. An extensive survey of black education conducted jointly by the United States Bureau of Education and the Phelps-Stokes Fund placed the number of black college students at 2,641 in 1915–16 (Holmes, 1969: 159). The enrollment figures for such schools remained virtually unchanged over this sixteen year period.

Besides exceedingly low enrollment figures, the 1916 survey pointed to other characteristic weaknesses of the black colleges. Among these were minuscule endowments, inadequate physical plants, and poorly trained faculties. The magnitude of the problems confronting the black colleges during this period is captured in the introduction to the "College and Professional Education" section of the Phelps-Stokes report: "no type of education is so eagerly sought by the colored people as college education. Yet no educational institutions for colored people are so poorly equipped and so ineffectively organized and administered as the majority of those claiming to give college education" (in Holmes, 1969: 159).

Spurred, in part, by the publication of these survey findings, philanthropic organizations such as the Peabody Education Fund, the John F. Slater Fund, and the Julius Rosenwald Fund significantly increased their contributions to black colleges during the 1920s. The twofold result of these efforts was a general improvement in the quality of higher education for blacks and a related rise in total enrollment over the same period of time. Still, as late as 1928, the total number of black college students had risen to just 12,922 or an average of only 130 per school. Other measures of institutional strength were similarly depressing. In 1930, at the close of the period under examination, the black colleges underwent accreditation for the first time in their history. Predictably, all but one school failed to obtain full accreditation. Although they made significant progress throughout the 1920s, the black colleges remained relatively weak and ineffectual institutions at decade's end.

The Southern Wing of the NAACP, 1910–30

Much the same conclusion is warranted in regard to the organizational situation confronting the network of southern NAACP chapters at the beginning of the Depression. While the association had greatly expanded its activities in the South during the preceding fifteen years, its strength in the region remained limited at the close of the 1920s.

The NAACP was officially incorporated in May, 1910, at a conference of black and white liberals in New York City. However, despite its claim of being a national association, it remained, for all intents and purposes, a strictly northern organization until James Weldon Johnson (later the association's first black executive secretary), was appointed, in 1917, to the position of field secretary and organizer. It was Johnson, in this dual capacity, who first recognized and acted on the opportunities for organizational expansion in the South. His organizing efforts there helped to stimulate an unprecedented period of growth in the association. In 1916, a year before Johnson's appointment, the NAACP had sixty-eight chapters, of which only three were located in the South (St. James, 1958: 53). Early in 1917 Johnson's work resulted in the creation of the Dixie District and the addition of thirteen southern chapters and 738 new members to the organization (Kellogg, 1967: 134).[11] By the end of that year, the association reported a total membership of 9,282. A year later the figure had risen sharply to 43,994, with yet another significant increase, to 91,203, the next year. Developments in the southern wing of the organization mirrored the national trend. Regional membership stood at 18,701, or 43 percent of the total figure as of December, 1918. A year later the regional total of 42,588 had grown to 47 percent of the association's membership (Kellogg, 1967: 135, 137).

As impressive as these figures are, they nonetheless represent the high-water mark of organizational expansion during this period. After briefly topping the 100,000 mark in 1920, membership declined throughout the decade to a figure of 88,227 in 1929 (Hughes, 1962: 197). Assuming that the proportion of southern to total membership remained constant over this period of time, the figure for southern membership would have stood at approximately 40,000 in 1929. This represents less than one-half of 1 percent of the total southern black population in 1930. By contrast, the proportion of northern blacks enrolled in the NAACP was 2 percent, or better than five times the comparable percentage among southern blacks. In short, though inroads had been made in the South, the NAACP remained largely a northern organization on the eve of the Depression.

ORGANIZATIONAL STRENGTH OF THE SOUTHERN BLACK POPULATION, 1931–54

At the close of the 1876–1930 period, the southern black population was only just beginning to develop the institutional strength so vital to the generation of social insurgency. However, so long as blacks remained a predominantly agricultural labor force, the extent of institutional development was destined to be limited. The decisive break once again coincided with the demise of "King Cotton." Precipitated by the mix of factors reviewed earlier, the decline of cotton farming triggered a demographic revolution in the South that was to leave blacks in a much stronger positon organizationally than ever before.

The Collapse of Cotton and the Demographic Transformation of the South

Despite developing contradictions, the South remained, on the eve of the Depression, essentially a semifeudal agricultural society. Nearly seven out of every ten southern blacks continued to live in rural areas as late as 1930. That same year, the number of black farm operators stood at

870,000, down only slightly from the record total reached in 1920. The apparent stability embodied in these numbers, however, was shattered by the Depression and the collapse of the world cotton market. Thereafter the combination of "push" factors reviewed earlier simply accelerated trends set in motion by the Depression. The extensiveness of this economic upheaval is captured in figure 5.3. From a total of 915,000 black farm operators in 1920 the number declined to only 267,000 in 1959 (U.S. Bureau of the Census, 1962). Increasingly, "the traditional tenant labor force of the South . . . found itself . . . obsolete, forced to search elsewhere for the means to subsist" (Piven and Cloward, 1979: 191).

Many of the displaced agricultural workers moved out of the South. However, many more stayed behind and were part of a massive rural to urban redistribution of blacks within the region. So thoroughgoing was this internal migration that by 1960 the proportion of southern blacks living in urban areas had increased to 58 percent, nearly double the figure for 1930 (Price, 1969: 11). Overall the increase in total southern black

Figure 5.3 Number of Black Farm Operators in the South, 1900–1959

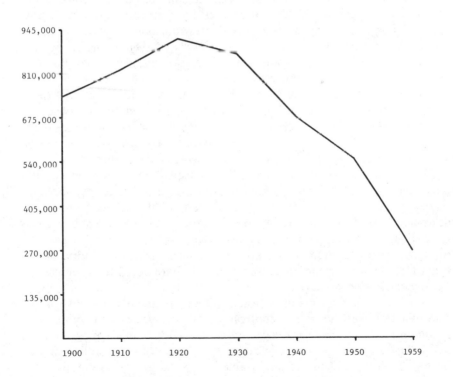

Source: U.S. Bureau of the Census (1962a): vol. 2, chap. 10.

population was only 18 percent between 1930 and 1960. By contrast, the increase among urban blacks living in the South was 118 percent over the same period of time.

Like the parallel northward migration, this regional movement was fueled by a mix of "push" and "pull" factors. The push, of course, was supplied by the decline in cotton farming. The pull was the result of expanding economic opportunities in urban areas. Numerous studies have documented the significant upgrading of the southern occupational structure that occurred during this period (Simpson and Norsworthy, 1965: 198–224; Spengler, 1963: 26–63; Thompson, 1971: 38–53). Thompson has summarized the occupational advances that occurred in the 1930s and 1940s: "in the drastic readjustment of its economy from 1930 to 1950 the South made more economic progress than in any four previous decades. This is evident in the sizeable shifts from extractive to manufacturing and service economies as shown by the occupational shift of the working force" (1971: 52–53). Data reported by Simpson and Norsworthy indicate that the general occupational upgrading of the southern economy noted by Thompson continued apace during the 1950s (1965: 199). That blacks benefited absolutely from these shifts in the southern occupational structure is also apparent from data presented by Simpson and Norsworthy. While continuing to lag well behind their white counterparts, southern blacks showed significant gains, between 1940 and 1960, in the proportion of their total work force employed in the higher-status occupations such as clerical and managerial positions, skilled craftsmen, and professionals (Simpson and Norsworthy, 1965: 209–10). As the authors note, "these shifts can be taken to mean improved occupational status for Negroes. Even their movement into operative, laboring, and service jobs was probably a step up from farming, in view of Negroes' low position within southern agriculture" (Simpson and Norsworthy, 1965: 207–8).

Through a combination, then, of decreased demand for agricultural labor and expanding occupational opportunities in urban areas, southern blacks were transformed, in the period from 1930 to 1960, from a predominantly rural to urban population segment. The dynamics of this transformation, however, concern us less than its effect on the pace of organizational development within the southern black community. In this regard, the demographic processes reviewed here acted to stimulate development in two principal ways.

First, the collapse of the cotton economy reduced the need for the oppressive system of social controls that had earlier been required to maintain it. Piven and Cloward comment: "with a massive agricultural and industrial transformation underway, a system of political domination based on terror and disenfranchisement was no longer essential to the southern ruling class in order to insure their labor needs on terms favorable to them" (1979: 192). The result was a gradual diminution after 1930 in the virulence of white control efforts. This trend is clearly visible in table 5.5. From an average of fifty-seven lynchings per year in the 1910–19 period, the number declined to twenty-eight during the 1920s, twelve in the 1930s, to only three a year between 1940 and 1949. This decline in supremacist violence encouraged organizing efforts in the black community both by diminishing the risks involved in such efforts and by signifying to insurgents that a certain "thaw" was underway in southern race relations.

The increased pace of urbanization after 1930 (and especially after 1940) served as a second stimulus to organizational development within the southern black community. Insofar as the incidence of supremacist violence was greater in rural than in urban areas, the move to the city granted an increasing number of blacks a measure of immunity from the more virulent forms of racism. More important, urbanization was accompanied by the occupational upgrading of the black population.

In turn, these occupational gains gave rise to an increase in personal income that afforded blacks more resources to support the growth of indigenous organizations. Burgess reports that median income for southern blacks, fourteen years of age or over, rose from $739 to $1,604 between 1949 and 1962, an increase the author links to the rapid urbanization of the southern black population over that same period of time (1965: 348–49). Though hardly stagggering, this rise did represent an increase in financial resources available to support institutional development.

As important as the actual dollar increase was the greater financial independence that resulted from urbanization and the accompanying diversification of the southern occupational structure. As long as the majority of blacks were employed as agricultural workers, their vulnerability to various forms of debt bondage remained a serious obstacle to organizing efforts. The expansion of occupational opportunities in southern cities thus contributed to a marked decline in the financial vulnerability of the black population both by pulling people out of southern agriculture and by concentrating them in numbers sufficient to support a growing occupational structure independent of white control. As Higgs has observed: "with these . . . occupational shifts went a measure of up-grading in the black labor force. Also significant was the increasing independence from direct white supervision achieved . . . in the emergence of a 'group economy' in the larger cities. In this respect the incipient ghettos had obvious advantages, for they promoted a modicum of independence and physical security for growing numbers of blacks" (1977: 121).

The advances noted in regard to occupation and income were paralleled in education. Studies have consistently documented higher levels of educational attainment for urban blacks in the South than for their rural counterparts. Given these rural/urban differentials, it is hardly surprising that the 1930–60 period was witness to a higher rate of educational advance among southern blacks than had occurred in any previous thirty-year period.[12]

By the mid-1950s, the demographic transformation of the South set in motion by the collapse of the cotton economy had created a growing class of urban black residents possessed of the personal resources (education, occupation, income) traditionally associated with organizational activity. Writing in 1954, Burgess discussed these trends and linked them to organizational developments within the black community: "It is in the city that the greatest educational opportunities have become available to the Negro. It is here that expanding occupational opportunities have been possible, and that a rise in income and standard of living have gradually been realized. In the urban black belts, Negro institutions . . . have flourished. These social institutions provide the breeding ground for a new kind of leadership trained in the values and skills of the middle class" (1965: 344).

It was not only the personal resources of this emerging black urban middle class, however, that encouraged the institutional development noted by Burgess. The physical proximity and improved communications characteristic of urban life were crucial factors as well. So too was the sheer increase in the size of the black community in urban areas.

Between 1931 and 1954 this complex mix of factors combined to produce an era of institutional development in the black communities of the urban South that was to give rise to the organizational structure out of which black insurgency was to develop in the 1950s and 1960s.[13] In the forefront of this process was the burgeoning black middle class and the three institutions discussed earlier: black churches, black colleges, and local NAACP chapters.

The Southern Black Church, 1931–54

Even while criticizing various aspects of the urban black church, numerous authors have acknowledged a greater propensity for social action among such churches than had been true for rural congregations (Bullock, 1967: 163; Johnston, 1954: 180; Mays and Nicholson, 1969). That the urban churches were much stronger organizationally than their rural counterparts has been amply documented as well. Conducted in 1930, the Mays-Nicholson study, *The Negro's Church*, provides relevant data on this point. Though not specifically designed as an organizational comparison of the urban and rural southern black churches, the study reports data that permit such a comparison. Table 5.6 summarizes a number of comparative measures of organizational strength reported by Mays and Nicholson.

TABLE 5.6
1930 Comparison between the Southern and Urban Black Churches on a Variety of Measures
of Organizational Strength

	Southern Rural Black Church	Southern Urban Black Church	Ratio of Southern Urban to Southern Rural Black Church
Mean membership size	145	442	3.0
% of ministers holding college or other degrees	2%	18%	9.0
Mean ministerial salary	$266	$1,268	4.8
Mean expenditure per year	$436	$3,472	8.0

Source: Mays and Nicholson (1969).

As can be seen, the urban church ranks significantly higher than the rural church on all measures of organizational strength. The differentials range from an average membership size three times greater in urban than in rural churches to a 900 percent difference in the proportion of ministers holding advanced degrees. Moreover, what sketchy evidence is available strongly suggests that the southern urban church grew apace with the general expansion in black urban population during the 1931–54 period. For instance, Joseph Washington, in summarizing developments in the southern black church in the period following the publication of the Mays-Nicholson study, observes that, "during the decades since this study was made, there has been a general upgrading of ministerial standards, religious education, financial responsibility, and institutional outreach to meet the needs of the community" (1964: 293–94). Ruby Johnston (1956) in *The Religion of Negro Protestants* offers evidence consistent with Washington's statement. Finally, a simple comparison of the rates of growth in number of black churches and total black church membership affords an indirect measure of the growing organizational strength of the black church between 1926 and 1962. While the number of black churches increased by only 17 percent, total church membership was up 93 percent over this period of time.[14] Thus, as one measure of organizational growth, the average size of the black congregation increased significantly during the period of interest here.

Simultaneously with these advances, and perhaps because of them, the southern urban black church also evidenced increased involvement in social action after about 1940. On the eve of the Montgomery bus boycott, Johnston discussed this increased church involvement in secular affairs. After noting that "urban churches tend to emphasize some aspects of these programs more than rural churches," Johnston goes on to specify the types of programs she is referring to. The churches, she writes, "urge members to register and vote, offer instruction and information on voting procedures and candidates for office, and organize the political community; and they support the National Association for the Advancement of Colored People" (Johnston, 1954: 180). Similar observations have been made by others. In one particularly interesting study, Tucker documents the growing secular orientation of the southern urban black church through a series of historical portraits of the leading black churchmen in Memphis, Tennessee. The author shows that while the dominant church leadership in the 1900–1940 period was decidedly accommodationist and otherworldly in orientation, an important shift in emphasis was already discernible by the early 1940s. So rapid and thoroughgoing was the transformation of church leadership that, according to Tucker, by the early 1950s, "the majority of local ministers . . . had become outspoken civil rights advocates" (1975: 106–7).

The organizational strength of the southern black church increased enormously between 1930 and 1954. A measure of this increased strength is attributable to the rapid urbanization of the black population during this period. Whereas nearly seven in ten southern black congregants were members of small, weak, rural churches in 1930, by the mid-1950s better than half held memberships in the larger and organizationally stronger urban churches. Add to this significant population shift the organizational advances made by the church, the socioeconomic upgrading of urban congregants, and the increasingly secular orientation of black church leadership during this period, and one begins to comprehend the enormous institutional strength embodied in the black church on the eve of the outbreak of widespread black protest activity in the mid-1950s.[15]

The Black Colleges, 1931–54

As impressive as the development of the black church was between 1931 and 1954, even more spectacular growth was registered by the black colleges over the same period of time. Perhaps the best evidence of this growth is that indicated in figure 5.4, which depicts the change in enrollment between 1900 and 1964. After experiencing little growth in the first decade and a half of this century, the enrollment for all black colleges increased sharply after 1915.

Figure 5.4 also serves as a useful means of illustrating the effect of various factors shaping the growth of the black colleges over time. The 1915–16 Phelps-Stokes survey of black colleges served as an early impetus to expansion by dramatizing the inadequacies of the existing system of higher education for blacks. A decade later a similar study, conducted jointly by the Phelps-Stokes Fund and the federal Bureau of Education, had much the same effect. That the period roughly bounded by these two

Figure 5.4   Total Enrollment in Black Colleges, 1900–1964

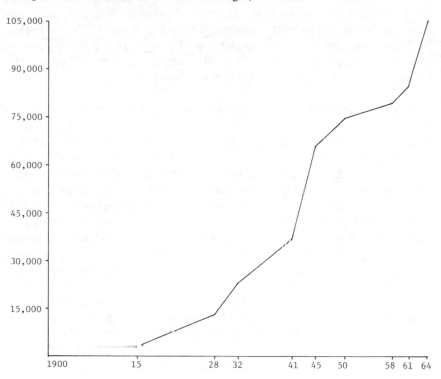

Sources: For 1900, Clift (1966: 382); for 1915, Holmes (1969: 154); for 1928, Atwood (1962: 249); for 1932, Badger (1951: 5); for 1941, Murray (1942:117); for 1945, Murray (1947: 143–45); for 1950, Clift (1966: 382); for 1958, Thompson (1960: 228–36); for 1961, Atwood (1962: 249); for 1964, Ploski and Marr (1976).

studies was one of significant growth for the black colleges is clear from an examination of figure 5.4. The growth stimulated by these two surveys was not simply in the area of enrollment, however. An especially beneficial result of the second study was the impetus it supplied for the upgrading of the educational programs of the colleges as a condition of obtaining full accreditation. While only one school merited full accreditation in 1930, five others achieved the distinction three years later (Holmes, 1969: 198–99). During this period there were other encouraging signs of institutional growth as well. Total income for all black colleges doubled between 1915 and 1930 (Bullock, 1967: 184). The number of degrees awarded rose by approximately 200 percent over the same fifteen-year period (Guzman, 1952: 218). It is with considerable justification, then, that Stephen Wright has characterized the 1916–38 period as one in which "the Negro college began to come of age" (1960: 288).

Nonetheless, as figure 5.4 shows, the period of greatest growth in the black colleges came after 1940. The rate of increase was especially pronounced in the 1940s, with enrollment doubling from 37,203 in 1941 to 74,526 at mid-century. This represents a 54 percent rise in the proportion of southern blacks attending college. By comparison, the rate of increase for southern whites during the same decade was only 18 percent (Bullock, 1967: 175).

This phenomenal rate of growth was, in large measure, the product of an equally dramatic rise in financial support for the black colleges. Total income for all black colleges rose from slightly more than 8 million dollars in 1930 to more than 38 million seventeen years later (Bullock, 1967: 184). A measure of this increased financial support is attributable to a rise in philanthropic sponsorship of black higher education during the postwar era. Financial data on 23 black church-affiliated colleges for the 1944–59 period support this assertion. Support for these schools, in the form of church donations or other gifts and grants, rose from just under a million dollars in 1944 to approximately 2.5 million by 1959 (Trent, 1960: 360). Similarly, the founding of the United Negro College Fund in 1944 served as another important impetus to the expansion of educational opportunities for blacks. During its first year in existence, the fund raised more than three-quarters of a million dollars in support of black colleges. By 1959 that figure had increased to nearly 2 million dollars (Trent, 1960: 363).

Increased financial support was also forthcoming during this period from an unexpected source: the governments of the southern states. Indeed, the rate of increase in support from the southern states far exceeded that for any other source during this period. In 1914–15, only $422,356, or approximately 10 percent of the total expenditures of the black colleges, was provided by the southern states (Bullock, 1967: 184). By 1947–48, the total amount had risen to $10,881,932, or more than 30 percent of total expenditures (Guzman, 1952: 219).

The major reason for this increased generosity is clear. In 1938 the Supreme Court ruled, in the *Gaines* case, that the state of Missouri had either to admit Lloyd Gaines, a black applicant, to the University of Missouri Law School or establish a separate school within the state to accommodate him. In effect, the Court was instructing the southern states to honor the "separate but equal" doctrine or face compulsory desegregation of their educational facilities. As Trent notes, the effect of this ruling, though indirect, was powerful:

> The southern and border states began to take more seriously the need for more adequate financing of their public colleges and teacher training institutions. They not only appropriated more funds for the general

educational program but also established new graduate and professional schools. It is clear that the purpose of this new concern was in the main to avoid admitting Negroes to the then white colleges and professional schools. But whatever the reason, the Negro public colleges began to grow and develop at a rapid rate (Trent, 1959: 267).

As a result, by mid-century the poorly supported, inadequately staffed black colleges of thirty years earlier had been transformed into some of the strongest and most influential institutions within the black community.

The Southern Wing of the NAACP, 1931–54

Finally, the southern wing of the NAACP experienced a period of rapid expansion between 1931 and 1954. In fact, for the three institutions under discussion here, the NAACP's rate of growth during this period was greater than that for either the black churches or colleges. Total association membership rose from approximately 85,000 in 1934 to around 420,000 in 1946 (NAACP, 1948: 92; Wolters, 1970: 302). This represents a nearly fivefold increase in only thirteen years. Over this same period of time, there occurred a comparable rate of growth in the number of separate units officially incorporated by the association.[16] The increase was from 404 units in 1934 to 1,613 in 1947 (NAACP, 1948: 3; Wolters, 1970: 302). In terms of the present argument, however, the NAACP's growth at the national level is not as significant as the rate of expansion in the association's southern wing. However, the figures on regional growth are, if anything, even more impressive than the national totals. Two separate observations are relevant here. First, growth in the association was disproportionately centered in the South throughout the period under examination here. St. James reports that, of the 310 units incorporated as of 1919, 131, or 42 percent, were located in the South (Hughes, 1962: 59; St. James, 1958: 53). By 1949 the proportion had increased to 63 percent, with 923 of 1,457 local units chartered in the South (NAACP, 1950: 63). This means that between 1919 and 1949 the number of nonsouthern units rose by some 200 percent while the rate of increase for southern units was approximately three times as great. In the context of the massive northward migration of southern blacks over the same period of time, these comparative figures are all the more significant.

Second, not only did NAACP growth between 1919 and 1950 take place disproportionately in the South, but the growth differential between the northern and southern wings of the association grew more pronounced as the period wore on. Evidence substantiating this observation is presented in figure 5.5. As the figure shows, the proportion of new southern branches increased steadily (with one decline between 1921 and 1925) throughout the association's history. By the 1946–50 period, nearly

Figure 5.5   Proportion of Southern and Nonsouthern NAACP Units Chartered in Successive Five-Year Periods, 1911–50

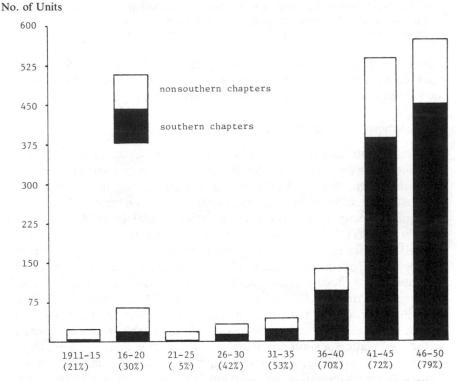

No. of Units

Source: for 1911–45, Anglin (1949: 128); for 1946–50, NAACP Annual Reports (1947–50).

Percentages indicate southern proportion of new units chartered during each five-year period.

eight of ten newly incorporated units were being chartered in the South. In terms of this analysis, though, the more relevant comparison involves the respective proportion of new units that were located in the South pre- and post-1930. In this regard, only 28 percent (38 of 137) of the units chartered between 1911 and 1930 were located in the South as compared to 74 percent (956 of 1,288) in the succeeding twenty-year period. Thus, the dramatic growth in the association after 1935 was clearly centered in the South.

The causes of this rapid regional expansion in NAACP strength are both difficult to pinpoint and, no doubt, numerous. However, a number of probable factors can be identified. The decline in supremacist violence after 1935 would seem to have served as an important impetus to the growth of the association's southern wing. The outbreak of World War II may also have facilitated NAACP organizing efforts in both substantive and symbolic ways. With regard to the latter, the glaring discrepancy between the thrust of American propaganda efforts during the war and the reality of Jim Crow racism at home no doubt served the association as an effective organizing device. As Dalfiume has observed:

> The hypocrisy and paradox involved in fighting a world war for the four freedoms and against aggression by an enemy preaching a master-race ideology, while at the same time upholding racial segregation and white supremacy, were too obvious. The war crisis provided American Negroes with a unique opportunity to point out, for all to see, the difference between the American creed and practice. The democratic ideology and rhetoric with which the war was fought stimulated a sense of hope and certainty in black Americans that the old race structure was destroyed forever (Dalfiume, 1970: 247).

Finally, it must be remembered that this rapid expansion in the association's southern wing occurred in the context of a dramatic rural to urban redistribution of the South's population. This transformation provided for larger concentrations of blacks in urban areas who possessed the characteristics associated with membership and were afforded a measure of protection from the more virulent forms of racism that probably inhibited organizing in rural areas. That southern NAACP chapters were overwhelmingly located in urban areas is clear from an analysis of their geographic distribution throughout the South. Of those newly chartered southern NAACP units listed in the organization's annual reports for the years 1940 through 1950, fully 85 percent were located in urban areas.

Regardless of the precise mix and weight assigned to the various factors facilitating the NAACP's growth in the region, the fact remains that by mid-century the association was firmly established as one of the strongest institutions in the southern black community. In combination with the black churches and colleges of the South, the local NAACP chapters afforded that population a strong, integrated institutional network capable of concerted and sustained collective action.

Finally, to this discussion of the shifting political opportunities and institutional development of the black community between 1876 and 1954, must be added a section on the changes in perception among blacks regarding the prospects for insurgency over this same period of time. For, as was argued in Chapter 3, the type of broad historical processes reviewed in this chapter only afford insurgents a certain "structural potential" for movement activity. Responsible for transforming this potential into collective action are people and the subjective meanings they attach to their situations. Specifically, it is the presence of two widely shared cognitions that are regarded as crucial to the generation of insurgency. The first of these cognitions is simply a consensus that the conditions the group is subject to are unjust or illegitimate. With respect to the black population, we can safely posit a certain constancy to this perception. That is, unlike in other segments of the population (farmers, women, etc.), large numbers of blacks have *always* been conscious of the oppressiveness of conditions in this country. In regard to this cognition, then, no fundamental "consciousness raising" was required to stimulate black protest activity.

A second cognition that has not always been widely shared—and apparently no longer is—within the black community is the belief that oppressive conditions are subject to change through collective action. Obviously, if people perceive themselves as powerless to change the fundamental conditions of their lives, the crucial motivation to organize a social movement will be lacking. In this sense, social movements are evidence that at least some members of the aggrieved population share a sense of political efficacy. It is to the development of this sense of efficacy that I now turn.

COLLECTIVE PERCEPTION OF THE PROSPECTS FOR INSURGENCY, 1876–1930

For the 1876–1930 period little needs to be said about the dominant perception among blacks regarding the prospects for collective action. Sitkoff describes the prevailing "mood" among blacks during the period: "segregation and discrimination now seemed so permanent, so immutable, so much an inevitable condition of life. Fatalism spawned hopelessness, and the majority of . . . Southern blacks succumbed to the new racial order" (1978: 10). It is not hard to understand why. The belief that conditions are subject to change is largely a function of the response of other groups to the aggrieved population. In effect, these responses constitute a set of "cognitive cues" signifying the vulnerability of the political system to collective change efforts by insurgents. Thus, a certain symbolic responsiveness on the part of other groups is likely to stimulate a widespread belief in the efficacy of insurgency among the population in question. Conversely, evidence of unmistakable hostility toward that same population is expected to impede the development of a belief in the mutability of existing conditions. From material presented earlier in the chapter, it should be obvious which of these two responses was most characteristic of black-white relations during the period from 1876 to 1930.

In the South, as we have seen, blacks were subject to a system of social control thoroughgoing and brutal in its effects. At a symbolic level, the daily manifestations of this system served to dramatize both the collective resolve of the white population to resist any challenge to the prevailing order and the personal risks embodied in even the most trivial instances of black defiance. What might have mitigated the symbolic significance of southern control efforts would have been evidence of supportive actions or statements at the national level. However, no such signs were forth-coming. Instead, the national political elite consistently opposed black interests during this period. Moreover, they did so in such a way as to forcefully symbolize the futility of insurgent efforts. A sampling of com-ments from various national figures during these years is illustrative of the trend. President Taft opposed the extension of voting rights to blacks, arguing that they were but "political children, not having the mental status of manhood" (in Du Bois, 1940: 23). Democratic presidential candidate William Jennings Bryan was even more forceful in defending the disen-franchisement of blacks "on the grounds that civilization has a right to preserve itself" (Meier, 1956). Finally, as late as 1921, President Harding could openly stress the "fundamental, eternal, and inescapable differ-ences" between blacks and whites as the basis underlying his pledge to "stand uncompromisingly against every suggestion of social equality. . . . Racial amalgamation there cannot be" (in Sitkoff, 1978: 27).

These and other manifestations of racism cannot be linked directly to a shared sense of pessimism among blacks regarding the prospects for successful collective action. Unfortunately, the period in question pre-dates the development of modern survey techniques. Thus, we must rely on sketchy impressionistic accounts of the "mood" of the black popu-lation rather than on any systematic attitudinal data drawn from surveys of blacks. Nonetheless, the consistency with which these accounts de-scribe the characteristic attitude of blacks during these years in terms of widespread feelings of pessimism, impotence, and fatalism supports the argument advanced here (cf. Sitkoff, 1978: 10). So too do the statements of black leaders during the period. In 1920, John Shillady resigned his post as executive secretary of the NAACP, citing a deep pessimism as one of the reasons for his action. He wrote, "I am less confident than heretofore of the speedy success of the Association's full program and of the probability of overcoming within a reasonable period the forces opposed to Negro equality by the means and methods which are within the Association's power to employ" (in Bennett, 1966: 111). Even Booker T. Washington, who tried as best he could to interpret the events of the period in a positive fashion, conceded that he had "never seen the colored people so discouraged and bitter as they are at the present time" (in Henri, 1975: 257).

Finally, the widespread support accorded Marcus Garvey's separatist movement can also be interpreted as evidence of a prevailing pessimism among blacks during these years. This interpretation is consistent with a more general relationship, noted by a number of observers, between white opposition to black interests and the relative strength of integra-tionist and separatist sentiment within the black community. According to Wilson, we are more likely to see "a push for integration during periods when blacks are optimistic about meaningful assimilation and a drive for separatism during periods of disillusionment and resignation" (Wilson, 1973: 97). Viewed in this context, Garvey's mass mobilization of blacks (estimates place the peak membership of his Negro Improvement Association at several million in the 1920s) would seem to reflect a deep pessimism among blacks regarding the prospects for change in this country's racial status quo.

Thus, the various strands of evidence reviewed above suggest the presence, during this period, of widespread feelings of pessimism and impotence within the black population. Nor is the fatalism embodied in this profile surprising in view of the thoroughgoing racism characteristic of the period. On the contrary, it seems a realistic response to the reality of a closed and coercive political system. Any change in the collective assessment of the prospects for black insurgency would have to await fundamental changes in the alignment of political forces in this country.

COLLECTIVE PERCEPTION OF THE PROSPECTS FOR INSURGENCY, 1931–54

In an earlier section of this chapter, the marked improvement in black political opportunities after about 1930 was discussed. The processes reviewed in that section greatly enhanced the political significance of the black population, which in turn prompted a decided shift in the response of other groups to blacks. Especially significant was the change in federal policy toward blacks. Beginning in the mid-1930s, both the Supreme Court and the executive branch under Roosevelt were increasingly responsive to the black community. The specific actions that followed from this fundamental shift in policy have already been reviewed. In any case, the symbolic effects of this shift were to far outweigh the limited substantive benefits that flowed from it. Indeed, the symbolic importance of the shift would be hard to overstate. It was responsible for nothing less than a cognitive revolution within the black population regarding the prospects for change in this country's racial status quo.

Viewed in a contemporary context, the impact of this shift in federal policy is hard to understand for two reasons. First, the present level of cynicism among blacks regarding the federal government makes it difficult for us to appreciate the importance blacks attributed to federal actions during the period in question. Second, it is simply impossible for us to comprehend the depths of official racism that prevailed prior to 1930. Accordingly, there is a tendency to disparage the federal actions of the New Deal era as so much tokenism and empty rhetoric. There is much truth in this criticism. What such characterizations miss is the dramatic *symbolic* contrast between these actions and those of earlier administrations. Writing in *Crisis* in 1934, no less a critic of federal racial policy than

W. E. B. Du Bois noted that, "It took war, riot and upheaval to make Wilson say one small word about lynching. Nothing ever induced Herbert Hoover to say anything on the subject worth saying. Even Harding was virtually dumb." But Roosevelt, Du Bois conceded, "has declared frankly that lynching is murder. We all knew it, but it is unusual to have a President of the United States admit it. These things give us hope" (*Crisis*, January 1934: 20). To observers of the day the shift was nothing short of extraordinary, signifying the first real prospects for change on racial issues since Reconstruction. In writing of his return to America in 1939, Paul Robeson describes the change in "climate" he sensed upon his arrival. "Conditions were far from ideal," he writes, "they were not even so much changed in fact as they appeared to be, in the hopefulness of liberals and Negro leaders. But change was in the air, and that was the best sign of all" (in Hoyt, 1967: 97).

Nor was this optimism regarding the prospects for change peculiar only to black notables. The results of several surveys conducted during this period suggest that such feelings were widespread within the black population. Table 5.7 summarizes the results of two such surveys. As the table shows, blacks exhibited considerably more optimism regarding future opportunities for advancement than did the total national sample. Moreover, there is some suggestion in the data of a widening gap between

TABLE 5.7
Summary of Two Surveys Asking Blacks Their Perception of the Prospects for Future Personal Gains

Year	Survey Organization	Question	National Totals	Blacks
1942	Roper	On the whole, after the war, do you think an average young man will have more opportunity, about the same opportunity, or less opportunity to get ahead than a young man had after the last war?		
		More opportunity	46.0%	50.0%
		Less opportunity	17.2	7.1
		Same as before	26.3	18.7
		Don't know	10.5	24.2
1947	Roper	Do you think your son's opportunities to succeed will be better than, or not as good as, those you have had?		
		Better than mine	62.1%	75.0%
		Not as good as mine	12.6	5.3
		Same as mine	12.3	7.2
		Don't know	13.0	12.5

Source: Adapted from Erskine (1969: 148).

the two populations as the period wore on. That is, the disparity in the proportion of "optimists" in each group was considerably larger in 1947 than five years earlier.

But it wasn't simply increased optimism regarding the prospects for racial gains that federal actions stimulated. More important, the shift in government policy triggered a growing sense of political efficacy among certain segments of the black community. Speaking at the opening of a three-day government-sponsored National Conference on Problems of the Negro and Negro Youth—a symbolically significant event in its own right—Mary McLeod Bethune remarked that "this is the first time in the history of our race that the Negroes of America felt free to reduce to writing their problems and plans for meeting them with the expectancy of sympathetic understanding and interpretation" (in Holt, 1964: 199). In place of the overt hostility and marked disinterest that had greeted black protests only a few years earlier, there was now the unmistakable signs of a new federal responsiveness. That this responsiveness was grudging and founded on the same manner of cold political calculation as earlier government opposition had been is less significant than the consequences that flowed from it. Political efforts by blacks now produced concrete results, thereby generating increased pressure for further remedial action. The result, throughout this period, was an accelerating cycle of black action and federal response, with a growing sense of political efficacy as the important psychological by-product of the process. Again, the lack of survey data for this period makes it difficult to measure the attitudinal consequences of this process directly. Instead, we must rely, as earlier, on contemporary descriptions of the "mood" of the black community as well as on other types of indirect evidence. The data presented in table 5.8 fall within the latter category.

What is shown in table 5.8 are the simple correlations between the annual number of new NAACP chapters and the yearly balance of favorable or unfavorable Supreme Court decisions between 1911 and 1950, with each measure lagged from one to six years behind the other. The

TABLE 5.8
Correlation between Annual Number of New NAACP Chapters and the Yearly Balance of Favorable or Unfavorable Supreme Court Decisions between 1911 and 1950

Independent variable		Number of Years Independent Variable Lagged					
	0	1	2	3	4	5	6
Supreme Court decisions		.325	.414	.578	.710	.716	.736
	.461						
NAACP chapters		.470	.621	.606	.525	.456	.542

Sources: For data on Supreme Court cases, see figure 5.2; for data on NAACP chapters, Anglin (1949: 128).

results of this analysis are important for the suggestive support they provide for the sort of reciprocal relationship alluded to earlier. First, the strong correlations produced by lagging the number of chapters two to three years behind the Supreme Court decisions suggest that the outcome of Court decisions was, at least in part, a function of the growing strength of the NAACP. Insofar as the association was the driving force behind the vast majority of these cases, this relationship makes intuitive sense. As the organization grew, and with it the resources to press the legal challenge to Jim Crow, so likewise did the pace of favorable Court decisions.

More important, in terms of the present discussion, are the apparent consequences of the Court's decisions. Of interest here are the extremely high correlations produced by lagging decisions four to six years behind the number of chapters.[17] The suggestion seems clear: the successful outcome of earlier association-sponsored cases over time contributed to a growing sense of political efficacy within the black community that in turn stimulated further growth in the association. Hence action begot success—however limited substantively—which in turn laid the cognitive foundation for further mobilizing efforts within the black community.

This view is also supported by an analysis of the effects of what was, arguably, the most important Supreme Court case of them all, the 1954 decision in *Brown* v. *Topeka Board of Education.*[18] Gerber (1962) sought to assess the effects of the decision on the "group cohesion of New York City Negroes." Among his measures of group cohesion were rates of participation in, and financial contribution to, "Negro organizations." As concerns both these measures Gerber's results are interesting. He found a significant increase in rates of participation and contributions to "Negro organizations," following the announcement of the Court's decision (Gerber, 1962: 300). In view of the often noted link between feelings of efficacy and organizational participation, it seems reasonable to suppose that the increased rates of participation reported by Gerber resulted, at least in part, from a commensurate rise in feelings of efficacy among his respondents. If this inference is correct, the expected sequence is again evident: successful political action generates the crucial psychological foundation for expanded insurgency.

Indeed, in a more general sense, this cycle accurately captures the broader dynamic that is thought to characterize the 1931–54 period. As the broad historical processes reviewed earlier combined to increase the political leverage available to blacks, the federal government (as well as other "members"), was forced to respond more favorably to black interests. The result was a cycle of black action and symbolic government response that produced only limited substantive gains but widespread feelings of optimism and political efficacy over the prospects for successful collective action. The full flowering of black insurgency in the 1950s and 1960s was to owe as much to these feelings as to the objective "structural potential" for collective action afforded blacks by the confluence of political opportunity and institutional growth.

THE DEVELOPING CONTEXT FOR INSURGENCY

In the preceding sections, three broad historical processes were analyzed that together encouraged the later development of black insurgency through a restructuring of political alignments more favorable to blacks, the rapid institutional development of the southern black community, and a process of "cognitive liberation" which left large numbers of blacks feeling optimistic and efficacious regarding the prospects for successful collective action. To afford the reader a thorough understanding of these processes, each has been discussed separately. Unfortunately, this method of presentation has tended to obscure the overall historical sequence under discussion, as well as the more dynamic relationships that exist between these three processes. In this summary section, then, the focus will be reversed, with these processes being discussed in the context of the broader historical sequence outlined in figure 5.6.

This figure underscores the central point of this chapter and illustrates a key difference between a political process and classical or resource mobilization interpretation of the origin of black insurgency. The movement is viewed not as a response to short-run changes in the years immediately preceding the outbreak of protest activity but as the culmination of a long developmental sequence that over time afforded insurgents the opportunity, organization, and cognitions needed to sustain collective action. Little needs to be said about the specific factors depicted in figure 5.6. All of them have been discussed earlier. The value of the figure derives instead from the broader view it affords of the overall historical dynamic resulting from the interplay of all these factors.

Unfortunately, the lack of operational measures for each of these factors precludes a quantitative assessment of the complete model. However, some idea of the model's explanatory worth can be gained through a path analysis involving only those variables for which comparable time-series data are available. The crucial dependent variables in this analysis are the realignment of political forces favorable to blacks, as measured by the outcome of Supreme Court decisions between 1900 and 1954, and the pace of institutional growth in the black community, operationalized as the number of new NAACP chapters charted in the South each year. The independent variables (with their operational measures in parentheses), are: overall consumer demand (annual per capita GNP in constant—1970—U.S. dollars, 1900–54), level of foreign migration (annual number

Figure 5.6   Model of Factors Contributing to the Development of a Favorable Context
for Black Insurgency, 1900–1954

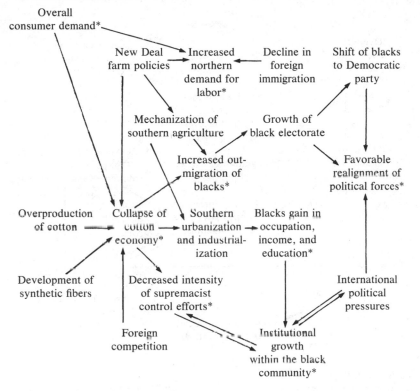

*variables included in path analysis

of foreign immigrants, 1900–54), northern demand for industrial labor
(annual number of wage earners in manufacturing, 1900–54), the decline
of the cotton economy (season average price per pound of cotton,
1900–54), out-migration of southern blacks (number of southern black out-
migrants between 1900 and 1954, measured in five-year intervals), the
level of supremacist control efforts (annual number of lynchings, 1900–54),
the extent of southern black urbanization (percentage of the southern
black population living in urban areas, 1900–54, measured in five-year
intervals), and the rate of black educational advances in the South (percentage of all southern blacks five to nineteen years of age attending
school between 1900 and 1954, measured in five-year intervals).[19] Figure
5.7 presents the results of this analysis.

As can be seen, the path coefficients between most of the variables are
significant and in the expected direction. Of the major relationships depicted, only those between cotton prices and urbanization, out-migration
and Court decisions, and lynching and NAACP growth run counter to the

Figure 5.7 Simplified Version of Model Outlined in Figure 5.6 with Path Coefficients for all Relationships

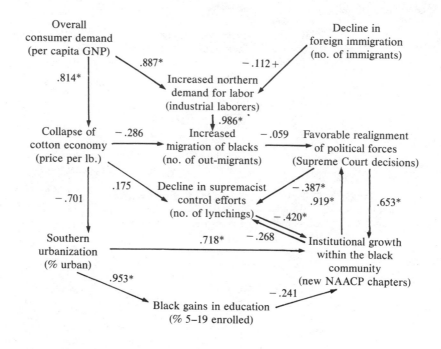

+ significant at .05 level
* significant at the .01 level

model outlined in figure 5.6. In the first case, the inconsistency is easily explained. Although cotton prices may be the best measure of the strength of the cotton economy, it was not the drop in cotton prices that directly stimulated the process of southern urbanization. More accurately, the drop in cotton prices led to a reduction in cotton acreage that in turn triggered the rural to urban exodus. When cotton acreage is introduced as an intervening variable between prices and urbanization, the expected relationship emerges. The correlation between prices and acreage is .32, while that between acreage and urbanization is −.62.

The other two anomalous findings are not so easily explained. The low partial correlation between out-migration and Court decisions may stem from a certain imprecision in my operational definition of out-migration.[20] But the inverse relationship between lynching and NAACP growth clearly runs counter to the argument offered here. Apparently, the decline in supremacist violence was not as significant a factor in the institutional development of the black community as was the pace of Supreme Court decisions or the more general process of southern urbanization.

Aside from these few findings, however, the coefficients reported are consistent with the model outlined in figure 5.6. As expected, consumer demand is strongly associated with the decline of cotton prices. This relationship is hardly surprising. As overall consumer purchasing power declined during the 1930s, so too did the capacity of the cotton market to sustain the higher prices enjoyed earlier. Also expected is the inverse relationship between cotton prices and the level of black out-migration from the South. The suggestion is that the displacement of agricultural labor triggered by the decline in cotton prices propelled blacks northward. At the same time, the strong positive relationship between the size of the industrial work force and the rate of black out-migration indexes the operation of a simultaneous "pull" factor, with expanding job opportunities in northern industry encouraging movement out of the South. The significant inverse relationship between numbers of industrial laborers and foreign immigrants, suggests that the decline in the latter may have acted as an indirect impetus to black out-migration by increasing northern demand for southern labor.

The decline in cotton prices is also positively associated with a simultaneous decline in supremacist violence. Here the implication is that the collapse of the cotton economy undermined the rationale behind the system of extreme social control that had earlier been required to sustain it. A second important link between the collapse of the cotton economy and the pace of organizational development within the black community concerns the important demographic processes set in motion by the demise of "King Cotton." As expected, the drop in cotton prices appears to have indirectly triggered the sizeable rural to urban migration among southern blacks. In turn, the pace of urbanization is positively related to both significant educational advances and institutional growth within the black community. Quite simply, the rural to urban transformation of the South's black population would appear to have been associated with an aggregate increase both in the personal characteristics generally associated with organizing efforts (education, income, etc.) as well as with the aggregation of community resources required to support institutional development. Figure 5.7 also indicates that the pace of institutional growth is itself related to both a decline in lynching and the outcome of Supreme Court decisions. Both relationships are intuitively reasonable. As the political strength of the black community grew apace of institutional expansion, organized segments within that community were able to bring effective pressure to bear on both the federal government and white supremacists. At the same time, the significant inverse relationship between Court decisions and number of lynchings would seem to suggest that some of the pressure on the supremacists was the indirect result of the success of the NAACP's legal campaign. Finally, the reciprocal relationship noted earlier between Court decisions and NAACP growth is also evident in the data, as the strong positive coefficients between the two variables indicate.

Having outlined the principal results of this analysis, I must caution against overemphasizing the significance of these findings. First, the unit of analysis for these calculations is time, as measured in yearly intervals. With only one observation per variable per year between 1900 and 1954, the analysis is based on just fifty-five data points.[21] Second, the lack of comparable time-series data has made it impossible to assess the effect of the other factors shown in figure 5.6. Almost certainly the introduction of these variables into the analysis would change the strength of some of the relationships depicted and alter considerably our understanding of the overall historical dynamic being studied. Finally, it is important to note that the findings presented here tell us nothing definite about causality. That the relationships between these variables are, for the most part, strong and in the expected directions is undeniable; that they are causally significant has not been demonstrated.

Emphasizing these necessary cautions, however, does nothing to diminish the significance of these findings. In combination, they provide consistent support for the broad historical processes of political realignment, institutional development, and "cognitive liberation" discussed in this chapter.

6 The Generation
of Black Insurgency
1955–60

In the previous chapter, a series of processes in the period from 1931 to 1954 were identified as facilitating the rise of the black movement in the 1950s by shaping not only the opportunities for successful collective action but the organizational capacity to exploit those opportunities. The focus of analysis, then, was clearly on the long-range processes that condition the likelihood of social insurgency. This in contrast to both the classical and resource mobilization models, which adhere to an underlying stimulus-response view of insurgency in which social movements are pictured as the direct result of recent changes in the larger sociopolitical environment confronting insurgents.

Having proposed (and applied) a markedly different time frame for the study of black insurgency than that suggested by the classical and resource mobilization perspectives, I must now assess the adequacy of the specific explanations of movement emergence embodied in these same two models.

The Classical Model Applied

Of the various classical formulations, two are found with great regularity in the literature on the black movement. These are the theories of rising expectations and relative deprivation. To these will be added a third, Davies' J-curve model, which although it appears less frequently in the discussions of black insurgency, has nonetheless assumed a prominent place in the general movement literature and will help further to illustrate the confusion that has resulted from the abundance of classical formulations. Each of these theories conforms to the causal sequence characteristic of the general classical model, with some form of system strain linked to the generation of insurgency by way of some intervening psychological state. In all cases, the source of strain is held to stem from a particular change in the socioeconomic status of this country's black population in the years immediately preceding the rise of widespread protest activity.

As applied to the black movement, the theory of rising expectations is based on the premise that black insurgency is a response to the psychological tensions generated by the *absolute* gains experienced by blacks in the immediate premovement period (Geschwender, 1964: 250–56; Gusfield, 1970: 12; Lewis, 1970: 154–55; Pettigrew, 1964: 170–91). Broom and Glenn offer a representative expression of this theory.

> During recent decades there have been improvements of the greatest consequences in the occupational and economic standing of Negro Americans. Viewed in absolute terms, these gains are impressive. . . . However, these substantial occupational and income gains have not been sufficient to forestall Negro restiveness. Advancement may bring not satiation of ambition but desire for even greater advancement. Success is companion to a discovery of the possible and an increase in aspiration (Broom and Glenn, 1970: 71).

Only slightly different from the rising expectation model is the theory of relative deprivation. Here the impetus to black protest activity is identified as the absolute gains experienced by blacks in the premovement period, coupled with their simultaneous failure to make any appreciable headway *relative* to whites (Geschwender, 1964: 250–56; Killian and Grigg, 1964: 178–79; Searles and Williams, 1962: 215–19; Williams, 1971: 24–33).

A very different idea underlies Davies' application of his J-curve or "rise and drop" model of revolution to the "Black Rebellion of the 1960s" (Davies, 1969). As the author argues, "revolution is most likely to take place when a prolonged period of rising expectations and rising gratifications is followed by a short period of sharp reversal, during which the gap between expectations and gratifications quickly widens and becomes intolerable. The frustration that develops, when it is intense and widespread in the society, seeks outlets in violent action" (Davies, 1969: 547). Thus, according to Davies, black insurgency is properly attributed, not to gains, but to *sharp reverses* in the economic fortunes of blacks in the period preceding the emergence of the movement.

As variations on the classical model, the three theories outlined above share the general deficiencies characteristic of that perspective. Insofar as those weaknesses have already been discussed in Chapter 1, there is no need to review them here. I am simply concerned with assessing the empirical accuracy of these models. In this regard, one conclusion is immediately apparent: the models offer contradictory interpretations of the changes in the socioeconomic status of the black population in the immediate premovement period. Obviously, not all the trends discerned by proponents of these theories can be accurate. However, far from clarifying the issue, an examination of several measures of the material status of the black population for the period in question only serves to heighten our confusion.

Table 6.1 reports nonwhite median family income and unemployment data for the 1948–76 period. In all, three yearly indicators of black economic status are included in the table: median nonwhite family income, ratio of nonwhite to white median family income, and nonwhite unem-

TABLE 6.1
Various Indicators of Black Economic Status, 1948–1976

Year	Median Nonwhite Family Income[a]	Ratio Nonwhite to White Median Family Income	Nonwhite Un-employment[b]
1948	1,768	.53	5.9
1949	1,650	.51	8.9
1950	1,869	.54	9.0
1951	2,032	.53	5.3
1952	2,338	.57	5.4
1953	2,461	.56	4.5
1954	2,410	.56	9.9
1955	2,549	.55	8.7
1956	2,628	.53	8.3
1957	2,764	.54	7.9
1958	2,711	.51	12.6
1959	2,917	.52	10.7
1960	3,233	.55	10.2
1961	3,191	.53	12.4
1962	3,330	.53	10.9
1963	3,465	.53	10.8
1964	3,839	.56	9.6
1965	3,994	.55	8.1
1966	4,691	.60	7.3
1967	5,094	.62	7.4
1968	5,590	.63	6.7
1969	6,190	.63	6.4
1970	6,516	.64	8.2
1971	6,714	.63	9.9
1972	7,106	.62	10.0
1973	7,596	.60	8.9
1974	8,265	.62	9.9
1975	9,321[c]	.65	13.9
1976	9,821[c]	.63	13.1

Sources: For income data, 1948–70, U.S. Bureau of the Census (1975) *Part 1*, Series G 189–204, p. 297; for income data, 1971–76, idem (1972–77): tables (in ascending order by edition) D 87-101, p. 135; for unemployment data, 1971–76, idem. (1972–77): table 642 in 98th ed. and table 351 in 93d ed.

[a]In current dollars.
[b]Percent of each group specified of persons 16 years old and over in the civilian labor force.
[c]Not strictly comparable with earlier figures due to revised statistical procedures.

ployment rate. However, even after limiting ourselves to these data, there is ample evidence to support any of the three classical interpretations discussed above. The task becomes deciding which set of figures represents the "true" indicator of black economic status in the years preceding the outbreak of widespread protest activity. The steady rise in median nonwhite family income between 1948 and 1976 supports the rising expectations hypothesis. Over the same period of time, however, the economic position of blacks relative to whites (as measured by the ratio of nonwhite to white median family income), showed little change, lending credence to a relative deprivation interpretation of black insurgency. On the other hand, what are we to make of the unemployment data? Certainly a cursory examination of the nonwhite unemployment rate for the years 1948–76 is consistent with Davies' rise and drop theory.

The economic data for the period in question are sufficiently varied as to support any number of interpretations of black insurgency, provided, of course, the investigator ignores the mass of contradictory data that is also available. Quite apart from the serious methodological weaknesses inherent in this approach, the ambiguous nature of these findings suggests a problem with research along these lines. Nonetheless, as one final "test" of these various classical formulations, the annual number of movement-initiated events reported in the annual *New York Times Index* for the years 1948–76 were correlated with the three sets of data presented in table 6.1 to assess the strength of the relationship between black insurgency and the various measures of system strain reviewed above.[1] Figure 6.1 depicts the number of movement-initiated events for the years 1948–76, while table 6.2 reports the simple correlations between the annual number of events and each of the yearly measures of black economic status reported earlier.

As expected, none of the economic indicators correlates significantly with the pace of movement activity over the course of the study period. Even lagging the economic data a year, on the assumption that the strains created by these trends might take time to develop, fails to alter the original finding. Contrary to the claims of the classical theorists, there does not seem to be any simple cause-effect relationship between the types of economic trends held to measure system strain and the yearly level of movement-initiated activity.[2]

The Resource Mobilization Model Applied

Equally important is the resource mobilization model and its empirical utility in accounting for the rise of widespread black protest activity in the 1955–60 period. Because of its relative recency, the resource mobilization model has rarely been applied to the black protest movement. An exception is the discussion and analysis of the movement presented by

Figure 6.1   Number of Movement-Initiated Events, 1948–76

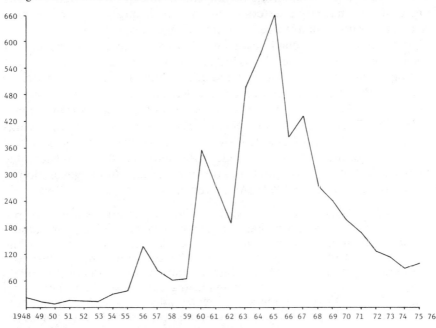

Source: Annual *New York Times Index*, 1948–76.

TABLE 6.2
Coefficients of Correlation between Various Indicators of Black Socioeconomic Status and the Annual Count of Movement-Initiated Events, 1948–76

	Median Nonwhite Family Income	Ratio Nonwhite to White Median Family Income	Nonwhite Unemployment Rate
Annual count of move-ment-initiated events	.111*	.108*	.060*

Sources: For number of movement-initiated events, annual *New York Times Index*, 1948–76; for sources of various measures of black socioeconomic status, see table 6.1.

*Not significant at the .05 level.

Anthony Oberschall as Chapter 6 of his excellent book *Social Conflict and Social Movements* (1973: 204–41). Elements of the model are also implicit in the work of other analysts. It is Oberschall's work, however, that will be most heavily relied upon in this discussion.

In contrast to the political process approach, the version of the resource mobilization model under discussion here tends to discount the importance of indigenous resources as a factor facilitating the generation of social insurgency. Rather, it is the expansion of external support opportunities that is held responsible for the emergence of protest activity. The suggestion is that rising external support for insurgent groups triggers insurgency rather than the reverse, as has been argued here.

To his credit, Oberschall has acknowledged (to an extent unusual for resource mobilization theorists), the importance of indigenous resources and organization in the origin of the Black Movement. Specifically, he discusses the role of the church as an organizational base and source of resources during several of the early movement campaigns (Oberschall, 1973: 126–27, 223). The central thrust of his argument, however, seems to run counter to this thesis. Consistent with the characteristic tenets of this version of the mobilization model, Oberschall attributes considerable significance to the actions and support of elite allies in the generation of black insurgency in the 1950s. As he remarks:

> one must realize that a negatively privileged minority is in a poor position to initiate a social protest movement through its own efforts alone. Especially in the early phases of a movement, outside support and the impact of outside societal events play an important role in bringing about a loosening of social control, which permits mobilization of the collectivity's resources. We shall document the extent to which the federal government, Northern liberals, college students, churches, and a host of other public and private associations, plus the effects of national news media coverage in generating broad public opinion support for increased federal government involvement and congressional legislation, had a decisive impact upon the civil rights and black movement (Oberschall, 1973: 214).

Or, as he asserts at another point, "there can be little doubt that *massive outside support* and the loosening of repressive social control brought about by increasing federal government involvement and support for civil rights created the conditions making possible the mobilization of the black movement" (Oberschall, 1973: 218–19; emphasis mine). However, notwithstanding the author's assertion that "there can be little doubt," the issue remains a matter of serious debate. Nowhere does Oberschall offer empirical evidence to bolster his claim that "massive outside support" precipitated indigenous protest efforts. What is missing are measures of external support and movement-initiated activity clearly showing the former preceding the latter. Fortunately, such measures are available, allowing for a systematic analysis of the relationship between these two important variables.

Introduced earlier, the *New York Times* count of the number of movement-initiated events will serve as a yearly index of the level of black insurgency between 1948 and 1970. To afford a rough measure of external support for the black movement, the total amount of income derived from

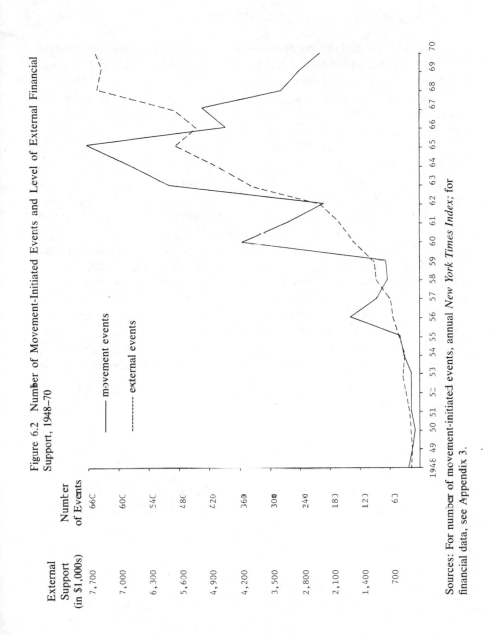

Figure 6.2 Number of Movement-Initiated Events and Level of External Financial Support, 1948–70

movement events
external events

External Support (in $1,000s)	Number of Events
7,700	660
7,000	600
6,300	540
5,600	480
4,900	420
4,200	360
3,500	300
2,800	240
2,100	180
1,400	120
700	60

1948 49 50 51 52 53 54 55 56 57 58 59 60 61 62 63 64 65 66 67 68 69 70

Sources: For number of movement-initiated events, annual *New York Times Index*; for financial data, see *Appendix 3*.

outside sources for all the major movement organizations operating during each year of the study period has been estimated and summed.[3] Figure 6.2 presents both sets of data graphically.

Based on an examination of these data, three observations are immediately apparent. First, there is no appreciable rise in the level of outside support in the years preceding the generation of widespread black insurgency.[4] Second, in direct contrast to the claims of some resource mobilization theorists, outside support rises sharply following, rather than preceding, increases in protest activity. This can be seen most clearly by computing the correlation between level of outside support and movement-initiated activity, lagging each measure from one to four years. The results of this analysis are reported in figure 6.3.

Far from suggesting that insurgency was a product of outside funding, figure 6.3 supports the opposite conclusion. Outside support seems to be a function of the level of movement-initiated activity rather than the reverse. Indeed, the correlation between the two sets of data increases steadily as the annual count of movement events is lagged against the yearly level of outside support.[5] The reactive nature of external support is a topic that will receive more attention later in this work. For now, it is important only to refer to the phenomenon and note the contradiction

Figure 6.3   Correlations between Annual Number of Movement-Initiated Events and External Financial support, by Years lagged

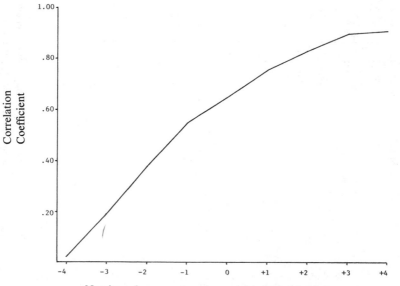

Number of years external support is lagged behind events

between it and the argument advanced by some resource mobilization theorists.

Finally, figure 6.2 documents continued high levels of external support for the movement during the late 1960s in the face of a rapid decline in movement-initiated activity. This finding should not be read to indicate that resources are antithetical or even irrelevant to the ongoing fortunes of a movement. It does, however, suggest that the ultimate causal importance attributed to resources by some mobilization theorists represents an overly simplistic reading of movement dynamics. As will be argued in Chapter 8, other factors were more responsible for the decline in black insurgency during the late 1960s than changes in the level of external support for movement organizations.

In general, then, the available data fail to support either a resource mobilization or classical interpretation of the emergence of black protest activity. Neither various measures of social strain nor the level of external support for the movement bear any significant relationship to the pace of movement activity between 1948 and 1970.

Instead, what seems to have accounted for the generation of black insurgency are the three factors discussed in Chapter 5. That is, it was the combination of expanding political opportunities and developing organizational strength mediated through a crucial process of collective attribution that facilitated the rise of the black movement. It was the rapid growth of the southern black churches, colleges, and NAACP chapters in the 1931–54 period that was to afford blacks the organizational strength needed to generate a campaign of collective insurgency. That growth has already been documented and discussed. However, it remains for me to document the disproportionate role played by these institutions during the crucial period of movement emergence.

CHURCHES, COLLEGES, AND THE NAACP: THE ORGANIZATIONAL BASE OF THE MOVEMENT

However impressive, the growth of these three institutions in the 1930–54 period tells us nothing of their role in the generation of black protest activity in the mid-to-late 50s. That they were heavily involved in this process is, however, clearly supported by an analysis of all movement-initiated activity reported in the *New York Times Index* for the years 1955–60.

Table 6.3 denotes the number of *Times*-reported actions attributed to major segments of the movement during the six-year period under examination here. This table clearly illustrates the dominant role exercised by these three institutions during the initial phase of movement activity. Of 487 movement-generated actions, 50 percent were initiated by church-

TABLE 6.3
Breakdown of All Movement-Initiated Actions, 1955–60, by Initiating Unit

Initiating Unit	No.	%	Cumulative %
Local NAACP units	33	7	7
Church based groups	57	12	19
Student groups	150	31	50
Black aggregate	126	26	76
Mixed aggregate	39	8	84
Formal movement organizations[a]	67	14	98
Others	15	3	101
Total	487	101	101[b]

Source: Annual *New York Times Index*, 1955–60.

[a]Including the National office and leaders of the NAACP.
[b]Due to rounding error.

or campus-based groups (or individuals), or by local chapters of the NAACP. Though substantial, this percentage actually underestimates the role of these institutions as catalysts of organized protest during the period. An additional 165 movement actions were attributed to either "black or racially mixed aggregates" about which the *Index* provides no identifying information except their racial identity and the geographic location of the action. By going back to the full *Times* story, however, additional information was obtained in 43 cases that justified switching the identity of the initiating unit from black or "mixed" aggregate to one of the three institutions identified earlier. That still leaves 122 actions attributed to unidentified "aggregates." Of these, 75, or 61 percent, occurred in locales marked by a protest campaign initiated either by church groups, students, or local NAACP chapters. While it is possible that these actions were unrelated to the larger campaign, it is more likely that the great majority were either initiated by one of these three groups or, at the very least, included group members as participants. When these two classes of actions are combined with those explicitly credited to church, campus, or local NAACP personnel, we are able to account for 74 percent of all movement-generated actions during the 1955–60 period.

In the calculation of this percentage, care was taken to exclude all actions initiated by formal movement organizations—or their leaders—that may have at one time been associated with either black churches or colleges. That is, despite their original church or campus ties, actions attributed to Martin Luther King, Jr., or the Southern Christian Leadership Conference (SCLC) after 1957, or the Student Nonviolent Coordinating Committee (SNCC) have been identified as the work of formal movement organizations rather than of the indigenous institutions out of which they developed.[6] Accurate as this categorization may be, the very existence of such groups is obviously dependent on the original institutions to which they were once linked. When one realizes, then, that the 74 percent of all movement actions cited above does not include the activities of Martin Luther King, Jr., SNCC, or SCLC, the significance of the black churches, colleges, and local NAACP branches in the South during the initial period of black insurgency becomes all the more apparent.

To cite the disproportionate involvement of these three institutions in the burgeoning movement is hardly to make an original observation. On the contrary, many investigators have discussed the central role played by these groups in the generation of black insurgency (Matthews and Prothro, 1966: 407–40; Morris, 1979; Oppenheimer, 1963; Orum, 1972; Record and Record, 1965: 92; Searles and Williams, 1962). With the exception of Morris and Orum, however, these authors betray an implicit adherence to the classical model and thus provide a useful contrast between that perspective and the political process model.

In the latter perspective, participants are distinguished from nonparticipants on the basis of their greater integration into the established organizational networks of the minority community. Thus, the perspective suggests a structural answer to the question of "Who participates?" By contrast, classical theorists have adopted a distinctly social-psychological position on the same topic. That is, participants are seen as distinct from nonparticipants on the basis of their characteristic psychological "profile." In many versions of the classical model, this profile serves to define movement participants as the marginal or poorly integrated members of society.

In the case of black insurgency, empirical analyses of movement participants have tended to adopt a "classical" focus. That is, to account for the involvement of black students, church members, or NAACP personnel in the movement, investigators have usually focused on individual characteristics of the participants rather than on the institutional settings in which they found themselves. Thus the atomistic approach evident in the work of classical theorists has been adopted by analysts of the black movement, as well.

Black student involvement, for instance, has been variously attributed to certain generational experiences peculiar to the student's age group (Brooks, 1974: 151; Zinn, 1965: 18), the transmission of liberal values through increased education (Matthews and Prothro, 1966: 430–31), "certain features of the developmental and group psychology of late adolescence" (Fishman and Solomon, 1970: 148), increased dissatisfaction with inequality resulting from the students' acceptance of the white middle class as their reference group (Searles and Williams, 1962: 215–19), and a growing awareness and "proximity to the dominant white culture"

(Orbell, 1971: 158).[7] Similarly, in seeking to explain the considerable civil rights activity of black ministers and other church members, investigators have been inclined to stress individual attributes as the cause of participation. Presumed to be especially significant in this regard is an ideological adherence to the demands of a "social gospel," emphasizing the realization of Judeo-Christian values in daily life (Marx, 1967: 105; Nelsen and Nelsen, 1975; Record and Record, 1965: 92).

The problem with these formulations is that they fail to distinguish adequately between movement participants and nonparticipants. That is, the distribution of the presumed causal characteristic is not limited to the population in question. Neither a "middle-class value orientation," exposure to liberal educational values, contact with the dominant white culture, nor idiosyncratic generational experiences are characteristics peculiar to college students. Nor is acceptance of the particular world view embodied in the "social gospel" restricted to churchgoers. Therefore, to account for the disproportionate involvement of black students or church members in the movement on the basis of such widely distributed character attributes is highly problematic. Morever, with respect to church members, the consistency with which other analysts have expressed a contrary view concerning the relationship of church attendance or religious beliefs to black protest activity renders the claims of these theorists all the more suspect (Dollard, 1957: 248; Duke and Clayton, 1963; Essien-Udom, 1962: 357–58).

In contrast, the perspective proposed here seeks to account for the disproportionate role played by these three institutions in the movement, not on the basis of the personal qualities of their individual members, but on the characteristics of the organizations themselves. Representing the most organized segments of the southern black population, the churches, colleges, and local NAACP chapters possessed the resources needed to generate and sustain an organized campaign of social insurgency. Three resources can be identified as having been especially critical in the initial protest campaigns.

Members

Perhaps the most important resource supplied by these institutions was a potentially mobilizable body of participants. By virtue of their integration into the most organized segments of the black community, the students, church members, and NAACP personnel were readily available for recruitment into the movement. This is merely to reassert a fundamental tenet of the political process model: social movements are collective phenomena arising first among those segments of the minority community characterized by a high level of prior organization. Only rarely and with great difficulty do previously isolated individuals emerge, band together,

and form movement groups. Rather, it is along established lines of interaction that movement recruitment usually occurs. It is this basic premise
that is ignored in the atomistic accounts of movement participation reviewed above. The fallacy in such accounts is that nothing so complicated
as shifts in reference groups, exposure to liberal educational values, and
the rest is required to explain the high rates of student, church, and
NAACP-member involvement in the movement. As noted in Chapter 3,
participants in a wide range of movements have been distinguished from
nonparticipants by virtue of their higher levels of integration into the
existent organizational spheres of the minority community. And so it is
with these three groups.

On one level, then, the importance of the churches, schools, and
NAACP chapters in the generation of insurgency can be attributed to
their role as established interactional networks facilitating the "bloc recruitment" of movement participants. That is, by building the movement
out of established institutions, insurgent leaders were able to recruit en
masse along existing lines of interaction, thereby sparing themselves the
much more difficult task of developing a membership from scratch. Impressionistic accounts of initial protest activity support this contention.
Martin Luther King, in describing the nature and importance of mass
church meetings during the Birmingham campaign, provides a vivid example of this phenomenon: "The invitational periods at the mass meetings, when we asked for volunteers, were much like those invitational
periods that occur every Sunday morning in Negro churches, when the
pastor projects the call to those present to join the church. By twenties
and thirties and forties, people came forward to join our army" (King,
1963: 59).

In his account of the Montgomery bus boycott, King describes much
the same dynamic (King, 1958: 76). Indeed, in the case of most church-
based campaigns, it was not so much that movement participants were
recruited from among the ranks of active churchgoers as it was a case of
church membership itself being redefined to include movement participation as a primary requisite of the role. As another observer of events
in Montgomery remarks, "It was their [the black church members'] religious duty now not only to go to church, visit the sick, and to pray, but
they must attend the mass meetings. To the Negro of Montgomery, Christianity and boycott went hand and hand" (Walton, 1956: 19). Former
SNCC president John Lewis echoes Walton's observation in the following
personal reminiscence of the early movement campaigns in which he was
involved: "Many Negroes . . . were involved in the movement out of a
strong moral, religious feeling, conviction. Sharecroppers, poor people,
would come to the mass meetings, because they were *in the church.*

People saw the mass meetings as an extension of the Sunday services''
(in Watters, 1971: 24; emphasis in original).

The same dynamic would appear to be operative in the case of student
involvement in the movement. Participation in protest activity simply
came to be defined as part and parcel of one's role as a student. Only by
positing such a dynamic is it possible to make sense of the extraordinarily
high levels of activism characteristic of black students during the emergent
phase of protest activity. Using interviews conducted in 1962, Matthews
and Prothro estimated that 39 percent of all black students were involved
in the movement (1966: 413). NORC survey data gathered two years later
placed the figure at 69 percent (Orum, 1972: 24–25). Regardless of which
estimate is more accurate, it is obvious that the level of student activism
was substantial, especially in view of the fact that many schools in the
Deep South experienced no protest activity whatsoever. If students from
such schools were excluded from the samples from which these estimates
were drawn, we would probably be talking about rates of activism of 60
to 80 percent or more. It is hard to reconcile such high rates of participation
with any of the theories that seek to explain student activism on the basis
of the individual characteristics of the participants themselves. That is,
it is hard unless one is willing to posit an extreme homogeneity to the
student body with respect to the background characteristic presumed to
be causally significant.

These high rates of activism simply provide additional evidence to support the assertion that throughout the 1955–60 period, indigenous protest
activity was, in large measure, a function of the degree of prior integration
into the black community. It is the density of integrative links on most
college campuses and not the individual characteristics of the students
themselves that accounts for the prominence of this group in the burgeoning movement. As noted in Chapter 3, this interpretation is consistent
with the central idea of diffusion theory. Like any other new cultural
pattern, social movements are expected to emerge first and spread fastest
among the most integrated segments of the population under study. Insofar
as they represented these segments, it is no surprise that church members,
students, and NAACP personnel exercised the dominant role within the
movement that they did.

Within these groups there was, of course, significant variation in participation rates. Even these differences, however, attest to the analytic
utility of the interpretation advanced here. Consistently, variation in participation rates within groups appears to be attributable to the strength
of a person's integration into that group. Most of the relevant findings in
this area concern variations in student involvement. For example, Searles
and Williams report significantly higher rates of activism among students
heavily involved, than among those less involved, in campus activities.

As they note: "One of the few statistically significant differences between active participators and those less active suggests the importance of previously established organizations for facilitating the organization and spread of such a movement. Those who were most active in the protest were more likely than those less active to participate in three or more extracurricular activities" (Searles and Williams, 1962: 219).

Orum reports a similar finding in his study of black student involvement in the movement. After dividing his student sample into groups based on the number of campus organizations they belonged to, Orum then computed participation rates for each group. The result is a consistent positive association between number of campus affiliations and rate of movement involvement, ranging from 67 percent for students who were members in no organizations to 91 percent for those who belonged to four (Orum, 1972: 50). Orum also found that student participation occurred earlier and was generally more extensive at residential than at commuter schools (1972: 68–69). Similarly, Sugarmon attributes the delayed outbreak of student protest activity in Memphis, Tennessee, to the fact that "most Negro students attending local colleges resided at home" (1964: 164). The implication is clear: assuming a more highly integrated student body at residential than at commuter schools, we would expect protest activity to occur earlier, and to be more extensive, at the former than at the latter.

Matthews and Prothro report that black student activism is correlated with class in school, with freshmen exhibiting the lowest rates of involvement and juniors and seniors the highest (1966: 430). The authors cite this finding to support their contention that it is exposure to "liberal educational values" that accounts for variations in protest participation. It would seem more likely, however, that these differences stem instead from class variations in level of integration into the campus community. Having attended school longer, juniors and seniors would have established the most extensive ties within the campus community and thus be more readily available for collective action.

All these findings, then, suggest the importance of integration as a factor effecting the likelihood of social insurgency. The *Times* data allow for one final assessment of this interpretation. If the disproportionate involvement of students in the movement is a function not of their individual characteristics but of the unusually dense set of integrative ties binding students to the campus community, we would expect the rate of student-initiated activity to decline during summer months when the campus is less active.

The data confirm this assumption. Regardless of whether summer is defined as the three months of June, July, and August, or as the four-month period ending September 30, the level of student-generated protest activity remains significantly lower than during the school year. If the time of year had no effect on the frequency of student activism, we would expect one-third of all such activity to be generated during the summer break. Instead, when September is defined as the last month of the summer, only 7 percent of all student-generated activity in 1960–61 occurs during the school break, as compared to 93 percent during the eight months of the year that school is in session. Nor would this finding seem to be merely an artifact of the increased difficulty in identifying students during the summer months. Impressionistic accounts of sit-in activity during this period are full of references to declining rates of student activism during the summer months (Brooks, 1974: 153; Oppenheimer, 1963: 181–82, 202, 223, 232–35; Walker, 1971: 381).[8]

Thus, the mass of findings reviewed here not only documents the disproportionate role played by these three groups in the emergent phase of the movement but suggests the reason for their dominance. Insofar as movement recruitment normally occurs along established lines of interaction, it makes sense that the churches, colleges, and NAACP chapters—the most highly developed associational networks in the black community—would also serve as the most readily mobilizable clusters of movement recruits.

Leaders

Besides supplying, to a considerable extent, the membership of the new movement, the black churches, colleges, and NAACP chapters also provided the bulk of its leadership. In fact, it could be argued that it was the willingness of the established leaders of these institutions to commit their energies and influence to the movement that convinced so many of the rank and file to do the same. The actions of these leaders served to convey to their natural constituents the importance and legitimacy of the movement, thereby encouraging participation. As a result, in most cases, the movement did not require the development of new institutional structures but was able instead simply to appropriate existing leader/follower relationships in the service of movement goals. The pattern established during the Montgomery bus boycott, and repeated in countless other church-based campaigns, nicely illustrates this dynamic.

In Montgomery, a handful of black ministers helped initiate the boycott, then secured the support of most of the city's remaining black clergy, who, in turn, actively solicited the cooperation of their congregations (King, 1958; Oberschall, 1973: 126–27). Impressionistic evidence points to a similar pattern of development in the case of campus-based protest activity during this period. Student demonstrators were drawn disproportionately from among those students most active in established campus organizations. Presumably this would also apply to the leaders of those organizations. Supporting this notion is the fact that a number of specific sit-in campaigns were either sponsored or led by elected leaders of the student government (Eschen, Kirk, and Pinard, 1971; Meier, 1961). This "top down" pattern of recruitment would also help to explain the rapidity and extensiveness of the movement's spread throughout the black college campuses of the South. Had the established student leadership opposed the demonstrations, the movement would almost surely have taken much longer to develop and attracted far fewer participants than it did.

Quantitative evidence of the extent to which representatives of these three institutions monopolized available leadership roles during this initial period of protest activity is lacking. Nothing resembling a complete list of movement leaders that would allow for such an analysis has been assembled for the period in question. What evidence is available regarding leadership patterns comes instead from descriptive accounts of the various direct action campaigns conducted during the early years of the movement. These accounts, however, leave little doubt as to the dominant leadership role played by individuals drawn from these three institutions. In fact, it is difficult in these accounts to find any mention of indigenous leaders who were *not* black clergymen, students, or local NAACP leaders. Evidence to support this statement is provided in appendix 4. No claim is made that this table is exhaustive. Nor was any effort made to verify the accuracy of designating any of these individuals as leaders. The intent was simply to represent in systematic fashion the information on indigenous protest leadership contained in the rich empirical literature on the movement. However incomplete, the resulting list is remarkable for the absence of leaders independent of the three institutions identified earlier. As expected, those identified as indigenous leaders were overwhelmingly drawn from the ranks of black ministers, students, or local NAACP personnel. Moreover, it is interesting to note that these three groups were represented in relatively equal numbers on the list. Finally, this tripartite leadership division roughly corresponds to three distinct types of protest activity initiated during this period and to the groups most closely identified with each (see table 6.4).

In the aftermath of the Supreme Court's 1954 school desegregation ruling, NAACP officials in the South took steps to insure local compliance with the ruling. These actions reflected the organization's long-standing preference for legalistic or other institutionalized forms of protest.[9] Table 6.4 shows that 75 percent of all local NAACP-initiated actions during this period were of this kind. These actions, of which the initiation of school desegration suits and the presentation of petitions requesting local school boards to comply with the Court's ruling were the most common, continued throughout the period, though with a considerable decline in frequency during the height of the supremacist attack on the association during the late 1950s.

TABLE 6.4

Breakdown of All Actions Initiated by Local NAACP Chapters, Church and Student Groups
between 1955 and 1960, by Type of Action

	NAACP Chapters		Church-based Groups		Student Groups		Total	
	%	(N)	%	(N)	%	(N)	%	(N)
Court action	45	(15)	9	(5)	2	(3)	10	(23)
Other institutionalized action (voter registration, petitions, campaign, etc.)	30	(10)	16	(9)	5	(8)	11	(27)
Economic boycott	12	(4)	25	(14)	5	(7)	10	(25)
Sit-in or other form of direct action	9	(3)	35	(20)	75	(113)	57	(136)
Violent action	3	(1)	0	(0)	3	(5)	2	(6)
Other	0	(0)	16	(9)	9	(14)	10	(23)
Total	99	(33)	101	(57)	99	(150)	100	(240)

Source: Annual *New York Times Index*, 1955–60.

Note: The 240 actions reported in this table represent 49 percent of all movement-generated actions that occurred during the 1955–60 period. For a breakdown of the remaining actions see table 6.3.

Two years after the Brown decision, the NAACP's hegemony over the movement was broken with the introduction and rapid spread of a second protest technique pioneered by church-based groups in various southern communities. These were the direct-action campaigns which sought through boycotts and other forms of mass action to desegregate local bus lines and other public facilities throughout the South. In the case of church-initiated actions, table 6.4 clearly mirrors the shift to these pioneering forms of protest. While only 21 percent of all NAACP-initiated actions were of the direct-action variety, the comparable percentage of church-generated actions was nearly three times as great. Though a potent force in the movement throughout this period, the church as the sole proponent of direct action had its heyday during the years from 1956 to 1959.

Student influence within the movement increased greatly with the introduction of a third and final protest technique. Beginning in early February, 1960, student-sponsored sit-ins, to protest segregated lunch counters, erupted in the states of the upper South. During the remainder of the year, use of the technique spread throughout the South (though it never reached the proportions in the Deep South it did elsewhere), and its application broadened to include segregation in institutions other than eating facilities (churches, bus terminals, movie theaters, etc.). The marked preference of student groups for this form of protest is clearly shown in table 6.4. Seventy-five percent of all student-initiated actions during the period involved use of the sit-in or other forms of direct action.

Though associated with different protest techniques, these three leadership groups are alike in one crucial respect. All represent segments of the black community protected, to a considerable extent, from white economic pressures. This point can be illustrated by reference to the NAACP leaders listed in appendix 4. Of the thirty-five leaders for whom occupational information was available, all but five earned their living in occupations independent of white control. Those who fall within this latter category include a business agent for an integrated union, two owners of funeral parlors, two students, a druggist, a field secretary employed by the NAACP, a housewife, a pullman porter, and no less than six ministers. Watters' discussion of the occupational basis of NAACP leadership during this period lends veracity to this finding: "The preacher, the mortician, doctor (if any), dentist, merchant, beautician . . . were the people in the Negro community who were the backbone of the old NAACP—people with independent means. It wasn't a matter merely of having money. Those whose means of income was dependent on white power were, sadly, not of the movement" (1971: 46).

As true as this characterization is for local NAACP officials, it is equally applicable in the case of the other two leadership segments represented in appendix 4. As any number of analysts have observed, the black church was free of white control to a greater extent than any other institution in the southern black community, thus affording the clergy a freedom of action unique to them (Brink and Harris, 1963: 103; Frazier, 1974; Matthews and Prothro, 1966: 185; Oberschall, 1973: 126, 220–22). Oberschall summarizes the common thrust of these observations: "The picture that emerges from Frazier and other writers is that the churches were the black institution least controlled and penetrated by whites. . . . Black ministers were the least exposed group among blacks to white sanctions since their salaries and church property depended entirely on contributions raised within the black community" (1973: 221).

That the black clergy, unlike NAACP leaders, were relatively immune to white pressure was not only a function of the fact that as individuals their means of livelihood was independent of white control but was also due to the protective institutional structure in which they lived and worked.[10] The same can be said for the final group of leaders listed in appendix 4. The protective confines of the black college afforded student leaders considerable immunity from white pressures. Thus, Smith, writing in reference to students at Florida A. and M., but with an obvious relevance to black students generally, notes that "[t]hey found . . . [they] enjoyed a kind of freedom from reprisal and a tolerance that was not shared by the non-student, adult citizens of the community" (1961: 225). As an example of this relative immunity, Smith and Killian cite the case of two Florida A. and M. coeds whose arrests for violating segregated seating patterns triggered the Tallahassee bus boycott. After their arrest, the two were released on bond and subsequently had their cases remanded to the college for disciplinary action. At the same time, charges against the pair were dropped (Smith and Killian, 1958: 7). In effect, the larger academic community functioned as an elaborate system of institutional support facilitating the involvement of student leaders in the movement.

Communication Network

Possessing both the leaders and the members needed for an effective protest campaign, many incipient movements nonetheless fail to grow beyond their localized beginnings. What is lacking is the extended communication network needed to link autonomous protest units in various communities into an integrated movement structure. What is being argued is nothing more than an extension of the basic principles of movement diffusion discussed earlier in this chapter. Just as established patterns of interaction facilitate the spread of a movement *within* a particular locale, similar links must exist *between* indigenous groups in various locales if the movement is to have any chance of expanding its geographical base of operation. Fortunately, in the case of the black movement, these same three institutions were able to supply this crucial resource.

As the movement developed, the links between these institutions multiplied rapidly, reflecting a growing need to coordinate the pace and extent of protest activities. In the early years of the movement, however, inter-institutional links were far fewer in number than those within each institution. Colleges were most closely linked to proximate colleges, churches to other churches, and local NAACP chapters to one another. The strength of these intra-institutional communication links is clearly suggested by the distinctive pattern of tactical specialization discussed in the previous section.

As noted above, the earliest insurgent actions during this period were local NAACP-sponsored attempts to speed compliance with the Supreme Court's school desegregation ruling. These attempts were set in motion at a strategy conference convened in Atlanta five days after the court's decision was announced. The conferees, representing local NAACP chapters in the seventeen affected states, resolved "to petition their local school boards to abolish segregation without delay" (in Brooks, 1974: 105). The consistency with which the southern chapters pursued this institutionalized approach to the problem is evident on reexamination of table 6.4. The tactical uniformity evident in the data suggests the strength of the communicative ties binding local NAACP units together. The implicit portrait is that of proximate chapters sharing information and experiences to produce a consistent tactical response to the problem of school desegregation.

However, it was not just a matter of tactical specialization. In addition, the very *issues* addressed by these three institutions attest to the strength of the communication network embodied in each. Table 6.5 documents a pattern of issue specialization on the part of these institutions to match the tactical specialization. Such distinct areas of concentration were to largely disappear by the early 1960s. Initially, however, patterns of specialization were apparent, reflecting both the presence of integrative links within each institution and the relative absence of similar ties between these same institutions. For their part, NAACP chapters were primarily concerned during these early years with the issue of school desegregation, as table 6.5 makes clear.[11]

Church-based groups, by contrast, devoted their energies initially to the problem of segregated bus transportation, only later shifting to the more general issue of public accommodations in response to student protests in that area. Here again, the involvement of church-based groups in this specialized issue is attributable, in large measure, to the set of interpersonal ties that served to link the clergy in various southern communities into a well-integrated institutional network. The event that triggered this particular phase of protest activity was, of course, the Montgomery bus boycott (1955–56), coordinated by the church-based Montgomery Improvement Association (MIA) headed by Martin Luther King, Jr.[12] The idea for a boycott was not, however, original to Montgomery. On at least one occasion, King sought advice from a friend and fellow clergyman, Theodore Jemison, who had in 1953 organized a bus boycott in Baton Rouge, Louisiana (King, 1958: 75).

The Montgomery campaign was nonetheless unique in the measure of success it achieved and the encouragement it afforded others to organize

TABLE 6.5
Breakdown of All Action Initiated by Local NAACP Chapters, Church and Student Groups between 1955 and 1960, by Issue Area

| | Initiating Unit | | | | | | | |
| | NAACP Chapters | | Church-based Groups | | Student Groups | | Total | |
Issue Area	%	(N)	%	(N)	%	(N)	%	(N)
Public accommodations	21	(7)	32	(18)	71	(107)	55	(132)
Transportation	6	(2)	39	(22)	5	(8)	13	(32)
Education	54	(18)	11	(6)	2	(3)	11	(27)
The economy	0	(0)	2	(1)	3	(4)	2	(5)
Politics (including voter registration)	12	(4)	12	(7)	7	(10)	9	(21)
Other	6	(2)	5	(3)	12	(18)	10	(23)
Total	99	(33)	101	(57)	100	(150)	100	(240)

Source: Annual *New York Times Index*, 1955–60.

similar efforts elsewhere. As might be expected, these succeeding campaigns developed along existing lines of communication that facilitated the transmission of tactical advice from the leaders of the Montgomery boycott to those involved in similar campaigns in other cities. As an example of this phenomenon, Brooks cites the case of the bus boycott in Tallahassee, Florida: "[t]he Reverend Charles K. Steele visited his friend Martin Luther King in the winter of 1956 and returned home to Tallahassee, Florida, to organize a bus boycott" (1974: 126). Soon after, other boycotts, patterned along the lines of the Montgomery campaign, were organized in Atlanta, New Orleans, Birmingham, Chattanooga, and Rock Hill, South Carolina. As in Montgomery, all were church-based operations headed by a minister. Besides inspiring other boycotts, the Montgomery campaign also served as an impetus to the development of indigenous church-based protest organizations in other southern cities. Writes Watters: "all over the South Negroes were forming organizations in imitation of the Montgomery Improvement Association" (1971: 50). It was out of these local organizations that the Southern Christian Leadership Conference (SCLC) was forged at a January, 1957, conference held in Atlanta (Clayton, 1964: 12).[13]

Students were the last of the three indigenous groups to initiate widespread insurgent activity during this period. However, this final phase of activism was to prove no less distinctive than the two that had preceded it. Rejecting both the institutionalized tactics of the NAACP and the issue focus adopted by the church-based protest groups, students forcefully addressed the problem of segregated lunch counters—and later other public accommodations—in a series of sit-in campaigns mounted throughout the South in 1960–61. The consistency of these campaigns, in terms of both the tactics utilized and the issues addressed, is clear on examination of tables 6.4 and 6.5. The former shows that 75 percent of all student-generated actions during the period were sit-ins or other forms of direct action. As for the issues addressed in these demonstrations, 71 percent of the time it was segregated public accommodations that served as the substantive focus of protest activity.

The uniform nature of these demonstrations again suggests the presence of a well-developed communication network linking the southern black college campuses into a loosely integrated institutional network. Intuitively, one would expect these integrative links to be especially strong between campuses geographically proximate to one another. If so, following diffusion theory, we would expect student-initiated protest activity to have occurred earlier at campuses close to the original protest site—Greensboro, North Carolina—and only later at schools some distance removed. To test this idea, I compiled a chronology of student sit-in demonstrations, using the *New York Times* data and several other sources of information on the sit-in movement (see Appendix 2). The number of miles from Greensboro was then computed for each protest site. This enabled me to determine the average distance (in miles) from Greensboro of the demonstrations occurring each week following the initial sit-in. The results of this analysis are presented in figure 6.4.

On the average, student-initiated protest activity *did* occur earlier in localities that were close to Greensboro than it did in towns farther away. Indeed, the data reported in figure 6.4 offer the most direct evidence of the pattern of diffusion discussed above in reference to both the earlier church and NAACP-initiated campaigns. In the nine-day period following the Greensboro demonstration, student protest activity was confined to North Carolina. From there demonstrations spread to neighboring states, with sit-ins occurring in Hampton, Virginia, on February 11; Rock Hill, South Carolina, on the twelfth; and Nashville, Tennessee, on the thirteenth. In succeeding weeks the movement surfaced in such traditional centers of southern black life as Tallahassee, Atlanta, and Montgomery, having finally encompassed the entire South (except for Mississippi) by the end of the six-week period depicted in figure 6.4. That interpersonal links between proximate campuses were crucial in accounting for this pattern of diffusion is a view supported by numerous observers (Brooks, 1974: 147; Oppenheimer, 1963: 61–62; Orum, 1972: 61). Oppenheimer, for instance, suggests a number of such links that may have facilitated the spread of the sit-in movement:

> As the movement caught on, often for idiosyncratic reasons to all appearances, colleges nearby would also pick it up, almost as a matter of competition—they could not permit themselves to be shown up. If a nearby college sat-in, so they also sat-in, hence continuing an image of a quickly spreading, dynamic, energetic, and spontaneous movement. In terms of these idiosyncratic factors, one student of the movement has pointed out that eleven of the first 15 sit-in communities are in the Piedmont region within a 100-mile radius of Greensboro. He suggests the presence of a basketball circuit, with Greensboro A & T playing five games in two weeks and students at each of the five opponent schools being involved shortly thereafter as a factor. In interviews, however, this writer has not been able to substantiate the basketball theory. Other idiosyncratic factors include letters from students at one college to friends and relatives at other institutions, dating patterns, etc. (Oppenheimer, 1963: 61–62).

As was true, then, in the case of both the NAACP and the black churches, the campuses afforded the burgeoning movement an effective communication network through which local protest units could be linked together to provide a broader geographical base for insurgency.

Figure 6.4 Location of Student-Initiated Demonstrations during the First Six Weeks Following the Initial Sit-in Demonstration, February 1, 1960

Numbers refer to the week during which the demonstration took place (for example, 2 means that the demonstration took place during the second week following the February 1 sit-in.

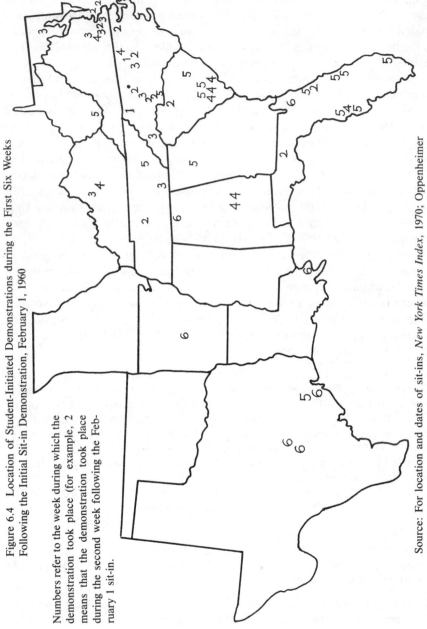

Source: For location and dates of sit-ins, *New York Times Index*, 1970; Oppenheimer (1963: 63); Southern Regional Council (1961: xix–xxv).

Other Resources

Nor were these the only resources the churches, colleges, and local NAACP chapters afforded insurgents. Besides members, leaders, and established communication networks, these three institutions supplied other important resources. The churches, for instance, functioned as the central meeting places during the vast majority of early campaigns. As one movement leader, Wyatt Tee Walker, explained: "If a Negro's going to have a meeting, where's he going to have it? Mostly he doesn't have a Masonic Lodge, and he's not going to get the public schools. And the church is the primary means of communication, far ahead of the second best, which is the Negro barbershop and beauty parlor" (in Brink and Harris, 1963: 103).

Reflecting the organization's legalistic bent, many local chapters of the NAACP included lawyers as members who willingly lent their expertise to the movement. Through these institutions insurgents also had access to a variety of lesser resources that are invaluable in sustaining any organized activity. Such things as mimeograph machines, secretarial help, and office supplies come to mind in this regard. This list of "other" resources could be added to indefinitely. Quite simply it was in their provision of all the organizational resources noted above that these three institutions functioned as the infrastructure out of which the Black Movement emerged in the period from 1955 to 1960.

So saying helps to underscore the central point of this chapter as well as to emphasize an important difference between the political process model and that version of the mobilization perspective under examination here. That difference can be easily summarized. The latter model attributes a degree of political powerlessness and general poverty to excluded groups that would seem to render them incapable of generating insurgency on their own. According to proponents of the model, such groups simply lack the organizational and political resources needed to initiate and sustain a social movement. Instead, insurgency must await the facilitative sponsorship of powerful external groups willing to commit their resources to the struggle. By contrast, the political process model challenges the mobilization perspective on both these counts. First, elite groups are not seen as willing, aggressive sponsors of social protest. And second, though clearly disadvantaged, challengers are assumed to possess sufficient resource strength to enable them—under favorable circumstances—to initiate a successful social movement.

Clearly, the evidence outlined in this chapter supports the latter rather than the former model. Data presented earlier documented the absence of any significant increase in external support for movement groups in the years preceding the outbreak of widespread black protest activity. Instead it was the indigenous institutions that provided insurgents with the organizational resources needed to exploit the expansion in political opportunities documented in Chapter 5. Far from constituting an inert mass, the southern black population, and not some combination of external support groups, triggered the initial wave of black insurgency.

THE RESPONSE TO INSURGENCY: THE MOVEMENT AND THE LARGER POLITICAL ENVIRONMENT

If a social movement is partially a response to shifting political conditions, the movement itself introduces new pressures for change into the political arena. Members and other challengers are expected to respond to these pressures in a fashion consistent with their own interests. In turn, the development of the movement is expected to be profoundly shaped by these responses even as it helps to condition them. Certainly this was true in the case of the black movement. During the period under analysis here the responses of two specific groups, southern white supremacists and the federal government, profoundly affected the pace and nature of black insurgency.

Perhaps most directly affected by indigenous black protest activity were the southern prosegregation forces. Reacting to what they perceived as the threat posed by black insurgency, these forces mobilized and grew increasingly active on two fronts during the latter half of the 1950s. At the local level, white supremacist groups mobilized, apparently in response to the outbreak of organized black protest efforts throughout the South. That local white supremacist activity rose sharply between 1955 and 1960 is apparent from an examination of the *New York Times* data. From 57 events initiated between 1948 and 1954 by white supremacist groups or unidentified local aggregates engaged in harassment or violent action against blacks, the number of such events increased to 352 in the subsequent six-year period. This demonstration of a simple rise in activity does not, however, substantiate the contention that this increased activism was a response to the emergence of the southern black protest movement during these years. However, as figure 6.5 shows clearly, the activity patterns of local movement and white supremacist groups do parallel one another quite closely.

It is conceivable, of course, that it was widespread supremacist activity that triggered black protest efforts. The overwhelming weight of impressionistic evidence, however, contradicts this interpretation. Especially significant are the many accounts documenting an increase in supremacist activity following the outbreak of direct action campaigns in various southern communities (Brooks, 1974: 116, 222; Muse, 1964: 52; Oppenheimer,

Figure 6.5   Distribution of Local Movement and White Supremacist Activity, 1955-1960

No. of Actions

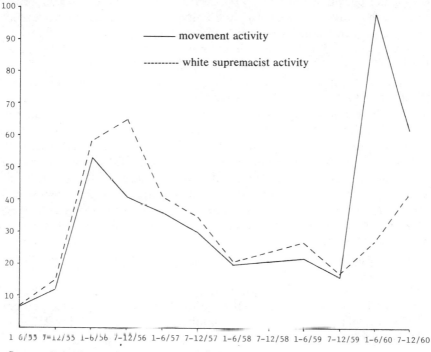

Source: Annual *New York Times Index*, 1955 60.

1963: 154, 206, 222, 236; Parker, 1974: 16, 18; Wakefield, 1960: 48–50; Woodward, 1966: 155).

✻The pronouncements made by white supremacist leaders also serve to validate the claim that local activity on the part of movement groups encouraged the mobilization of an extralegal force of southern segregationists.‧ For example, in the summer of 1956, one official of the White Citizens' Council in Alabama explained the growth of his organization in the following manner: "[t]he bus boycott made us. Before the niggers stopped riding the buses, we had only 800 members. Now we have 13,000 to 14,000 in Montgomery alone. We've got 75,000 members in 80 chapters all over the state. They made us'✻(in Brooks, 1974: 116). A leader in the Mississippi council movement alluded to the same dynamic in explaining the growth of the councils in his state. "Our Jackson Council started in April, 1955 with only sixty members . . . and by mid-July we had 300. But after the NAACP petition was filed in late July we went over 1,000 in two weeks time" (in Wakefield, 1960: 48). Even allowing for exaggeration, such evidence remains impressive. In general, the membership of the various Citizens' Councils affiliates represents an accurate "fever chart" of grass-roots conflict between movement and supremacist forces during this period (McMillen, 1971). Although the first council was formed in 1954, the movement had attracted only 60,000 members by November, 1955. However, in the three months following the initiation of the Montgomery bus boycott a month later, nearly a quarter of a million new members were added to the lists (Brooks, 1974: 128–29). As another analyst of the resistance movement observed, "[t]he councils quickly discovered that their best recruiting impetus was provided by specific moves toward integration which aroused local citizens to the dangers in their own community" (Wakefield, 1960: 48).

During this period, prosegregation activity was not confined to the local conflict arena just described. In addition to the grass-roots activity of white supremacist groups, the institutionalized arm of the southern resistance movement was engaged in a conventional political struggle with the federal government aimed at minimizing or delaying the effects of the Supreme Court decision. In the forefront of this struggle were the elected state officials of the region.

As reported in the *New York Times*, the number of government-initiated events attributed to southern state officials rose from 48 to 472 between 1948–54 and 1955–60. Over the same period of time, the proportion of state-initiated events coded prointegration dropped from 47 to 26 percent. Relative to this increase in antiintegration activity at the state level, federal activity declined between 1955 and 1960. The proportion of all government-initiated events attributed to federal officials dropped from 37 to 28 percent over these same two periods. However, as figure 6.6 suggests, rather than representing two independent patterns of activity, these two trends appear to be related. In the absence of decisive federal support for integration in the years immediately following the Supreme Court decision, the prosegregation forces were allowed to mobilize and grow ever more active. Benjamin Muse describes the period: "With the legislatures of the eleven southern states the Brown decision . . . became a continuing obsession. . . . The volume of pro-segregation legislation grew steadily. In 1956 state assemblies launched upon a legislative binge. . . . By the end of the year the number of enactments in the eleven southern states had reached a total of a hundred and six and the flood showed no signs of subsiding" (1964: 65–66).

Consistent with the data, Muse's description also captures the essence of the dynamic relationship that existed during this period between the federal government and the elected state officials of the South. It was in reaction to the Supreme Court's decision that state officials first mobilized. It was in response to an initial federal reluctance to enforce the Court's decision that political resistance gained momentum throughout the South.

Figure 6.6   Distribution of Pro-Integration Activity by Federal Officials and Anti-Integration Activity by State Officials, 1955–60

No. of Actions

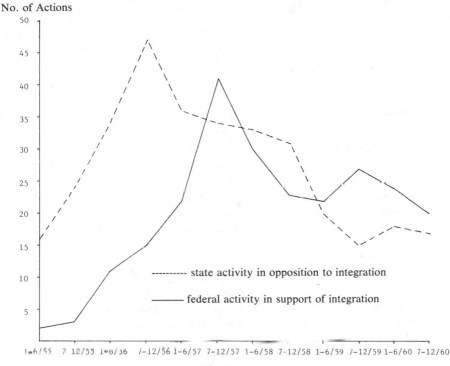

Source: Annual *New York Times Index*, 1955–60.

And, finally, it was a sharp increase in supportive federal involvement during the last three years of the Eisenhower administration that critically weakened the South's institutionalized assertion of state's rights.

The suggestion is that the so-called southern resistance movement actually represented two separate conflicts involving two different sets of participants. On the one hand, there was the political structure of the region mobilized in resistance to the federal government. And on the other, local white supremacist groups organized to counteract the perceived threat posed by indigenous black protest activity. Only by conceptualizing the developments of the period in this fashion have I been able to make sense of the different activity patterns exhibited by the various parties to the conflict.

7 The Heyday of
   Black Insurgency
   1961–65

One of the key tenets of the political process model is that social movements occur during periods marked by a significant increase in the vulnerability of the political establishment to pressure from insurgent groups. At such times, the power disparity between members and challengers is reduced, thus rendering insurgent action more likely, less risky, and potentially more successful. Consistent with this argument, the ongoing development of insurgency is expected to reflect fluctuations in the degree of political leverage exercised by the movement. Should the power disparity between insurgents and members return to premovement levels, the prospects for successful insurgency will necessarily decline. If, on the other hand, the political leverage exercised by insurgents remains high, the movement is likely to survive—perhaps even expand—over time.

Conditioning these fluctuations in political leverage is the same mix of external opportunity, internal organization, and shared attributions discussed earlier in connection with the process of movement emergence. This indicates a certain continuity in the evolution of a social movement over time. What marks the ongoing development of insurgency as discontinuous with the emergent phase of protest activity is the extent to which these three factors are shaped by the responses of other groups to the movement. In effect, the emergence of a movement introduces a new contender into the larger political arena. The contender's actions and the reactions they provoke constitute the fourth, and perhaps most important, factor shaping the development of the movement over time. After briefly discussing the organizational strength of movement forces, the "structure of political opportunities," and the shared perception among blacks of the prospects for insurgency characteristic of the early 1960s, I will turn to this dynamic.

ORGANIZATIONAL STRENGTH, 1961–65

In stressing the importance of existing institutions in the process of movement emergence, I made no claim that their dominance over the movement would last beyond the initial period of protest activity. In fact, the ar-

146

gument is quite the opposite. To survive over time, insurgent groups must be able to parlay their initial successes into the increased resource support needed to place the movement on a more permanent footing. The ad hoc groups and informal committees that typically coordinate the movement at its outset are ill-equipped to direct an ongoing campaign of social protest. To effect the transformation from a short-lived insurgent episode to a sustained political challenge, the movement must be able to mobilize the resources required to support the creation or expansion of a structure of formal movement organizations. If this effort proves successful, we can expect these organizations gradually to replace indigenous institutions as the dominant organizational force within the movement. That this transformation did occur in the case of the black movement is apparent from the data presented in table 7.1.

Table 7–1 clearly shows the dominance of indigenous institutions in the movement during the 1955–60 period. Equally clear, however, is the dramatic transformation of the movement's organizational structure that occurred between 1961 and 1965. While only 29 percent of all movement-generated events between 1955 and 1960 were attributed to formal movement organizations, the comparable figure for the succeeding five-year period was 50 percent. Simultaneously, the proportion of all movement-generated events initiated by church or campus-based groups dropped from 46 to 13 percent.

The Mobilization of External Support

Fueling this organizational transformation was a dramatic increase in the resources available to support black insurgency. Interesting in itself, the dynamics of this expansion in resource support also help to illustrate another important difference between the political process model and a

TABLE 7.1
Distribution of Movement-Initiated Events by Year, 1955–65

	1955–60		1961		1962		1963		1964		1965		1961–65	
	%	(N)	%	(N)	%	(N)	%	(N)	%	(N)	%	(N)	%	(N)
Campus/church-based groups or individuals	46	(342)	33	(90)	22	(43)	14	(70)	9	(53)	6	(39)	13	(295)
Formal movement organizations	29	(218)	42	(115)	57	(110)	53	(264)	53	(305)	47	(313)	50	(1107)
Black or mixed aggregate	22	(165)	24	(64)	19	(36)	30	(148)	31	(179)	44	(293)	33	(720)
Unaffiliated individuals	2	(18)	1	(3)	2	(4)	3	(17)	6	(34)	3	(19)	4	(77)
Total	99	(743)	100	(272)	100	(193)	100	(499)	99	(571)	100	(664)	100	(2199)

Source: Annual *New York Times Index*, 1955–1965.

certain version of the resource mobilization perspective. The latter perspective seems to describe the involvement of at least some elite groups in social insurgency as a form of active, even aggressive, sponsorship. The implication is that, without such sponsorship, insurgency would not occur. By contrast, political process theorists acknowledge the involvement of elite groups in social movements but dispute the account of that participation offered by mobilization theorists. Specifically, the involvement of external groups is seen as reactive, occurring only as a response to the perceived threat or opportunity posed by an indigenous protest campaign.

The contrast between the two perspectives is marked, indeed. Nothing less than opposite accounts of the causal sequence linking movement activity and external support are embodied in the two models. As to which sequence better fits the history of the black movement, we need only reexamine figure 6.2 (see p. 123).

Contrary to the central thrust of the resource mobilization model, the figure shows that peaks in black protest activity clearly precede, rather than follow, increases in external support. Figure 6.2 thus carries with it a strong suggestion that external support, far from triggering insurgency, is actually a product of it. Historical accounts of the movement during this period support this conclusion. The experiences of the Congress of Racial Equality (CORE) are typical of those of other movement organizations and thus are worth discussing at some length. In the years immediately preceding the Montgomery bus boycott, CORE was virtually moribund, with nearly all affiliates inactive and the national office lacking the funds to initiate activity on its own (Meier and Rudwick, 1973: 40–71). However, the momentum generated by the Montgomery campaign and similar boycotts elsewhere, changed all this. By consciously tying fund-raising appeals to the indigenous protest campaigns then underway in the South, CORE's leaders were able to stimulate a revival that was to leave the organization in a stronger position than ever before. CORE's historians describe this phase in the organization's development: "The rush of events in the South confirmed . . . that CORE should bend its efforts . . . there; the parallel growth in national concern for the black man's rights was reflected in the success of CORE's fund-raising appeals, which permitted the organization to increase its staff, expand its work in the South, and stimulate the revival of CORE activity in the North" (Meier and Rudwick, 1973: 80).

CORE's experience was not unique. Having remained virtually constant through 1955, external support for all movement organizations rose significantly in the two years following Montgomery. Figure 6.2 also shows that much the same phenomenon occurred in the wake of the 1960 student demonstrations. While support rose very little in 1958–59, sharp increases were recorded in 1960–61. Again this trend can be illustrated by reference to developments within CORE:

> CORE . . . on the eve of the outbreak of the southern black student movement, was still a small organization. Nor did the organization's leaders foresee rapid growth in its size or influence in the near future. . . . [But] the effects of these student demonstrations on . . . the Congress of Racial Equality were momentous. . . . As a consequence, it expanded its foothold in the South. . . . At the same time, the courageous example of the black youth and CORE's sponsorship of sympathy demonstrations in the North helped the revival of CORE work there. Moreover the excitement generated by the sit-ins boosted CORE's income, enabling the organization to enlarge its field staff greatly, and thus to take further advantage of the broadening opportunities (Meier and Rudwick, 1973: 97, 101–2).

Meier and Rudwick's description captures, in a more general sense, the relationship between insurgency and external support that prevailed throughout this period. By stimulating a significant expansion in the available support opportunities, each new wave of insurgency effectively subsidized ever higher levels of protest activity which, in turn, stimulated new increases in funding support. This basic activity/support cycle was to continue uninterrupted until the mid-1960s, insuring over this period of time the presence of the permanent movement organizations required to sustain an ongoing campaign of social protest.

There is one note of irony connected with the successful mobilization of external support during this period. The wave of reactive funding triggered by the initial movement campaigns allowed for the formal organizations to grow ever more active and, in short order, to displace the indigenous institutions whose actions had triggered the increase in support in the first place. This is not to say, however, that these groups and the indigenous resources they controlled ceased to be important during the movement's heyday. On the contrary, the incorporation of these groups and their resources into the campaigns increasingly initiated by the formal movement organizations helps to account for the high levels of activism characteristic of the early 1960s.

The Co-optation of Indigenous Resources

One of the reasons the transfer of organizational control from the established institutions of the black community to the formal movement organizations was effected so quickly and successfully stems from the fact that the latter, rather than trying to build an operational base independent of the former, sought instead to incorporate the indigenous resources of the southern black community into their programs. Their success in doing so enabled insurgents to retain the indigenous resource strength mobilized during the emergent phase of protest activity, even while putting the movement on a more permanent organizational footing. Thus, the indigenous institutions and the resources they supplied—leaders, members, etc.—were not sacrificed in the process of institutionalization. On the contrary, these institutions and resources remained vital to the success of the movement during the early 1960s.

Black college students and church members continued to serve as the foot soldiers of the movement, even if they no longer initiated most of the actions themselves. A 1963 CORE-sponsored campaign in Greensboro serves as a good example of this change. Though the campaign was initiated by CORE, it is clear from Meier and Rudwick's description of it that students from North Carolina A. and T. made up the bulk of the participants (Meier and Rudwick, 1973: 218–19). Moreover, during this period, black students and church members functioned in much the same capacity in any number of other campaigns initiated by formal movement organizations.[1]

Similarly, the southern black church continued to function as the institutional base of operation for many protest actions, even though these campaigns were rarely initiated by local church-based groups. In their respective accounts of the Albany movement, Zinn and Watters offer a by no means unique example of this phenomenon (Watters, 1971; Zinn, 1965: 126).[2]

As for the church and student leaders who directed the early movement campaigns, many remained active in the movement through their affiliation with the newly created or revitalized movement organizations that increasingly dominated black protest activity in the early 1960s. Indeed, the co-optation of indigenous leadership facilitated the institutionalization of insurgency by providing continuity in the direction of movement affairs during the transformation of the movement's organizational structure. The extent of this co-optation is reflected in appendix 5, which reports the later organizational affiliations of all the indigenous movement leaders identified in the previous chapter (see appendix 4).[3]

Fifty-one percent of those leaders were later to become staff members of at least one of the major movement organizations. Of the three main leadership groups, only the "independents" were to remain largely untouched by this process of leadership co-optation. For their part, black clergy were logically inclined toward participation in the Southern Christian Leadership Conference, while the students, because of their tactical bent, were recruited by all three of the major direct action organizations: SCLC, SNCC, and CORE.

The point made earlier in regard to the movement's rank and file is equally applicable to its leaders: during the movement's heyday, many of its resource requirements continued to be satisfied by the indigenous institutions of the southern black community. This happened despite the fact that the institutions themselves were increasingly being displaced by formal movement organizations as the dominant force directing black insurgency. By mobilizing the external support of elite groups and co-opting the indigenous resources of the southern black community, these formal organizations managed to establish a broad base of support that facilitated the rapid expansion of their operations and the generation of the high levels of activity characteristic of the early 1960s.

The Concentration of Movement Forces

If support for the movement was both broad-based and substantial in the early 1960s, another factor contributed to the organizational strength of the movement during this period. In any conflict situation the strength of a particular group is determined as much by the deployment of its re-sources as by their absolute quantity. On both counts movement forces were in good shape in the early 1960s. By confining their attack to targets that were narrowly defined, both substantively and geographically, move-ment groups were able to concentrate their forces so as to offset the basic resource discrepancy between themselves and their opponents. The result was a narrowly circumscribed, highly focused, effective insurgent campaign.

Geographic Concentration. One form this concentration of movement forces took was geographic. With the outbreak of the indigenous cam-paigns of the mid-1950s, the movement took on a decidedly southern cast, an emphasis it was to retain throughout the period under analysis here.

Table 7.2 provides a breakdown of all movement-initiated actions, by geographic region, for the years 1955–65. As can be seen, the overwhelm-ing majority of those actions occurred in the seventeen southern and border states. Though the later trend toward insurgency in the northern and western regions of the country is clearly foreshadowed in the data, as late as 1965 nearly 70 percent of all movement actions still took place in the South.[4] Even within the region, insurgent campaigns were usually centered in a particular area or town, thus serving to further concentrate the strength of movement forces. For example, the initial wave of activism in 1955–57 was almost exclusively centered in those half-dozen Deep South towns that experienced bus boycotts.[5] The 1960 sit-in campaigns, by contrast, were disproportionately centered in such upper South states as North Carolina, Tennessee, and Virginia. In 1961, the focus of move-ment activity again shifted to the Deep South with the initiation of CORE-

TABLE 7.2
Location of All Movement Initiated Actions, 1955–65

Geographic Region	1955–60 %	(N)	1961 %	(N)	1962 %	(N)	1963 %	(N)	1964 %	(N)	1965 %	(N)	1961–65 %	(N)
Deep South	37	(184)	54	(99)	60	(71)	36	(138)	25	(85)	59	(267)	47	(688)
Middle South	42	(207)	22	(40)	3	(15)	22	(82)	23	(76)	5	(23)	14	(208)
Border States	10	(47)	12	(23)	15	(18)	9	(36)	13	(45)	5	(23)	10	(144)
Total South	89	(438)	88	(162)	88	(104)	67	(256)	61	(206)	69	(313)	71	(1040)
New England	1	(7)	1	(2)	1	(1)	2	(7)	2	(7)	3	(14)	2	(32)
Middle Atlantic	6	(29)	4	(7)	7	(8)	18	(70)	26	(89)	13	(60)	16	(234)
East North Central	2	(12)	5	(9)	3	(4)	8	(30)	6	(19)	11	(51)	8	(113)
West North Central	0	(1)	1	(2)	0	(0)	2	(8)	0	(1)	0	(0)	1	(11)
Mountain	0	(1)	0	(1)	0	(0)	1	(2)	1	(4)	0	(2)	1	(9)
Pacific	1	(3)	1	(2)	1	(1)	2	(9)	3	(11)	3	(12)	2	(35)
Total	99	(491)	100	(185)	100	(118)	100	(382)	99	(337)	99	(452)	101	(1474)

Source: Annual *New York Times Index*, 1955–65.

Note: Except for geographic divisions within the South, the system of classification employed in this table derives from standard census categories. As regards the southern states, the following categories were used: *Deep South,* Alabama, Georgia, Louisiana, Mississippi, South Carolina; *Middle South,* Arkansas, Florida, North Carolina, Tennessee, Texas, Virginia; *Border states,* Kentucky, Maryland, Missouri, Oklahoma, West Virginia, District of Columbia.

sponsored Freedom Rides in Mississippi. In 1962, another Deep South state, Georgia, and in particular the town of Albany, was the focal point for considerable activity growing out of a campaign variously credited to SNCC, SCLC, or the local Albany movement. Finally, in 1965, the last concentrated mobilization of movement forces took place in Alabama, with the Selma campaign serving as the focal point. By marshalling their forces in this fashion, insurgents were able, throughout the period, to effect a concentration of forces that offset the numerous tactical and resource disadvantages they would later face as a result of the geographic diffusion of protest activity.

Issue Concentration. More important than this geographic concentration was the broad-based issue consensus that prevailed within the movement during this period.[6] Table 7.3 provides evidence of just how strong this consensus was during the early 1960s.

Broadly defined, it was racial integration, in a variety of settings, that served as the fundamental goal of the movement until the mid-1960s. Whatever its limitations as a solution to America's racial problems, this substantive consensus nonetheless contributed to the organizational strength of the movement in two ways. First, it encouraged the regional

TABLE 7.3
Issues Addressed in Movement-Initiated Events, 1955–65

Issue	1955–60 %	(N)	1961 %	(N)	1962 %	(N)	1963 %	(N)	1964 %	(N)	1965 %	(N)	1961–65 %	(N)
Integration	84	(625)	78	(214)	65	(125)	76	(379)	48	(272)	34	(226)	55	(1216)
Public accommodation	38	(284)	42	(115)	37	(72)	49	(243)	35	(201)	15	(102)	33	(733)
Public transportation	15	(112)	16	(44)	8	(16)	2	(10)	0	(0)	0	(0)	3	(70)
Housing	1	(5)	1	(2)	1	(2)	0	(2)	0	(2)	2	(10)	1	(18)
Education	28	(212)	16	(43)	16	(31)	20	(99)	10	(55)	13	(88)	14	(316)
Other	2	(12)	4	(10)	2	(4)	5	(25)	2	(14)	4	(26)	4	(79)
Black political power	0	(2)	2	(4)	5	(10)	2	(8)	8	(46)	20	(132)	9	(200)
Black economic status/power	1	(9)	1	(3)	3	(5)	1	(3)	0	(3)	12	(78)	4	(92)
Black culture	0	(3)	0	(1)	1	(1)	0	(1)	0	(0)	1	(9)	1	(12)
Legal equality	5	(35)	6	(17)	5	(10)	2	(10)	4	(24)	5	(30)	4	(91)
White racism	1	(7)	2	(5)	2	(3)	2	(9)	3	(17)	1	(7)	2	(41)
Police brutality	0	(0)	1	(2)	1	(1)	2	(10)	6	(32)	4	(29)	3	(74)
General plight of black America	4	(31)	2	(6)	4	(8)	0	(1)	2	(12)	3	(18)	2	(45)
Others	3	(19)	3	(7)	11	(22)	13	(64)	20	(115)	19	(124)	15	(332)
Too vague to categorize	2	(14)	5	(13)	4	(8)	3	(14)	9	(50)	2	(11)	4	(96)
Total	100	(745)	101	(272)	100	(193)	101	(499)	100	(571)	101	(664)	99	(2199)

Source: Annual New York Times Index, 1955–65.

concentration of movement forces discussed above, by suggesting that the fundamental problem confronting black Americans was their exclusion on racial grounds from the American mainstream. Obviously nowhere were such exclusionary practices so visible or oppressive as in the South.

Second, this substantive consensus provided movement leaders with a highly salient issue around which diverse factions within the movement could be mobilized in the effective mass action campaigns characteristic of the period. However, as this consensus began, under myriad pressures, to deteriorate, it became increasingly difficult to mount or sustain such united efforts, and the organizational strength of the movement declined accordingly. The beginnings of this deterioration are clearly visible in the decline in the salience of the issue during 1964–65.

Organizational Concentration. Movement forces were also "concentrated" organizationally in the early 1960s. Table 7.4 shows that the movement's organizational structure was dominated by four major groups during the 1961–65 period. This was in marked contrast to the NAACP's

TABLE 7.4

Distribution of All Events Initiated by Formal Movement Organizations, 1955–60

Organization	1955–60 %	(N)	1961 %	(N)	1962 %	(N)	1963 %	(N)	1964 %	(N)	1965 %	(N)	1961–65 %	(N)
NAACP	70	(153)	30	(35)	25	(27)	30	(80)	20	(60)	20	(63)	24	(265)
CORE	3	(6)	24	(28)	15	(16)	27	(72)	29	(88)	13	(40)	22	(244)
SCLC	6	(12)	19	(22)	25	(28)	18	(47)	13	(40)	38	(120)	23	(257)
SNCC*	0	(1)	9	(10)	9	(10)	7	(18)*	4	(11)*	4	(13)*	6	(62)
Other movement organizations	20	(43)	12	(14)	23	(25)	13	(35)	22	(68)	9	(27)	15	(169)
Multiple movement organizations	2	(3)	5	(6)	4	(4)	4	(12)	12	(38)	16	(50)	10	(110)
Total	101	(218)	99	(115)	101	(110)	99	(264)	100	(305)	100	(313)	100	(1107)

Source: Annual *New York Times Index*, 1955–65.

*The figures for SNCC understate the volume of its activity to a greater extent than is true for any of the other movement organizations during these same years. The reason stems from the fact that during these years SNCC committed most of its personnel and resources to voter registration campaigns in the South. Ostensibly, these campaigns were only part of a larger effort uniting all the major movement organizations in a broad-based coalition called the Council of Federated Organizations (COFO). In fact, SNCC was the driving force and dominant organization within COFO and therefore responsible for much activity attributed to that organization. Much the same could be said for the political by-product of the COFO campaign in Mississippi, the Mississippi Freedom Democratic Party (MFDP). While again theoretically distinct from SNCC, the MFDP was to a large extent an extension of SNCC's Mississippi operation and thus the party's activities are properly attributed to the latter organization.[8] However, consistent with the coding categories employed in this phase of the study, COFO-initiated events were attributed to "Multiple Movement Organizations," while those generated by the MFDP were coded as "Other Movement Organizations." Had the events attributed to these two groups been credited to SNCC, the latter's yearly totals for the years 1963–65 would have been as follows: 1963—24(9%); 1964—49(16%); 1965—35(11%).

hegemony over the movement's formal organizational structure during the latter half of the 1950s. It was the indigenous campaigns of this latter period that decisively ended the NAACP's dominance by stimulating a dramatic increase in external support that allowed for the creation and revitalization of competing movement organizations. The result was the highly competitive situation depicted in table 7.4. Throughout the period from 1961 to 1965 the so-called "Big Four" organizations—NAACP, SCLC, SNCC, CORE—jockeyed with one another for influence over the movement, as well as for the increased shares of publicity and money generated by protest activity.[7] On the strength of Martin Luther King's extraordinary popular following and media appeal, SCLC was frequently able to preempt the stage.[8] Despite this fact, it should be clear from an examination of table 7.4 that none of these four groups succeeded in dominating the movement's formal structure in the way the NAACP had been able to do earlier. Still, their attempts to do so lent much-needed vitality and diversity to the movement. Each organization came to carve out for itself a unique program, expressive style, and mode of operation that broadened the movement's recruiting and financial bases by offering a range of organizational alternatives from which potential members and benefactors could choose. Writing during this period, Clark noted this phenomenon:

> The civil rights groups vary in organizational efficiency as well as in philosophy, approach, and methods. The rank and file of liberal or religious whites might be more responsive to the seemingly nonthreatening, Christian approach of Martin Luther King, Jr. More toughminded and pragmatic business and governmental leaders might find a greater point of contact with the appeals and approaches of the NAACP and the Urban League. The more passionate Negroes and whites who seek immediate and concrete forms of justice will probably gravitate toward CORE and SNCC. . . . The variety of organizations and "leaders" among Negroes may be viewed as . . . the present strength of the movement rather than as a symptom of weakness. . . . Each organization influences the momentum and pace of the others. The inevitable interaction among them demands from each a level of effectiveness and relevance above the minimum possible for any single organization (Clark, 1970: 295).

Clark's description accurately captures the dynamic quality and functional consequences of the organizational competition that prevailed during the movement's heyday. In addition to the positive effect these organizations had on one another, their collective presence also posed problems for movement opponents. Movement opponents were confronted with no less than four sources of pressure, rather than with a single insurgent group, increasing tremendously the difficulties and cost of defeating or containing the movement.

If the movement benefited from this proliferation of groups, it managed to do so without sacrificing the minimal concentrations of power and resources required to sustain an effective insurgent challenge. Together, the Big Four dominated the movement in the early 1960s and over that span of time afforded insurgents the centralized organizational forms usually associated with successful collective action (Gamson, 1975: 93–94).

It should also be noted that, when the occasion demanded, these organizations were quite capable of joining forces for an even more concentrated attack on selected targets. In fact, nearly all of the events attributed to "multiple movement organizations" in table 7.4 represent some combination of the Big Four engaged in this very sort of joint protest action. In fact, the frequency of this form of cooperative action increased as the period wore on. This is not to say that the cooperation between these organizations was unlimited or that their relationships with one another were free of conflict. Actually the opposite was true. But so long as the overwhelming issue consensus discussed earlier prevailed within the movement, it exerted considerable pressure on these organizations to set aside their rivalries and differences in pursuit of common goals. The result was a remarkably powerful coalition of insurgent forces responsible for some of the significant victories of this period. As Watters remarks:

> in the sit-ins and freedom rides, the different organizations worked together beautifully with improvisation, spontaneity. SNCC, SCLC, NAACP youth councils, and CORE sent forth demonstrators; SCLC and the NAACP provided bases and wise consultation; the NAACP Legal Defense and Educational Fund came in with attorneys and legal maneuvers; the local churches, the local organizations, the local leaders were available in various supporting roles. Behind the scenes, these diverse elements might be involved in all kinds of rivalries and differences of opinion; but in the crises they overcame their differences and were remarkably effective (Watters, 1971: 126).

In summary, certain processes internal to the movement combined, during this period, to create the organizational strength productive of the high rates of activism characteristic of the early 1960s. The initial protest campaigns of 1955–60 triggered a rapid expansion in external support which encouraged the creation of new movement organizations and the revitalization of others. Increasingly, these formal organizations came to displace the established institutions of the southern black community as the dominant organizational force in the movement, even as they were usurping their strength through the co-optation of many of the indigenous resources crucial in the early campaigns (leaders, meeting places, etc.). By confining their attack to rather narrow targets, both substantively and geographically, these organizations were able to effect a certain concentration of forces that further strengthened the organizational position of insurgents during the period in question.

STRUCTURE OF POLITICAL OPPORTUNITIES, 1961–65

During the early 1960s movement expansion was also facilitated by a variety of external political pressures that functioned to sustain the supportive political context that had emerged as a result of the broad socio-economic processes reviewed in Chapter 5. Indeed, several of those earlier processes remain crucial to an understanding of the political conditions under which black insurgency flourished in the early 1960s.

Growing Importance of the Black Vote

Developments in the 1950s and early 1960s increased the significance of the black vote and, in turn, the pressure on national politicians to appear responsive to that constituency. Three factors contributed to this trend. The first was the continuing high rate of black out-migration from the South. Between 1950 and 1965 more than 2 million blacks left the region. And, as had been true in the 1930–50 period, it was the large industrial states of the North and West that continued to attract the majority of these migrants. Seven states in particular—New York, Pennsylvania, New Jersey, Ohio, Michigan, Illinois, and California—controlling 212, or 79 percent, of all the electoral votes required to win the presidency, received 86 percent of the southern black migrants during the 1950s and approximately 80 percent between 1960 and 1965. The political significance of these numbers should be apparent on their face.

A second factor contributing to the growing importance of the black vote during this period was the increase in the size of the southern black electorate. Though continuing to lag well behind the comparable proportion of whites, the absolute number of southern blacks registered to vote rose sharply between 1950 and 1965 (see figure 7.1). From approximately

Figure 7.1   Number of Southern Blacks Registered to Vote, 1950–65

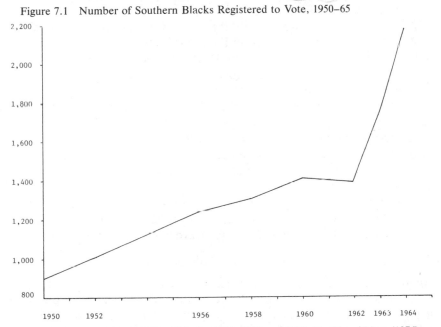

Sources: For 1950, Bullock (1971: 227); for 1952, 1956 and 1960, Ploski and Marr (1976); for 1958, Oppenheimer (1963: 35); for 1962 and 1963, Muse (1968: 58, 152); for 1964, Brooks (1974: 242).

900,000 registered black voters in the South in 1950, the number rose to more than 2,250,000 over the next fifteen years. Thus, by 1965, the black vote had become a significant factor in southern as well as national politics.

Finally, besides the absolute increase in black voters stemming from these trends, the outcome of the presidential contests during this period further enhanced the political significance of the black electorate. In both of the Stevenson-Eisenhower contests the Republican candidate was able to reverse the trend toward ever larger black Democratic majorities that had begun with Roosevelt's election in 1936. Republican gains were especially pronounced in 1956 with Eisenhower capturing an estimated 40 percent of the black vote (Lomax, 1962: 228). The practical result of this reversal was to render the black vote a more volatile political commodity than it had heretofore been, prompting both parties to intensify their efforts to appeal to black voters. Writing prior to the 1960 election, Glantz comments on the heightened party competition triggered by the surprisingly strong Republican showing four years earlier: "[n]either party can afford to ignore the numerical weight of the Negro vote. In the next campaign the Democratic candidate will have the responsibility of reversing the changing image of the Democratic party, while the Republican candidate will have the responsibility of enlarging . . . the appeal of the Republican party" (1960: 1010).

The 1960 presidential election did little to diminish the political significance attributed to the black vote. For the third time since 1936, the votes of black Americans were widely credited with deciding the contest. Lawson's assessment is typical of those offered in the wake of Kennedy's election: "An analysis of the returns demonstrated that Negro ballots were enough to give the Democratic contender a winning margin in New Jersey, Michigan, Illinois, Texas, and South Carolina, all states that had supported Eisenhower in 1956. Had the Republican-Democratic division in the black districts of these states broken down in the same way as four years earlier, Richard Nixon would have become the thirty-fifth President" (1976: 256).

Thus, Kennedy's election reinforced, in a dramatic way, a political perception whose salience had been growing since the early 1930s. In a close presidential election, black votes were likely to decide the outcome.

Continuing Importance of Cold War Political Pressures

Another factor strengthening the political position of blacks in the early 1960s was the continuing importance of the cold war political pressures generated by the United States ongoing battle with the Soviet Union for influence among the emerging third world nations of the world. These pressures stemmed from the obvious conflict between this country's professed democratic values and the reality of white racism at home. That this conflict retained as much salience in the early 1960s as it had in the immediate postwar era is attested to by statements made during this period by various political figures. For example, in supporting integration at the University of Georgia in 1961, Attorney General Robert Kennedy defended his position on the basis of international political considerations. Said Kennedy, "[i]n the worldwide struggle, the graduation at this University of Charlayne Hunter and Hamilton Holmes [the first two black students admitted to the university] will without question aid and assist the fight against communist political infiltration and guerrilla warfare" (in Brooks, 1974: 157). In defending his party's 1960 civil rights platform, Richard Nixon had advanced much the same argument a year earlier during his unsuccessful run for the presidency. To accede to black demands for equality, Nixon said, was tactically advisable because it would deprive "the Communist leaders any arguments against America and what she stands for" (in Lawson, 1976: 254). The continuing international tensions of the period imposed on America's political elite a certain interest in seeing the country's racial conflict resolved in favor of black equality, if not for idealistic reasons then for the obvious propaganda value that such a resolution would entail.

Growing Salience, Support for the Issue

From 1961 to 1965, the salience of the "Negro question" reached such proportions that it consistently came to be identified in public opinion surveys as the most important problem confronting the country. Evidence to this effect is provided in fig. 7.2. In six of eleven national opinion polls conducted between 1961 and 1965, "civil rights" was identified as the most important problem facing the country. In three other polls it ranked second. Only twice did it rank as low as fourth.[9]

Over the same period of time, public support for many of the stated goals of the movement also showed a steady increase. In an interesting article, Burstein has documented the consistent gains in white support registered during the 1950s and early 1960s across a wide range of specific issue areas (1978). That this support was grudging or hypocritical in many cases, and no doubt erosive in the face of a more meaningful test of support (fund-raising, willingness to participate, etc.), hardly diminishes its significance. The fact remains that this growing body of supportive opinion introduced a new set of political considerations into the calculations of other parties to the conflict and, in so doing, helped constrain their responses to the movement. No longer could the cost of openly racist rhetoric or policies be measured only in terms of the loss of black support that inevitably followed from such actions. In addition, the disaffection of the white liberal community became an ever more likely occurrence as their sensitivity to the issue increased throughout this pe-

Figure 7.2   Proportion of General Public Identifying Civil Rights as the "Most Important Problem Confronting the Country," 1961–65

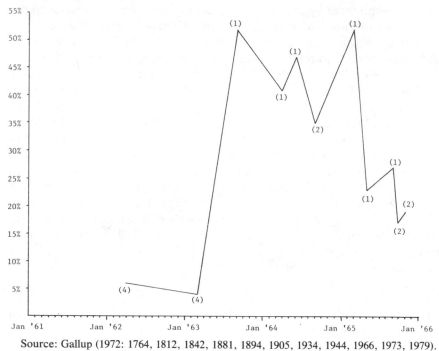

Source: Gallup (1972: 1764, 1812, 1842, 1881, 1894, 1905, 1934, 1944, 1966, 1973, 1979).

Note: Civil rights was the usual designation given the problem. However, in some polls it was identified as the "Racial Problem." The numbers in parentheses refer to the rank of civil rights among all the problems identified in that poll.

riod. James Q. Wilson accurately captured the significance of this dynamic: "The principal value of the white liberal," wrote Wilson, "is to supply votes and the political pressures . . . that make it almost suicidal for an important Northern politician openly to court anti-Negro sentiment" (1965: 437). The mobilization of liberal support acted, then, to further enhance the bargaining position of blacks by increasing the political consequences of opposing "acceptable" black demands.

In summary, a variety of external political pressures continued, in the early 1960s, to render the political establishment vulnerable to pressure from black insurgents.[10] Among these pressures were increased public awareness of, and support for, civil rights, the growing size and significance of the black vote, and the continued salience of certain international political tensions.

COLLECTIVE ASSESSMENT OF THE PROSPECTS FOR INSURGENCY, 1961–65

If there existed a favorable confluence of external political conditions and internal movement characteristics in the early 1960s it nonetheless was the sense of optimism prevalent among blacks regarding the prospects for insurgency that furnished the motive force for heightened movement activity. Evidence of this optimistic "state of mind" is again sketchy, but is so consistent as to leave little doubt that it was shared by large numbers of blacks in the early 1960s. Data gathered in 1963 by Hadley Cantril showed blacks to be more optimistic about the future than were whites (Cantril, 1965: 42–43). Using a "self-anchoring-ladder" question, blacks were asked to rank themselves and the United States on a scale from one to ten in terms of how they stood five years ago, where they stand at present, and where they expect to be five years from now. The results of this analysis are shown in table 7.5.

As can be seen, blacks were more optimistic about the prospects for both personal and national gains than were the white respondents. Interestingly, the discrepancy between these two groups was more pronounced on the matter of national than personal progress. Given the salience of the civil rights issue at the time of the survey, it would seem logical to interpret this discrepancy as at least a partial reflection of an underlying black-white difference in the value placed on what, in 1963, was perceived to be the likely direction of change in racial matters.

A *Newsweek*, Brink-Harris survey also conducted in 1963 yielded considerable evidence consistent with that reported by Cantril. Table 7.6 summarizes the responses of blacks to a series of questions asking them to assess how they expected their situation five years from now to compare with their present status on a number of dimensions. The level of optimism

TABLE 7.5
Mean Rankings of Black and White Respondents to a 1963 Survey Assessing Past, Present and Future Perceptions of Personal and National Standing

	5 Years Ago	At Present	5 Years from Now	Past-Future Differential	Past-Present Differential
"Where do you stand?"					
Blacks	4.6	5.2	6.6	+2.0	+1.4
Whites	5.7	6.3	7.5	+1.8	+1.2
"Where does America stand?"					
Blacks	5.3	6.6	7.7	+2.4	+1.1
Whites	6.3	6.7	7.3	+1.0	+0.6

Source: Adapted from Cantril (1965: 43).

TABLE 7.6
Personal Assessment of Blacks in 1963 Concerning the Prospects for Future Gains

Issue Area	Percentage of Nonleaders				Percentage of leaders			
	Better-off	Worse-off	About Same	Not Sure	Better-off	Worse-off	About Same	Not Sure
Pay	67	2	14	17	81	7	11	1
Work situation	64	3	15	18	76	5	10	9
Housing accommodations	62	2	24	12	52	4	44	0
Being able to get children educated with white children	58	1	21	20	66	2	30	2
Being able to eat in any restaurant	55	1	31	13	56	2	39	3
Being able to register and vote	42	1	48	9	15	2	81	2
White attitudes[a]	73	2	11	14	93	0	4	3

Source: Adapted from Brink and Harris (1963: 234, 238).

[a]The data reporting black estimates of white attitudes were taken from a question separate from the others.

revealed in these responses is striking. Only in regard to voting did a majority of blacks fail to respond optimistically. And even here, those expecting an improvement in voting rights outnumbered those anticipating a deterioration, 42 percent to 1 percent. Similarly, by a margin of 73 percent to 2 percent, blacks expected white attitudes to improve "over the next five years" (Brink and Harris, 1963: 136). Reflecting even greater optimism were the comparable responses of 100 black "leaders" interviewed as a separate part of the survey. Fully 93 percent of the leaders questioned felt white attitudes would improve in the future, while none felt they would get worse. Given that these leaders were initiating much of the protest activity occurring at the time, their overwhelming optimism regarding the prospects for favorable change is significant indeed.

But perhaps the most striking evidence of the prevalent mood within the black community during this period comes from the responses to another question taken from the Brink-Harris survey. The item read as follows: "Some people have said that since there are ten whites for every Negro in America, if it came to white against Negro the Negroes would lose. Do you agree with this or disagree?" Only two in ten blacks agreed with this statement, while 52 percent disagreed, arguing that blacks would win despite the numerical superiority of whites (Brink and Harris, 1963: 74). These figures suggest the extraordinary sense of political efficacy (not to mention "moral destiny") shared by blacks in these years. They also

TABLE 7.7

Percentage of Blacks in 1963 Reporting a Willingness to Participate in Various Forms of Collective Action

Form of Action	Percentage of Nonleaders	Percentage of Leaders
March in a demonstration	51	57
Take part in a sit-in	49	57
Go to jail	47	58
Picket a store	46	57

Source: Adapted from Brink and Harris (1963: 203).

help to explain one final set of findings reported by Brink and Harris. When asked whether they would be willing to participate in various forms of protest activity, an amazingly large number of the respondents replied affirmatively. The exact percentages responding in this manner are reported in table 7.7.

Obviously, an expressed willingness to participate in protest activity is not the same as actual involvement. We would expect many of these "attitudinal participants" to fall by the wayside when faced with the real-life risks associated with insurgency. This caveat notwithstanding, these figures remain impressive testimony to the psychological resources insurgents had to draw upon in this period. Can one imagine 47 percent of the American population professing a willingness to go to jail for *any* contemporary cause? Not likely. Quite simply, these figures reflect a unanimity of purpose and sense of political efficacy to be found only in periods of intensified political activity. It was these attitudes, then, as much as favorable political conditions and strong organizations, that account for the high rate of insurgency characteristic of the civil rights phase of the movement.

THE RESPONSE TO INSURGENCY, 1961–65

Finally, the responses of other organized parties to the movement also contributed to the dramatic expansion in movement activity during the early 1960s. Indeed, perhaps more than any of the aforementioned three factors it was these responses that were to shape the fortunes of the movement by determining the balance of supporting and opposing forces confronting insurgents. In the next chapter I will argue that in the late 1960s these responses proved detrimental to the movement by defining a growing opposition to black insurgency. In the period from 1961 to 1965, however, the response of other parties to the conflict generally served to facilitate the expansion of protest activity.

As important as these responses were, they can only be understood by reference to certain characteristics of the black movement during this period. This is simply to acknowledge the rather basic, but nonetheless important, point that such responses are themselves shaped by the actions of insurgents. Specifically, it is the degree of threat or opportunity embodied in any insurgent challenge that largely determines the line of action taken by other groups toward the movement. In turn, the "degree of threat or opportunity" is largely a function of two factors: the goals sought by insurgents and the tactics used to pursue those goals. In the case of the black movement, then, a review of the goals and tactics adopted by insurgents during this period is crucial to an understanding of the responses engendered by these choices..

With respect to the goals of the movement, little needs to be added to the earlier discussion of the dominant issue-focus of insurgent activity during this period. A reexamination of table 7.3 shows that the aims of insurgents in the early 1960s centered more on the integration of blacks into various areas of American life rather than on any major restructuring of the dominant economic and political institutions of society. Accordingly, the goals of the movement posed little threat to the fundamental imperatives of class rule in this country. As Clark has commented: "The civil rights organizations were never revolutionary. Their assumptions and strategy and tactics were essentially conservative, in that they did not seek to change and certainly made no attempt to overthrow the basic political and economic structure. The social changes they sought were limited to the inclusion of the Negro in the existing society" (1970: 278).

The issue of tactics is more complicated than that of movement goals. One of the key challenges to insurgents is that of overcoming the basic powerlessness that has long confined them to a position of institutionalized political impotence. Groups whose interests are routinely "organized out" of institutionalized politics are excluded precisely because they lack the traditional political resources that are a prerequisite to effective bargaining within "proper channels." To overcome this powerlessness insurgents must bypass routine decision-making channels and seek, through use of noninstitutionalized tactics, to force their opponents to deal with them outside of established arenas within which the latter derive so much of their power. The emergence of a social movement testifies to at least limited success in this regard. To survive, however, a movement must be able to sustain the leverage generated by the use of such novel tactics. To do so often requires further experimentation with noninstitutionalized forms of protest.

It was in their use of such tactics that black insurgents proved particularly adept during the early 1960s. Indeed, the pace of insurgency throughout this period can be seen largely as a function of a series of tactical innovations pioneered by movement activists. Figure 7.3 helps illustrate this point. As the figure shows, peaks in movement activity do tend to correspond to the introduction of new protest techniques. The first example of this relationship involves the sit-ins. Pioneered by four North Carolina A. and T. students, the first sit-in occurred February 1, 1960, in Greensboro, North Carolina. The effect of this tactical innovation on the pace of movement activity can be seen clearly in figure 7.3. After low levels of activity prior to the first sit-in, the pace of insurgency jumped sharply in February, peaked in March, and remained at a high level throughout the remainder of the spring. The next major peak in movement activity occurred in February-March of 1961, simultaneously with the introduction and spread of the "jail-in." This tactic, pioneered by CORE and SNCC workers in Rock Hill, South Carolina, involved courting arrest and then refusing to accept bail. The intention was to dramatize the op-pressiveness of southern racism through mass jailings, while at the same time straining the law enforcement resources of the affected municipali-ties. Close on the heels of this innovation came another in the form of the CORE-sponsored Freedom Rides, stimulating a commensurate rise in movement activity that was to last through the summer of 1961. December,

Figure 7.3   Movement-Initiated Actions, January 1960 through April 1965

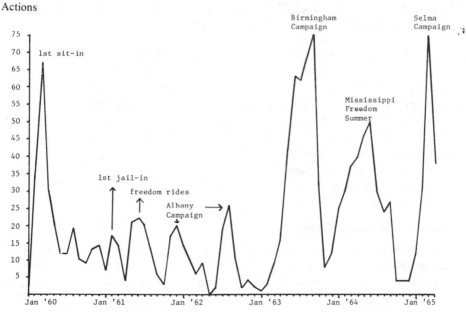

Source: Annual *New York Times Index*, 1960–65.

1961, brought the first of the comprehensive community-wide civil rights campaigns and another peak in black insurgency. Based in Albany, Georgia, the campaign was the prototype of similar movements in Birmingham and Selma that show up in figure 7.3 as the peaks in protest activity during the summer of 1963 and the spring of 1965. Finally, the period of heightened activism in the summer of 1964 coincides with the mass voter-registration campaigns of Mississippi Freedom Summer. In short, the fit between the pace of movement activity in the early 1960s and the introduction and spread of various tactical innovations is a good one. With the introduction of a new protest technique the movement's local opponents were temporarily caught off guard, making them more vulnerable to concerted insurgent efforts. Accordingly, the pace of movement activity rose. As local supremacists adjusted to the technique and devised effective tactical responses to it, insurgency once again declined.

The purpose of discussing these innovations, however, is not so much to account for the ebb and flow of insurgency as it is to provide the reader with a context for understanding the responses of other groups to the movement. The key point is that the tactics adopted during this period by insurgents were inherently more threatening than the goals they were pursuing. In this respect, the genius of the movement during its heyday was preeminently tactical. In bypassing the opposition-controlled "proper channels," insurgents posed a fundamental challenge to the established political system. Such a challenge demanded a direct response from other parties to the conflict. It is to those responses that I now turn.

Besides the movement organizations themselves, the other major parties to the conflict during this period were the federal government, white supremacists, and external support groups. The latter category represents a congeries of groups drawn from among the ranks of labor, northern students, organized religion, and such traditional liberal organizations as the American Civil Liberties Union and the Taconic Foundation. Together, these three broad categories of participants constitute the organizational environment within which the movement operated during the period in question. It was the ongoing interaction between these groups and insurgents that produced the unique and ultimately facilitative conflict dynamic characteristic of the early 1960s.

External Support Groups

The involvement of external support groups in the black movement affords us another opportunity to assess the relative merits of the political process model and one version of the resource mobilization model. The implicit argument advanced by proponents of the latter perspective would seem to hold that external support is absolutely essential for a movement, given the abiding powerlessness and poverty of excluded groups. By contrast, the political process model is based on the notion that the interests of insurgents and external support groups are likely to diverge, thereby exposing the movement to the rather ominous control possibilities embodied in such linkages.

In the case of the black movement, both perspectives would seem to be partially correct. In the short run, the establishment of external support links proved beneficial to the movement. Over time, however, developments within the movement were ultimately to render these linkages a distinct liability rather than an asset. In the period under discussion both the immediate benefits and long-range costs of these linkages are evident.

In an earlier chapter, the reactive pattern of external support triggered by the outbreak of indigenous protest activity was documented (see figure 6.2). This pattern persisted throughout the early 1960s, affording movement groups ever larger operating budgets. This rapid expansion in support opportunities was made possible by the substantive focus of insurgency during this period. In the face of the moderate reform approach adopted by insurgents and the limited threat it posed to member interests, there was no shortage of external groups willing to support the movement. Accordingly, financial support rose steadily between 1961 and 1965. This expansion in external support contributed greatly to the growth in insurgency by providing movement organizations with the resources required to broaden and intensify their programs. On one level, then, the high rates of activism characteristic of the movement's heyday can be seen as a function of the ability of insurgents to establish and maintain lucrative support links to external groups.

However, these linkages were not to prove wholly beneficial to the movement. Specifically, three important costs followed from the establishment of these external support links. The first was simply increased competition among the major movement organizations for the external support required to sustain their programs and the media coverage needed to generate that external support. The rapid expansion of support opportunities encouraged movement groups to channel their energies into the cultivation of external links. As a result, they came increasingly to depend on the same general sources for support and the same news media for publicity, thus exacerbating the normal range of tensions inherent in interorganizational relations. As Watters observes: "Inherent in the inability of the organizations to work together cohesively in such an important campaign as Greenwood or in such a serious matter as the timing of the Freedom March and Birmingham was—beyond personal and ideological conflicts—the increasing rivalry among them for financial support" (Watters, 1971: 264). The pursuit of external support linkages introduced a new source of uncertainty into the organizational environment of these groups. This uncertainty took the form of new constituencies—the news media, external support groups—whose demands had to be balanced against other competing pressures such as the need for interorganizational cooperation.

A second problem arising from the cultivation of elite linkages was the tactical inadvisability of accepting support from parties that the movement, in other contexts, was trying to influence. Acquiring resources in this way grants some measure of control over the movement organization's program to the supporting institution. Owing to the general "acceptability" of movement goals, this control was more often an implied capability than an actual constraint during the early 1960s. Still there were enough instances where this control was exercised to support the conclusion that external support linkages served, at times, to constrain or "tame" insurgent activities. Perhaps the most obvious example of this phenomenon involved the pressure brought to bear on SNCC president John Lewis to alter the speech he had intended to deliver as part of the 1963 March on Washington. That pressure came from representatives of many of the external support groups active in the march who objected not only to the "immoderate" tone of the speech but to its substantive focus as well. As part of SNCC's southern field staff, Lewis had all too often suffered the consequences of the federal government's failure adequately to protect civil rights workers from violent attack by southern supremacists. Accordingly, he came to Washington to question publicly the depth of the federal commitment to black equality. As an example, one line of Lewis's speech read: "I want to know, which side is the Federal Government on?" (Zinn, 1965: 215). Ultimately, this and other "offensive" passages were omitted by Lewis in response to pressure from march sponsors. When finally delivered, the speech represented little more than a standard attack on the traditional southern enemy, uninformed by the broader—and more threatening—questions and issues Lewis had hoped to raise.[11]

Another instance involving external control of insurgency occurred in 1964, when a cutback in voter registration funds was threatened in an effort to pressure civil rights groups to declare a moratorium on demonstrations until after the November presidential election. That this effort was largely successful is suggested by the sharp decline in movement activity that took place during the fall of 1964 (see figure 7.3). Of course, one could argue, as those threatening the cutback did, that the moratorium benefited the movement by helping to prevent the widely predicted conservative backlash that threatened to sweep Barry Goldwater into the presidency that fall. Even if one attributes a modicum of truth to this view—which it is difficult to do in view of Goldwater's crushing defeat in the election—the potential for co-optation inherent in the external support links established by insurgents during this period should be apparent from this and the other example cited above.

Finally, quite apart from any special dangers posed by the establishment of elite linkages, exclusive dependence on *any* particular funding source raises the possibility of a rapid decline in insurgency should support be withdrawn. The relevance of this observation for the Black Movement stems from a recognition of the extent to which the major movement organizations were coming, in the early 1960s, to rely on this general class of support groups for the bulk of their funding. Among the Big Four, only the NAACP maintained a diverse basis of support throughout the period (Aveni, 1977). By contrast, the survival of SNCC, CORE, and SCLC was growing ever more dependent on the vagaries of external support.[12] Initially, of course, this dependence posed few difficulties for the movement. This is attributable to the compatibility of interests that marked the relationship between insurgents and support groups during this period. So long as the latter found the aims of insurgents consistent with their own interests, dependence on external sources of support posed no serious problems for the movement. However, changes within the movement during the mid-1960s were to undermine the legitimacy earlier accorded movement organizations by these external support groups, thus rendering the movement's continued financial dependence on such groups increasingly problematic.

The Federal Government

One view of the federal government's relationship to the black movement has the government assuming the role of a committed ally aggressively working for the realization of movement goals. This view underlies many traditional liberal accounts of the movement. Representative of this perspective is the following statement by Benjamin Muse:

> The Supreme Court was a mighty bulwark of the revolution; the national administration a towering ally. . . . The Administration's drive for civil rights was centered in the Department of Justice. . . . These men and their assistants had drafted the President's omnibus civil rights bill, and were working intensively to secure its enactment. They were carrying on a volume of litigation related to school desegregation and voting rights that strained the capacity of the Civil Rights Division's forty overworked lawyers (Muse, 1968: 40–42).

Muse's statement conveys the image of a federal government wholly supportive of the movement, even to the point of taxing its available manpower in an effort to advance the cause.

In contrast to this view, the argument advanced here is that the federal government attempted to maintain a stance of tactical neutrality vis-à-vis the South's unfolding racial conflict throughout the 1955–65 period. In the face of the growing electoral strength of blacks and the continued strategic importance of the South, the national political elite sought to refrain from antagonizing either side through forthright support of the other. Their interest lay, instead, in curbing the disruptive excesses of both sides so as to avoid a dangerous confrontation that would force their involvement in the conflict. Only by avoiding such involvement could federal officials hope to continue to court the political favors of both groups. Thus, the watchword of every administration during this period was "the preservation of public order" rather than the realization of black equality.

The 1962–64 Voter Education Project (VEP) offers perhaps the best and most significant example of the government's efforts to direct movement activity into channels it viewed as less threatening. Though ostensibly sponsored by the Taconic Foundation, the real driving force behind VEP were officials in the Kennedy administration who viewed voter registration as a way of curbing the disruptive tendencies of the movement while, at the same time, systematically swelling the ranks of likely Democratic supporters.[13] Piven and Cloward elaborate:

> In the wake of the student sit-ins and the freedom rides, the Kennedy Administration attempted to divert the civil rights forces from tactics of confrontation to the building of a black electoral presence in the South. The Kennedy Administration's posture on these matters is not difficult to understand. Tactics of confrontation, together with the police and mob violence which they provoked, were polarizing national sentiments. The excesses of southern police violence and of white mob violence generated one excruciating political dilemma after another for the Kennedy Administration as to whether it should intervene to protect civil rights demonstrators and uphold the law. Each intervention, or the lack of it, angered one or the other major constituency in the civil rights struggle, thus worsening the electoral lesion in the Democratic Party (Piven and Cloward, 1979: 231).

Writing in 1963, another chronicler of the movement concurred, if a bit tersely, with Piven and Cloward's interpretation of the motives underlying VEP: "it seems obvious that prevention of mayhem is one idea involved here" (Cleghorn, 1963: 14). Again, one could argue that, regardless of these ulterior motives, the project benefited the movement by underwriting crucial southern registration campaigns. Perhaps, but one could just as easily point to the federal government's failure to deliver on their promise of protection for civil rights workers, the rather insignificant gains registered during VEP's early years, the ultimate corrosive effect the campaign had on the workers themselves, and the weak empirical link between electoral strength and substantive policy outputs (Alford and Friedland, 1975: 440–41) to support the thesis that the project actually hurt the movement by containing and defusing the disruptive tactics that had proved so effective in earlier campaigns.[14]

Kennedy sponsorship of VEP was only the most obvious example of a federal strategy very much in evidence throughout the late 1950s and early 1960s. It was also evident in Kennedy's oft-praised call for legislative action in the midst of a Birmingham-inspired escalation in protest activity during the early summer of 1963. Said Kennedy in a televised speech on June 11 of that year: "fires of frustration and discord are burning in every city, North and South. . . . Redress is sought in the streets, in demonstrations, parades and protests, which create tensions and threaten violence" (in Watters, 1971: 271). Thus, as Watters perceptively notes, "the non-violent demonstrations were not a magnificent achievement within a violence-prone society, but rather, in the eyes of the . . . lawmakers, a threat to be quieted, a creator of tensions to be avoided" (1971: 271). No doubt, similar considerations underlay Robert Kennedy's call for a "cooling-off" period following the initial Freedom Rides as well as the previously noted pressure campaign to effect a moratorium on demonstrations in advance of the 1964 presidential elections.[15] Finally, the same fear of significant public disorder would appear to help account for variations in federal responses to ostensibly similar crises that arose in various southern locales during the movement's heyday. In Montgomery in 1961, the administration intervened to protect Freedom Riders after law enforcement officials failed to, while in Albany, a year later, protests similar to those in Montgomery failed to produce federal intervention. Apparently, the substantive similarities of the two protest campaigns were not as significant as their contextual differences. Brooks explains: "in Montgomery, there was a major breakdown of civil order while in Albany, relatively speaking, there was no such breakdown. As long as the local police maintained order, no matter how many went to jail in violation of their constitutional rights to freedom of assembly, petition, and speech, there would be no federal intervention" (1974: 187).

The tacit federal support for segregation evident in Albany is a far cry from the portrait of an aggressive, supportive federal presence implicit in the "liberal" perspective touched on at the beginning of this section. Even this less than forthright position, however, represented a marked improvement over the blatant opposition to black interests displayed by the federal government from 1900 to 1930. What is more, the federal government's strong aversion to violent racial confrontations actually encouraged protest activity during the early 1960s by affording insurgents a ready-made strategy with which to press their claims. As Brooks notes, the federal government, by responding only to crisis, "bought a short-run civil peace at a long-run cost—the escalation of civil disobedience to confrontation, the deliberate courting of violence in order to provoke federal action'' (1974: 187). In the final section of this chapter, this crucial dynamic will be analyzed in greater detail. For now, the important point is that the federal response to the movement during this period was facilitative of insurgency both in its absence of overt opposition to movement goals and in its decisive, if grudging, support for black rights when insurgents were able to provoke the violent confrontations that would necessitate government intervention.

White Supremacists

In Chapter 6, supremacist activity was shown to be reactive in nature from 1955 to 1960. That is, local supremacist forces seemed to mobilize primarily in response to the initiation of direct action campaigns by black groups. This characteristic pattern appears to have persisted throughout the period in question here. Certainly, the accounts of numerous local conflicts in the South during the early 1960s suggest a continuation of the stimulus-response pattern of movement-supremacist interaction. For example, one source documents a dramatic rise in supremacist violence following the initiation of SNCC-sponsored voter registration activity in southwest Georgia in 1962 (Keesing's Reports, 1970: 126). Similarly, in regard to COFO's stepped-up campaign of voter registration in Mississippi two years later, the same authors note that the ''White Knights of the Ku Klux Klan launched a terrorist campaign in Mississippi in the spring of 1964, largely as a reaction to the movement for the registration of Negro voters led by civil rights organizations'' (Keesing's Reports, 1970: 171). In addition to these accounts, many others report the same reactive pattern of supremacist activity in other southern locales during the early 1960s (Chalmers, 1965: 370–71, 378–80; Muse, 1968: 140–41, 165–68; Skolnick, 1969: 220).

More systematic evidence suggestive of this characteristic pattern of supremacist activity comes from an analysis of the *New York Times* data discussed earlier. By simply tallying the number of movement and white supremacist actions for each month of the period in question, we are in a position to quantitatively assess the relationship between these two groups. The results of this analysis are reported in figure 7.4. The best fit between the activity patterns of these two groups is achieved by lagging the actions of insurgents one month behind those of the supremacists. The simple time-series regression produces an r^2 of .599 and a total variance explained of .358.

If the pattern of supremacist activity remained unchanged during this period, its frequency did not. Reflecting the intensified pace of black protest activity in the early 1960s, white supremacist activity increased substantially over this same period of time (see table 7.8). This increase may also reflect the geographic shift of black insurgency to more recalcitrant areas of the Deep South where white resistance to integration was stronger. Table 7.2 shows that the proportion of movement-generated actions taking place in the Deep South rose from 37 percent in the 1955–60 period to 47 percent in the succeeding five-year period. Certainly, this shift helps to account for the rise in supremacist violence during the latter period.

Figure 7.4   Correlations between Monthly Number of Movement-Initiated Actions and White Supremacist Actions (1961–April, 1965), by Number of Months Correlation Is Lagged

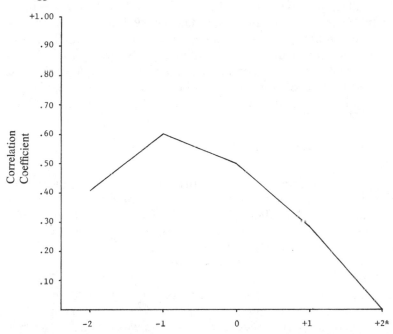

Number of months movement actions are lagged behind supremacist actions

*Correlation at +2 is −.019

TABLE 7.8
Number and Proportion of All White Supremacist Events That Involved Violence against Blacks, 1955–65

	1955–60		1961		1962		1963		1964		1965		1961–65	
	%	(N)	%	(N)	%	(N)	%	(N)	%	(N)	%	(N)	%	(N)
Involved violence	25	(176)	18	(26)	29	(24)	25	(45)	71	(98)	41	(55)	37	(248)
Violence absent	75	(540)	82	(118)	71	(58)	75	(132)	29	(40)	59	(79)	63	(427)
Total	100	(716)	100	(144)	100	(82)	100	(177)	100	(138)	100	(134)	100	(675)

Source: Annual *New York Times Index*, 1955–65.

Ironically, the increased pace of supremacist activity during the early 1960s and the greater violence associated with it contributed greatly to the expansion in black insurgency over the same period of time. Indeed, supremacists were as responsible for the full flowering of black insurgency as any other party to the conflict, save the insurgents themselves. President Kennedy's famous "tribute" to Bull Connor, Birmingham's notorious commissioner of public safety, suggests the importance of supremacist violence during the movement's heyday. In a remark to Martin Luther King, Kennedy said: "our judgment of Bull Connor should not be too harsh. After all, in his own way, he has done a good deal for civil rights legislation this year" (in King, 1963: 144). On one level, what supremacists such as Connor brought to the movement were highly dramatic symbols of segregation contributing greatly to the insurgents' ability to mobilize the resources of both the black community and elite support groups. More important, local white opposition could be counted on to provide the flagrant disruptions of public order that, when publicized, prompted federal intervention.

Supremacists, Insurgents and the Federal Government:
The Critical Dynamic

The above discussion brings us back to the critical dynamic touched on earlier in the section on the federal government. The importance of this dynamic cannot be underestimated. It was, in fact, the recognition and conscious manipulation of this dynamic by insurgents that produced the particularly high rates of activism and significant victories characteristic of the years from 1961 to 1965.

The dynamic can be described simply. Lacking sufficient power to defeat the supremacists in a local confrontation, insurgents sought to broaden the conflict by inducing their opponents to disrupt public order to the point where supportive federal intervention was required. As a by-product of the drama associated with these flagrant displays of public violence, the movement was also able to sustain member commitment, generate broad public sympathy, and mobilize financial support from external groups.

Obviously, this dynamic involved an element of conscious provocation on the part of movement groups. This provocation, in turn, implies a level of tactical awareness and command on the part of insurgents that is generally missing from both the classical and resource mobilization models. In these two perspectives insurgency is held to be shaped more by processes external to the movement than by the actions of insurgents themselves. By contrast, the argument advanced here suggests that the pace of insurgency depends, to a large extent, on the ability of movement groups to gauge accurately the interests and likely responses of other parties to the conflict and then to orchestrate a campaign designed to exploit these characteristics. Certainly this was true in the civil rights phase of the black movement. 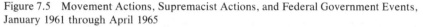 It was the insurgents' skillful use of the "politics of protest" that shaped the unfolding conflict process and keyed the extent and timing of federal involvement and white opposition. Data presented in figure 7.5 support this contention. In their respective patterns of activity, both supremacist forces and the federal government betray a consistent reactive relationship vis-à-vis the movement. With regard to the first of these groups, the pattern of movement stimulus and supremacist response is quite evident. In figure 7.5 peaks in supremacist activity are clearly shown to follow similar peaks in black insurgency.

The relationship between the federal government and the movement is a bit more complex. Government activity is still responsive to the pace of black insurgency, but, as expected, much of this responsiveness derives from the ability of the movement to provoke disruptive supremacist activity. This can be seen more clearly by running a path analysis between

Figure 7.5   Movement Actions, Supremacist Actions, and Federal Government Events, January 1961 through April 1965

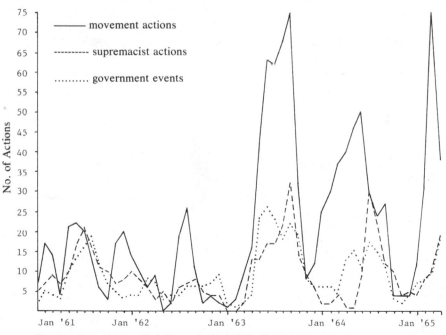

Source: Annual *New York Times Index,* 1961–65.

Note: The final eight months of 1965 have been excluded from this figure because they mark the termination of the dynamic under analysis here. In large measure this is due to the shifting northern location of movement activity.

movement and supremacist actions (lagging the former one month) and government events. The multiple correlation between the two independent variables and the dependent variable is .78, with the combined effect of movement and supremacist activity accounting for approximately 60 percent of the variance in government events. Of more immediate interest, however, is the strength of the respective "paths" through the dependent variable. Figure 7.6 shows that both movement and supremacist action exert a significant positive effect on the pace of government events. It is the relationship between supremacists and the federal government, however, that is the stronger of the two. More accurately, then, much of the strength of the relationship between federal and movement activity is indirect, with the stimulus to government involvement supplied by the intervening pattern of supremacist activity.

Returning to figure 7.5, we can identify four periods that, in varying degrees, reflect this characteristic three-way dynamic linking black protest activity to federal intervention by way of an intermediate pattern of white resistance. To identify and briefly discuss these periods, as well as one other in which the dynamic is noticeably absent, will help to document the process and span of time over which the interplay between these groups typically evolved.

Chronologically, the first instance of this three-way dynamic occurred between May and August, 1961, during the peak of activity associated with the Freedom Rides. Figure 7.5 clearly identifies this period as one of unusually high rates of activism by all three groups. For their part, supremacists responded to the threat posed by the rides with a series of violent and highly publicized acts of resistance such as the bus-burning at Anniston, Alabama, on May 14 and the mob attack on the Freedom

Figure 7.6   A Path Model of the Relationship between Movement, White Supremacist, and Federal Activity Patterns

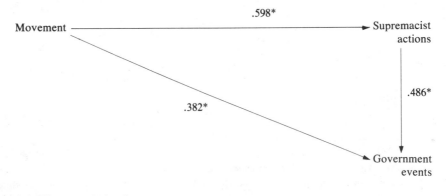

*significant at .01 level

Riders six days later in Montgomery. In turn, these flagrant disruptions of public order forced a reluctant administration to intervene in support of black interests. The Justice Department asked a federal district court in Montgomery to enjoin various supremacist groups from interfering with interstate travel; Robert Kennedy ordered six hundred marshals to Montgomery to protect the riders; and under administration pressure the Interstate Commerce Commission issued an order barring segregation in interstate travel effective November 1, 1961.[16] That these favorable federal actions were in some sense coerced is suggested by former CORE director James Farmer in his account of the strategy underlying the rides: "our intention was to provoke the Southern authorities into arresting us and thereby prod the Justice Department into enforcing the law of the land" (Farmer, 1965: 69).

The next major movement campaign provides an interesting contrast to the others reviewed here, not so much for what transpired as for what did not. The campaign took place in Albany, Georgia, during the final two months of 1961 and throughout the summer of the following year. Figure 7.5 again mirrors a rise in movement activity during these two periods. What is absent are corresponding increases in white supremacist and government activity. This is consistent with accounts of the campaign.[17] Those accounts stress the firm control exercised by police chief Laurie Pritchett over events in Albany. While systematically denying demonstrators their rights, Pritchett nonetheless did so in such a way as to prevent the type of major disruption that would have prompted federal involvement: "the reason . . . [the movement] failed in Albany was that Chief Pritchett used force rather than violence in controlling the situation, that is, *he effectively reciprocated the demonstrator's tactics*" (Hubbard, 1968: 5; emphasis in original). Even in "defeat," then, the dynamic is evident.[18] Failing to provoke the public violence necessary to prompt federal intervention, insurgents lacked sufficient leverage to achieve anything more than a standoff with the local supremacist forces in Albany.

The experience of Albany was not without value, however, as the following remarkable passage by Martin Luther King attests:

There were weaknesses in Albany, and a share of the responsibility belongs to each of us who participated. However, none of us was so immodest as to feel himself master of the new theory. Each of us expected that setbacks would be a part of the ongoing effort. There is no tactical theory so neat that a revolutionary struggle for a share of power can be won merely by pressing a row of buttons. Human beings with all their faults and strengths constitute the mechanism of a social movement. They must make mistakes and learn from them, make more mistakes and learn anew. They must taste defeat as well as success, and discover how to live with each. Time and action are the teachers.

When we planned our strategy for Birmingham months later, we spent many hours assessing Albany and trying to learn from its errors (King, 1963: 34–35).

The implication of King's statement is that a fuller understanding of the dynamic under discussion here was born of events in Albany. No doubt, a part of this fuller understanding was a growing awareness of the importance of white violence as a stimulus to federal involvement. As Hubbard argues, this awareness appears to have influenced the choice of Birmingham as the next major protest site. "King's Birmingham innovation was pre-eminently strategic. Its essence was not merely more refined tactics, but the selection of a target city which had as its Commissioner of Public Safety 'Bull' Connor, a notorious racist and hothead who could be depended on *not* to respond nonviolently" (Hubbard, 1968: 5).

The view that King's choice of Birmingham was a conscious, strategic one is supported by the fact that Connor was a lame-duck official, having been defeated by a moderate in a runoff election in early April, 1963. Had SCLC waited to launch the protest campaign until after the moderate took office, there likely would have been considerably less violence *and* less leverage with which to press for federal involvement. "The supposition," in the words of Watters, "has to be that . . . SCLC, in a shrewd . . . strategem, knew a good enemy when they saw him . . . one who could be counted on in stupidity and natural viciousness to play into their hands, for full exploitation in the press as archfiend and villain" (Watters, 1971: 266).

The results of this choice of protest site are well known and clearly visible in figure 7.5. The Birmingham campaign of April–May, 1963, triggered considerable white resistance in the form of extreme police brutality and numerous instances of terrorist violence. In turn, the federal government was again forced to intervene in defense of the movement. The ultimate result of this shifting posture was administration sponsorship of a civil rights bill that, even in a much weaker form, had earlier been described as politically inopportune by administration spokesmen. Under pressure by insurgents, the bill was ultimately signed into law a year later as the Civil Rights Act of 1964.

Finally there was Selma, the last of the massive campaigns of this period. It was in this campaign, as Garrow has argued in his definitive book on the subject, that the characteristic protest dynamic under discussion here was most fully realized: "it is clear that by January 1965 King and the SCLC consciously had decided to attempt to elicit violent behavior from their immediate opponents. Such an intent governed the choice of Selma and Jim Clark [Selma's violence-prone sheriff], and such an intent governed all of the tactical choices that the SCLC leadership made throughout the campaign" (Garrow, 1978: 227). These choices achieved the desired result. Initiated in January, 1965, the campaign reached its peak in February and March, triggering the typical reactive patterns of white resistance and federal involvement noted above in connection with protest actions elsewhere. With regard to supremacist violence, the campaign provoked no shortage of celebrated atrocities. On March 9, state troopers attacked and brutally beat some 525 persons who were attempting to begin a protest march to Montgomery. Later that same day, the Reverend James Reeb, a march participant, was beaten to death by a group of whites. Finally, on March 25, following the triumphal completion of the twice interrupted Selma-to-Montgomery march, a white volunteer, Mrs. Viola Liuzzo, was shot and killed while transporting marchers back to Selma from the state capital. In response to this consistent breakdown of public order, the federal government was once again forced to intervene in support of black interests. On March 15, President Johnson addressed a joint session of Congress to deliver his famous "We Shall Overcome" speech. Two days later he submitted to Congress a tough voting rights bill containing several provisions that movement leaders had earlier been told were politically too unpopular to be incorporated into legislative proposals. The bill passed by overwhelming margins in both the Senate and House and was signed into law on August 6 of the same year.

However, for all the drama and momentum associated with Selma it was to represent the last time insurgents were able successfully to orchestrate a campaign designed to exploit the characteristic response of the other two major parties to the conflict. The heyday of the movement was over.

Summary

The period from 1961 to 1965 proved to be one of heightened activity and significant accomplishment for the movement. Consistent with a political process interpretation, the expansion of insurgency during these years would appear to have been the product of four broad sets of factors. First, throughout the period, insurgents were able to maintain organizational strength sufficient to mount and sustain an organized campaign of social protest. This strength stemmed in part from the profitable linkages movement groups were able to establish with external support groups. In addition, the narrow geographic and substantive focus of insurgency in the early 1960s contributed to the strength of the movement by enabling insurgents to concentrate their forces for an effective attack on limited targets.

Second, a series of external factors facilitated movement growth during this period by sustaining the supportive political context that had begun to develop in the 1930s. These factors had the effect of enhancing the political significance of the black population, thus granting organized elements within that population increased leverage with which to press their claims. Among the factors contributing to this favorable "structure of political opportunities" was the accelerated pace of northward migration among blacks, the growing public salience of the civil rights issue, and the continuing significance of certain international political pressures.

A third factor facilitating the growth of the movement during this time was the sense of optimism and political efficacy prevalent among blacks. In effect, these shared attributions provided insurgents with the will to act, while the confluence of external opportunity and internal organization afforded them the structural capacity to do so.

Finally, the responses of other groups to the burgeoning movement also contributed to a rapid expansion in insurgency. External groups were forthcoming with vital resource support, even if such support was neither as aggressive nor nonproblematic as some resource mobilization theorists have suggested. For its part, the federal government, though wary of the movement, could ill afford to oppose openly what were widely regarded as legitimate demands. Thus, it chose a stance of tactical neutrality that allowed it to court both insurgents and supremacists. However, through their successful orchestration of the "politics of protest," movement groups were able to pressure the government into supportive action by provoking white supremacists into violent disruptions of public order. Thus, even the characteristic response of the supremacists to the movement played a facilitative role in the unfolding conflict dynamic.

8 The Decline
of Black Insurgency
1966–70

In Chapter 3 the noticeable absence of material on the decline of insurgency in the movement literature was noted. This omission is equally characteristic of the vast collection of writings specifically concerned with the black movement. Indeed, to my knowledge, no sociological analysis of the decline of the movement has, to date, appeared in the literature.[1] That such a decline did take place is suggested by figure 6.1. After peaking in 1965, black insurgency dropped off sharply in 1966 and continued to decline steadily thereafter. In this chapter I will analyze this crucial period in the development of the movement with an eye to identifying those factors that contributed to this decline. This analysis will also provide a final opportunity to assess the relative merits of the political process and resource mobilization perspectives.

It is important to note that in ascribing a position on the decline of insurgency to proponents of the mobilization perspective, I am not so much drawing on any explicit resource mobilization model of movement decline as attempting to use the key tenets of the perspective to deduce such a model. Resource mobilization theorists seek to account for insurgency on the basis of the resources available to support it. It is not grievances, discontent, or any subjective "states of mind" that vary, but the resources needed to sustain a movement. Thus, it is a significant expansion in resource support that is held to provide the crucial impetus behind movement emergence and expansion. Given this causal proposition, it would seem reasonable to presume that movement decline would result from a significant *contraction* in the resources available to support insurgency. Later in this chapter evidence will be presented that seriously contradicts this scenario, at least as regards the black movement.

As for the political process view of movement decline, a basic continuity between this and earlier phases of movement development has been posited. That is, the factors responsible for the decline of the movement are not held to be unique to this phase of insurgency. Rather, I will argue that changes in the same four factors discussed in the previous chapter were responsible for the decline of black insurgency in the late 1960s. Before doing so, however, I should qualify the characterization of the late 1960s as a period of declining black insurgency.

Labeling these years as ones of movement decline serves to obscure the extraordinary nature and intensity of black insurgency during the period. This was, after all, the peak period of urban rioting. No less than 290 "hostile outbursts" were recorded for the years 1966–68 alone. In connection with these disorders, 169 persons were killed, 7,000 wounded, and more than 40,000 arrested (Downes, 1970: 352). These are extraordinary figures.[2] It would not seem an overstatement to argue that the level of open defiance of the established economic and political order was as great during this period as during any other in this country's history, save the Civil War. It is hard to reconcile the magnitude of this "open defiance" with any simple notion of movement decline.

And yet, just as surely, such a decline did take place during these years. If the riots of this period conveyed an image of escalating racial conflict, they also masked a series of more subtle processes that were simultaneously at work undermining the efforts of insurgents to develop the organizational and tactical forms needed to sustain the leverage attained by the movement during the mid-1960s. The result of these processes was dramatic and quickly felt. By 1970, the movement, as a force capable of generating and sustaining organized insurgency, was moribund, if not dead.

DECLINING ORGANIZATIONAL STRENGTH, 1966–70

The first of four general factors facilitating the expansion of black insurgency in the early 1960s was the organizational strength of insurgent forces. During its heyday, the movement was characterized by a strong centralized organizational structure, substantial issue consensus, and a certain "geographic concentration" of movement forces. In the late 1960s all three of these functional characteristics were to disappear.

Organizational Proliferation

In Chapter 7 the dramatic transformation that took place between 1960 and 1963 in the movement's organizational structure was noted. During those years, formal movement organizations gradually replaced the indigenous institutions of the black community as the driving force behind black protest activity. In the period under analysis here, the relative importance of formal organizations remained virtually unchanged. Between 1966 and 1970 53 percent of all movement-initiated events were attributed to formal movement organizations, as compared to 50 percent in the preceding five years.

On closer examination, however, this apparent stability proves illusory. If the overall importance of formal movement groups remained unchanged, the organizational composition of the movement did not. The change is evident in table 8.1, which presents a comparison of the events initiated by formal movement organizations in 1961–65 and 1966–70. An examination of that table clearly reveals a diminution over time in the dominance of the movement's formal organizational structure by the "Big Four." While NAACP, CORE, SNCC, and SCLC were credited with initiating 75 percent of all events attributed to formal movement organizations between 1961 and 1965, the figure dropped to 56 percent for 1966–70. However, even this latter figure understates the drastic decline in the role played by these previously dominant groups in the second half of the 1960s. The more revealing comparison is between the years 1967 and 1970. In the earlier year, the Big Four retained their dominant role in the movement, initiating 74 percent of all events credited to formal movement organizations. By 1970, the proportion attributed to these same groups had declined by more than one-half, dropping to barely 32 percent. This represented only 15 percent of all movement-initiated events during the year.

What had occurred was a drastic disintegration of the centralized structure that had dominated the movement in the early 1960s.[3] At the root of this disintegration was a growing disagreement within insurgent ranks over the proper goals of the movement and the most effective means of attaining them. These two fundamental points of contention effectively divided the movement into two wings, increasingly distinct and antagonistic as the decade wore on.

TABLE 8.1
Distribution of All Events Initiated by Formal Movement Organizations, 1961–70

Organization	1961–65 %	(N)	1966 %	(N)	1967 %	(N)	1968 %	(N)	1969 %	(N)	1970 %	(N)	1966–70 %	(N)
NAACP	24	(265)	21	(50)	27	(53)	16	(25)	16	(21)	21	(20)	21	(169)
CORE	22	(244)	4	(10)	18	(36)	7	(10)	6	(8)	2	(2)	8	(66)
SCLC (including) M. L. King)	23	(257)	23	(56)	25	(49)	36	(55)	18	(24)	8	(8)	23	(192)
SNCC	6	(62)	9	(22)	4	(8)	1	(2)	0	(0)	1	(1)	4	(33)
Other movement organizations	15	(168)	23	(55)	17	(34)	33	(49)	56	(76)	59	(56)	33	(270)
Multiple movement organizations	10	(110)	20	(49)	8	(15)	7	(11)	4	(6)	8	(8)	11	(89)
Total	100	(1106)	100	(242)	99	(195)	100	(152)	100	(135)	99	(95)	100	(819)

Source: Annual *New York Times Index*, 1961–70.

Lined up on one side were traditional integrationists who continued to eschew violence as an unacceptable or ineffective means of pursuing movement goals. Among the Big Four, SCLC and NAACP shared this position. A further distinction can be made between these two groups on the basis of the principal method used to pursue integrationist aims. With its reliance on noninstitutionalized protest techniques, SCLC can be seen as constituting the "radical" faction within the integrationist wing, while the NAACP, on the basis of its continued emphasis on institutionalized forms of protest, comprised a "conservative" integrationist faction. Aligned in increasing opposition to the integrationists was the so-called "black power" wing of the movement, with its rejection of integration as *the* fundamental goal of black insurgency and its approval of violence (either in self-defense or as an offensive tactic), as an acceptable addition to the movement's tactical arsenal. The remaining two members of the Big Four—CORE and SNCC—were in varying degrees associated with this wing of the movement.

This typology is not meant to capture fully the divergent characteristics of the various "wings" of the movement but rather to help demonstrate that the decline in insurgency during the late 1960s was not evenly distributed over these three factions. Instead, as figure 8.1 indicates, the extent and timing of the decline was different for each.

The decline was not nearly so pronounced for the NAACP as for the other two wings of the movement. Later in this chapter an explanation for this difference will be proposed. For now, it is important only to note the relatively stable position of this "conservative" faction within the movement. As for the "radical" component of the movement's integrationist wing, fluctuations in SCLC activity during the decade reflect the organization's extraordinary dependence on Martin Luther King, Jr. In contrast to the other major insurgent groups, SCLC's relative importance within the movement actually increased up until King's death in 1968. Thereafter, deprived of King's proven abilities as fund-raiser, tactician, and conciliator of diverse factions, the organization declined sharply in importance within the movement.

Among the movement's three wings, the decline occurred earliest and was the most pronounced for CORE and SNCC—the black-power segment of the Big Four. While the two groups combined for 28 percent of all events initiated by formal movement organizations between 1961 and 1965, their proportion of that total dropped to 13 percent as early as 1966 and declined still further to a mere 3 percent by the decade's end. The effect of this decline was the creation of an organizational void in the movement's black-power wing that stimulated a period of intense organizing on the part of myriad fledgling groups intent on filling the void. Commenting on this period, Meier and Rudwick observe: "with both

Figure 8.1   Proportion of all Events Initiated by Movement Organizations Attributed to Various Wings of the Movement, 1961–70

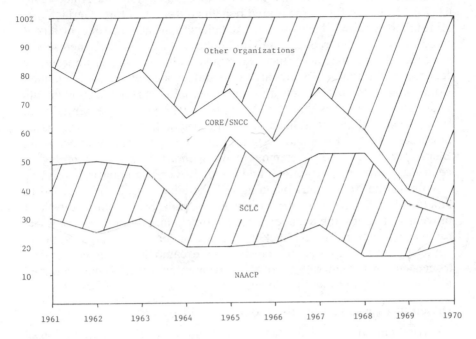

Source: Annual *New York Times Index*, 1961–70.

SNCC and CORE weakened and in decline, the banner of Black Power and black nationalism passed to other groups, mostly locally based" (1973: 425). King's assassination in 1968 greatly exacerbated this trend toward organizational proliferation by critically weakening the only remaining strong group that was action-oriented. With the NAACP heavily committed to institutionalized protest, the way was clear, upon King's death, for a host of new groups to compete for the loyalties of those seeking an activist alternative.

By 1970, then, the centralized structure of strong national groups that had dominated the movement in the early 1960s had been replaced by a highly fluid, segmented structure of small, loosely connected local organizations: "the guiding genius of The Movement had passed from the . . . Big Five [including the National Urban League] . . . to a ghetto-bred generation with reputations no larger than a single city or neighborhood or even a particular block" (Goldman, 1970: 77). In their study of the black-power wing of the movement, Gerlach and Hine have referred to this as a "decentralized, segmented, reticulate" structure, citing the well-known Communist cell structure as another example (1970: 67). The authors then go on to ascribe numerous functional benefits to this structure such as the "maintenance of security," "multipenetration," "social in-novation," and the "minimization of failure" (Gerlach and Hine, 1970: 63–78). However, for all the touted benefits of this structure, Gerlach and Hine fail to acknowledge its singular deficiency: the absence of centralized direction required to render it a potent political force. As they themselves concede, the analogy with the Communist cell structure is imperfectly realized in the Black Movement: "One difference between this planned Communist structure of cell differentiation and that of the movements under consideration is that the Communist cell system is essentially an institutionalized and routinized insurgency plan. It is a result of a series of conscious acts of will and design. Similar cell differentiation occurs in Black Power . . . and other movements *without conscious planning or centralized direction*" (Gerlach and Hine, 1970: 67; emphasis mine).

Without the "conscious planning or centralized direction" needed to link together the growing collection of autonomous protest units, the black movement had, by the decade's end, become a largely impotent political force at the national level. Lacking the strong centralized organizational vehicles required to sustain the disruptive campaigns that earlier had forced supportive federal action, the movement was increasingly confined to limited efforts at the local level.

Dissensus over Goals and the Proliferation of Issues

As noted earlier, one of the factors contributing to the disintegration of the movement's previously strong organizational structure was the col-lapse of the broad-based issue consensus that had prevailed among in-surgents during the early 1960s. Table 8.2 mirrors this collapse. Whereas the substantive focus of black insurgency had, for all intents and purposes, been dominated by the single issue of integration during the early 1960s, the same can hardly be said for the succeeding five-year period. Instead of a single overriding issue, the movement came to embrace nearly as many distinct issues as there were groups around to lobby for their adop-tion. Indeed, this proliferation of issues no doubt contributed to the rapid expansion in new movement groups during the late 1960s. The absence of a single dominant issue around which the various insurgent factions within the movement could rally created a substantive vacuum that fledg-ling groups sought to fill by mobilizing support for a variety of alternative issues. That no single or even limited combination of issues filled this void from 1966 to 1970, is evident from the data in table 8.2. No issue was implicated in more than 12 percent of all movement-initiated events during this period. This is in contrast to the 56 percent share amassed by the single issue of "integration" between 1961 and 1965. With regard, then, to the substantive focus of black insurgency during the late 1960s, the increasing rejection of integration as *the* goal of the movement trig-

TABLE 8.2
Issues Addressed in Movement Initiated Events, 1961–70

Issue	1961–65 %	(N)	1966 %	(N)	1967 %	(N)	1968 %	(N)	1969 %	(N)	1970 %	(N)	1966–70 %	(N)
Segregation/ integration	56	(1237)	9	(34)	9	(40)	12	(34)	12	(28)	22	(45)	12	(181)
Public accommodations	34	(752)	4	(16)	2	(9)	0	(1)	0	(0)	0	(0)	2	(26)
Public transportation	3	(70)	0	(0)	0	(0)	0	(0)	0	(0)	0	(0)	0	(0)
Public education	14	(318)	3	(13)	2	(9)	8	(22)	10	(24)	20	(41)	7	(109)
Housing	1	(18)	1	(3)	1	(5)	1	(2)	1	(2)	0	(0)	1	(12)
Other	4	(79)	1	(2)	4	(17)	3	(9)	1	(2)	2	(4)	2	(34)
Black political power	8	(179)	12	(45)	5	(21)	4	(11)	4	(9)	4	(7)	6	(93)
Black economic status	4	(92)	2	(7)	3	(14)	4	(12)	7	(16)	3	(6)	4	(55)
Legal equality	4	(91)	16	(60)	3	(15)	3	(7)	2	(6)	6	(13)	7	(101)
Black culture	1	(12)	1	(5)	1	(6)	1	(2)	1	(2)	2	(5)	1	(20)
White racism	2	(41)	14	(55)	5	(23)	3	(7)	12	(28)	5	(10)	8	(123)
Police brutality	3	(74)	4	(17)	2	(10)	6	(16)	5	(12)	8	(15)	5	(70)
General plight of black America	2	(45)	3	(11)	6	(24)	8	(21)	7	(16)	7	(14)	6	(86)
Internal dissent	10	(228)	14	(54)	13	(58)	18	(49)	5	(11)	2	(3)	11	(175)
Other	5	(104)	16	(60)	20	(85)	14	(39)	16	(39)	10	(20)	16	(243)
Too vague to be coded	4	(96)	10	(37)	32	(137)	29	(79)	31	(75)	31	(62)	25	(390)
Total	99	(2199)	101	(385)	99	(433)	102	(277)	102	(242)	100	(200)	101	(1537)

Source: Annual *New York Times Index*, 1961–70.

gcred a process of issue proliferation that left the movement without the single dominant issue around which diverse insurgent factions could be organized.

The Rise of Inter-movement Conflict

Even at the peak of black insurgency in the early 1960s there was considerable animosity between various organizations within the movement. Especially pronounced was the frequently divisive competition between the Big Four movement groups for the money and publicity needed to sustain their operations and position within the movement. However, owing to the substantial consensus with regard to goals and tactics that prevailed within the movement during this period, these conflictual relations failed to preclude the type of extensive cooperation discussed in Chapter 7. In fact, a good many of the major victories during the movement's heyday were the product of joint efforts on the part of some combination of the major movement organizations. The 1961 Freedom

Rides and the COFO-sponsored Voter Education Project are only the two
most noteworthy examples of such cooperative campaigns. In the late
1960s, however, the growing dissensus over movement goals foreshadowed the virtual termination of significant cooperation between the major
movement groups.

The dissension within movement ranks was to diminish the organizational strength of the movement in two important ways. First, the growing
rifts in the movement made it increasingly difficult, and ultimately impossible, to organize and sustain the type of cooperative campaign that
had proven so successful in the movement's early days. As early as 1963,
substantive points of contention between the NAACP and other COFO
members had prompted the former to reconsider its role in the proposed
Voter Education Project. Subsequently, the association's national office
did choose to participate but, owing to some serious reservations about
the project, did so only in a role much reduced from that originally
envisioned. The high point of the VEP, the 1964 Mississippi Freedom
Summer, was itself marked by increasing evidence of friction between
COFO members, culminating in the bitter in-ranks debate sparked by the
compromise-seating proposal offered the Mississippi Freedom Democratic Party (MFDP) delegation by party regulars at the 1964 Democratic
convention.[4] The debate also contributed to a growing disenchantment
on the part of SNCC members with Martin Luther King and with SCLC
more generally. King had counseled acceptance of the compromise seating
arrangement, while the SNCC contingent within the MFDP had bitterly
opposed it as an unconscionable sellout.

By the time of the Selma campaign some six months later, the rift
between SCLC and SNCC had grown to such proportions that the two
organizations openly opposed one another at various points in the campaign. Still there was sufficient strength in the Selma coalition to prevent
the SNCC-SCLC conflict from damaging the outcome of events there.
Nonetheless, relations between the various movement groups were to
deteriorate still further in the days following Selma, thus marking it as
the last successful cooperative campaign waged by the major movement
groups: "the movement—in the special sense of organizations and leaders
working together toward agreed goals . . . fell apart after Selma" (Watters,
1971: 330). Thereafter, the divisions within the movement simply grew
too large, as the disastrous Meredith march of the following summer
indicated, to support a working coalition of movement organizations.[5]
And with such unified campaigns no longer a possibility, gone too was
the movement's capacity to marshal the organizational strength inherent
in such efforts.

The growing divisions within the movement diminished the organizational strength of insurgents in yet another way. As a result of internal

dissension a portion of insurgent resources and energies was expended on divisive intermovement conflict instead of being used in pursuit of substantive movement goals. To a far greater extent than had been true in the 1961–65 period, insurgents found themselves engaged in conflict with one another rather than with recognized movement opponents. The result was a predictable diminution in the internal strength of the movement.

Though atypical in the extreme form it took, one incident dramatically symbolizes the depths of factionalism within the movement during this time. Sixteen blacks, drawn largely from the ranks of a group called the Revolutionary Action Movement, were arrested on June 21, 1967, on charges of conspiring to murder Whitney Young, Roy Wilkins, and other "moderate" civil rights leaders (Keesing's Reports, 1970: 253).

Less dramatic, but ultimately more significant than this incident, were the numerous factional disputes that served to undermine the insurgent capacity of many local protest groups. Meier and Rudwick have documented the role such disputes played in the decline of CORE affiliate strength in the mid to late 1960s. Representative of these disputes was one that split the Seattle chapter of CORE into a "conservative" faction and a dissident group called the Ad Hoc Committee:

> Ad Hoc members were charged with circulating "divisive and derog-
> atory allegations" that the chapter leaders had conspired to thwart
> direct action projects and had "foisted a compromising agreement on
> the membership." Ad Hoc people attacked the chapter's black chairman
> and vice-chairman as "too respectable" and too fearful of losing their
> jobs and homes by participating in militant tactics. . . . Defeated in its
> attempt to oust the chapter's established leadership in the next election
> and hoping to function independently as a ghetto-oriented organization,
> the Ad Hoc Committee withdrew, and soon after disintegrated. Mean-
> while, amid the accusations and counteraccusations, a number of others
> left the Seattle chapter, disgusted by the "lack of faith and trust we
> CORE people now have in each other." Thus the result of the conflict
> was to leave Seattle CORE seriously weakened (Meier and Rudwick,
> 1973: 311).

As recounted by Meier and Rudwick (1973: 319), the same fate befell other CORE affiliates rent by similar disputes. Indeed, the Seattle incident was symptomatic of a trend widespread throughout the movement. Once effective insurgent organizations were rendered impotent by factional disputes that drained them of the unity, energy, and resolve needed to sustain protest activity. The growing divisions within the movement not only reduced the possibility of cooperative action *between* movement groups but further diminished the organizational strength of insurgent forces by stimulating disputes *within* these groups that reduced their effectiveness as autonomous protest vehicles.

Geographic Diffusion of the Movement

Finally, the organizational strength of the movement was adversely affected by the geographic shift in insurgent activity that took place between 1966 and 1970. The extent of this shift is clearly shown in table 8.3. Whereas 71 percent of all movement-initiated events in the years 1961 to 1965 occurred in the South, the comparable proportion for the succeeding five-year period was less than half (34 percent) the earlier figure.

This transfer of movement activity from the South to the North and West was accomplished only at the considerable cost of abandoning the strong indigenous links that insurgents had established in the South over the course of the previous decade. While no longer the dominant organizational force they had once been, the indigenous institutions of the southern black community nonetheless continued to play an important role in the movement during the early 1960s. However, with the shift to the North, this role was drastically curtailed and the movement was deprived of the strength that these institutions had earlier brought to the struggle.

Actually, to be more accurate, it was not the shift per se that damaged the movement so much as the failure of insurgents to establish indigenous roots in the North to supplant those they abandoned in the South. Not that the failure to do so resulted from any lack of effort on the part of the established movement groups. On the contrary, the early riots triggered

TABLE 8.3
Location of Movement-Initiated Actions, 1961–70

Geographic Region	1961–65 %	(N)	1966 %	(N)	1967 %	(N)	1968 %	(N)	1969 %	(N)	1970 %	(N)	1966–70 %	(N)
Deep South	47	(688)	34	(77)	16	(41)	4	(5)	15	(21)	25	(33)	20	(177)
Middle South	14	(208)	8	(18)	8	(20)	5	(7)	19	(26)	12	(16)	10	(87)
Border South	10	(145)	5	(11)	2	(6)	10	(13)	1	(2)	8	(10)	5	(42)
Total South	71	(1041)	46	(106)	26	(67)	19	(25)	35	(49)	45	(59)	34	(306)
New England	2	(31)	1	(2)	7	(17)	8	(11)	6	(8)	9	(12)	6	(50)
Middle Atlantic	16	(234)	18	(42)	32	(84)	28	(38)	31	(43)	26	(34)	27	(241)
East North Central	8	(113)	17	(38)	26	(68)	27	(36)	21	(30)	15	(20)	21	(192)
West North Central	1	(11)	3	(6)	3	(7)	7	(9)	1	(1)	2	(3)	3	(26)
Mountain	1	(9)	1	(3)	1	(2)	1	(2)	1	(1)	2	(2)	1	(10)
Pacific	2	(35)	14	(31)	6	(16)	10	(13)	6	(8)	2	(2)	8	(70)
Total	101	(1474)	100	(228)	101	(261)	100	(134)	101	(140)	101	(132)	100	(895)

Source: Annual *New York Times Index*, 1961–70.
Note: For geographic classification of states, see table 7.2.

a veritable northward stampede by movement leaders to establish organizational footholds in the ghetto as a means of regaining control over a movement that was beginning to slip away from them. As CORE director James Farmer observed in the aftermath of Watts, "Civil rights organizations have failed. No one had any roots in the ghetto" (Killian, 1975: 94). CORE itself pioneered in the northward exodus, behind an ambitious call for "community organization" on the part of its affiliates. Community organization called for the establishment of programs based on the expressed needs of ghetto residents. Likewise, Martin Luther King came North to Chicago in 1966 to establish roots through SCLC's "End-the Slums" campaign. SNCC, too, shifted its geographic focus from the depressed rural areas of the South to the northern slums in the hope that its brand of radicalism would allow it to develop an organizational base among ghetto youth. For all this resolve and effort, however, the establishment of strong indigenous operations in the North proved an elusive goal for all these groups. Meier and Rudwick have painstakingly documented the discrepancy between CORE's concept of community organization and the limits of its programmatic realization (1973: 329–73). SCLC's northern campaign also foundered on King's inability to mobilize the extensive community support that his earlier efforts had generated in the South. Weakened by internal cleavages and the withdrawal of financial support, SNCC too was unable to effect the desired northern transplant. Writing in 1966, Jacobs and Landau accurately summed up the situation: "the masses of poor Negroes remain an unorganized minority in swelling urban ghettos, and neither SNCC nor any other group has found a form of political organization that can convert the energy of the slums into political power" (Jacobs and Landau, 1966: 26).

The failure to establish an indigenous base of operation in the North deprived the movement of one crucial source of strength it had enjoyed in the earlier southern campaigns. Moreover, these failures only aggravated the movement's growing dependence on external sources of support. Without adequate roots in the North and increasingly estranged from the indigenous institutions of the South, the action-oriented wing of the movement found itself increasingly vulnerable to the vagaries of external support. And the willingness of external sources to continue supporting this wing of the movement was rapidly diminishing as well.

THE CONTRACTION OF POLITICAL OPPORTUNITIES, 1966–70

The internal factors reviewed above contributed to the declining rate of black insurgency in the late 1960s by diminishing the organizational strength of movement forces. Simultaneously, several external processes—some a response to the above factors and others strictly independent—

were further weakening the movement by redefining the political significance of blacks in such a way as to afford them less leverage with which
to press their demands. These developments marked a reversal of a trend
dating from the 1930s wherein blacks had confronted a political environment increasingly vulnerable to insurgent political action. If the years
from 1954 to 1965 amounted to a "Second Reconstruction," as numerous
commentators contend, then just as surely the late 1960s are properly
viewed as the "end of the Second Reconstruction."

Mobilization of Political Reaction and the Devaluation of the Black Vote

As early as 1963, political commentators began to speak presciently of
"thunder on the right" in American politics. The stimulus for such discussions was the Goldwater campaign, replete with its vituperative attacks
on "big government," charges of softness in our prosecution of the Vietnam War, and thinly veiled rhetoric of racial reaction. Ultimately, of
course, the threat posed by the Goldwater candidacy proved inconse-
quential in the face of Johnson's landslide victory in the 1964 elections.
Nonetheless, the potential negative consequences that conservative reaction could have on black insurgency were foreshadowed by one incident
during the presidential race that year. This was the pressure brought to
bear on the civil rights organizations to curtail protest activity during the
crucial months of the campaign. As Brooks tells it:

> white liberal money men were persuaded to threaten a cutoff in funds
> for civil rights activity as a means of containing the wilder enthusiasm
> of civil rights activists. The Democratic National Committee held back
> releasing funds allocated for voter registration drives among blacks to
> assure their use for registration and not hell-raising. The message was
> "cool it," and Roy Wilkins called civil rights leaders together to work
> out a "moratorium" on demonstrations. Wilkins, King, Young, and
> Randolph signed a call, after three hours of debate on July 29, "to
> observe a broad curtailment, if not total moratorium, of all mass
> marches, mass picketing, and mass demonstrations until after election
> day" (Brooks, 1974: 237).

That the moratorium may have been in the best interests of the movement
is less important than the broader implications of the incident. The crucial
point is that the conservative threat posed by Goldwater altered the context in which insurgency was occurring to such an extent that black protest
was redefined, even by its allies, as a political liability that had to be
curtailed. As conservative strength increased throughout the remainder
of the decade, this perception grew ever more salient.

By the off-year elections of 1966 the degree of racial polarization in this
country was such that openly to court the black vote was to invite de-

fections among one's white constituents. Prematurely prophesied three years earlier, the much-heralded "white backlash" had indeed set in. Certainly, the imprint of the backlash on the 1966 elections is unmistakable. As Brink and Harris said: "the backlash vote of 1966 helped install sizeable numbers of conservative congressmen who threaten even the modest goals of the Great Society" (1967: 182). Much the same view was expressed by Killian: "[t]he congressional elections of 1966 did not reveal a growing alliance between the 'have nots,' . . . of the United States. Instead, they reflected the existence of a backlash against the welfare programs of the Great Society" (1975: 132).

Contests for statewide office reflected a similar mobilization of conservative strength. A prime example was the California governor's race, in which a liberal Democrat, Pat Brown, was defeated by a conservative Republican, Ronald Reagan. And as the results of a preelection survey indicate, the success of the Reagan candidacy owed much to a racially motivated form of political reactionism. Specifically, on the question of whether incumbent Governor Brown had been "soft" in his handling of the racial issue, California split about 50-50 in the preelection survey. However, of those who viewed him as too "soft" with regard to the issue, nine of ten voted for Reagan. Thus, in the view of Brink and Harris, "the California outcome could have been foretold on the single issue of race alone . . . the facts . . . prove that three out of every four people who voted for Reagan found it easier to do so because they felt they could register a protest in varying forms to the riots and racial unrest that had taken place" (1967: 111). Moreover, as the authors note, the analysis of 1966 election returns from other key industrial states—notably Michigan and Illinois—suggested a more general significance to the pattern of racial reaction evident in California (Brink and Harris, 1967: 111–14).

The specific electoral victories enjoyed by conservatives in 1966, however, were probably less damaging to the long-range prospects for black insurgency than another more general by-product of the racial backlash. More significant were the mass defections from the traditional Democratic electoral coalition that had swept both Kennedy and Johnson into office. Chief among the defectors were the white urban ethnic groups of the industrial North that had been an integral part of the traditional Democratic coalition first forged by Roosevelt. By 1966 the affiliation of these groups with the Democratic party had been rendered tenuous by the transfer of the racial conflict from the South to the very cities in which these groups lived. Worried by northern riots and threatened by open-housing demonstrations in their own neighborhoods, these groups were no longer willing, en masse, to support a party that had come to be identified with "unacceptable" black demands. Writing in 1964, Samuel Lubell accurately forecast this trend:

In the past, Democratic strategists have assumed that the civil rights issue helped hold together the "big city" vote. This may have been a valid political strategy as long as the civil rights cause appeared mainly a matter of improving the treatment of Negroes in the South.

But the new demands of Northern Negro militants have posed sharp conflicts with what many white voters see as their own rights. Agitation over civil rights . . . could alienate enough white voters to disrupt the Democratic majorities in the urban areas (Lubell, 1964: 127–28).

In 1966 Lubell's prediction came true. Far from solidifying the Democrats' hold on the "big city" vote, the racial issue tended to polarize the various components of their traditional urban coalition. While the black vote held generally firm, the white ethnics abandoned the party in droves. Brink and Harris recount some of the major defections:

in Illnois, the Polish and Eastern European precincts showed a precipitous drop of 17 points in the Democratic vote from two years before, and a full 22 points off the high-water mark of 75 percent registered for Kennedy six years earlier. In Ohio, Polish precincts plummeted to 44 percent Democratic in the contest for governor there, off 39 points from 1964 and 45 below JFK's showing in 1960. The drop in Pennsylvania's Polish precincts was not as precipitous, but still fell 7 points below Johnson's showing and 12 below Kennedy's (Brink and Harris, 1967: 108).

The symbolic political importance of this sampling of findings would be hard to overstate. As a result of these defections, there occurred a significant devaluation of the black vote, as political strategists of both parties came to weigh the advantages of courting the black electorate against the costs of antagonizing a large and ever expanding segment of the white population. In the context of a society increasingly polarized along racial lives, the black vote had ceased to be an unqualified asset.

The Capstone of White Reaction: Nixon and Wallace in 1968

Events between 1966 and 1968 did little to reverse the trend discussed above. If anything, the increased frequency and destructiveness of the 1967–68 riots, combined with the growing use of an inflammatory and opportunistic "law and order" rhetoric by white politicians, accelerated the racial polarization already evident in the 1966 elections. Together with one other aspect of American politics in the late 1960s, this trend served to diminish further the electoral leverage of the black population. Goldman explains:

The most important single fact about Negroes in American party politics is that they are stubbornly, incorrigibly Democratic. . . . And though the affiliation was reasonable enough . . . it left the Negro community painfully vulnerable. The Democratic Party could become for them, as it had for other beleaguered American minorities, a source of jobs, prestige, and power at the local level. But their deep party loyalty tended to mark them in national politics as the special wards of the Democracy—a fact that was by no means lost on the strategists of a victory-hungry GOP (Goldman, 1970: 101).

Thus, while the mass defection of blacks to Eisenhower in 1956 and the reasonably competitive distribution of black votes between the two major parties in 1960 had served to define the black vote as a potentially variable, and thus strategically significant, commodity, the staggering Democratic majorities returned for Johnson in 1964 and the choice of long-time civil rights champion Hubert Humphrey as the party's nominee in 1968 changed things dramatically. And where once the Democrats would have welcomed the predictable support of blacks, by 1968 their votes promised to insure the defection of still more whites to the Republican party.

In 1968 the Republicans sought to exploit this dilemma by devising a campaign strategy designed to play on both the country's deepening racial cleavage and the traditional association of blacks with the Democratic party. By reminding voters of the latter, the Republicans hoped to tap the growing undercurrent of racial antagonism engendered by the shifting patterns of black insurgency in the mid to late 1960s. The following sampling of findings from an analysis of the election results reflects the wisdom of the Republican strategy:

—the Democratic share of the popular vote dropped nineteen percentage points, from approximately 61.5 to 42.5 percent, between 1964 and 1968.
—fully 50 percent of those who voted for Nixon in 1968 had cast ballots for Lyndon Johnson four years earlier.
—a breakdown of the popular vote along racial lines reveals that blacks retained their traditional loyalty to the Democratic party by casting 97 percent of their votes for Humphrey. By contrast only 35 percent of the white electorate concurred with that choice (Converse et al., 1969: 1084, 1085).

Perhaps the last of these findings is also the most significant. The extreme polarization of the electorate along racial lines accurately reflects the declining political power of blacks, as the value of their support had come, by 1968, to be weighed against the inevitable loss of white votes that followed from it.

The election did more than simply mirror the declining political fortunes of blacks; it contributed to them as well. With precious little political debt to blacks and considerable to their opponents, Nixon's election promised to reduce further the already limited political leverage available to insurgents. And as Goldman, writing in 1970, accurately reported, nothing in the substantive performance of the Nixon administration's first two years in power contradicted this expectation: "Nixon . . . came to office with substantial political debts to the South—and, as his advisers were frank to say, none at all to the blacks. The most moderate Negro leaders found their lines of communication to the White House abruptly cut. Judicial conservatives were posted to vacancies on the Supreme Court. Pressure on the South to integrate its schools relented" (1970: 23).

However, for blacks the negative political consequences of the 1968 elections were not confined to the substantive policy outcomes that resulted from Nixon's accession to office. At least as damaging was the effect the election had on the political expectations and strategies of the two major parties. In this, the remarkable success enjoyed by George Wallace in the 1968 elections exercised a marked influence.

The significance of the Wallace phenomenon for the future electoral prospects of both Republicans and Democrats was clear on the face of the 1968 election returns. With the two major parties evenly dividing 86 percent of the popular vote, the remaining 14 percent who supported Wallace clearly emerged as a potential balance of power in future elections. As Converse and his associates noted in the wake of the election, "it is obvious to any 'rational' politician hoping to maximize votes in 1970 or 1972 that there are several times more votes to be gained by leaning toward Wallace than by leaning toward [Eugene] McCarthy" (1969: 1105).

For the Republicans, Nixon's narrow victory suggested that the party's future lay not in the 43 percent of the popular vote he achieved but in the 57 percent he shared with Wallace. Republican strategists believed this total represented a potentially dominant conservative majority that, if successfully tapped, could well insure the electoral success of the party for years to come: "it suggested a course of strategy that could keep the Presidency Republican for a generation—precisely by isolating the Democrats as the party of the blacks and building the rickety Nixon coalition of 1968 into a true majority of the white center" (Goldman, 1970: 102).

Similarly, because of Wallace's success, many Democratic leaders became convinced that the party's future prospects rested in their ability to recapture the affiliation of the sizeable segment of unionized labor that had supported Wallace in 1968 (Converse et al., 1969: 1102). If this attempt were to fail, the prospects for a successful Republican realization of the campaign strategy outlined above seemed extremely good. The crucial point, then, regarding the Republican and Democratic electoral strategies that emerged from the 1968 campaign was that both were founded on an appeal to the perceived political interests of Wallace's supporters. As such, these strategies could only serve to diminish further the political leverage exercised by blacks. As Ross and his colleagues noted in concluding their assessment of Wallace's continuing influence on American electoral politics in the early 1970s: "competing for the support of a small minority of Wallace supporters in the North, both parties have come to feel they must oppose the type of civil rights programs that characterized the 1960's" (Ross, Vanneman, and Pettigrew, 1976: 89–90).

The Declining Salience of the "Racial Problem" and the Rise of Competing Issues

One final factor contributing to the general diminution in black political power in the late 1960s was the declining salience accorded the racial issue by the American public. As Goldman has sardonically observed, "Negroes did not precisely fall from grace at . . . [this] juncture, but they did go out of fashion" (1970: 201). This decline is depicted graphically in figure 8.2, which reports the proportion of survey respondents who identified "civil rights" as the "most important problem facing" America in a series of Gallup opinion polls between 1962 and 1971. From its peak in the years 1963–65, the issue of civil rights experienced a general decline in salience during the late 1960s and early 1970s. The extent of this decline was such that by February, 1971, only 7 percent of the people surveyed identified "race relations" as the country's most important problem. This was in contrast to the 52 percent who had done so only six years earlier.

One of the chief reasons for the decline was the emergence of competing issues that served to divert attention from the ongoing racial conflict. As Killian has accurately observed: "In spite of the evidences of continued tension and growing polarization, the racial conflict that had seemed to threaten American society soon dropped from its preeminent position in public concern. Vietnam, ecology, inflation, the Arab-Israeli conflict, the energy crisis, and Watergate took their turns in preempting both the headlines of the newspapers and the interest of white Americans" (Killian, 1975: 146). Far and away the most important of these emergent issues was the war in Vietnam, as figure 8.3 attests. First identified as a distinct problem in the May, 1965, Gallup Poll, Vietnam quickly supplanted civil rights as the dominant social issue in America. And as figure 8.3 shows, it retained this distinction throughout the remainder of the decade. In addition, other issues arose in the late 1960s that further reduced public concern over the racial problem. Among the issues accorded more importance than civil rights in various opinion surveys after 1967 were crime, campus unrest, drug addiction, and the "state of the economy." Indeed, late in 1971, the latter issue replaced Vietnam as the number one problem in the country in the eyes of the general public (Gallup, 1972: 2338).

The decline in public concern over racial matters, however, stemmed from more than just the emergence of competing issues. Indirectly, the trend can also be linked to the declining organizational strength of the

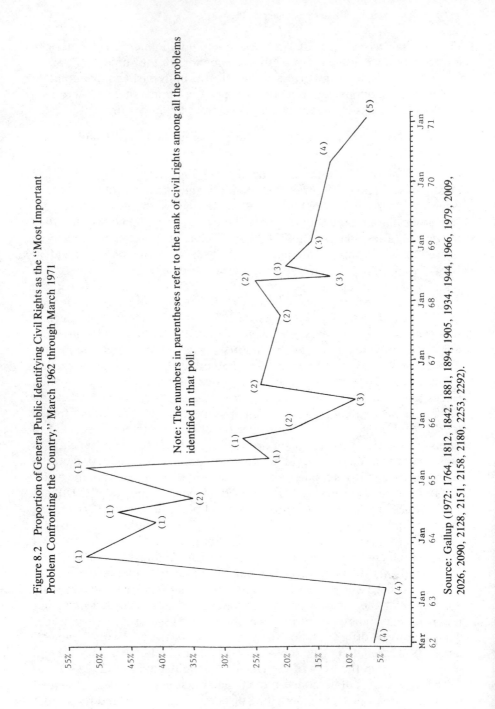

Figure 8.2 Proportion of General Public Identifying Civil Rights as the "Most Important Problem Confronting the Country," March 1962 through March 1971

Note: The numbers in parentheses refer to the rank of civil rights among all the problems identified in that poll.

Source: Gallup (1972: 1764, 1812, 1842, 1881, 1894, 1905, 1934, 1944, 1966, 1979, 2009, 2026, 2090, 2128, 2151, 2158, 2180, 2253, 2292).

Figure 8.3 Proportion of General Public Identifying Civil Rights or Vietnam as the "Most Important Problem Confronting the Country," March 1962 through February 1971

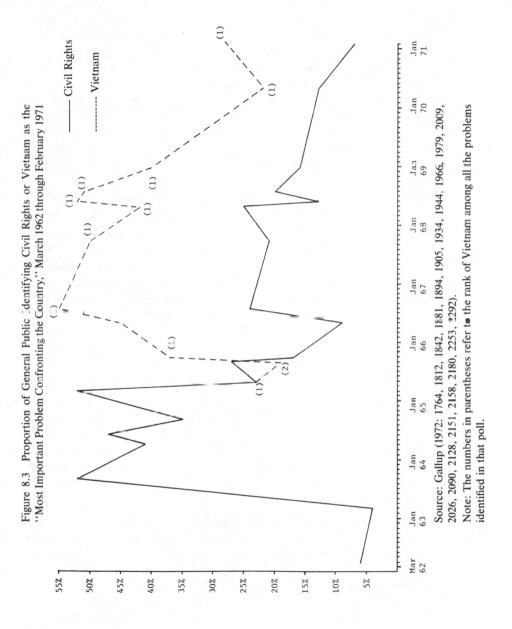

Source: Gallup (1972: 1764, 1812, 1842, 1881, 1894, 1905, 1934, 1944, 1966, 1979, 2009, 2026, 2090, 2128, 2151, 2158, 2180, 2253, 2292).

Note: The numbers in parentheses refer to the rank of Vietnam among all the problems identified in that poll.

movement. In the face of the disintegration of the movement's organizational core, insurgents found it increasingly hard to mount the dramatic campaigns that had earlier insured public consciousness of the issue. That popular awareness of the "racial problem" was, to a considerable extent, a function of the movement's ability to keep the issue before the public is evidenced by figure 8.2. The first three public opinion "peaks" in the figure coincide perfectly with the Birmingham, Mississippi Freedom Summer, and Selma campaigns. Conversely, the noticeable "valley" between the second and third of these peaks corresponds to the often mentioned moratorium in movement activity during the 1964 presidential campaign. Given this close fit between insurgency and issue salience, it is hardly surprising to see public consciousness of "civil rights" decline sharply after 1965, just as insurgents began to experience serious difficulties in trying to sustain the pace of earlier protest campaigns.

Finally, the decline in public concern for racial issues during the late 1960s must also be seen as a function of the efforts of elected officials and political candidates to discredit the shifting patterns of black insurgency characteristic of the period. This phenomenon is most apparent in regard to the urban riots of the late 1960s. Despite a mass of contradictory findings, "responsible" public officials persisted in interpreting ghetto disorders as either insurrections instigated by subversive elements or exercises in rampant criminality.[6] The former interpretation was embraced by the acting mayor of New York, in the wake of the 1964 Harlem riot. As he noted at the time: "I would like to point out, however, that anyone who has been on the scene—and I've had first hand reports from people outside the Police Department too—will tell you that the whole operation, is directed toward the so-called fringe groups; including the Communist Party and some of the more radical groups, and not involving the rank-and-file persons living in the Harlem Community" (in the *New York Times*, July 22, 1964, p. 18). Meanwhile, Senator Byrd (D.-Va.), provided a good example of the "criminal element" interpretation of the riots in a statement he made in April, 1968, at the height of the disorders that followed the assassination of Martin Luther King.

I wonder when our leaders in Washington are going to come to their senses and take a firm, unequivocal, unmistakable stance against rioters and all those who commit acts of violence. Such a stand is long overdue . . . the criminal element should be warned that if they persist in rioting and committing acts of violence, they will do so at the risk of life and limb. And then, if they persist, let the criminal element suffer the consequences. The criminal element understand one language, and understand it well—and that is the language of force (in the *Congressional Record*, April 25, 1968).

In view of the legitimacy most Americans accord public officials (see Almond and Verba, 1965; Lane, 1962), it would have been surprising if statements like those quoted above had *not* resulted in a certain erosion of public support for black insurgency. Instead it is evident from poll data that such official pronouncements did shape public perceptions of the riots to a considerable extent. A 1967 Louis Harris poll showed that 45 percent of the whites surveyed believed "outside agitation," "Communist backing," or "minority radicals" to be the cause of the riots, as compared to the 40 percent who placed the blame on the socioeconomic circumstances confronting blacks (Muse, 1968: 309).

As perceptions such as these developed, white support for racial issues declined sharply. In turn, this diminished public concern for the issue of black inequality eliminated one more source of pressure on the nation's political elite to undertake more aggressive action to combat the problem. While never decisive in its own right, this pressure, as Burstein notes (1978), was certainly a contributing factor in some of the significant legislative victories scored earlier in the decade. The declining strength of that pressure thus contributed to the general diminution in the political leverage exercised by blacks in the late 1960s.

COLLECTIVE ASSESSMENT OF THE PROSPECTS FOR INSURGENCY, 1966–70

If the generation of insurgency depends on the presence of certain shared cognitions within the movement's mass base, then just as surely the absence of these same cognitions contributes to movement decline. Certainly this was true in the case of the black movement. A growing sense of pessimism and impotence among blacks regarding the prospects for racial change was as significant as the collapse of the movement's centralized organizational structure and the general erosion in black political leverage in accounting for the declining pace of insurgency in the late 1960s. In fact, these three processes are undoubtedly related.

With regard to the link between organizational structure and cognition, it was argued in Chapter 3 that feelings of optimism and political efficacy are more likely to develop in stable group-settings. If this is true, then, it could be assumed that the collapse of the large direct-action organizations in the late 1960s contributed to the decline in the salience of these feelings by depriving insurgents of the collective settings in which the feelings are most likely to arise.

Likewise, the contraction in political opportunities discussed in the preceding section no doubt also encouraged the development of those feelings of pessimism and political impotence destructive of insurgency. Thus, the widely heralded "white backlash" did not simply reduce the leverage available to insurgents but also probably discouraged their mobilization in the first place. At a symbolic level, the growing stridency of calls for "law and order" and "swift justice for urban anarchists" served to convey an unambiguous message to insurgents: the risks associated with insurgency were growing greater every day. Nor was the significance of Nixon's election and the general conservative sweep of 1968 lost on the black community. The election results appear to have been widely—and accurately—interpreted by blacks as a clear portent of a growing official hostility toward the interests of the black community. Less than four months after Nixon's inauguration, blacks were asked as part of a nationwide *Newsweek*-Harris poll whether they felt "the federal government under Nixon has been more helpful or more harmful to Negro rights." Only a quarter of all respondents answered "helpful," as compared to 74 and 83 percent who gave the same response when questioned in connection with similar polls conducted in 1966 and 1963 (Goldman, 1970: 256). Whether the earlier Johnson and Kennedy administrations had, in fact, been so "helpful to Negro rights," is a matter of serious debate. But it is not the substance of federal policy that is so important here as its symbolic impact. And on this count, these findings suggest that the shifting political realities of the late 1960s had indeed been defined as significant by large numbers of blacks. From there it would seem but a small inferential leap to assume that these perceptions furnished the crucial impetus in the late 1960s to the growth of widespread feelings of pessimism and fatalism within the black community regarding the prospects for insurgency. However, in the absence of hard evidence establishing such a link, this relationship remains implied rather than demonstrated.

If the causal factors shaping these shared perceptions remain hard to document, their presence within the black community is not. First there are the clear indications of a growing sense of pessimism among blacks as the decade came to a close. Indicative of this trend are the responses blacks gave to another question on the *Newsweek*-Harris survey. The item read: "in the next five years, do you think the attitude of white people about Negro rights will get better, worse or stay about the same?" This question is especially interesting because it was also asked on the two earlier surveys conducted in 1963 and 1966, thus affording a clear-cut comparative measure of the shifting "mood" of the black community during the 1960s. The trend in these data is clear. The percentage of black respondents indicating that they felt white attitudes would improve "over the next five years" dropped from 73 in 1963, to 69 in 1966, to 61 in 1969 (Goldman, 1970: 252).

These data suggest a consistent incremental growth in pessimism among blacks during the 1960s regarding the prospects for progressive change in the racial attitudes of whites. This would seem to be the clear implication of a second set of comparative responses to another question asked on all three *Newsweek*-Harris surveys. As part of each survey blacks were asked whether they thought that "most white people want to see Negroes get a better break, or do they want to keep Negroes down, or do you think they don't care one way or another?" Again the answers suggest a growing pessimism within the black community. While 27 percent of those responding in 1966 thought most whites wanted "Negroes to get a better break," only 20 percent thought so three years later. By contrast, the proportion of those who felt that most whites "wanted to keep Negroes down" rose from 38 to 43 percent between 1966 and 1969 (Goldman, 1970: 250).

Finally, one could cite the dramatic growth of separatist sentiment among blacks during the late 1960s as another indirect measure of the decline in optimism characteristic of the period. This is simply to reassert the general relationship cited in Chapter 5 between the strength of separatist/integrationist ideologies within the black community and the dominance of widespread feelings of pessimism or optimism regarding the prospects for significant racial change. The claim is that support for integration will be greatest during times when feelings of optimism about future racial prospects are prevalent within the black community. Conversely, segregationist sentiment "will tend to be high . . . when struggles against racial inequality appear hopeless or when subordinate members have experienced intense disillusionment and frustration after a period of heightened expectations" (William Wilson, 1973: 200). If this relationship is accurate, the consistent increases in black support for separatism recorded in the late 1960s and early 1970s (see Goldman, 1970: 266) strongly suggest a corresponding rise in feelings of pessimism concerning the likelihood of significant racial progress.

However, perhaps more important than the pessimism itself was the apparent decline in feelings of political efficacy that accompanied it. Not only were blacks growing less optimistic about their future prospects, they were also less confident of their ability to change the situation. The two survey findings reported in figure 8.4 are clearly relevant here. Both involve a comparison of the answers given by national samples of blacks to standard survey items asked several times between 1958 and 1970. These answers are particularly important for the clear trend-data they provide. The trend itself is strong and consistent. In their responses to both questions blacks evidence a dramatic decline in feelings of personal efficacy over time. However, the decline is especially marked after 1964. For instance, the proportion of blacks reporting that they "usually get to carry things out the way" they planned declined from 45 percent in 1964 to just 23 percent in 1970.

Figure 8.4   Black Perceptions of Personal Efficacy, 1958–70

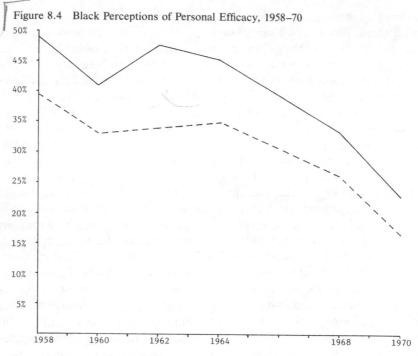

Source: Converse et al. (1980: 8, 12).

Note: Solid line represents the percentage of black respondents answering "Things generally work out the way I expected" to the following question: "When you do make plans ahead, do you usually get to carry out things the way you expected, or do things usually come up to make you change plans?" Broken line represents the percentage of black respondents answering "Pretty sure" to the following question: "Have you usually felt pretty sure your life would work out the way you want it to, or have there been more times when you haven't been sure about it?"

Admittedly one's feelings of *personal* efficacy are not the same as one's perception of *collective* power. Nonetheless, it seems logical to assume that these two cognitions would influence each other. This would seem especially true in the case of a population whose hopes for personal advancement had long been inextricably linked to the success or failure of collective action. So long as the movement flourished, so too did the widespread feelings of personal efficacy on which insurgency depends. However, as the movement began to founder in the late 1960s, these feelings began to dissipate. The crucial cycle of movement success followed by enhanced feelings of efficacy had been broken. And in its place a new and ultimately destructive cycle took hold. Defeat and white reaction bred feelings of frustration, pessimism, and ultimately fatalism that, in turn, reduced the willingness of blacks to participate in collective protest activity. The data presented in table 8.4 illustrate this shift in feeling.

TABLE 8.4
Comparison of the Percentage of Blacks in 1966 and 1969 Reporting a Willingness to Participate in Various Forms of Insurgency

Form of Action	1966	1969
March in a demonstration	54%	44%
Take part in a sit-in	52	40
Go to jail	45	33
Picket a store	49	41
Stop buying at a store	69	57
Participate in a riot[a]	15	11

Source: Adapted from Goldman (1970: 242, 249).

[a]Data on this item were generated by a separate question.

The data reported in the table are significant in two senses. First, they clearly suggest a marked decline in the number of potential recruits available for movement participation in the late 1960s. Second, and just as important as this explicit finding, is the implicit "cognitive profile" of the black population embodied in the data. Given the strong empirical link between feelings of political efficacy and participation in political activity, any significant decline in expressed willingness to participate would seem also to imply a commensurate drop in feelings of political efficacy. Obviously if people perceive themselves as powerless to alter their situation, they are not likely to express a willingness to participate in collective change efforts. These data, then, provide strong suggestive support for the broader dynamic under discussion here. Even as the "structural potential" for insurgency declined, under myriad pressures, in the late 1960s, so too did the salience of the cognitions needed to transform this potential into action.

THE RESPONSE TO INSURGENCY, 1966–70

In addition to the movement's weakened internal structure, a rapidly deteriorating political context, and the growth in the late 1960s of widespread feelings of pessimism and fatalism within the black community, the movement was further handicapped during this period by the shifting patterns of interaction between the movement and the other major parties to the conflict. Chief among these were the same three groups discussed in the previous chapter: external support groups, white opposition, and the federal government. Throughout the 1960s, these groups constituted the most significant components of the larger political environment confronting insurgents. If, however, the involvement of these groups was continuous throughout the 1960s, the nature and impact of their relationships on the movement were to change dramatically over the course of the decade. As shown in Chapter 7, the responses of these three groups to the movement served to encourage insurgency in the early 1960s. While imposing important constraints on insurgents, external support groups were nonetheless forthcoming with vital financial backing. For its part, the federal government eschewed direct supportive action but could be forced to intervene in support of black interests when white opposition to the movement occasioned a significant disruption of public order. Thus, even the violent excesses of the supremacists contributed to the early successes of the movement.

These characteristic responses—external financial support, federal intervention, and supremacist violence—were, however, the product of the substantive and tactical thrust of black insurgency characteristic of the early 1960s. Accordingly, as the goals and tactics of insurgents began to change around mid-decade, so too did the response of these groups to the movement. Thus, an understanding of the changing focus—both substantive and tactical—of black insurgency during this period is necessary to appreciate the shifting response patterns these changes triggered.

With respect to movement goals, the collapse of the strong issue-consensus that had prevailed among insurgents during the civil rights phase of the movement has already been documented. Ironically, this development owed much to the early successes enjoyed by insurgents who, in eradicating many of the vestiges of Jim Crow racism, had come to realize the limited significance of the victories they had won. Bayard Rustin gave succinct expression to this realization when he asked rhetorically, "what is the value of winning access to public accommodations for those who lack money to use them?" (1965: 25). As John Howard wrote: "New black organizations arose, not because the civil rights movement had failed, but because its successes had created an awareness of a new set of issues. Once melioration had been realized on matters of ordinary civil liberties, once affronts to the basic humanity of blacks had decreased, a new set of issues, more fundamental and more subtle, came to the fore" (1974: 13).

These emergent issues had the effect of shifting the focus of insurgency from questions of caste to those of class. The issue of an anachronistic regional caste system was replaced by fundamental questions concerning the equity of the prevailing distributions of wealth and power in America. As Stokely Carmichael asserted, "Integration is irrelevant. Political and economic power is what the back people have to have" (in Killian, 1975: 106).

The substantive shift advocated by Carmichael also entailed a redefinition of who the principal targets of insurgency should be. In place of such traditional enemies as the southern sheriff, the hooded night-rider, and the ax-wielding restaurant owner, insurgents increasingly came to attribute the ultimate responsibility for the perpetuation of inequality to the dominant political and economic elite of the country. This shift in targets also reflected the movement's growing hostility toward a federal establishment that had shown itself in the tough southern campaigns of the early 1960s to be a less than aggressive advocate of black rights. Viewed in this light, the shift in movement goals can be seen as a logical response to the federal government's consistent failure to support, in substance, what it purported to advocate symbolically. This "government as enemy" theme was given moderate expression by James Farmer in his address to the 1965 CORE national convention:

> The major war now confronting us is aimed at harnessing the awesome political potential of the black community in order to effect basic social and economic changes for all Americans. . . . This job cannot be done for us by the government. In the first place, the establishments—Federal, State and Local—have too much built-in resistance to fundamental change. Any establishment by definition seeks its own perpetuation and rejects that which threatens it (in Broderick and Meier, 1965: 422).

By the decade's end this view had been embraced and extended by various insurgent groups. For instance, a 1970 release by the Black Panthers read in part:

> The Black Panther Party stands for revolutionary solidarity with all people fighting against the forces of imperialism, capitalism, racism and fascism. Our solidarity is extended to those people who are fighting these evils at home and abroad . . . our struggle for our liberation is part of a worldwide struggle being waged by the poor and oppressed against imperialism and the world's chief imperialist, the United States of America (in Foner, 1970: 220).

Notwithstanding the declining strength of insurgent forces, the substantive shift implied by this statement obviously posed a far greater threat to existing political and economic interests in this country than had the focus of the earlier civil rights phase of the struggle. The changing tactics advocated by insurgents during the late 1960s also came to be viewed as threatening by the nation's political elite. Moving from a position of strict adherence to nonviolence, to the justification of self-defense, many insurgents ultimately came openly to espouse violent insurrection as a viable tactic in the ongoing struggle. In the following passage, Bell discusses this tactical evolution within CORE, and in so doing, suggests the crucial impetus behind the trend:

> At its 1966 convention, CORE drastically revised its official position on nonviolence and asserted the natural right of self-defense. This

change was aimed mainly at legitimizing self-defense organizations in Southern communities and the right of demonstrators to defend themselves when attacked. By the summer of 1967, however, CORE's executive director, Floyd McKissick, was implying approval of the Detroit insurrection by stating that the old-style civil rights tactics were out of date and that the insurrection heralded a new era in the Negro revolution. Indeed, the impression is inescapable that some leaders have tried to put themselves in the forefront of developments which, in fact, they neither organized nor controlled (Bell, 1971: 110).

The "developments" to which Bell was referring were, of course, the series of urban riots that began in 1964. The riots precipitated a major dilemma for insurgent leaders who, while traditionally committed to nonviolence, nonetheless had to respond to the disruptions in such a way as to retain their credibility as leaders. "Their reaction," as Killian has observed, "was essentially to use the riots as a weapon of protest. . . . It was this response that brought illegal rioting into the mainstream of the revolution and made it part of the strategy of protest" (1975: 93).

Perhaps even more than the substantive shift in goals discussed earlier, the riots and their rhetorical exploitation by black leaders embodied an insurgent challenge of much greater threat to the established politico-economic order than that posed by the earlier direct-action campaigns. For now the violent disruptions of public order were being mounted not by white supremacists but by black insurgents. It was this fundamental tactical shift, then, as much as the substantive change in movement goals noted earlier, that prompted the other major parties to the conflict to alter their earlier responses to the movement.

External Support Groups

Earlier in the chapter an implicit resource mobilization account of movement decline was outlined. I return to it now as a natural sidelight to my discussion of the evolving relationship between the movement and external support groups in the late 1960s.

If, as mobilization theorists argue, insurgency is a function of the resources available to support it, we would expect the demise of a social movement to coincide with a significant decline in resource support. Did such a decline occur in the case of the black movement? There is both a simple and a complex answer to this question. The simple answer is no. A reexamination of figure 6.2 shows that the dramatic decline in black insurgency in the latter half of the 1960s was accompanied, not by any decrease in external support, but by continued high levels of external funding. On one level, then, the available evidence contradicts the paramount importance attributed to resources by proponents of the mobilization model.

A closer examination of the evolving patterns of financial support for the Black Movement, however, suggests that the pace of insurgency and the level of available resources are related. Figure 6.2 obscures what, on examination of figure 8.5, actually appear to be three distinct funding patterns involving the various organizational wings of the movement. Taken together these patterns indicate a decided shift in the response of external support groups to the movement, beginning about mid-decade. By the decade's end, this shift had drastically diminished the insurgent capabilities of the direct-action wing of the movement, even as it spelled continued high levels of support for the movement generally.

The shift involved a tripartite funding pattern based on the relative "acceptability" of the goals and tactics embraced by the various components of the movement shown in figure 8.5. In the face of the widespread legitimacy ascribed to movement goals in the early 1960s and the nearly unanimous issue consensus that prevailed within insurgent ranks over the same period of time, all three wings of the movement enjoyed a consistent rise in their level of external support until the mid-1960s. However, after 1965, only the NAACP continued to do so.

Of the major movement organizations, SNCC and CORE were the first to experience the disaffection of liberal supporters. Funding for these two groups, which had commanded the largest share of external support gar-

Figure 8.5   External Financial Support for SCLC, NAACP, and CORE-SNCC, 1961–70

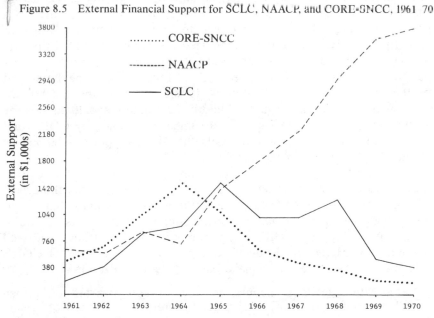

Sources: See Appendix 3.

Note: Where absolute dollar amounts were unavailable, knowledgeable estimates were substituted.

nered by the major movement groups between 1962 and 1965, fell off rapidly after 1965. Precipitating this drastic change in the response of external support groups was the substantive shift in insurgency advocated by both groups. In the words of Brink and Harris, "the onset of black power produced sharp birth pangs for its principal advocates . . . both CORE and SNCC were reduced to serious financial straits as white sympathizers deserted in droves" (1967: 62). That the decline in external support was clearly related to the changing goals of the two organizations is clearly seen in figure 8.6. So long as SNCC and CORE adhered to the traditional integrationist goals of the civil rights phase of the movement, external support showed a steady rise. When, however, the substantive orientation of the two groups began to shift in the mid-1960s, so likewise did the response of external support groups. Having abandoned the "acceptable" goals upon which the external support links had originally been predicated, SNCC and CORE found themselves cut off from those sources of funds they had come to depend on (Laue, 1965: 125; Meier and Rudwick, 1973; Muse, 1968: 23; Zinn, 1965: 10).

The experiences of CORE and SNCC help explain why external support linkages profitable at one point in time may, in the long run, prove damaging to a movement. It is not simply that such linkages may be withdrawn as the interests of insurgents and funding sources diverge. More important, the initial availability of external support frequently dissuades insurgents of the need to develop a strong grass-roots structure as a protection against the uncertainty of elite support. There is nothing inherently wrong with externally supported insurgency provided that the interests of the movement organization and funding source remain compatible. However, should the interests of the funding source be threatened by the actions of insurgents, then the latter, in light of the dependence that has developed, faces the likelihood of extinction should support be withdrawn. This was precisely the dilemma occasioned by CORE and SNCC's increasing advocacy of goals that their supporters defined as inconsistent with their own interests.

That leaders of both organizations appreciated the tenuous position they had created for themselves was not enough to forestall the crisis. Though efforts were made to develop the grass-roots links that would have offset the rapid decline in external support, such efforts proved to be too little, too late. CORE's experience is both illustrative and well documented. Meier and Rudwick describe the early efforts of CORE officials to restructure the financial basis of the organization:

> Faced with a declining income, and increasingly attracted to the idea of black self-help, many CORE leaders found the notion of raising money from blacks appealing. In early 1965 the Steering Committee

Figure 8.6 Proportion of All Events Initiated by CORE and SNCC that Were Coded Pro-Integration or Anti-Black Power, and External Financial Support for Those Organizations, 1961–70

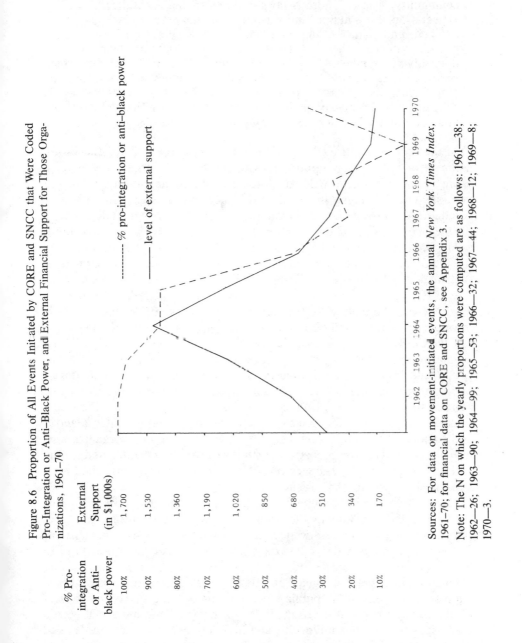

--------- % pro-integration or anti-black power

————— level of external support

Sources: For data on movement-initiated events, the annual *New York Times Index*, 1961–70; for financial data on CORE and SNCC, see Appendix 3.

Note: The N on which the yearly proportions were computed are as follows: 1961—38; 1962—26; 1963—90; 1964—99; 1965—53; 1966—32; 1967—44; 1968—12; 1969—8; 1970—3.

decided to make intensive efforts to seek substantial funds in the Negro community, where "there is no pattern of giving to CORE." . . . But expectations for a major fund-raising campaign among blacks were not realized, and Gantner, who had become CORE's full-time fund raiser in June, informed the NAC [National Action Council], "We have not done anywhere near as well as we had hoped." In fact, as he informed Farmer, he had concluded that it was time to renew efforts among the group which had always supplied most of CORE's financial resources, "the much and properly maligned but nevertheless moneyed white liberal community" (Meier and Rudwick, 1973: 336).

In the face of continued liberal abandonment, the call for the establishment of indigenous support links to the black community was once again renewed by certain CORE officials at the organization's 1966 convention. The deepening financial crisis faced by the organization is mirrored in the following excerpt from an address given by a CORE official on the opening day of the convention. Advocating an aggressive fund-raising campaign in the black community, the official argued that, "in fund-raising, until blacks support the movement we can't go anywhere. . . . We don't need professional fund-raisers. Start asking the people in the streets [for nickels and dimes] . . . Go to the barroom. Talk to the people. That's where the money is" (in Meier and Rudwick, 1973: 403; emphasis in original). Notwithstanding this and similar admonitions, the declining rate of CORE-sponsored insurgency, shown in table 8.1, attests to the organization's failure to develop successfully the indigenous base of support needed to offset the decline in external sponsorship. Having developed an organizational structure and mode of operation based on one form of support, CORE ultimately found it impossible to effect the transformation to another. The same can, and has, been said of SNCC (Jacobs and Landau, 1966: 26; Oberschall, 1973: 237). While both organizations initially benefited from the external support links they established, in the end their exclusive dependence on such links drastically diminished their capacity for sustained insurgency.

Less immediate, but ultimately as significant as the decrease in support for CORE and SNCC, was the similar decline in external funding experienced by SCLC. Figure 8.5 shows a steady increase in external support for SCLC through 1965, followed by a general decline thereafter. In SCLC's case, however, the decline doesn't seem to owe as much to any substantive change in the goals pursued by the organization as it does to simple fluctuations in the public's perceptions of the organization's chief fund-raiser: Martin Luther King, Jr. The successful and much-publicized campaigns in Birmingham in 1963 and in Selma two years later enhanced his reputation tremendously and triggered pronounced increases in external support for SCLC in those same two years. Conversely, a statement made by King late in 1965, asking President Johnson to issue an "unconditional and unambiguous" call for Vietnam peace talks was widely—and correctly—interpreted as antiwar in sentiment. Reflecting the continued popular support which the war enjoyed in 1965, external funding for SCLC declined sharply the following year. Finally, King's assassination in 1968 stimulated a brief resurgence of external support that, unfortunately, lasted only as long as the feelings of sympathy and guilt occasioned by his death.

The more far-reaching consequence of his death (clearly visible in figure 8.5), had, ironically, been anticipated by Kenneth Clark in an early assessment of SCLC's enviable financial position. Writing in 1966, Clark observed that SCLC "financially . . . seems strong; it seems relatively easy for SCLC, through King, to attract a majority of the nonselective contributions to the civil rights movement, despite the minimal organization of SCLC itself. It is reasonable to conclude that *if King were not its leader there would be no SCLC*" (1970: 293; emphasis mine). Insofar as SCLC had come to rely on King's extraordinary appeal as the basis of its fund-raising efforts, his death left the organization in nearly as vulnerable a position financially as that of CORE and SNCC. Certainly by 1970, all three organizations seemed to be in deep trouble financially.

In marked contrast to the withdrawal of external support experienced by SCLC, SNCC, and CORE, the NAACP enjoyed a steep and steady rise during this period in its level of outside funding. Figure 8.5 shows that the NAACP's level of external support remained virtually constant between 1961 and 1964, while the dollar amounts received by both SCLC and SNCC-CORE increased steadily over the same period of time. After 1964, however, this pattern was reversed, with the latter two wings of the movement experiencing the general decline noted earlier while the NAACP benefited from a sharp increase in external support.

Together these patterns suggest an inescapable conclusion: over time the NAACP came to be seen by external support groups as virtually the only "acceptable" funding option available to them.[7] In response, first to the substantive radicalization of SNCC and CORE, and later to King's antiwar stance, many groups that had earlier contributed to one of these three organizations shifted their support to the NAACP. As a result, the relatively even distribution of external support characteristic of the early 1960s was replaced in later years by the gross funding disparities evident in figure 8.5. By the end of the decade, this dramatic redistribution of external support had helped to reduce the once formidable Big Four to a single strong movement organization. As much as from internal dissension, then, the disintegration of the movement's organizational structure in the late 1960s resulted from a fundamental shift in the response of external support groups to the pace and substance of black insurgency.

White Opposition

Just as the changing nature of black insurgency in the mid to late 1960s produced a fundamental shift in the response of external support groups to the movement, so too did it elicit a very different reaction from white America. In effect, white opposition to the movement was transformed during the decade from a regionally based, relatively well-organized force of counterinsurgents, into a geographically dispersed mass of people recognizable only on the basis of their common opposition to trends within the movement. This so-called "white backlash" represented little more than a much-publicized shift in public opinion, rather than the organized white resistance encountered earlier by insurgents in the South. Nonetheless, this change was to have important negative consequences for the movement.

This transformation was fueled largely by the shifting patterns of black insurgency reviewed earlier. Specifically, it was the substantive changes in the goals embraced by insurgents and the geographic change in the location of movement activity that presaged this transformation. On a substantive level, the goals embraced by insurgents during the civil rights phase of the movement called for little more than the dismantling of an anachronistic caste system in which few people outside the South had any stake. Over time, however, the movement's critique of America was broadened to embody a more holistic attack on the complex patterns of institutional racism in which the interests of many who had earlier "supported" the movement were implicated. The effect of this change was to broaden opposition to the movement. Geographically, the shift of the movement out of the South had much the same effect. Confined almost exclusively to the former Confederate states during the early 1960s, the movement posed little threat to residents of other regions of the country. However, with the advent of riots, open-housing marches, and court-ordered busing, the comfortable illusion that the racial problem was a distinctly southern dilemma was shattered. Suddenly, the movement posed a threat to population segments that had earlier been removed from the conflict. Accordingly, opposition to the movement expanded into those areas newly effected by the shifting geographic focus of black insurgency. By the late 1960s opposition to the movement was more nearly a northern than a southern phenomenon.

As important as were the factors producing this transformation, it is the effects that flowed from it that hold special significance for this analysis. In particular, two especially debilitating consequences can be identified. The first comes from the radically different form that white resistance took in the North as opposed to the South. One of the functional characteristics of the southern supremacists was that they could be counted on, when sufficiently provoked, to create the violent disruptions of public order needed to produce federal intervention. No such convenient foil was available to the movement outside the South. In fact, more often than not during this period, insurgents resembled a movement in search of an enemy. Clark has captured the amorphous quality of the opposition the movement came increasingly to confront during the late 1960s:

> What do you do in a situation in which you have the laws on your side, where whites smile and say to you that they are your friends, but where your white "friends" move to the suburbs leaving you confronted with segregation and inferior education in schools, ghetto housing, and a quiet and tacit discrimination in jobs? How can you demonstrate a philosophy of love in response to this? What is the appropriate form of protest? One can "sit-in" in the Board of Education building, and not a single child will come back from the suburbs or from the private and parochial schools. One can link arms with the Mayor of Boston and march on the Commons, but it will not affect the housing conditions of Negroes in Roxbury (Clark, 1970: 288).

In short, the very different character of northern white resistance deprived insurgents, in the late 1960s, of one of the crucial elements in the tactical dynamic that had earlier served as the cutting edge of black insurgency in the South. Without the dramatic instances of overt white oppression, the movement was deprived of both the visible manifestations of racism so valuable as organizing devices and the leverage needed to force supportive government involvement. Having developed an affective mode of tactical interaction vis-à-vis one opponent, insurgents were unable to devise a similarly suitable response to the changed pattern of northern resistance.

Even if insurgents had been able to provoke in the North a "southern form" of disruptive white opposition, the federal government would probably not have intervened as readily in support of black interests as it had earlier in the South. Quite simply, as opposition to the movement broadened and shifted northward the political repercussions of supportive federal action changed accordingly. No longer was opposition to the movement confined to a relatively small, politically expendable segment of the population. The changing composition of movement opposition is discussed by Killian: "The white people who are now resisting the movement are not the ancient foe, the southern whites. They are Jews, traditional liberal friends of blacks, now defending their middle-class suburban neighborhoods and their neighborhood schools. They are Americans of Irish, Italian, or Polish descent defending their labor unions, their neighborhood schools, and the imagined integrity of their neighborhoods.

. . . And there are, finally, the old American Protestants as well" (Killian, 1975: 117).

The important characteristic shared by all these groups, is that, unlike the white South, they represented population segments vital to the political fortunes of both major parties. The practical result of this shift was a predictable decline in the enthusiasm of the national political elite even for symbolic action in support of black interests. Indeed, the mobilization of broad-based white opposition to the movement between 1966 and 1970 prompted a general political devaluation of blacks and a simultaneous tactical swing to the right on the part of both major parties.

The changing nature of white opposition to the movement in the late 1960s contributed to the decline in black insurgency in two ways. First, reflecting the shift of the movement northward, white opposition during this period was not characterized by the violent disruptions of public order that had earlier served as the cutting edge of black insurgency in its exclusively southern phase. And second, as opposition to the movement broadened in the late 1960s, in response to the shifting substantive and geographic focus of insurgency, the political gains to be derived from supportive action declined as well. In effect, the "white backlash" served to undercut the leverage insurgents had earlier enjoyed as a consequence of their limited and popular attack on a politically expendable target, namely, the South.

The Federal Government

The federal government's response to the movement during the early 1960s can be characterized as one of tactical neutrality with directly supportive action forthcoming only as a consequence of the severe disruptions of public order occasioned by the movement's successful use of the "politics of protest." The urban riots of the mid to late 1960s continued this tradition of disruptive protest and, for awhile, stimulated a form of reactive federal support not unlike that characteristic of the civil rights phase of the movement. The public disruptions of this later period did, however, differ in one crucial respect from those that occurred in the southern direct-action campaigns of the early 1960s. In the latter case, the breakdown of public order, though provoked by black insurgents, was nonetheless initiated by white supremacists. In the urban riots, the challenge to the state's "legitimate" monopoly over the means of coercion was being mounted directly by the insurgents themselves. This fundamental tactical challenge, coupled with the movement's increasing espousal of goals that threatened the basic prerogatives of class rule in this country, prompted a predictable reversal in the state's response to the movement. After 1965—and especially 1967—the grudging support that had been forthcoming in earlier years gave way to an increasingly repressive federal response to the movement. The consequences of this reversal were to prove especially damaging to the ongoing prospects for successful black insurgency.

To be sure, not all components of the movement were initially affected by the government's policy shift. Those movement organizations such as the NAACP and Urban League that continued to adhere to substantive and tactical policies acceptable to the federal elite continued to receive the same mix of abundant symbolic and limited substantive support as before. In this sense the government's reaction to the changing patterns of insurgency more nearly resembled the differentiated response of external support groups described earlier. Nonthreatening components of the movement continued to receive some semblance of support, while those embracing the new goals or tactics received increased social-control attention. The development and persistence of this bipartite government response to the movement is reflected in table 8.5. As can be seen, the years 1966–70 are distinguished from the preceding five-year period by virtue of the mobilization of governmental opposition to the black-power wing of the movement. Twenty-four percent of all events initiated by federal officials or national political candidates between 1966 and 1970 were coded as anti–black power, as compared to only 2 percent during the earlier five-year period. Even this sharp increase vastly understates the actual level of government-initiated control activities directed at the "radical" wing of the movement in the late 1960s. Owing to the illegality of much of the activity and the covert nature of even some strictly legal forms of repression, the numbers reported in table 8.5 should only be regarded as indicative of a general trend rather than as accurate in any strict numerical sense.

A full description of the extent of government control activities against the movement is beyond the scope of this book. As a general summary though, two broad categories of control activities can be identified. First, there were the countless instances of violence, intimidation, harrassment,

TABLE 8.5
Distribution of All Events Initiated by Federal Officials or National Political Candidates, by Direction, 1961–70

	1961–65		1966		1967		1968		1969		1970		1966–70	
	%	(N)	%	(N)	%	(N)	%	(N)	%	(N)	%	(N)	%	(N)
Pro-integration	85	(554)	70	(113)	66	(82)	67	(123)	73	(103)	65	(102)	68	(523)
Pro–black power	0	(1)	4	(7)	0	(0)	2	(4)	1	(2)	0	(0)	2	(13)
Anti-integration	12	(81)	1	(1)	6	(7)	5	(9)	11	(15)	11	(17)	6	(49)
Anti–black power	2	(13)	25	(41)	29	(36)	26	(47)	15	(22)	24	(37)	24	(183)
Totals	99	(649)	100	(162)	101	(125)	100	(183)	100	(142)	100	(156)	100	(768)

Source: Annual *New York Times Index*, 1961–70.

and surveillance directed at the myriad black-power groups active during the late 1960s. Second, much energy was expended over this same period of time in devising an effective control response to the urban riots. In both cases, as will be seen, it is difficult to distinguish between the efforts of federal, state, and local officials. Moreover, to do so would, in most instances, be misleading. The fact is, officials at all three levels worked together in a loosely coordinated effort to counter the substantive and tactical threat posed by the black-power wing of the movement. Taken together, then, the activities of all three constitute the overall response of the state to the shifting patterns of insurgency in the late 1960s.

Repression of Black-Power Groups. Certainly official efforts to damage specific movement organizations or leaders occurred prior to the period under examination here. Perhaps the most infamous of these early instances was the FBI's use of electronic surveillance to obtain information on the alleged sexual improprieties of Martin Luther King, Jr., for the purpose of dissemination to the press (Marx, 1976: 5). However, the pace of such efforts increased markedly during the late 1960s in the face of the escalating rhetorical militance of certain insurgent leaders. Indeed, from a tactical standpoint, many of these leaders can be criticized for pursuing what Gamson describes as the "strategy of speaking loudly and carrying a small stick" (1975: 87). That is, many insurgent groups aggressively advocated the use of violence without ever practicing it systematically. As Gamson points out, this strategy makes little tactical sense given the social control costs that the open advocacy of violence is likely to entail. Groups that pursue this strategy, "seem to pay the cost of violence without gaining the benefits of employing it. They are both threatening and weak, and their repression becomes a low-cost strategy for those whom they attempt to displace" (Gamson, 1975: 87).

Certainly this description can be accurately applied to a number of black-power groups active during the late 1960s. Perhaps the most celebrated of these was the Black Panther party founded in Oakland in October, 1966. The Panthers were subjected to a wide array of official control efforts ranging from infiltration, to harassment through arrests for minor offenses, to efforts to involve them in violent encounters with other black-power groups, to violent confrontations with law enforcement personnel (Goldstein, 1978: 523–30; Major, 1971). Some idea of the extensiveness of these control efforts can be gained by reading Major (1971), who presents a selective compilation of acts of official repression directed against the Panthers between 1966 and 1970.

Though unique in the extent of official attention they received, the Panthers were by no means the only insurgent group subjected to government-initiated control activities. Several other examples will help illustrate the pervasiveness of such efforts:

—In Cleveland, three members of a black nationalist group died in a 1968 shoot-out with police triggered by an unsubstantiated report by an FBI informant that the group, the Black Nationalists of New Libya, were stockpiling weapons to carry out an assassination plot against moderate black leaders (Masotti and Corsi, 1969).
—FBI officials planted a series of derogatory articles in papers during the SCLC-sponsored Poor Peoples Campaign in 1968 as a means of discrediting it (Marx, 1976: 5).
—Police raided the Los Angeles office of SNCC on April 5, 1968, while chapter members were attending a memorial service for Martin Luther King (Major, 1971: 297).
—In his study of a local black-power group, Helmreich reports countless instances of official violence, harassment, and intimidation directed at the organization's leadership. In the most flagrant incident, two leaders were arrested on a charge of faulty brake lights, taken to the police station, and beaten severely (Helmreich, 1973: 120–21).
—No fewer than twenty-four known black insurgent groups were subjected to tax surveillance as part of a larger effort to use the IRS to harass "extremist" groups of varying (though primarily leftist) political philosophies (U.S. Congress, Senate Select Committee, vol. 3, 1975: 50–52).

Such instances could be multiplied indefinitely without adding appreciably to our understanding of the phenomenon. Suffice to say, in the late 1960s law enforcement officials at all levels of government responded to what they perceived to be the growing threat posed by insurgents by initiating a stepped-up campaign of repression designed to destroy the black-power wing of the movement. This campaign served to diminish the ongoing prospects for black insurgency in a number of important ways. At the most basic level, stepped-up control efforts increased significantly the risks associated with movement participation. Accordingly, the recruitment of new members grew especially difficult as repression against insurgents intensified in the period from 1968 to 1970.

Just as damaging to the movement were the programmatic constraints insurgents had to endure as a result of their increasingly antagonistic encounters with government officials. The escalating conflict forced black-power groups to assume a defensive stance that transformed the substantive thrust of their programs from community organizing to efforts aimed at preserving and defending the organization against external threats. Quite apart from the substantive impotence embodied in this transformation, this shift also reduced the ability of insurgents to withstand repression by undermining their support within, and ties to, the larger black community (Helmreich, 1973: 147).

Official repression also imposed extraordinary financial burdens on insurgents that further diminished their capacity to act. Indeed, as Oberschall perceptively notes, the precipitation of financial crisis may well have been the real motive underlying the federal government's aggressive prosecution of movement activists in the late 1960s: "the government's strategy appeared to be to tie down leaders in costly and time consuming legal battles which would impede their activities and put a tremendous drain on financial resources regardless of whether the government would be successful in court" (1978: 277–78). On the local level, as Helmreich notes in his study of a particular black power group, law enforcement officials achieved much the same results through constant harassment of insurgents: "raising bail money was a constant problem for the organization. This drained their financial resources to the point where they had tremendous difficulty in even surviving as a group, not to mention expanding their activities within the community" (1973: 147–48).

Finally, it would be hard to overestimate the divisive internal effect that increased government surveillance had on insurgents. Fear of informers was sufficient in many cases to generate the climate of suspicion and distrust needed to precipitate serious internal problems. And where fear itself failed to produce the desired results, social control agents could be counted on to stir up dissension. As one example, Gary Marx cites a 1970 memo in which "FBI agents were instructed to plant in the hands of Panthers phony documents (on FBI stationery) that would lead them to suspect one another of being police informers" (1974: 435). He concludes, "Sociologists who have often observed the bickering and conflict among sectarian protest groups holding the same goals, and their ever-present problems of unity, must ask what role 'counterintelligence' activities may be playing" (Marx, 1974: 436).

The net effect of increased governmental repression, then, was to seriously weaken the capacity of the black-power wing of the movement to sustain insurgency. As Killian observed in 1975, movement activity

has subsided not because the racial crisis has passed but because white power has demonstrated that open black defiance is extremely dangerous and often suicidal. The ranks of the most dramatically defiant black leaders were decimated by imprisonment, emigration, and assassination. The best-known black nationalist organizations, such as the Black Panthers, the Republic of New Africa, the Revolutionary Action Movement, and the Student Nonviolent Coordinating Committee, have dwindled in strength (Killian, 1975: 155–56).

Governmental Response to the Riots. One of the consistent themes of this book concerns the effectiveness of disruptive forms of political action. The suggestion is that such forms of action may constitute the only available means by which excluded groups can overcome their traditional powerlessness within institutionalized political channels. Thus, the extraordinary pace of black insurgency during the early 1960s and the significant victories that followed from it must be seen, in large measure, as a tribute to the tactical genius of movement activists. Through their pioneering use of the various tactical innovations discussed in Chapter 7, insurgents were able to provoke the significant disruptions of public order required to insure federal intervention in the conflict. In effect, they had succeeded in "nationalizing" the issue, thereby insuring that the conflict would be resolved outside of the South's closed and coercive political system. In this way, insurgents were able to offset the clear disparity in power that existed between themselves and the southern supremacists.

The urban riots of the mid to late 1960s can be seen as a final extension of the "politics of protest." That there were differences between the riots and the earlier southern campaigns should be obvious. Underlying these differences, however, are two basic similarities. Both forms of action occasioned a dramatic breakdown in public order. And both served to stimulate or hasten federal action favorable to blacks. In regard to the riots, evidence to support this contention is drawn from a number of sources. Of particular interest is Button's (1978) detailed quantitative analysis of the federal response to the "urban disorders" between 1964 and 1968. Using a variety of methods, Button has documented a strong (though by no means consistent) pattern of increased federal expenditure for programs benefiting blacks in forty American cities following urban riots in those same locales. He concludes: "the major riots affected national socioeconomic reform policies to a varying but sometimes great degree, and in some instances even more than conventional forms of political participation. . . . Those who argue that collective violence is necessarily beyond the pale of effective political action and is totally counterproductive in terms of achieving any of the goals set forth by the practitioners of violence are, on the basis of this study, in serious error" (Button, 1978: 167).

Consistent with the general thrust of Button's work are the data reported in tables 8.6 and 8.7. Together the tables suggest a close connection between disruptive insurgency and the pace of federally sponsored school desegregation efforts. As can be seen, such efforts increased sharply during and immediately following the peak period of urban rioting. Then, as the level and intensity of the "urban disorders" slackened in the early 1970s, so too did the pace of federal initiative in this area.

TABLE 8.6

Number of School Districts Desegregated, by Source of Intervention and Year of Greatest Desegregation

Source of Inter-vention	1901–53 %	(N)	1954–65 %	(N)	1966–67 %	(N)	1968–69 %	(N)	1970–71 %	(N)	1972–73 %	(N)	1974–75 %	(N)	1901–75 %	(N)
Courts	a		15	(12)	11	(8)	41	(53)	50	(107)	22	(12)	28	(15)	34	(207)
HEW	a		22	(18)	26	(19)	33	(42)	28	(61)	9	(5)	13	(7)	25	(152)
Total federal inter-vention	a		37	(30)	38	(27)	74	(95)	78	(168)	31	(17)	42	(22)	59	(359)
State-local	100	(6)	63	(52)	62	(45)	26	(34)	22	(46)	69	(38)	58	(31)	41	(252)
Total	100	(6)	100	(82)	99	(72)	100	(129)	100	(214)	100	(55)	99	(53)	100	(611)

Source: Adapted from U.S. Commission on Civil Rights (1977), p. 18.

[a]None in sample.

TABLE 8.7

Growth in Hostile Outbursts, 1963–68

Data on Hostile Outbursts	1963	1964	1965	1966	1967	1968	Total
Number of cities having outbursts	8	16	20	44	71	106	254[a]
Number of outbursts	12	16	23	53	82	155	341[b]
Total number of days of hostilities	16	42	31	92	236	286	703

Source: Adapted from Downes (1970: 352).

[a]Many of the same cities had more than one incident each year, which is why this figure is so high. Of the 676 cities which had 25,000 or more persons in 1960, 149 (22 percent) had experienced one or more hostile outbursts since 1963. In these 149 cities, 283 incidents of collective racial violence occurred, with an additional 58 incidents taking place in cities under 25,000 persons.
[b]Smaller (less violent) incidents are underreported.

The evidence reviewed here provides consistent support for the view that the urban riots of the mid to late 1960s did help to stimulate a reactive pattern of favorable federal action across a wide range of policy areas of interest to blacks. However, as implied earlier, such efforts did not exhaust the federal response to the urban disorders of this period. In addition, the late 1960s were marked by intensified social-control efforts designed to contain the expanding threat posed by the riots. In fact, after 1967 this control response came to overshadow the pattern of ameliorative federal action.

At the federal level, this social-control emphasis was evident in numerous actions. Two important pieces of congressional legislation bore its imprint. First, Congress attached to the 1968 Civil Rights Act antiriot provisions that provided harsh penalties for persons found guilty of crossing state lines or using interstate communications facilities to incite riots. Significantly, it was this legislation that provided the Justice Department with the legal basis for many of the prosecutions of black leaders that proved so debilitating to the movement in the late 1960s. A second piece of legislation framed in partial response to the ghetto disorders was the Omnibus Crime Act of 1968. Among the act's many provisions were ones providing for the establishment of a national training center to instruct local police in riot control techniques and a program of fiscal aid to local law enforcement agencies seeking to bolster their antiriot capabilities. The latter program provided 75 percent federal funding for local riot control efforts. That there was no shortage of takers for the newly available funds is clear from statistics cited by Feagin and Hahn. They report that "nearly $4 million in initial grants to 40 states for riot prevention, detection, and control had been made by the end of the first month of operation" (Feagin and Hahn, 1973: 232). The authors conclude: "measured in terms of dollars disbursed over a short period of time, the federal law enforcement response to ghetto rioting and other civil disturbances does seem to have been perhaps the most substantial reaction at any level of government" (1973: 232).

These two pieces of legislation did not exhaust the federal control response to the riots. On the heels of the 1967 summer riot season, President Johnson ordered all National Guard units to undergo an intensive thirty-two-hour program of riot control training. Additionally, he called for the establishment of 125 new Guard units, the majority of which were to be "specifically oriented to state riot control requirements" (in Allen, 1970: 201). Not to be outdone, the U.S. Army announced in April, 1968, that it too was raising the number of troops assigned expressly to riot control duty from 15,000 to 25,000. To provide for more centralized coordination of these disparate units the Pentagon, in July, 1969, established a civil disturbance directorate. As Killian observes, "while it was still fighting an undeclared war in Indochina, the United States army maintained a domestic command post, on twenty-four hour alert, to coordinate the suppression of a revolution at home" (1975: 144).

This federal response was augmented by control efforts at the state and local levels. Numerous states, for example, added stiff antiriot sections to their penal codes. Stimulated by the massive rioting in Watts a year earlier, the California legislature established the precedent in July, 1966, by approving the following addition to its penal code:

404.6   Every person who with the intent to cause a riot does an act or engages in conduct which urges a riot or urges others to commit acts

of force or violence, or the burning or destroying of property, and at
a time and place and under circumstances which produce a clear and
present and immediate danger of acts of force or violence or the burning
or destroying of property, is guilty of a misdemeanor (in Feagin and
Hahn, 1973: 234).

According to Feagin and Hahn, no less than twenty states followed California's lead and passed similar statutes between 1966 and 1969 (1973:
235).

Locally, officials responded in similar fashion to counter the escalating
disorders. Ordinances were passed in many cities granting the mayor
expanded powers to deal with civil disturbances as he or she saw fit. In
effect, these ordinances gave the mayor legal authority to declare martial
law in the event of ghetto disorders. A more common response was simply
to strengthen the riot control capabilities of local law enforcement agencies. In a retrospective analysis of the trend, Allen noted that, "cities
across the country were stockpiling arms, buying tanklike armored vehicles, building up huge caches of ammunition and tear gas, and arming
their policemen with helmets and highpowered rifles and shotguns" (1970:
197). As examples of the trend, Allen goes on to cite Newark's $300,000
expenditure for riot equipment, the acquisition by Virginia state police
of six armored cars designed for riot duty, and the request by Detroit's
police commissioner for 9 million dollars worth of exotic riot equipment,
"including battle cars and machine guns" (1970: 197–98).[8] A more systematic overview of this trend was provided by Horace Webb in an article
written for the 1969 *Municipal Yearbook*, entitled "Police Preparedness
for Control of Civil Disorders" (1969). Webb reports that by 1969 75
percent of the 1,267 cities providing information had instituted some form
of police riot-control training. He also presents data showing a 45 percent
increase in the number of cities reporting the development of riot control
plans and a 25 percent rise in those reporting that they had obtained or
prepared their own riot control manuals (Webb, 1969: 320–21).

Thus, the repressive response documented earlier for the state and
federal levels was no less dominant locally. Indeed, the composite picture
that emerges is of a massive control response at all levels of government
designed to counter the threat posed by the escalation in ghetto rioting.
That these combined efforts had a measurable effect on the actual handling
of urban disorders is suggested by a comparison of data on the 1967 and
April, 1968, riots, the latter occurring in the wake of Martin Luther King's
assassination. The first finding of note involves a comparison of the number of law enforcement personnel used in quelling these two sets of disturbances. An examination of tables 8.8 and 8.9 indicates that the force
levels used in the 1968 disorders were on the average 50 percent greater

TABLE 8.8
Manpower Levels Used in Controlling the Major Racial Disorders of 1967

| | | 1967 Disorders | |
City	Date of Disorder	National Guard/ Federal Troops	Average Force Deployment per Day of Disorder
1. Baton Rouge, La.	8/20–21	2,150	1,075
2. Cairo, Ill.	7/16–19	100	25
3. Cambridge, Md.	7/24–26	700	233
4. Cincinnati, Ohio	6/12–18	800	100
5. Detroit, Mich.	7/23–30	12,977	1,622
6. Durham, N.C.	7/19–20	120	60
7. Jackson, Miss.	5/10–13	600	150
8. Lorain, Ohio	7/27	100	100
9. Memphis, Tenn.	7/27	4,000	4,000
10. Milwaukee, Wisc.	7/30–8/8	4,800	480
13. Minneapolis, Minn.	7/19–25	600	86
12. Montgomery, Ala.	6/12–14	200	67
13. Newark, N.J.	7/12–17	3,000	500
14. Plainfield, N.J.	7/14–21	200	25
15. Prattville, Ala.	6/11, 14–15	150	50
16. Tampa, Fla.	6/11–15	500	100
17. Wilberforce, Ohio	11/13–15	300	100
18. Winston-Salem, N.C.	11/2–7	1,150	192
Total	75 (days of disorder)	32,447	433

Source: Adapted from Lemberg Center for the Study of Violence (1968): 65–66.

than those used the previous year. As Skolnick notes: "1968 represented a new level in the massiveness of the official response to racial disorder. In April alone . . . more National Guard troops were called than in all of 1967 . . . and more federal troops as well. . . . *Never* before in this country has such a massive military response been mounted against racial disorder" (1969: 173). A dramatic example of what Skolnick was writing about was the occupation by National Guard troops of one city, Wilmington, Delaware, from April, 1968, through January, 1969—the longest domestic military occupation since the Civil War.

The presence of increased numbers of enforcement personnel facilitated the more thoroughgoing containment efforts desired by those charged with controlling the disorders. As the data in table 8.10 indicate, all major indices of official repression, save one, showed increases between 1967 and April, 1968. The average number of injuries per disorder in 1968 was nearly 40 percent higher than in 1967. Even more dramatic was the nearly twofold increase in average number of arrests between the two years.

In the face of this massive control response, it is hardly surprising that the intensity and pace of racial disorders dropped sharply in the final two years of the period under study (Feagin and Hahn, 1973: 193–94; Skolnick,

TABLE 8.9
Manpower Levels Used in Controlling the Racial Disorders of April, 1968

City	Date of Disorder	National Guard/ Federal Troops	Average Force Deployment per Day of Disorder
1. Baltimore, Md.	4/6–9	11,000	2,750
2. Cambridge, Md.	4/7	60	60
3. Chicago, Ill.	4/4–11	11,700	1,462
4. Columbia, S.C.	4/6–8	600	200
5. Detroit, Mich.	4/5–9	3,000	600
6. Durham, N.C.	4/5–10	950	158
7. Gainesville, Fla.	4/6–8	130	43
8. Goldsboro, N.C.	4/5–8	150	38
9. Greensboro, N.C.	4/4–5	1,100	550
10. Hampton, S.C.	4/7	100	100
11. Joliet, Ill.	4/6–7	130	65
12. Kansas City, Mo.	4/9–12	1,700	425
13. Memphis, Tenn.	4/4–6	400	133
14. Nashville, Tenn.	4/5–8	4,000	1,000
15. Pine Bluff, Ark.	4/5–6	500	250
16. Pittsburgh, Pa.	4/4–11	3,400	425
17. Raleigh, N.C.	4/4–8	1,200	240
18. Washington, D.C.	4/4–9	15,100	2,517
19. Wilmington, Del.	4/5, 8–14	1,400	175
20. Wilmington, N.C.	4/6–7	1,100	550
21. Wilson, N.C.	4/6–7	300	150
22. Youngstown, Ohio	4/8–9	600	300
Total	85 (days of disorder)	58,620	690

Source: Adapted from Lemberg Center for the Study of Violence (1968): 65–66.

1969: 173). Confronted by government forces increasingly willing and able to forcefully suppress ghetto disorders, and painfully aware of the costs incurred in the earlier rioting, insurgents gradually abandoned the tactic. As Feagin and Hahn observe:

by the end of the 1960's many residents and leaders in a ghetto that had had a riot or riots were probably eager to avert further violence of the type seen in ghetto rioting—violence that might result in excessive casualties and suffering to local black civilians. Efforts by black urbanites, including militants, to avoid additional outbreaks of ghetto rioting probably have been inspired not only by the recognition of the superior force available to police agencies but also by a realization that excessive force on the part of police control agents during previous riots had inflicted devastating and irreplaceable damage on the lives and property of the residents of the black community (Feagin and Hahn, 1973: 193).

TABLE 8.10
Comparative Statistics on Racial Disorders during 1967 and April, 1968

	1967	1968	Totals
Number of disorders	217	167	384
Cities	160	138	298
States	34 (+ Wash., D.C.)	36 (+ Wash., D.C.)	70 (+ Wash., D.C.)
Arrests	18,800	27,000	45,800
Average number of arrests per disorder	87	162	119
Injured	3,400	3,500	6,900
Average number injured per disorder	16	22	18
Killed	82	43	125
Property damage[a]	$69,000,000	$58,000,000	$127,000,000
National Guard			
times used	18	22	40
numbers used	27,700	34,900	62,600
Federal troops			
times used	1	3	4
numbers used	4,800	23,700	28,500

Source: Adapted from Lemberg Center for the Study of Violence (1968): p. 60.

Note: Excluded from the totals reported in this table are "equivocal" disorders, so-termed by the authors of the Lemberg study because of sketchy information on the racial aspects of the event.

[a]Property damage refers to physical damage to property or loss of stock (usually through looting) and is estimated in dollars.

Though no doubt tactically sensible, the abandonment of rioting as a form of protest deprived insurgents of their only major tactical innovation during the late 1960s. In effect, the government's massive control efforts had proved an effective counter to the riots.

SUMMARY

Thus, by the decade's end, the pace and intensity of black insurgency were much diminished from what they had been even a few years earlier. This decline was a product of the four sets of factors discussed here. First, the organizational structure of the movement grew progressively weaker as the decade wore on. In the face of the collapse of the strong consensus on issues and tactics that had prevailed within the movement during its heyday, insurgents found it increasingly difficult to organize the strong, focused campaigns characteristic of the early 1960s. Instead, by 1970, insurgent activity had taken on a much more diffuse quality with a veritable profusion of small groups addressing a wide range of issues by means of an equally wide range of tactics. Unfortunately, the variety inherent in this approach was too often offset by a political impotence that stemmed from the absence of the strong protest vehicles that had earlier dominated the movement.

Second, reversing a trend begun during the 1930s, the "structure of political opportunities" available to insurgents contracted in the late 1960s in response to a variety of burgeoning pressures. Chief among these was the mobilization of a strong conservative "backlash" in this country fueled both by the turbulence of the era and the conscious exploitation of a "law and order" rhetoric by public officials. When combined with the emergence of other competing issues and the declining salience of the black vote, this "backlash" served to diminish the overall political leverage exercised by insurgents and therefore the prospects for organized insurgency.

The shifting political realities reviewed above also set in motion a third process that was to prove detrimental to the movement. As the political context deteriorated in the late 1960s, so too did the widespread feelings of optimism and political efficacy that had earlier furnished the motive force behind insurgency. Deprived of these crucial attitudinal supports, insurgents found it increasingly hard to mobilize the significant collections of people needed to sustain the movement.

But perhaps the most important factor contributing to the decline of the movement during this period was the substantive and tactical shifts evidenced by insurgents themselves. Abandoning the limited-reform goals and nonviolent forms of direct action characteristic of the civil rights phase of the movement, insurgents triggered a drastic alteration in the responses of the other principal parties to the conflict. Based on the greater perceived threat posed by insurgents, these altered responses increasingly involved outright opposition to the movement rather than the mix of neutrality and grudging support forthcoming during earlier phases of the struggle.

Pointing up the dangers of external support, the movement's liberal "sponsors" abandoned the movement in droves, as the interests of insurgents increasingly diverged from their own. This development critically weakened the direct-action wing of the movement, which displayed a marked inability to cultivate the grass-roots support that might have been able to offset the loss of the external "sponsorship" on which it had grown exclusively dependent.

Finally, both continuity and change marked the government's response to the movement during the late 1960s. In the urban riots of the period, insurgents developed yet another disruptive form of political action that was successful in stimulating the reactive pattern of federal action so familiar by now. As the decade wore on, however, the state's early ameliorative response to the riots was increasingly overshadowed by a stepped-up campaign of repression designed both to destroy the "black power" wing of the movement and to put down forcefully the urban rebellions. The rapid decline in black insurgency after 1968 attests to the success of this campaign.

9 Political Process and Black Insurgency

I began this book by outlining four distinct objectives that were to underlie the analysis. In this chapter I return to those objectives as a way of summarizing the complex mix of theory and empirical analysis contained in the first eight chapters. My first objective was simply to assess the current state of sociological theorizing in the field of social movements. Toward that end, I outlined and criticized two existing perspectives, the classical and resource mobilization, and proposed a political process model as an alternative to them.

The book's second objective called for an assessment of the predictive utility of the aforementioned models as applied to a single instance of insurgency: the black movement of the 1950s and 1960s. This second objective is hard to separate from the third, that of providing a comprehensive empirical analysis of the emergence and subsequent development of black insurgency from 1876 to 1970. Insofar as these two objectives are clearly related, the relevant findings with regard to both will be summarized together.

First, neither the classical nor resource mobilization models appear to adequately explain the emergence and subsequent development of the black movement over the course of the study period. Neither various measures of social strain nor the level of external support for the movement bear any significant relationship to the pace and extent of movement activity between 1948 and 1970.

Instead, what seems to account for the generation of black insurgency in the mid-1950s are the three factors discussed in connection with the political process model. First, as shaped by several broad social processes, the "structure of political opportunities" confronting blacks gradually improved during the period from 1930 to 1954, thus affording insurgents more leverage with which to press their demands. Second, this expansion in political opportunities contributed to a growing sense of political efficacy within the black population as insurgents came to redefine existing conditions as subject to change through collective action. And third, with the simultaneous growth of three institutions—the black churches and colleges, and NAACP chapters—the southern black population developed the indigenous organizational strength needed to mount and sustain a social movement. Certainly, the data suggest the disproportionate role played by these institutions in the emergent phase of insurgency.

Finally, a comparison of the movement in the periods from 1961 to 1965 and from 1966 to 1970 suggests the continuing significance of internal organization and external opportunity mediated through an intervening process of collective definition in accounting for both the peak of insurgency in the earlier period and the decline of the movement thereafter. To these three factors, however, must be added a fourth: the shifting response of other organized groups to the movement. Owing to the widespread legitimacy accorded insurgent goals in the early 1960s, opposition to the movement remained relatively limited. However, with the shift to goals and tactics that posed a greater threat to established interests, the movement, in the late 1960s, encountered an opposition increasingly willing to use repressive social-control measures to contain insurgency.

That leaves only the fourth and final objective outlined in the Introduction. What has this analysis of the black movement told us about the broad topic of power in America? What is the relationship between the "politics of protest" and more institutionalized forms of political action? These questions remain crucial to this study. But while implicit throughout, they have often taken a back seat to the more narrowly empirical focus of the book. In this final chapter, it is necessary to return to them.

At the outset of this book I argued that all theories of social movements imply adherence to a more general model of institutionalized power. Accordingly, any empirical analysis of a social movement will have important implications for such models as well as for the specific theories of insurgency derived from them. And so it is with this analysis. Having found the classical and resource mobilization models wanting as explanations of the black movement, I am led to question the adequacy of the more general models of political power on which they rest. Specifically, neither the pluralist model nor certain versions of the elite model fit well with the history of black insurgency between 1930 and 1970.

With regard to the pluralist model, two contradictions are immediately apparent. First, pluralists argue that noninstitutionalized forms of political action are unnecessary to advance the collective interests of organized groups in society. This contention is based on the fundamental assumption that power is so widely distributed in America as to insure the openness and responsiveness of the political system to virtually all groups. Second, this wide distribution of power also serves, according to the pluralists, to "tame" the political system. That is, it renders force and violence ineffective as political tactics. The reason given for this is simple. In a situation where power is widely distributed, the power disparity between any two groups will not be great enough to allow one party to withstand the likely political reprisals that the use of force and violence is almost certain to provoke. Thus, noninstitutionalized, coercive forms of political action are both unnecessary and tactically ineffective, according to proponents of the pluralist model.

The history of recent black insurgency in this country clearly contradicts the pluralist model on both counts. Throughout their stay in America, blacks have been the victims of institutionalized political powerlessness. Contrary to the claims of the pluralists, blacks have consistently found themselves barred from participation in a system of institutionalized politics that has proven to be generally unresponsive to their interests. In the context of this closed and unresponsive system, black insurgency has been anything but unnecessary. Indeed, historically it has been, as it remains today, the only real avenue of political influence available to blacks.

Nor has it proven to be an ineffective one. It is popular in light of our contemporary awareness of the limits of the racial reforms of the 1960s to disparage the "minimal accomplishments" of the black movement. Such criticism is both ingenuous and inaccurate. It must be remembered that the movement was able, in a matter of years, to dismantle a thoroughgoing system of caste restrictions that had remained impervious to change for some seventy-five years. It was also responsible, in three years' time, for the passage of more civil rights legislation than had been enacted in all the previous congressional sessions in U.S. history. One effect of that legislation has been to more nearly equalize voting rights in the South, thereby contributing to a dramatic reduction in violence against blacks. Insofar as blacks now constitute a potent electoral force in southern politics, elected officials—especially sheriffs—can ill afford to engage in, or encourage through inaction, the virulent forms of racist violence so commonplace in the South prior to the mid-1960s. These gains are hardly insignificant.

That the movement failed to eliminate the last vestiges of racial discrimination in this country is undeniable, but the failure is hardly proof of the ineffectiveness of the "politics of protest." Instead, the persistence of discrimination attests to the combined power of the forces arrayed against the sorts of fundamental systemic changes that would be required to eliminate institutional racism. In terms of the pluralist model, the obvious implication of the black movement is that the system is neither as open nor as responsive to the interests of all social groups as the model's proponents contend. Neither, then, can the political system be based on as wide and equitable a distribution of power as the model suggests. If blacks can be rendered so impotent within the institutionalized political arena that they must seek to mobilize leverage outside of "proper channels,'' then obviously certain groups in society do possess sufficient power to bar others from meaningful participation in political decision-making.

This would seem to lend credence to the elite model of the American political system. Certainly, the findings reported here are more consistent with this interpretation than the one offered by the pluralists. At the same time, nearly all versions of the model attribute to elite groups a measure of control over the larger political environment that is inconsistent with the history of recent black insurgency in this country. The image that emerges from the writings of most elite theorists is of a political system controlled by narrow interests that exercise virtually exclusive control over decision-making processes. This view consigns all other segments of society to a state of impotence that virtually precludes the exercise of any significant political influence. It is but a short inferential leap from this view to the conclusion that significant social change can only result from elite action.

Such a conclusion is clearly at odds with the development of black insurgency in the middle decades of this century. As shown earlier, elite groups did not so much stimulate black protest activity as seek to respond to it in ways that would minimize the threat it posed to their interests. Thus, the recent history of black protest would seem to grant excluded groups a measure of indigenous power that is denied them in most versions of the elite model. This is not to resurrect the ghost of pluralism (it is not that all segments of society *routinely* exercise power *through institutionalized means*, as the pluralists argue). Instead, it is simply to stress the latent, disruptive power all groups possess by virtue of their location within systems whose smooth functioning depends on their willing cooperation.

The experiences of the black movement argue for a serious modification in the characteristic elite view of the distribution of power in America. In place of our image of an elite comfortably in control of the political environment, it would seem more accurate to see the elite as a harried group scrambling to manage or contain numerous challenges that arise to threaten the fundamental prerogatives of class rule. Not that we need overstate the extent of elite vulnerability to insurgent challenge. Most of the time the threat to their interests is more an implied capability than an actual fact. The important point here, though, is that the absence of routine challenge to elite control more often results from a shared sense of political powerlessness than from any inherent impotence on the part of the challengers.

And what does all this suggest about the future prospects for black insurgency in this country? By way of a specific timetable, nothing. However, there is little question but that widespread black insurgency will develop again in the not too distant future. Jim Crow may be dead, but its legacy lives on in the form of grinding poverty, persistent institutional discrimination in jobs, housing, and education, and the continued social estrangement of blacks and whites in this country. Sooner or later organized black insurgency, aimed at this litany of inequities, will no doubt arise. And when it does we can expect it to be preceded by a fundamental shift in political alignments favorable to blacks, the mobilization of the indigenous organizational strength of the black community, and the transformation of existing feelings of cynicism and hopelessness into a shared vision of collective political power.

Appendix 1: Methodology and Presentation of Coding Manual

Use of the annual *New York Times Index*, or newspapers in general, as a data source has been frequently criticized as methodologically problematic (Bagdikian, 1972; Breed, 1958; Danzger, 1975; Molotch and Lester, 1974). Consistent with some of the objections raised by critics, newspaper data would appear to be poorly suited to the study of various aspects of social insurgency. Specifically, the method is poorly suited to the study of subtle social-psychological processes or the effect of psychological conditions on the unfolding insurgent process (Gurr, 1972: 34). Nor does it seem that newspapers provide a suitable source of data for any but the most newsworthy insurgent challenges. Thus, to use the *Index* as the sole data source to analyze "gay" activism prior to 1965 would be problematic simply because such activity did not constitute "copy" until several years later. Finally, it would seem indefensible to use the technique to study aspects or forms of insurgency that are readily subject to reporter distortion. Here Tuchman's distinction between "hard" and "soft news" provides a useful guideline (Tuchman, 1973: 113). That is, newspaper accounts of the "hard" or factual aspects of an event are likely to be reliable. On the other hand, the interpretive or "soft" aspects of the story are particularly vulnerable to reporter distortion and thus logical candidates for exclusion from analysis. In support of this distinction, Danzger argues that "in a case of conflict whether an action was a march or a boycott, involved ten or one hundred, the police or the clergy, are all clear facts. The attitudes of rioters—i.e., are their actions part of a 'Christmas in August' looters' syndrome or are they trying to get a message through to the power structure; is an attempt to break up a mob intentional harassment or a reasonable action—all these are open to question. These are the kinds of facts which are easily subverted by bias and difficult to establish beyond question. Newspaper reports may be unreliable data sources here" (1975: 577).

At the same time, however, I strongly argue that several factors highly recommend the methodological technique of content coding for the historical analysis of insurgency. In the first place the technique allows for replication by others, as well as for the systematic formulation and testing of research hypotheses. Such advantages are hardly insignificant.

Second, the technique is ideally suited to provide rough measures of the sorts of broad macro-level processes that over time shape insurgency (Gurr, 1972: 34). Crucial facets of the unfolding conflict process otherwise resistant to quantification can be crudely measured. Such important aspects of insurgency as the rate of involvement of various groups over time, the different patterns of activity manifest by various parties to the conflict, the shifting geographic location of insurgent events and the interaction of various groups over time can all be given rough quantificative expression.

A final factor encouraging use of data drawn from newspapers is the extraordinary paucity of alternative data sources for those engaged in conflict research. Indeed, as Danzger notes, even some of these "alternative" sources are, in fact, drawn from newspaper accounts of insurgent events. As examples, he cites the *Congressional Quarterly's Civil Disorder Chronology*, the Lemberg Center's *Riot*

Data Review, and the *Report of the National Advisory Commission on Civil Disorders*. As Danzger writes, "Although they appear to be a variety of sources, in reality they are all based on a single source of data, newspaper reports, and several of them are based on the *New York Times*" (Danzger, 1975: 572).

To exclude from use all newspaper data would thus seriously impair research into these important topics. No one is seriously suggesting this. Danzger, in his important article, is not so much criticizing the use of newspaper data as its utilization without any awareness of the limitations inherent in the source (Danzger, 1975: 573). In this study an effort was made to utilize *Index* data only when it was methodologically defensible to do so. As I argued above, newsworthiness, avoidance of social-psychological topics, and variables resistant to reporter distortion are necessary prerequisites for the viable use of the technique under discussion. The research reported here conforms to all three conditions.

In regard to the first of these conditions, it seems safe to say that the extensive media attention devoted to the black movement was only an extension of the substantial coverage accorded blacks prior to the generation of widespread insurgency in the mid-1950s. A qualitative analysis of the stories contained in the *Index* for the years 1948–54 supports this assertion. The following examples drawn from those years serve to illustrate the point:

—Army and Navy Chaplains' Association held opposed to segregation (May 11, 1948)
—T.J. McKee, who lived forty-five years as a white man, dies (August 19, 1948)
—Abyssinian Baptist Church to send seventy-five Negro children to Vermont white families for vacations (April 24, 1948)
—Cross burned at home of L. Hutson, believed only Negro in Wall Township, New Jersey (June 13, 1948)
—Two Negroes jailed, Ozark, Alabama, for donning masks to scare two Negresses seen with white man (August 6, 1949)
—Cadet D. Campbell is first flight commander in Pensacola Naval Air Station preflight graduating class (October 22, 1950)
—White and Negro neighbors repair home of 109-year-old Negro woman, Jefferson, Georgia (March 26, 1950)
—Two white policemen, charged with beating Negro prisoner to death, Lafayette, Alabama, acquitted by white jury (March 23, 1950)

These few examples, which could be multiplied many times over, accurately convey a level of media awareness that suggests a receptivity to the general topic of black America significantly predating the movement. As a result, I feel confident in interpreting the findings reported here as reflective of actual social processes rather than as artificial by-products of increased media attention.

Moreover, the extreme importance attributed to the black struggle by the media would make it seem unlikely that the *Times* was guilty of failing to report a major story relevant to the movement. It is hard to believe that any major story involving a movement that had captured the imagination of the country, would have escaped the attention of the paper that has long prided itself on being the most comprehensive in the world. Indeed, 83 percent of all dated events between 1955 and

1962 (447 of 536), mentioned in nine descriptive accounts of the movement (Bergman, 1969; Brooks, 1974; Hughes, 1962; Keesing's Research Report, 1970; Killian, 1975; Muse, 1964; Oppenheimer, 1963; Woodward, 1966; Zinn, 1965), were reported in the *Times*. When the comparison is reversed, the descriptive accounts report only 9 percent (447 of 4,817) of all events contained in the *Index*.

Finally, in the choice of the basic variables utilized in this analysis, care was taken to omit those that seemed especially vulnerable to reporter distortion or misrepresentation. Thus, while newspaper accounts of events relevant to the movement (court actions, sit-ins, demonstrations, etc.) may systematically misinterpret the motives of the participants involved, it is unlikely that such accounts will contain inaccuracies as to the date and location of the event or the general identity of those involved, (black students, state police, etc.). In short, the selection of major variables reflects an acute awareness of the inability of newspaper accounts to depict accurately every aspect of a complex social event. Besides increasing confidence in the accuracy of the data under analysis, this careful selection of variables also resulted in impressive intercoder reliability coefficients. By way of conventional assurances, ratings for the coding of all variables were consistently around 90 percent. But in regard to the key variables utilized in the final analysis, coder reliability ratings were never below 95 percent.

The coding manual used in this research read as follows.

Coding Manual

I.   *Introduction*

The basic aim of the analysis is to content code all story synopses relevant to the topic of black insurgency that are contained in the annual indexes of the *New York Times* corresponding to the years of the study period. Specifically, in the yearly indexes from 1948 to 1970, all story synopses listed under the two headings, "Negroes-U.S.-General," and "Education-U.S.-Racial Integration," are to be read and, if relevant, coded in accordance with the criteria and categories set forth below.

How summaries are to be coded. The first code is to be used in coding actions (riots, sit-ins, protest marches, etc.), while the second code is designed to handle all speeches and statements. The "speech code" consists of the following seven dimensions along which a synopsis can be coded:
1)   date of event
2)   initiating unit
3)   direction of the event (pro or anti movement)
4)   level of initiating unit (local, state, or national)
5)   geographic target of the event
6)   issue(s) at stake
7)   racial identity of the initiating unit
The "action code" includes these same seven dimensions as well as the five additional categories listed below:
8)   location of event (what state?)
9)   size of locality (rural/urban)

10) nature of event
11) violence (yes/no)
12) resources (did the action involve the allocation of resources?)

It is hoped that together these two codes will afford rough measures of the sorts of broad macro-level processes that over time shape insurgency (interaction between various parties to the conflict, shifting substantive and geographic focus of insurgency, etc.).

II.   *General Coding Instructions*

Perhaps the single most difficult determination in regard to any story is whether or not to code it in the first place. It is hoped that the following simple rules will help to eliminate some of the difficulties associated with this initial coding decision.

A)   Only synopses relevant to the general topic of black insurgency are to be coded. No doubt you will find other story summaries under the two headings listed above that bear little or no relationship to the topic under study. For example, stories documenting the achievements of black athletes or entertainers are commonplace. To repeat, such stories should not be coded.

B)   Besides this general criteria of relevance, summaries are to be coded only if they are judged to be unambiguous with regard to 1) the identification of the event; 2) its location (where relevant); and 3) the individual(s) or group(s) who were responsible for initiating the event.

C)   All *New York Times*-generated stories will not be coded. This rule will apply to all letters (lr), comments, Sunday opinion-type stories (designated by Roman numerals), surveys, ads, and editorials (ed).

D)   Two separate codings on one story should only occur when the activities in question are discrete. That is, a given speech or action will usually generate only one coding. For example, no matter how many different points a speaker should make, the speech itself should only be coded once.

E)   On stories that hinge on a preceding event, code the present activity and only if it warrants coding under the criteria set out earlier. For example:

> "Two 18 year old white youths arrested in con-
> nection with the shooting death of a civil rights
> worker a week ago."

In this case the arrest would be coded, *not* the shooting itself.

III.   Black Insurgency Codes

A.   *Action Code*

13–18   Dates of action

19–22   Pages in *Index*

23–24   Area (Where did the action take place?)

          00   No specific location   27   Nebraska
          01   Alabama*   28   Nevada

02	Alaska	29	New Hampshire
03	Arizona	30	New Jersey
04	Arkansas*	31	New Mexico
05	California	32	New York
06	Colorado	33	North Carolina*
07	Connecticut	34	North Dakota
08	Delaware	35	Ohio
09	Florida*	36	Oklahoma*
10	Georgia*	37	Oregon
11	Hawaii	38	Pennsylvania
12	Idaho	39	Rhode Island
13	Illinois	40	South Carolina*
14	Indiana	41	South Dakota
15	Iowa	42	Tennessee*
16	Kansas	43	Texas*
17	Kentucky*	44	Utah
18	Louisiana*	45	Vermont
19	Maine	46	Virginia*
20	Maryland*	47	Washington
21	Massachusetts	48	West Virginia*
22	Michigan	49	Wisconsin
23	Minnesota	50	Wyoming
24	Mississippi*	51	NYC Metropolitan area
25	Missouri*	52	District of Columbia (local)*
26	Montana	53	District of Columbia (national)

25   Size of Locality (Where did the event take place?)
1 Urban
2 Rural

26   Target Area
0 No specific target
1 North
2 South
3 Regional
4 National
5 Federal

27   Unit Level (Importance or "level" of those involved)
1 Local
2 State
3 Regional
4 National

28–29   Initiating Unit
Political
11 Candidates (explicitly acknowledged)
12 Party spokespersons
18 2 or more candidates

Governmental
21 Executive head
22 Executive body, agency, or official (including cabinet members)
23 Legislator
24 Legislative body
25 Individual jurist
26 Judicial body
27 Law enforcement personnel
28 Multiple gov. figures, bodies, etc.
29 U.S. Civil Rights Commission
Religious
31 Protestant spokesperson or body
32 Catholic spokesperson or body
33 Jewish spokesperson or body
34 Other religious spokesperson or body
38 Multiple religious spokespersons or groups
Labor & Professional Bodies
41 Labor spokespersons
42 Business spokespersons
43 Medical personnel or associations
44 Social scientist
45 Legal profession
46 Educational associations (school boards, etc.)
47 Human relations councils
48 Multiple labor or professional spokespersons or associations
49 Foundations
Interest or "Reactionary" Groups
51 Miscellaneous interest groups
52 KKK
53 John Birch Society
54 Citizens Council
55 Other white Supremacist groups
56 "Leftist" groups
57 Other sociocultural organizations
58 Multiple interest or "reactionary" groups
59 Sports commission or authority
Media
61 Newspaper
62 Television
63 Artists/actors
Education
71 Black colleges (administrative spokesperson)
72 White or interracial colleges (administrative spokesperson)
73 Black students and/or faculty

74 White students and/or faculty
75 Interracial group of students and/or faculty
78 Multiple educational units
Movement Groups
81 NAACP
82 The Black Muslims
83 CORE
84 SNCC
85 SCLC
86 Panthers
87 Martin Luther King
88 Multiple movement groups or spokespersons
89 Other specifically identified movement groups or spokespersons
Others
91 Black aggregate
92 White aggregate
93 Interracial aggregate
94 Other aggregates (racial composition unknown)
95 Unknown notables
96 Known notables
97 Individual actor
98 Black cultural organization
99 Multiple units cross-categories

30   Racial Composition of Initiating Unit
1 Black
2 White
3 Mixed

31–34   Issue
11 Segregation-integration
12 Equality under the law
13 Political power
14 Economic power/jobs/poverty
15 Black culture/black pride
16 Racism (black)
17 Racism (white)
18 Separtism/self determination
19 Internal dissent
21 Organizational concerns
22 Black extremism
23 The general plight of the black American
24 Impoverished sociocultural environment/ghettos
25 Voter registration
27 Police brutality
28 Riots/law and order

35–36   Issue Area
     11   Public facilities and accommodations
     12   Public transportation
     13   Housing
     14   Education
     15   Military
     16   Labor/the economy/employment
     17   Administration of justice
     18   Politics
     19   Media
     21   Sports
     22   Health and medicine
     23   Religion
     24   Business
     25   The arts
     26   The family
37   Specificity
     1   Identification of specific issue
38–39   Event
     11   Institutionalized government action (passage of bill, institution of new program, executive actions, elections, appointments, or formation of new committees, commissions, etc.).
     12   Private group materially aids the movement/foundation grants.
     21   Internal dynamics of black movement (formation of new group, leadership changes, mergers, conventions, conferences, etc.).
     22   Internal dynamics of white supremacy movement.
     31   Institutionalized insurgency (i.e., campaign to enact legislation, elect a public official, register voters, petition campaign, etc.).
     32   Threat or warning made by a group or individual who possess the resources to carry out the threat, mentioning specific target and date.
     33   Movement group materially aides local population.
     34   Court action (either its initiation or resolution).
     35   Desegregation of facility, event, or organization.
     36   Continued segregation of facility (attempt at desegregation fails).
     41   Boycott/strikes (except school boycott).
     42   Mass action (sit-in, protest march, demonstration, rally, etc.).
     44   Harassment or intimidation of blacks or their supporters by antimovement forces.
     45   Other illegal acts.

46   Violent action (riot, lynching, murder, etc.).
47   State control (arrests, jailings, convictions, indictments, fines, suspensions, subpoenas, etc.).
48   Freedom Ride
49   Black cultural event
50   School boycott
51   Termination of aid to insurgent group.

40   Violence
0   The event wasn't violent
1   The event was violent

41   Direction
0   Ambiguous
1   Pro-integration
2   Pro–"black power"
3   Neutral
4   Anti-integration
5   Anti–"black power"

42   Resources
1   Legislation
2   Money
3   Program
4   Combination of 2 and 3
5   Jobs/physical facility
6   Other

43   Related Movement Connections
1   Gay movement
2   Peace movement
3   Women's movement
4   Other minority movement
5   Other leftist movement

B.   *Speech Code*
13–18   Date of speech
19–22   Page in *Index*
45–46   Initiating Unit
         (same as "Initiating Unit" in Action Code)
47   Direction
         (same as "Direction" in Action Code)
48   Unit Level
         (same as "Unit Level" in Action Code)
49   Target Area
         (same as "Target Area" in Action Code)
50–53   Issue
         (same as "Issue" in Action Code)
54–55   Issue Area
         (same as "Issue Area" in Action Code)
56   Rhetoric

        1   Segregation-integration
        2   Discrimination
        3   Civil rights
        4   Racism
        5   Separatism
        6   Extremism
        7   Nationalism

57   Racial Composition
        (same as "Racial Composition" in Action Code)

IV. *Explanation of Code Categories*
(Listed below are explanations for those code categories that would seem to be less than self-explanatory. The general categories are listed by column number with the specific codes within each category listed in accordance with the numbers assigned them above.)

13–22   *Date and Page of the Article*

23–24   *Area*—The code would appear to be self-evident except for the last three categories.

    51   *NYC Metropolitan Area*—refers only to actions that occur within the immediate NYC Metropolitan area.

    52   *Dist. of Colum. (local)*—refers specifically to those related movement activities that are concerned with conditions in the District of Columbia as a place of habitation rather than as the seat of national government.

    53   *Dist. of Colum. (national)*—refers to any story that deals with the workings of national government.

25   *Size of Locality*—in coding size of locality, the coder should refer to the attached sheets for a list of the major cities in each state. For the purposes of this study, cities with a population of 10,000 or more in 1960 will be referred to as "urban" while all others will be coded "rural."

26   *Target Area*—refers to the geographical target that is implied in movement and movement-related events. In other words that geographical area that the relevant actors are concerned with affecting. For example:

        "650 marchers hold prayer services on the steps of City Hall, Birmingham, Alabama, to protest continued harassment of those blacks seeking to register to vote."

The demonstrators are clearly concerned with conditions in Birmingham, or more generally, the South. Therefore, the target area is the "South."

Those states under the general coding category "Area" that are followed by an asterisk will be coded as "South" while all others will be designated as "North."

The target area "National" refers not to a specific geographical area but rather to the United States as a whole. "Federal" will be coded only in regard to statements or actions that involve the federal government as the focus or target of the event.

28–29   *Initiating Unit*—refers to the individual or individuals whose actions or statments have prompted the story. For the most part, all coding categories would appear to be self-evident, except for the following:

11   *Candidate*—refers to any person explicitly designated as a candidate in the *Index*. If the person is an elected official but identified as a candidate in the synopsis, he should be coded as a candidate.

71   *Black Colleges*

72   *White or Interracial Colleges*—in both these cases I refer to the actions or statements by administrators and/or faculty members acting, not as individuals, but as spokespersons for the school itself.

73   *Black Students and/or Faculty*

74   *White Students and/or Faculty*

75   *Interracial Group of Students and/or Faculty*

The above categories refer to the statements or activities of students and/or faculty members acting autonomously from their respective educational institutions.

91   *Black aggregate*

92   *White aggregate*

93   *Interracial aggregate*

94   *Other aggregate*

In the above categories, an aggregate refers to a collection of people who act in consort, but who nevertheless are not specifically identified as a formally constituted group.

95   *Unknown notables*—refers to those individuals, unknown to the coder, who are listed in the *Index* without additional identifying information.

30   *Racial Composition of Initiating Unit*—In many cases it will be difficult to ascertain the racial composition of the initiating unit. This especially is true in reference to activities generated by the various movement organizations. In this determination the coder must, of necessity, rely on the information contained in the story itself.

31–34   *Issue*—It should first be noted that four columns have been set aside for the coding of issues rather than two. This permits the coder to identify two issues per story and thus enables us to handle the bulk of multiple issue stories. As one might expect, if the story deals with only one issue, columns 33 and 34 will be marked 0.

An examination of the specific coding categories listed under this heading reveals a set of vague, general issues whose coding

criteria are too complex to be clearly stated here. The specifics
of each issue remain to be transmitted from author to coder
during his/her training period. A general feel for each issue,
however, may be gained by reading the following short summaries:

11   *Segregation-Integration*—concerns the general question of
the institutional separation of blacks and whites in America,
with reference to such specific spheres of everyday life as
housing, education, public accommodations, and transportation.

12   *Equality under the law*—involves the demand that the rights
and responsibilities of black Americans be adequately leg-
islated *and* enforced. For example:

> "600 blacks picket the White House to demand
> federal protection for beleaguered voter regis-
> trars in the Deep South."

13   *Political power*—the recognition of the importance of political power as a tool to facilitate the socioeconomic advancement of blacks.

14   *Economic power/jobs/poverty*—an explicit focus on the
economic problems (jobs, poverty, etc.) confronting blacks
or the need to generate greater economic power to facilitate
the realization of movement goals (i.e., black capitalism).

15   *Black culture*—represents a concern for the preservation
and perpetuation of black culture. Implicit in this concern
is the belief that the black cultural heritage has been systematically suppressed and denigrated by the dominant
white society and that blacks must recover their lost heritage if they are to maintain a sense of collective identity.

16   *Black racism*—refers to the charge made by some movement opponents in the late 60s that the "wilder excesses"
of the black movement had fostered a reverse racism in
which blacks were prejudiced against whites (frequently
Jews).

17   *White racism*—Rejecting the reformist ideology of the early
movement, white racism represents a more comprehensive
indictment of American society in which discrimination and
racial prejudice are seen as inextricably woven into the
institutional fabric of everyday life.

18   *Separatism/self-determination*—As with segregation-integration this issue concerns the general question of the institutional relationship between blacks and whites in America.
In this case, however, the preferred relationship involves
the maintenance of separate institutions (or perhaps even
whole communities or nations) rather than the integration
of same.

19   *Internal dissent*—To code this issue the event in question
must involve either a clear-cut instance of dissension be-

tween movement groups or a discussion of the phenomenon itself. The following two examples will illustrate both types of events.

> "Rap Brown brands Roy Wilkins and Whitney Young as Uncle Toms; says two pose greater threat to black interests than George Wallace."

> "Martin Luther King, in speech to National Student Association, says, 'internal divisiveness' is eroding previously strong civil rights coalition; calls for renewed unity."

21   *Organizational concerns*—involves any explicit concern with the organizational dynamics of movement or movement-related groups. For example:

> "Roy Wilkins, Executive Director of the NAACP, cites 'mistaken belief that the crusade is over' as reason for drop in organization's membership."

22   *Black extremism*—involves the explicit approval of tactics or strategies more extreme than those advocated during the era of nonviolent direct action. Thus, any story dealing with the debate over the desirability of these "extreme" tactics will be coded 22.

23   *The general plight of the black American*—A catchall, this category is designed to handle those movement-related stories in which no specific issue is identified. For example:

> "Nelson Rockefeller, in speech before joint session of NY legislature, reports that he 'deplores the general plight of the black American,' and pledges his continued support for further civil rights legislation."

24   *Impoverished sociocultural environment*—involves the explicit recognition of the sociocultural disadvantages imposed on blacks by means of the institutional arrangements of American society.

25   *Voter registration*—would appear to be self-explanatory.

27   *Police brutality*—would appear to be self-evident.

28   *Riots/law and order*—involves any explicit discussion of the urban riots as a phenomenon or the numerous calls for "law and order" in the face of those riots.

35–36   *Issue Area*—The general coding category, *Issue Area*, will be used in two distinct ways:

1)   In some instances it will be impossible to identify one of the 16 specific issues listed under the coding category *Issue* but possible to identify a specific issue area. For example:

> "In an outbreak of racial hostilities, 50 black and white sailors clash aboard the U.S.S. Enterprise."

Issue: too vague to be coded

Issue Area: Military

2) For the most part, however, the *Issue Area* code will be used in conjunction with the specific issues of Segregation-Integration, Black and White Racism, and Equality Under the Law as listed under the coding category *Issue*. That is, the *Issue Area* code will be used to provide more specific information in regard to stories involving the issues mentioned above. For example:

> "100 black demonstrators converge on the Albany, Georgia, City Hall to protest alleged segregation in municipal bus service."

Issue: Segregation-Integration

Issue Area: Public transportation

37   *Specificity*—A story will be coded specific if it is tied to a *local* effort to deal with it. This effort may be either pro- or anti-movement. For example:

> "Eleven black students stage lunch counter sit-in, Fayetteville, North Carolina, in effort to force desegregation of city's public facilities."

> "Threats of violence by white citizens force discontinuation of integrated church services, Greenwood, Mississippi."

38–39   *Event*—For the most part the event code is self-explanatory. Several coding categories, however, demand further explanation.

11 *Institutionalized government action*—This first coding category includes all those events listed in the code plus their converses. In other words, not only is the passage of a bill coded number 11, but the *defeat* of a bill, as well.

12 *Private group materially aids the movement*—This category will be used to code those stories involving private contributions designed to benefit the movement. For example:

> "Fund for the Republic contributes $150,000 to Southern Regional Council to help support current inter-racial programs."

31 *Institutionalized insurgency*—This coding category seeks to capture those instances in which *movement participants* engage in institutionalized political action. Thus only those campaigns in which blacks are reported to be actively involved will be coded 31.

32 *Threat or warning*—Two conditions must be satisfied before a threat or warning can be coded. First of all, the individual or group issuing the threat must be in a position to carry it out. If not, the threat is not likely to provoke a

reaction from the opposition. Secondly, the threat must make reference to a specific target. By insisting on this condition we hope to eliminate the rash of vague threats that proliferate in all instances of social conflict. Examples:

> "Bobby Seale issues warning to white America to expect 'protracted guerrilla warfare' if economic exploitation of black masses continues much longer."

> "Lyndon Johnson issues statment in which he threatens 'non-cooperation' on impending legislation unless Voter Rights Bill is on his desk by mid-September."

In the above examples, only the second story should be coded.

36 *Continued segregation of facility, event, or organization*—Under increased pressure to desegregate, a continued refusal to do so becomes noteworthy. Thus the continued segregation of any facility (public park), event (Memorial Day Parade), or organization (Lions Club) will be coded 36 under the Event code. Again, an example may prove helpful:

> "Lyric Theatre, Baltimore, closes when local black leaders fail to reach a satisfactory agreement with management regarding racial admissions policies."

46 *Violent action*—refers to those events which are *exclusively violent*. By this criterion, then, a peaceful march, marred by violence, would not be coded.

51 *Termination of aide to insurgent group*—represents the converse of 12. Here private groups withdraw, reduce, or suspend resource support they earlier granted movement groups.

40   *Violence*—An event will be coded violent if violence is in any way associated with it. For instance, a peaceful march, marred by violence, would be coded under this category.

41   *Direction*—refers to the actors intent on undertaking the activity in question. That is, regardless of the ultimate impact of the event on the movement, so long as it was intended to promote the aims of the movement it will be coded Pro.

In this code, however, the movement is not presumed to be monolithic but rather to consist of two main divisions. The first is the traditional civil rights coalition stressing integration as its goal and nonviolent direct action as its means. The second "wing" of the movement are the "Black Power" proponents distinguished not so much by specific goals or means but rather by their rejection of integration as a viable goal and nonviolence as *the* only means. The direction code has been drafted in such a way as to reflect this division. Movement related activities can be either Pro or Anti "Black Power."

Finally, a Neutral activity refers to any noncommital stance in regard to the movement. This particular category will most often be used to code statements of condition, as in the following example:

> "Economist Herbert Stein cites recent gain in black per capita income as evidence of economic progress."

42   *Resources*

 1 *Legislation*—The enactment of a piece of legislation designed primarily to benefit black Americans.
 2 *Money*—The allocation of a significant monetary sum (over $5,000) designed in some way to benefit black Americans.
 3 *Program*—The institution or continuation of some program designed to benefit black Americans.
 4 *Combination of 2 and 3*—Refers to any story involving the allocation of a significant monetary sum in conjunction with a specific program designed to benefit black Americans.
 5 *Jobs/physical facility*—would appear to be self-evident.

43   *Related movement connections*—here I am concerned with capturing those events where a clear connection between the black movement and the various insurgent challenges listed under this category is indicated. For example:

> "Huey Newton meets with representatives of the anti-war movement; afterwards issues call for the establishment of closer ties between all elements working to 'defeat' American imperialism at home and abroad."

53   *Rhetoric*—This code is designed to measure, however crudely, the shifts in movement rhetoric from 1948 to 1970, and will be employed only when the story summary indicates that the speaker in question used one of the seven words listed under this coding category. For example:

> "Eldridge Cleaver attacks what he terms diseased, racist society, at press conference in Oakland, California."

Rhetoric Code: Racism

Appendix 2: Chronology of Sit-in Demonstrations, February 1–March 31, 1960

Date	*Location*
February 1	Greensboro, North Carolina
February 8	Durham, North Carolina
	Winston-Salem, North Carolina
February 9	Charlotte, North Carolina
	Fayetteville, North Carolina
February 10	Raleigh, North Carolina
February 11	Elizabeth City, North Carolina
	Hampton, Virginia
	High Point, North Carolina
February 12	Concord, North Carolina
	Portsmouth, Virginia
	Deland, Florida
	Norfolk, Virginia
	Rock Hill, South Carolina
February 13	Nashville, Tennessee
	Tallahassee, Florida
February 16	Salisbury, North Carolina
February 17	Chapel Hill, North Carolina
February 18	Suffolk, Virginia
	Shelby, North Carolina
February 19	Chattanooga, Tennessee
February 20	Richmond, Virginia
	Baltimore, Maryland
February 22	Whaleyville, Virginia
	Frankfort, Kentucky
	Newport News, Virginia
February 25	Montgomery, Alabama
	Orangeburg, South Carolina
	Henderson, North Carolina
	Charleston, South Carolina
February 27	Lexington, Kentucky
	Petersburg, Virginia
	Tuskegee, Alabama
February 29	Denmark, South Carolina
	Tampa, Florida
March 1	Monroe, North Carolina
March 2	St. Petersburg, Florida
	Daytona Beach, Florida
	Columbia, South Carolina
	Sarasota, Florida

251

Date	Location
March 3	Atlanta, Georgia
March 4	Miami, Florida
	Florence, South Carolina
	Sumter, South Carolina
	Orlando, Florida
	Houston, Texas
March 7	Knoxville, Tennessee
	Sanford, Florida
	Bluefield, West Virginia
March 8	New Orleans, Louisiana
March 10	Little Rock, Arkansas
	Huntsville, Alabama
March 11	Galveston, Texas
	Austin, Texas
March 12	Jacksonville, Florida
March 13	San Antonio, Texas
March 15	St. Augustine, Florida
	Statesville, North Carolina
	Corpus Christi, Texas
March 16	Savannah, Georgia
March 17	New Bern, North Carolina
March 18	Memphis, Tennessee
March 19	Wilmington, North Carolina
	Arlington, Virginia
	Lenoir, North Carolina
March 24	Pine Bluff, Arkansas
March 26	Lynchburg, Virginia
	Charleston, West Virginia
	Marshall, Texas
March 28	Baton Rouge, Louisiana
March 31	Birmingham, Alabama

Source: *New York Times Index*, 1960; Oppenheimer, 1963: 63; Southern Regional Council, 1961: xix–xxv.

Appendix 3: Estimated Total External Income for Five Major Movement
Organizations, 1948–70

Year	NAACP	NAACP LDEF	CORE[b]	SCLC	SNCC	Total
1948	96,302	94,092	5,000	c	c	195,394
1949	100,000[a]	70,734	3,000[a]	c	c	182,734
1950	100,000[a]	100,000[a]	2,000[a]	c	c	202,000
1951	105,000[a]	133,561	2,500[a]	c	c	241,061
1952	107,000[a]	210,923	3,000[a]	c	c	320,423
1953	135,806	226,205	5,000[a]	c	c	368,011
1954	142,870	200,021	7,700	c	c	350,591
1955	200,695	285,000[a]	10,514	c	c	496,110
1956	250,000[a]	346,947	14,332	c	c	611,279
1957	307,405	319,537	21,072	35,000[a]	c	683,014
1958	579,701	315,081	46,446	60,000[a]	c	1,000,228
1959	523,631	357,988	69,854	100,000[a]	c	1,051,473
1960	630,301	489,540	241,669	180,000	5,000	1,546,510
1961	654,678	560,808	455,212	193,000	14,000	1,877,698
1962	593,713	669,428	556,279	400,000[a]	120,000	2,339,420
1963	901,508	1,131,889	733,378	875,000	309,000	3,950,775
1964	707,494	1,538,099	837,611	975,000	650,000	4,708,204
1965	1,402,244	1,705,615	624,851	1,500,000	449,000	5,681,710
1966	1,808,497	1,719,467	310,000	1,000,000	325,000[a]	5,162,964
1967	2,220,235	2,054,217	200,000[a]	1,000,000	250,000[a]	5,724,452
1968	2,980,495	2,887,688	200,000[a]	1,250,000	150,000[a]	7,468,183
1969	3,546,000	3,135,990	150,000[a]	500,000[a]	50,000[a]	7,381,990
1970	3,796,430	3,152,449	150,000[a]	400,000[a]	25,000[a]	7,523,879
	21,890,005	21,714,279	4,649,319	8,468,000	2,347,000	59,068,103

Sources: For the NAACP, *Annual Report of the National Association for the Advancement of Colored People*, 1948–70; for CORE, Meier and Rudwick (1973: 40–42, 78, 82, 97, 149, 225, 335, 411, 429–30); for NAACP Legal Defense and Education Fund, information supplied directly by the organization; for SCLC, Brink and Harris (1963: 115); Clayton (1964: 14); Lomax (1962: 94); Muse (1968: 276); for SNCC, Carson (1981: 71,108,173); Meier (1971: 25); Oberschall (1978: 259); Zinn (1965: 10).

[a] My estimate.
[b] CORE's fiscal year ran from June 1 to May 31 thus requiring a further estimating procedure to obtain an income figure for the normal calendar year.
[c] Organization not yet in existence.

Appendix 4: List of Indigenous Protest Leaders, 1955–60

Ministers	*Local NAACP Leaders (Occupations)*
Ralph Abernathy	Daisy Bates (Housewife)
Joshua Barney	Rev. William Bender (College Instructor)
L. Roy Bennett	L. A. Blackman (Contractor)
Charles Billups	C. C. Bryant
J. W. Bonner	D. V. Carter
William H. Borders	A. J. Clement
Henry Clay Bunton	Gus Courts (Grocer)
B. Elton Cox	Rev. D. S. Cunningham (Minister)
W. T. Crutcher	John Edwards (Student)
G. G. Daniels	James C. Evers (Mortician)
A. L. Davis	Medgar Evers (NAACP Staff)
Grady Davis	George Ferguson (Mortician)
J. A. DeLaine	Billy Fleming
W. A. Dennis	Mrs. George Gibbs (Housewife)
Julius T. Douglas	Rev. L. Francis Griffin (Minister)
K. S. Dupont	Rev. J. S. Hall (Minister)
E. N. French	Aaron Henry (Pharmacist)
R. J. Glasco	Rev. James Hinton (Minister)
Robert S. Graetz	Rev. Julius Caesar Hope (Minister)
Edward Graham	Ruby Hurley (NAACP Staff)
W. H. Hall	Rev. C. A. Ivory (Minister)
Ben L. Hooks	Rev. E. F. Jackson (Minister)
H. H. Hubbard	Emory Jackson (Editor)
Robert E. James	Lillie M. Jackson
E. W. Jarrett	Rev. Dwight V. Kyle (Minister)
Theodore Jemison	W. W. Law
Vernon Jones	John LeFlore
Clarence Jones	Dr. H. A. Logan (Doctor)
D. E. King	Alexander Looby (Lawyer)
Martin Luther King, Sr.	Rev. Van J. Malone (Minister)
Martin Luther King, Jr.	James T. McCain (High School Principal)
Samuel B. Kyles	Dr. A.A. McCoy (Doctor)
George Lee	Amzie Moore (Farmer)
Roy Love	Harry T. Moore
Matthew McCullum	Rev. I. Dequincy Newman (Minister)
Douglas E. Moore	E. D. Nixon (Pullman porter)
J. L. Netters	W. C. Patton (NAACP Staff)
J. S. Phifer	Mrs. H. F. Pierce (Housewife)
W. J. Powell	Barbara Ann Posey (Student)
Solomon Seay	R. D. Robertson (Business agent for integrated union)
Fred Lee Shuttlesworth	Walter Scott

Ministers

B. J. Simms
Kelly Miller Smith
Daniel Speed
A. K. Stanley
Charles K. Steele
John L. Tilley
Wyatt T. Walker
Leon Whitney
Hosea Williams
A. W. Wilson
Calvin W. Woods
Virgil Wood
R. K. Young

Independent

Euretta Adair
Dr. W. G. Anderson
Wiley Branton
R. H. Craig
David H. Dwight
Charles Gomilion
Fred Gray
Richard Haley
Dr. Vivian Henderson
David Hood, Jr.
Luther Jackson
Dr. Moses Jones
C. W. King
George W. Lee
Julia Lewis
Professor Rufus Lewis
Dr. Gilbert Mason
John H. McCray
Floyd McKissick
William P. Mitchell
Professor James E. Pierce
Jo Ann Robinson
Blevin Stout
J. J. Thomas
William Thomas
Dr. J. E. Walker

Local NAACP Leaders (Occupations)

Dr. George Simpkins (Doctor)
Emmett Stringer (Dentist)
J. M. Tinsley
Rev. Samuel Wells (Minister)
Robert Williams (Machinist)
T. B. Wilson

Students

Marion Barry
James Bevel
Ezell Blair, Jr.
Julian Bond
Robert Booker
Amos Brown
Callas Brown
Lee Butler
Stokeley Carmichael
David Carter
Oretha Castle
MacArthur Cotton
Courtland Cox
David Dennis
Dion Diamond
Paul Dietrich
Rev. Elroy Embree
Tom Gaither
Lennie Glover
Lawrence Guyot
John Hardy
Frank Holloway
Timothy Jenkins
Major Johns
Joseph Charles Jones
Ed King
Lonnie King
Bernard LaFayette
Rev. James Lawson
Bernard Lee
John Lewis
Rudy Lombard
Bill Mahoney
Franklin McCain
Charles McDew

Students

Joseph McNeil
Fred Moore
Ronnie M. Moore
Donald Moss
Diane Nash
Richard Frank Parker
Charles Person
George Raymond, Jr.
Cordell Reagon
David Richmond
Marvin Robinson

Weldon Rougeau
Charles Sherrod
Jerome Smith
Ruby Smith
Patricia Stephens
Priscilla Stephens
Matt Suarez
Henry Thomas
Joan Trumpauer
C. T. Vivian

Sources: Brink and Harris (1963); Brooks (1974); Clayton (1964); Hughes (1962); King (1958); Lawson (1976); Lomax (1962); Meier and Rudwick (1973); Oppenheimer (1963); Parker (1974); Peck (1960); Proudfoot (1962); Quint (1958); Tucker (1975); Wakefield (1960); Watters (1971); Zinn (1965).

Appendix 5 Indigenous Protest Leaders and Their Later Organizational Affiliations within the Movement

Students	Later Organizational Affiliations
Marion Barry	SNCC
James Bevel	SCLC
Ezell Blair, Jr.	
Julian Bond	SNCC
Robert Booker	
Amos Brown	NAACP
Callas Brown	NAACP
Lee Butler	
Stokely Carmichael	SNCC
David Carter	
Oretha Castle	CORE
MacArthur Cotton	SNCC
Courtland Cox	
David Dennis	CORE
Dion Diamond	SNCC
Paul Dietrich	SNCC
Rev. Elroy Embree	
Tom Gaither	NAACP, CORE
Lennie Glover	
Lawrence Guyot	SNCC
John Hardy	SNCC
Frank Holloway	SNCC
Timothy Jenkins	
Major Johns	CORE, SCLC
Joseph Charles Jones	SNCC
Ed King	SNCC
Lonnie King	
Bernard LaFayette	SNCC
Rev. James Lawson	SCLC, NAACP
Bernard Lee	SCLC
John Lewis	SNCC, SCLC
Ruby Lombard	CORE
Bill Mahoney	SNCC
Franklin McCain	
Charles McDew	SNCC
Joseph McNeil	
Fred Moore	
Ronnie M. Moore	CORE
Donald Moss	NAACP
Diane Nash	NAACP
Richard Frank Parker	NAACP
Charles Person	

Students	*Later Organizational Affiliations*
George Raymond, Jr.	CORE
Cordell Reagon	SNCC
David Richmond	
Marvin Robinson	CORE
Weldon Rougeau	CORE
Charles Sherrod	SNCC
Jerome Smith	CORE
Ruby Smith	SNCC
Patricia Stephens	CORE
Priscilla Stephens	CORE
Matt Suarez	CORE
Henry Thomas	SNCC
Joan Trumpauer	
C. T. Vivian	SCLC

Ministers	*Later Organizational Affiliations*
Ralph Abernathy	SCLC
Joshua Barney	
L. Roy Bennett	
Charles Billups	SCLC
J. W. Bonner	
William H. Borders	SCLC
Henry Clay Bunton	SCLC
B. Elton Cox	
W. T. Crutcher	
G. G. Daniels	
A. L. Davis	SCLC
Grady Davis	
J. A. DeLaine	
W. A. Dennis	SCLC
Julius T. Douglas	
K. S. Dupont	
E. N. French	
R. J. Glasco	
Robert S. Graetz	
Edward Graham	SCLC
W. H. Hall	SCLC
Ben L. Hooks	SCLC
H. H. Hubbard	
Robert E. James	SCLC
E. W. Jarrett	
Theodore Jemison	SCLC
Vernon Johns	

Ministers	Later Organizational Affiliations
Clarence Jones	
D. E. King	SCLC
Martin Luther King, Sr.	SCLC
Martin Luther King, Jr.	SCLC
Samuel B. Kyles	
George Lee	
Roy Love	
Matthew McCullum	SCLC
Douglas E. Moore	SCLC
J. L. Netters	
J. S. Phifer	
W. J. Powell	
Solomon Seay	SCLC
Fred Lee Shuttlesworth	SCLC
B. J. Simms	
Kelly Miller Smith	SCLC
Daniel Speed	SCLC
A. K. Stanley	
Charles K. Steele	SCLC
John L. Tilley	SCLC
Wyatt T. Walker	SCLC, NAACP
Leon Whitney	
Hosea Williams	SCLC
Samuel Williams	SCLC
A. W. Wilson	
Calvin W. Woods	
Virgil Wood	SCLC
R. K. Young	SCLC

Independent	Later Organizational Affiliations
Euretta Adair	
Dr. W. G. Anderson	
Wiley Branton	
R. H. Craig	
David H. Dwight	
Charles Gomillion	
Fred Gray	
Richard Haley	CORE
Dr. Vivian Henderson	
David Hood, Jr.	
Luther Jackson	
Dr. Moses Jones	
C. W. King	
George W. Lee	
Julia Lewis	CORE

Independent	*Later Affiliations*
Professor Rufus Lewis	
Dr. Gilbert Mason	
John H. McCray	
Floyd McKissick	CORE
William P. Mitchell	
Professor James E. Pierce	
Jo Ann Robinson	
Blevin Stout	
J. J. Thomas	
William Thomas	
Dr. J. E. Walker	

Sources: Brink and Harris (1963); Brooks (1974); Clayton (1964); Hughes (1962); King (1958); Lawson (1976); Lomax (1962); Meier and Rudwick (1973); Oppenheimeer (1963); Parker (1974); Peck (1960); Proudfoot (1962); Quint (1958); Tucker (1975); Wakefield (1960); Watters (1971); Zinn (1965).

Notes

INTRODUCTION

1. Evidence supportive of this assertion comes from a cursory analysis of the ways in which social movements have been conceptualized in recent introductory sociology texts (Bassis et al., 1980: 240–46; Leslie et al., 1980: 256–60; Popenoe, 1980: 537–40; Storer, 1980: 411–14). These texts betray a continued adherence to the classical approach to movement analysis, albeit without the hints of pathology and blatant assertions of irrationality characteristic of the more extreme versions of that approach. I am indebted to Arnold Anderson-Sherman for bringing this evidence to my attention.

CHAPTER 1

1. At the risk of lapsing into simplistic functionalism, I think that Durkheim was probably correct, when he wrote that "a human institution cannot rest upon an error and a lie" (Durkheim, 1965; 14).

2. My comments in this section are based largely on William Kornhauser's book *The Politics of Mass Society* (1959). For other writings in this tradition, see Arendt (1951) and Selznick (1970).

3. For a useful summary of the concept as applied to movement participation, see Louis Kriesberg, *The Sociology of Social Conflicts* (1973: 70–76).

4. In this section I draw heavily on Neil Smelser's *Theory of Collective Behavior* (1962). Other versions of the model can be found in Lang and Lang (1961) and Turner and Killian (1957).

5. At a more fundamental level, classical theorists can also be criticized for failing to adequately define strain. Indeed, in many versions of the model the strains presumed to account for social movements are defined in such ambiguous fashion as to virtually guarantee their existence in the immediate premovement period. Thus, we appear to be engaged in little more than a form of post-hoc analysis. Rule and Tilly express this point nicely in reference to a particular version of the classical model, Davies' J-curve theory of revolution: "Davies appears to start with the accomplished fact of revolution, then cast about in the period immediately preceding it for evidence of the sharp reversal of some need within some part of the population, then look farther back for needs that have undergone increasing satisfaction for some length of time. Given that different groups in any population experience the satisfaction and frustration of various needs at various times, such a search has a high probability of success" (Rule and Tilly, 1975: 49).

6. Adoption of the classical perspective would force us to argue, for example, that the level of strain in American society was significantly lower in the 1980s than it was during the turbulent 60s. Quite apart from the methodological difficulties inherent in operationalizing

the independent variable, I'm not sure there would be much intuitive support for this assertion.

7. Consistent with this point, it is entirely possible that the influence of the various models under discussion here are far more dependent on the ideological demands of the day than on the objective merits of the theories themselves. In this regard, the dominance of the classical model in the 1950s can be seen as stemming from the need of liberal academics to devise a "scientific" theory to discredit the antidemocratic movements (i. e., McCarthyism, Nazism) they were studying. The various classical models, with their heavy suggestions of irrationality, were ideally suited to the task. However, with the emergence of popular left-wing protest movements (i.e., civil rights, antiwar) in the 60s, liberal academia faced a new challenge: positing a revised perspective that cast these "progressive" movements in the favorable light of rationality and courageous resistance to oppression. In short, the development of both the resource mobilization and political process models must be seen in the context of the shift in political climate between the 1950s and 60s and the consequent change in the ideological needs of the academic community.

8. In general, Pinard's summary and critique of psychological models of social movements is as good a one as can be found in the literature (Pinard, 1971: 223–42).

9. For other studies documenting the social integration of movement participants, see Caplan and Paige (1968); Flacks (1967); Fogelson and Hill (1968); Keniston (1968); Oberschall (1971); and Rogin (1967).

10. One exception is Geschwender's article "Social Structure and the Negro Revolt: An Examination of Some Hypotheses" (1964). Here the author attempts to document both a net increase in the proportion of status inconsistents in the black population and a rise in the aggregate level of relative deprivation for the same population. As I note though, Geschwender relies exclusively on objective data to infer the presence of the subjective states of mind he is concerned with.

11. A related weakness concerns the causal ordering of these various psychological states and movement participation. The classical model rests on the assumption that the former serves as the immediate cause of the latter. But empirical studies cited as supporting the classical model consistently lack the time-series data needed to document the causal ordering of the two variables. It may well be that movement participation actually triggers feelings of alienation, relative deprivation, etc., rather than the reverse. At least in the absence of unambiguous time-series data on both variables, this remains as likely a causal proposition as the classical interpretation.

CHAPTER 2

1. Placing people in different theoretical schools is always a tricky and somewhat arbitrary exercise. As I note in the next chapter, Jenkins and Perrow (1977); Leites and Wolf (1970); and Oberschall (1973) also incorporate important aspects of the political process model into their work. Their inclusion in this list, then, does not suggest that their work is synonymous with the resource mobilization model. Rather, they were included because key propositions derived from that model are evident in their work.

2. In referring to resource mobilization theory, I am engaging in a bit of fiction. In truth, resource mobilization is little more than a label that has been applied rather indiscriminately to a disparate group of theorists. So divergent are some of the perspectives to which the label has been applied, that continued adherence to the present use of the term threatens to obscure important differences between distinct schools of thought. To remedy this confusion, Perrow has suggested a distinction between what he calls "RM [resource mobilization] I" and "RM II." RM I refers to the works of Gamson and Tilly among others, while RM II is represented by the work of McCarthy and Zald. As laudable as Perrow's attempt

at clarification is, I think the retention of the resource mobilization label will only serve to confuse the issue further by suggesting a degree of theoretical compatibility that, in fact, is lacking in the two versions of the model he outlines. The basic distinction between these two theoretical perspectives is, however, sound and is evident in this work. That is, many of the ideas of the theorists that Perrow groups under the heading of RM I have been incorporated into the alternative "political process" model of insurgency outlined in the next chapter. What is more, the critique of resource mobilization offered in this chapter is aimed at a version of the mobilization model that roughly corresponds to what Perrow has termed RM II.

3. While not himself a proponent of the resource mobilization model, Michael Schwartz has perhaps most succinctly summarized the "rationalist" view of movement participation when he writes that "people who join protest organizations are at least as rational as those who study them" (1976: 135). More generally, Schwartz's discussion of the rationality/irrationality issue, with respect to movement participation, is as thorough and useful a one as can be found in the literature (1976: 135–45).

4. For several general discussions of the exchange perspective, see Blau (1964); Eisenstadt (1965. 22–49); and Gouldner (1960).

5. Though not specifically concerned with movement organizations, numerous studies have stressed the importance of interorganizational linkages as a means of obtaining resources. For examples of such studies see Esman and Blaise (1966); Levine and White (1961); and Zald (1969).

6. Recent theoretical developments in social psychology have rendered any straightforward link between conditions and behavior increasingly problematic. In place of theories based on unconscious drives and the various mechanistic reinforcement models that for so long dominated the field, social psychologists are beginning to stress the analytic utility of cognitive models that depict the individual as an active participant in the "meaning making" process that continually shapes his or her behavior (see Neisser, 1967).

CHAPTER 3

1. Besides the Rule-Tilly piece, other writings by political theorists have had considerable influence in shaping the perspective outlined here. Indeed, a rapidly growing body of literature on social movements has emerged in recent years and precipitated something of a conceptual revolution in the field. The political process model draws heavily on that literature, even as it reflects a critical stance toward much that has been written. Of those contributing to the literature, the following theorists have advanced specific insights that have been incorporated into the model proposed here: Aveni (1977); Edelman (1971); Ferree and Miller (1977); Freeman (1973); Gamson (1975); Gerlach and Hine (1970); Jenkins (1981); Jenkins and Perrow (1977); Marx (1976); McCarthy and Zald (1973); Oberschall (1973); Pinard (1971); Piven and Cloward (1979); Schwartz (1976); and Wilson and Orum (1976).

2. Even such perceptive analysts as Piven and Cloward seem to echo this line of argument. They assert, for instance, "that it not only requires a major social dislocation before protest can emerge, but that a sequence or combination of dislocations probably must occur before the anger that underlies protest builds to a high pitch, and before that anger can find expression in collective defiance" (Piven and Cloward, 1979: 8). Consistent with the classical model, the image is that of disruptive social change, triggering a rise in aggregate discontent which eventually erupts into collective protest. For reasons noted in Chapter 2, this caual sequence remains problematic.

3. Indeed, the search for micro-level correlates of individual participation has frequently provided evidence of the central importance of existent associational networks. Orum, in his analysis of protest participation among black college students, compared nonparticipants

and participants on a number of background variables such as family income, father's education, incidence of parental desertion, and size of place of residence. In general, the variables tested failed to produce any significant association with protest participation. There was, however, one exception. The variable that best distinguished participants from non-participants was simply the student's integration into the campus community, as measured by number of memberships in campus organizations (Orum, 1972: 27–50).

4. Judging from the passage of Proposition 13 in California we can be reasonably sure that the lack of a "pre-established communication network" was remedied in the twenty-odd years that intervened between the earlier tax revolt and the successful 1978 version.

5. For a general review or introduction to the literature on cultural diffusion, see Brown (1981), Lionberger (1960), or Rogers (1962).

6. Zald and Ash (1970) were but the first to challenge the inevitability ascribed to the process by Weber and Michels (Gerth and Mills, 1946: 297–301; Michels, 1959). Moreover, there now exists impressive empirical evidence supportive of the facilitating, rather than retardant, effect of organization on insurgency (Gamson, 1975: esp. chap. 7; C. Tilly, L. Tilly, and R. Tilly, 1975). Accordingly, current research in the field has shifted from describing the process of oligarchization to specifying the conditions under which movement organizations can be expected to develop in conservative or radical ways (Beach, 1977; Gillespie, 1980).

7. These observations are not made to suggest that insurgent groups should avoid goals and tactics that are likely to be seen by the political establishment as threatening. Indeed, my earlier assertion that the strength of insurgent forces is also a determinant of other groups' responses to the movement carries with it the implicit suggestion that insurgents can pursue any goal or tactic so long as they maintain the strength needed to withstand the social control response these choices produce. Instead, my aim has simply been to discuss the relationship between these various choices and the level of movement opposition they engender. The key point is that movement groups largely determine, by means of the goals and tactics they adopt, the level of opposition they must confront. As Schwartz notes, "in choosing movement activities, a protest group can attain a degree of control over who the opposition will be, and to what degree it will be mobilized" (1976: 162). It therefore behooves insurgents to base their choice of tactics and goals on some realistic assessment of their strength. If they are to survive, movement groups must avoid mobilizing an opposition that is capable of successfully repressing the movement.

Chapter 5

1. Actually the compromise is more accurately viewed as a symbol of the close of Reconstruction rather than an absolute return to regional rule on racial issues. Exclusive southern dominance over the "Negro question" was only truly achieved in the period from 1896 to 1932. The years 1876–96 are more properly seen as a crucial transition period in which the foundations of the South's later hegemony on racial matters were laid (Hirshson, 1962). In this view, the Compromise of 1876 merely demarcates the beginning of this transition period.

2. In fact, insofar as planters no longer had to maintain a slave population, it could be argued that their actual capital outlay was less under the tenant system than under slavery.

3. Nor did the antipathy of the northern industrial elite to the "war issues" diminish with the reestablishment of economic stability. Rather, most industrialists retained, throughout the period, their aversion to such issues, fearing a reoccurrence of sectional strife and the economic disruption characteristic of Reconstruction. As a consequence, the dominant segment of the industrial elite consistently opposed any program designed to benefit southern blacks. The following statement from an 1879 *New York Journal of Commerce* story ex-

emplifies the position adopted by northern industrialists throughout the period. Commenting on a proposed plan to finance the migration of freed blacks to several northern states, the journal noted that the southern planters were "justly sensitive . . . to every word and deed in the North which bear the construction of interference between the late slave and the late master. We can assure the Southerners, once and for all, that, excepting a few incurable fanatics who have little money or influence, the people of the North feel no desire to break up the present Southern labor system, and will contribute a hundred dollars to transport the refugees back to their homes from Kansas, to every dollar given by any rabid hater of the South toward depriving the capitalists of the only labor available to them" (in Hirshson, 1962: 71).

4. Blacks were not the only segment of the southern population to lose the vote as a result of the disenfranchisement campaigns. The voting strength of poor whites also declined, leaving the southern electorate with a highly upper-class flavor.

5. The poor white farmers of the South were also victimized by the Populist defeat, sacrificing a potentially effective electoral coalition with blacks for the dubious emotional gratification of "white supremacy."

6. This relationship holds over time. That is, those states with the highest black out-migration totals remained, well into the 1960s, the states with the lowest black voter-registration rates. For example, the correlation between the percent of the black voting-age population registered to vote in 1964 and the total number of black out-migrants between 1910 and 1960 is −.76.

7. The NAACP opposed Parker's nomination because of his "clear supremacist views." As a candidate for governor of North Carolina in 1920, Parker had, for example, remarked that the "participation of the Negro in politics" was "a source of evil and danger to both races." And later, that "the Negro has not yet reached that stage in his development when he can share the burden and responsibilities of government" (in Sitkoff, 1978: 85).

8. For an interesting account of the March on Washington movement, see Garfinkel (1959).

9. For instance, in his 1953 study of the "Organizational Activities of Rural Negroes in Mississippi," Payne reported an average of more than one church membership per person. Moreover, he found that church memberships outnumbered all other organizational affiliations combined by a margin of more than three to one (Payne, 1953: 3–4).

10. Many analysts have acknowledged the dominant role played by the rural black church during this period in helping to encourage accommodation rather than resistance to the prevailing racial status quo. See, for example, Dollard (1957: 248); Johnson (1941: 135–36); Mays and Nicholson (1969); Myrdal (1944: 852).

11. The urban basis of the NAACP is readily reflected in the location of these thirteen chapters. They were located in the following southern cities: Atlanta, Tampa, Richmond, Savannah, Columbia, Jacksonville, Athens, Raleigh, Charleston, Augusta, Greensboro, Norfolk, and Durham (Kellogg, 1967: 134).

12. For figures confirming this statement see Johnson (1930: 232); U.S. Bureau of the Census, Census of the Population: 1950, vol. 2 (1952); U.S. Bureau of the Census, Census of the Population: 1960, Characteristics of the Population, U.S. Summary (1962: table 239).

13. That the later protest campaigns were disproportionately centered in urban areas is obvious from an examination of available data. Of the 394 movement-initiated events reported by the New York Times that occurred in the South between 1955 and 1961, 386, or 98 percent, took place in urban areas. From "newspaper files and accounts published by the Southern Regional Council," Oppenheimer compiled a list of 102 sites that were witness to student-initiated protest activity during 1960. Of these, 98, or 96 percent, occurred in urban, as opposed to rural, locales (Oppenheimer, 1963: 63–64). Since only 58 percent of the southern black population was residing in urban areas in 1960, the disproportionate urban locus of the demonstrations is indeed impressive. There may, of course, be a slight

underestimation of rural protest activity built into these figures as a consequence of the decreased publicity that normally accompanies any event that occurs in an isolated locale (Danzger, 1975). But any such bias would probably be too small to reduce the significance of these figures. The fact remains that the migration to urban locales within the South facilitated insurgency by affording blacks the personal resources, physical proximity, and protection from the more virulent forms of white racism that they had lacked in rural areas.

14. The number of black churches rose from 42,585 in 1926 to 49,882 in 1962. The comparable increase in total church membership was from 5,203,487 in 1926 to 10,048,493 in 1962 (Murray, 1942: 94–95; Washington, 1964: 233).

15. One additional characteristic of the urban church strengthened its position as a potential vehicle for collective protest. Quite simply, in comparison to rural congregations, the urban church was, as a rule, far more independent of white control. This was true in two senses. First, the vast majority of urban churchgoers were themselves not as economically dependent on whites as their rural counterparts, a large percentage of whom remained tied to the tenant farm system. Second, as an institution, the urban church usually relied less on white support than the rural church did. As many observers have remarked, the black church, especially, in urban areas, represented the institution within the black community that was least controlled or "penetrated" by whites (Matthews and Prothro, 1966: 185; Mays and Nicholson, 1969: 279–80; Washington, 1964: 229). Oberschall, in the following passage, touches on both these points: "In the middle-sized and large cities . . . the position of the large and relatively affluent black churches was much stronger. Its ministers and finances were truly independent of white control. Its middle-class, professional congregation enjoyed social leadership and prestige within the entire black community and possessed considerable financial resources independent of white control" (1973: 222).

16. The term "units" refers to all local NAACP-affiliated membership bodies. This includes all regular branches, youth councils, and college chapters.

17. Even when all earlier values of the independent variable are controlled for by running a lagged path-analysis on both dependent variables, the reciprocal relationship between Supreme Court decisions and NAACP chapters is still evident. The only change is that the effects of NAACP growth on Court decisions are even more immediate than the simple correlations suggest. When chapters are treated as the independent variable, the only significant partial correlations occur with chapters lagged 0 to 1 years behind Court decisions. When the causal order is reversed, the relationship between the two variables conforms to that shown in table 5.8. That is, the highest partial correlations are produced by lagging Court decisions from 4 to 6 years behind chapters.

18. *Brown* v. *Board of Education of Topeka*, 349 U.S. 294 (1954).

19. The sources of data for these various measures are: annual per capita GNP, U.S. Bureau of the Census, *Historical Statistics of The United States, Colonial Times to 1970, Bicentennial Edition, Part 1* (1975: 224); annual number of foreign immigrants, ibid., p. 105; season average price per pound of cotton, ibid., pp. 516–17; annual number of wage earners in manufacturing, ibid., p. 137; yearly balance of Supreme Court decisions, see figure 5.2; annual number of new NAACP chapters, Anglin (1949: 128); annual number of lynchings, Ploski and Marr (1976: 275–76); percent of the black population living in urban areas, Price (1969: 11); percent of all sourthern blacks 5–19 years of age in school, for figures from 1900–1930, Johnson (1930: 232); for same figures for 1930–50, U.S. Bureau of the Census, *Census of the Population: 1950*; for same figures for 1950–60, U.S. Bureau of the Census, *Census of the Population: 1960*, Characteristics of the Population, U.S. Summary (1962, table 239).

20. This imprecision is a function of the small number of data points on which the measure of black out-migration is based. Estimates of black out-migration were only available for

the years of the decennial census and at mid-decade. Therefore, all coefficients involving black out-migration are based on only eleven data points.

21. My operational definitions of black out-migration, black urbanization, and southern black educational advances rest on only eleven data points. Therefore, special caution should be exercised in interpreting the significance of any of the relationships involving these three variables.

CHAPTER 6

1. This count of movement-initiated events was obtained through content-coding of news abstracts contained in the annual *New York Times Index*. More specifically, in the indexes corresponding to the years 1948–70, all story synopses contained under the two headings "Negroes—U.S.—General," and "Education—U.S.—Racial Integration," were read and coded according to criteria drawn up prior to the start of research. The decision to restrict coding to these two headings was based on a careful examination of the classification system employed in the *Index*. This examination convinced me that the overwhelming majority of events relevant to the movement were contained under the two general headings listed above. In all, better than 12,000 summaries were coded from a total of about 29,000 read. Only information relevant to the general topic of black insurgency was coded. As a result, many other topics were excluded from the analysis, for example, stories documenting the achievements of black athletes or entertainers. Besides this general criterion of relevance, summaries to be coded also had to be judged unambiguous with regard to the identification of the event, its location, and the individual(s) or group(s) who were responsible for initiating the action. If the story was ambiguous on any one of these three dimensions it was excluded from the analysis. When completed, the coding afforded rough measures of the extent and nature of black insurgency over the course of the study period.

Obviously, this constitutes only the most general description of the coding procedures employed in this study. For a more detailed discussion of these procedures as well as a description of the specific coding categories used, the reader is referred to Appendix 1.

2. The analysis presented here hardly constitutes an exhaustive test of the classical account of movement emergence. It was never intended as such. Instead, I have sought merely to analyze the simple relationship between various economic indices presumed (by proponents of the model) to measure system strain and the incidence of black insurgency over the course of the study period. No doubt, more sophisticated operational definitions of strain could be devised and their association with black protest activity assessed using techniques other than those employed here. However, there is little reason to suspect that these attempts to salvage the classical model would prove any more successful than the one reported in the text. This suspicion rests both on the damaging evidence presented here and the more general theoretical deficiencies discussed in Chapter 1. Moreover, even if such attempts yielded evidence more consistent with the classical interpretation, we would still be stuck with the seemingly insoluble problem of assessing the significance of these conflicting findings.

3. The operationalization of external resource support is not without its difficulties. The problem stems from the failure of mobilization theorists to advance a precise definition of resources. We are thus left to operationalize the concept ourselves. Obviously, one could propose a number of such definitions, but probably the most defensible, and the one to be utilized here, is that which defines resources solely in monetary terms. That is, the level of external resource support is simply operationalized as the dollar amount of financial contributions, grants, etc. made by outside groups to formal movement organizations.

This definition has a number of methodological and theoretical advantages to recommend it. First, the definition is clearly quantitative, thus facilitating statistical analysis. Second, it would seem to be face valid. That is, as ambiguous as the term "resource" is, it would be hard for any proponent of the mobilization perspective to quarrel with applying that designation to money. Indeed, insofar as it can be used to purchase other goods and services, money may well be the most "flexible" of resources (Perrow, 1968). Finally, unlike other commodities one might base a definition on, money has the added advantage of generating records available to investigators.

4. In constructing this measure of external support, I adopted several simplifying guidelines. First, because of a paucity of information on lesser-known movement groups, data were gathered on only the five major civil-rights organizations. These five groups are the NAACP, Congress of Racial Equality, Southern Christian Leadership Conference, Student Nonviolent Coordinating Committee, and the NAACP Legal Defense and Education Fund. Second, an inability, in all cases, to distinguish between income derived from indigenous and external sources led to the adoption of the following convention: all income for each organization, except the NAACP, was counted as outside support. In the case of the NAACP most of its annual reports listed both the total yearly income of the organization and the amount received from regular branch memberships. By subtracting the latter figure from the former, I arrived at a consistent means of distinguishing between indigenous and external support. In the case of the other organizations, the decision to define total annual income as synonymous with external support stemmed from impressionistic descriptions and scattered data that confirmed the organization's heavy reliance on external as opposed to indigenous sources of support. Various sources of financial data were employed in constructing this measure. In the case of CORE, Meier and Rudwick's definitive account of the organization served as a consistent source of information. As just noted, data for the NAACP were taken from that organization's annual reports for the years of the study period. Questionnaires requesting the relevant data were sent to the NAACP Legal Defense and Education Fund and SCLC, of whom only the former returned a completed questionnaire. Income information for SCLC and SNCC was obtained from a variety of impressionistic accounts of those organizations. Appendix 3 presents the full range of income information obtained through these varied efforts.

5. Even when we control for the effects of earlier values of the independent variable (by means of a distributed lag analysis), the effect of events on income remains greatest when the former is lagged three and four years behind the latter, with only small partial effects thereafter.

At the same time, running a distributed lag analysis treating income as the independent variable again fails to yield evidence consistent with the resource mobilization model. Although the partial correlations produced by lagging income three and four years behind events are significant, they are in the opposite direction than the mobilization model predicts. That is, the correlations are negative. All correlations at other points in time are not significant.

6. More accurately, no actions attributed to Martin Luther King, Jr., or SCLC after January 10–11, 1957, are included in the category of church, student, or NAACP-initiated activity. Over the course of those two days, SCLC was formally established as a movement organization at a conference held in Atlanta (Clayton, 1964: 12).

7. These last two models could have as easily been relied upon to explain NAACP's role in the generation of social insurgency. Numerous impressionistic descriptions of NAACP membership have asserted its disproportionate interracial and middle-class character; these are attributes consistent with the aforementioned formulations. However, I have been unable to find in the literature any specific attempt to account for NAACP involvement in the movement on the basis of the individual characteristics of its members.

8. In his analysis of the People's Democracy, a Northern Irish civil rights organization composed primarily of students, Beach also notes the decline of activism during the summer

recess: "In August 1969 widespread rioting broke out in Belfast. The PD [People's De-
mocracy], shrunken in size due to summer recess, took no active part as a group in the
fighting" (1977: 309).

9. No doubt the lack of drama associated with these institutionalized forms of insurgency
accounts for the relative obscurity of the NAACP leaders listed in appendix 4.

10. Martin Luther King, Jr., provides a concrete example of how this protective institutional structure facilitated his assumption of a leadership role in the specific case of the
Montgomery bus boycott. In *Stride Toward Freedom* he writes: "In this crisis the officers
and members of my church were always nearby to lend their encouragement and active
support. As I gradually lost my role as husband and father, having to be away from home
for hours and sometimes days at a time, the women of the church came into the house to
keep Coretta company. Often they volunteered to cook the meals and clean, or help with
the baby. Many of the men took turns as watchmen, or drove me around. . . . Nor did my
congregation ever complain when the multiplicity of my new responsibilities caused me to
lag in my pastoral duties. For months my day-to-day contact with my parishioners had
almost ceased. I had become no more than a Sunday preacher. But my church willingly
shared me with the community, and threw their own considerable resources of time and
money into the struggle" (King, 1958: 141).

11. Later in the period, local NAACP youth councils in Oklahoma turned their attention
to segregated public accommodations in a series of sit-in demonstrations that foreshadowed
the widespread outbreak of similar student-initiated actions several years later. Here again,
though, the spread of the Oklahoma sit-in campaign illustrates the dynamic under discussion.
Existing links between the local youth councils provided a means by which news of the
campaign could be disseminated, thus encouraging the initiation of similar protests in nearby
towns. Oppenheimer's description of the campaign serves to illustrate this phenomenon:
"On Sunday, August 24, 1958, 20 pairs of Negro youths attended 20 white churches; they
were refused admittance at only three, making Oklahoma City the first city to have a 'pray-
in'. . . . On August 29, 1958, the NAACP Youth Council in Wichita, Kansas, staged a sit-
in at the Dockum Drug Store. The idea had come through official NAACP channels from
Oklahoma City. After four days of sitting, the manager of the store called the NAACP
branch president and told him the policy of the store would be changed to serve everyone
equally. The news spread and sit-ins took place in Enid, Tulsa, and Stillwater, Oklahoma,
and in Kansas City, Kansas, with varying success" (Oppenheimer, 1963: 52).

12. Unlike most campaigns during this period, the Montgomery boycott is unique in the
amount of descriptive historical material it generated. For information on the boycott, see
Brooks (1974: 95–119); King (1958); Walton (1956).

13. Actually the organization formed at the January conference in Atlanta was a forerunner
of the SCLC and was called the Southern Leadership Conference on Transportation and
Nonviolent Integration.

CHAPTER 7

1. See Zinn's account of the Albany campaign (1965: 123, 146); Meier and Rudwick's
description of a 1963 CORE-sponsored protest movement in Tallahassee (1973: 221); or
King's book on the Birmingham campaign (1963).

2. The compilation of a complete list of the cases in which the church served as an
institutional focal point for campaigns initiated by formal movement organizations could
easily constitute a separate book. The reader will have to settle for the following illustrative
examples: King (1963); Lomax (1962: 125, 130); Meier and Rudwick (1973: 166, 267); Walker
(1971: 380).

3. The list in appendix 5 is identical to the one in appendix 4 except for the fact that it omits all local NAACP chapter leaders. Obviously all such leaders are already affiliated with a formal movement organization. In addition, I would like to acknowledge my debt to Aldon Morris, who verified the later affiliation of many ministers with SCLC.

4. However, even the outbreak of protest activity in the North, on many occasions, reflected the movement's essential southern basis. In fact, most of the early northern protest activity took the form of sympathy demonstrations or aggressive picketing in support of southern campaigns. For an example, see Meier and Rudwick's discussion of the effect that the outbreak of the sit-ins had on the revitalization of CORE activity in the North (1973: 101–2, 121).

5. Of the eight towns in which boycotts are known to have occurred, only two, Chattanooga, Tennessee, and Tallahassee, Florida, are not in the Deep South. Of the other six towns, two are in Alabama (Birmingham and Montgomery), two in Louisiana (New Orleans and Baton Rouge), and one each in Georgia (Atlanta) and South Carolina (Rock Hill).

6. The question of how this consensus developed is an interesting topic in its own right. While integration had long constituted a powerful ideology in black sociopolitical thought, so had a well-developed separatist philosophy. What makes the period from 1930 to 1965 so unusual is the nearly exclusive dominance of the former over the latter. To account for the causes of this ideological dominance is beyond the scope of this book. No doubt part of the answer lies in the success of the campaign to discredit Marcus Garvey, the last significant proponent of separatism prior to this period. The myth, championed by elements within both the black and white communities, made Garvey out to be part charlatan, part buffoon. In truth, he was neither, but the strength of his following in the 1920s made him a threat to vested interests in both communities and resulted in the campaign of public vilification that reduced support for separatism within the black population.

7. Some have argued that the movement was actually dominated during this period by five, rather than four, organizations. The fifth group mentioned is the National Urban League. Certainly the Urban League was an influential organization, but its influence was far greater in social welfare and business circles than within the movement itself. Indeed, the organization's visibility within the "liberal establishment" (foundations, academia, social welfare groups) may help to account for the prominent role ascribed to it by many of the movement's contemporary chroniclers who were largely drawn from the same "establishment" (cf. Clark, 1970). At the same time, one will search vainly in the accounts of actual movement campaigns for any mention of the involvement of the Urban League. This is not to disparage the organization, only to report that its efforts were expended in arenas other than those of local insurgency. This conclusion is supported by the *New York Times* data, which attribute the following yearly event-totals to the Urban League: 1961, 7 (6 percent); 1962, 13 (12 percent); 1963, 21 (8 percent); 1964, 25 (8 percent); 1965, 7 (2 percent).

8. For historical documentation of SNCC's dominant role in both COFO and the MFDP see Watters (1971: 298–322) and Zinn (1965).

9. This analysis was based exclusively on comparable Gallup polls conducted between 1961 and 1965. Smith (1980) has assembled a richer data set consisting of all such surveys conducted by the major polling organizations between 1946 and 1976. In all, he reports the results of nineteen such polls between 1961 and 1965. His findings, however, are consistent with those reported here. While he does not report the rank order of "civil rights" among all problems identified in each survey, the percentage of respondents listing that as the "most important" problem remained high throughout the period. In ten of the nineteen surveys, at least 20 percent of the respondents identified civil rights as the country's most important problem, while in another three the figure was between ten and 20 percent (Smith, 1980: 170–71).

10. While analytically defensible, the distinction between factors internal and external to the movement is frequently hard to maintain empirically. For instance, in regard to both the black vote and the international political pressures discussed in the text, the facilitative effect of each on protest activity stemmed, at least in part, from the conscious efforts of black leaders to capitalize on their obvious potential as bargaining tools. With respect to the black vote, as early as the mid-1930s black leaders were beginning aggressively to publicize and exploit its significance in their dealings with national political figures. In a memorandum quoted by Freidel (1965), one-time NAACP executive secretary Walter White recounts a meeting with President Roosevelt that illustrates this phenomenon. Conceiving of the meeting as an opportunity to lobby for an antilynching bill then before Congress, White sought through documentation to remind the president of the growing significance of the black vote. His memo reads in part: "the Secretary . . . called the President's attention to . . . tables . . . in which 17 states, with a total electoral vote of 281, have a Negro voting population, 21 years of age and over, sufficient to determine in a close election" (in Freidel, 1965: 90).

In similar fashion, movement leaders sought to exploit the international political pressures noted in the text. Amid growing concern over expanding Russian influence in Eastern Europe, the NAACP's monthly magazine, Crisis, warned shortly after the close of World War II that "only if our system distributes . . . the rewards of democracy to all citizens regardless of race, will it prevent Russia from dominating certain European states and prevent sneers and snickers to our righteous words" (in Lawson, 1976: 122).

In the case of both these external factors, then, processes internal to the movement contributed to the favorable effect they had on the structure of black political opportunities during the period in question. With respect to the final "external" factor, growing public support for the movement, the interplay between internal and external processes is all the more apparent. Obviously, one of the primary forces contributing to the growing salience of civil rights was the movement itself, which sought, through dramatic protest, to generate support from other segments of society. However, once mobilized, this supportive body of public opinion came to constitute an independent force promoting expanded protest opportunities.

11. For several accounts of the controversy surrounding Lewis's speech and its resolution, see Muse (1968: 15); Zinn (1965: 190, 208, 211–12, 215).

12. For example, Oberschall reports that SNCC in 1965 drew its $800,000 budget from "churches, foundations, friends of SNCC groups and direct mail appeals" (1978: 259). Other accounts of SNCC's financial situation during the early 1960s are consistent with this general portrait (Laue, 1965: 125; Muse, 1968: 23; Zinn, 1965: 10). According to Meier and Rudwick's definitive history of the organization, CORE displayed much the same pattern of financial dependency as SNCC. As the authors note at several points in their book, CORE's funds were drawn almost entirely from northern liberal supporters, with only minimal contributions coming from the local chapters themselves (Meier and Rudwick, 1973: 78, 81, 107, 119, 127, 225). Finally, during this period, SCLC's support base was drawn disproportionately from the same general sources mentioned above in connection with the other civil rights organizations (Clark, 1970: 293; Clayton, 1964; Oberschall, 1973: 218).

13. This account of the Kennedy administration's role in the 1962–64 Voter Education Project is based on the descriptive accounts contained in Brooks (1974: 171–72); Lawson (1976: 260–65); Piven and Cloward (1979); Watters (1971: 132–34); and Zinn (1965: 58–59).

14. This thesis is advanced quite persuasively by Pat Watters in his book Down to Now: Reflections on the Southern Civil Rights Movement (1971).

15. For representative accounts of these two episodes, see Brooks (1974: 165 and 237).

16. For accounts of the Freedom Rides see Brooks (1974: 159–67); Meier and Rudwick (1973: 135–45); Peck (1962); and Zinn (1965: 40–61).

17. For a more detailed account of events in Albany the reader is referred to Watters (1971: 141–229) and Zinn (1962).

18. In what is perhaps the most moving of the impressionistic accounts of the black movement, Watters (1971) argues that concepts such as "defeat" and "victory" are irrelevant in view of the moral victory achieved by movement participants even in the face of what would objectively be termed defeat. He advances this argument most forcefully in his discussion of the movement's "defeat" in Albany, evoking as he does the extraordinary beauty, inspiration, and exhilaration inherent in the movement, qualities all too often ignored in dispassionate social scientific accounts of black insurgency during this period. While I do not fully subscribe to Watters view that the movement's greatest achievements were spiritual and not material, his is, nonetheless, a healthy and necessary corrective to the opposite view and its dominance in the literature.

CHAPTER 8

1. The only material to appear in the literature that bears on the topic of movement decline is contained in three references whose relationship to the subject is tangential at best. First, there is an article entitled, "The Disintegration of the Negro Non-violent Movement," by Von Eschen, Kirk, and Pinard (1969). In this work, however, the authors are concerned not with the ultimate decline of black insurgency in the late 1960s but rather with the movement's gradual rejection of nonviolence in the mid-1960s. A second piece bearing some relationship to the topic is Oberschall's 1978 article, "The Decline of the 1960's Social Movements." Again, however, Oberschall does not address the topic of black insurgency directly; he is concerned with a more general analysis of the factors conditioning the overall decline in movement activity in the early 1970s. Finally, there is the impressionistic account of the movement's demise contained in Pat Watter's book *Down to Now, Reflections on the Southern Civil Rights Movement* (1971). Watters's work, however, shares with the others a focus slightly different from the one pursued here. Instead of a sociological analysis of the general decline in black insurgency in the late 1960s, Watters offers only an impressionistic account of the termination of the distinctly nonviolent, southern civil rights movement in the period from 1960 to 1965.

2. Yet, if we are to believe other observers, even Downes's figures seriously underestimate the level of "urban disorders" during these years. For example, the Civil Disorders Clearinghouse at Brandeis University recorded 233 disorders for the single year 1967, and an additional 295 in just the first four months of 1968 (Lemberg Center for the Study of Violence, 1968: 60).

3. This collapse is also reflected in changes over time in the way blacks evaluated the performance of the major movement groups. As part of a series of national surveys of blacks conducted by *Newsweek* and Louis Harris in 1963, 1966, and 1969, respondents were asked to "rate the job done" by various movement groups or leaders as either "excellent," "pretty good," "only fair," or "poor." The rankings are interesting both for the indirect evidence they provide for the strength of the movement's organizational structure in 1963 and for the clear indication of the collapse of that structure after 1966. A sampling of findings will convey the general trend in these rankings. Seventy-five percent of all respondents gave the NAACP a rating of "excellent" in 1963. Only 37 percent did so in 1969. Similarly, the percentage rating CORE's performance as "excellent" slid from 38 to 16 between 1963 and 1969. For SNCC the drop was from 23 percent in 1966 to 11 percent three years later. And so it went for nearly all major groups or figures in the movement. Only Martin Luther King's ranking improved over the period. The irony in this, of course, is that King had already been dead a year when the last survey was conducted.

4. For accounts of the convention challenge mounted by the MFDP and the subsequent disagreement within the movement as to the merits of the seating compromise offered insurgents by Democratic party regulars, see Lawson (1976: 301–6); and Zinn (1965: 253–57).

5. The Meridith march began inauspiciously enough when on June 5, 1966, the first black student at the University of Mississippi, James Meridith, set forth from Memphis en route to Jackson, Mississippi, in his walk to dramatize the "all-pervasive and overriding fear that dominates the day-to-day life of the Negro in the United States" (in Brooks, 1974: 273). On the second day of the journey, however, Meridith was shot, prompting the major movement organizations to organize an expanded march ostensibly in his honor. What resulted was nothing so simple. In the chaos and haggling that insued, both the NAACP and Urban League withdrew early on to protest the sweeping march resolution proposed by SNCC and CORE, leaving only the latter two groups and SCLC to stage the march. However, even this reduced coalition proved unstable, as Stokely Carmichael and King wound up competing for the loyalties of march participants and staging a kind of traveling public debate over the merits of their respective visions of the movement. That neither emerged the clearly dominant figure was far less significant than the divisions revealed by the march and the wounds inflicted along the way.

6. Numerous empirical investigations of riot participation have failed to turn up evidence of disproportionate criminal involvement in the disorders (see for example, Fogelson and Hill, 1968; Oberschall, 1971). With regard to the presence of "outside agitators," or "subversive elements," even such official reports as those compiled by the FBI, CIA, and Kerner Commission have failed to uncover evidence of significant involvement by any such elements (Fogelson, 1971: 149–50; Keesing's Reports, 1970: 168–70).

7. More accurately, by the late 1960s, the NAACP represented the bounds of acceptability when it came to contributing to black organizations. That is, the NAACP was the most "radical" organization still commanding significant external support. Other organizations—the majority not specifically those of a "movement" nature—also benefited from a marked increase in external support. This overwhelming conservative bias in external funding is well documented in a 1970 study of corporate America's financial contributions to urban affairs programs (Cohn, 1970). In a section of the article entitled "Shift of Funds," the author offers the following summary of the major organizations benefiting from corporate support: "Organizations benefitting most from corporate donations are those specifically oriented to minority-group problems. Both the Urban Coalition and the National Alliance of Businessmen are favored, as are the National Association for the Advancement of Colored People, the United Negro College Fund, and the Urban League.

Approximately one-fourth of the 247 companies have added at least one of the latter three to their donations list since 1967; another 23 companies, which had contributed to these organizations before 1967, are now giving significantly more. . . . Corporate liberality is less evident, however, where the more militant minority-group organizations such as CORE, SNCC, and the National Welfare Rights Organization are concerned . . . only 3 of 247 companies surveyed responded with cash contributions" (Cohn, 1970: 71, 73).

8. A particularly chilling portrait of the mentality underlying the dominant law enforcement response to the riots is provided by Gary Wills in his book *The Second Civil War* (1968).

Bibliography

BOOKS AND ARTICLES

Abeles, Ronald P. 1976. "Relative Deprivation, Rising Expectations, and Black Militancy" *Journal of Social Issues* 32 (no. 2): 119–37.

Alford, Robert R., and Roger Friedland. 1975. "Political Participation and Public Policy." *Annual Review of Sociology* 1: 429–79.

Allen, Michael Patrick. 1974. "The Structure of Interorganizational Elite Cooptation: Interlocking Corporate Directorates." *American Sociological Review* 39 (no. 3): 393–403.

Allen, Robert L. 1970. *Black Awakening in Capitalist America.* Garden City, New York: Doubleday.

Almond, Gabriel, and Sidney Verba. 1965. *The Civic Culture.* Boston: Little, Brown.

Anglin, Robert A. 1949. "A Sociological Analysis of a Pressure Group." Ph.D. diss., Indiana University.

Arendt, Hannah. 1951. *The Origins of Totalitarianism.* New York: Harcourt, Brace.

Atwood, Rufus. 1962. "The Origin and Development of the Negro Public College with Special Reference to the Land-grant College." *Journal of Negro Education* 31 (no. 3): 240–50.

Aveni, Adrian F. 1977. "Organizational Linkages and Resource Mobilization: The Significance of Linkage Strength and Breadth." Paper delivered at the American Sociological Association meetings, Chicago, 1977.

Aya, Rod. 1979. "Theories of Revolution Reconsidered: Contrasting Models of Collective Violence." *Theory and Society* 8 (no. 1): 39–99.

Bachrach, Peter, and Morton S. Baratz. 1973. "Two Faces of Power." In William E. Connolly, ed., *The Bias of Pluralism.* New York: Lieber-Atherton.

Badger, Henry G. 1951. *Statistics of Negro Colleges and Universities: Students, Staff, and Finances, 1900–1950.* Circular no. 293 (April). Washington, D.C.: Office of Education, Federal Security Agency.

Bagdikian, Ben H. 1972. "The Politics of American Newspapers." *Columbia Journalism Review* 10: 8–13.

Baron, Harold M. 1971. "The Demand for Black Labor: Historical Notes on the Political Economy of Racism." *Radical American* 5 (no. 2): 1–46.

Bassis, Michael S., Richard J. Gelles, Ann Levine. 1980. *Sociology: an Introduction.* New York: Random House.

Beach, Stephen W. 1977. "Social Movement Radicalization: The Case of the People's Democracy in Northern Ireland." *Sociological Quarterly* 18 (Summer): 305–18.

Beale, Calvin L. 1966. "The Negro in American Agriculture." In John P. Davis, ed., *The American Negro Reference Book*. Englewood Cliffs, N.J.: Prentice-Hall, 161–204.

Bell, Inge Powell. 1971. "Status Discrepancy and the Radical Rejection of Nonviolence." In John H. Bracey, Jr., August Meier, and Elliott Rudwick, eds., *Conflict and Competition: Studies in the Recent Black Protest Movement*. Belmont, Calif.: Wadsworth Publishing Company.

Bennett, Lerone, Jr. 1966. *Confrontation: Black and White*. Baltimore, Md.: Penguin Books.

Berger, Morroe. 1950. *Equality by Statute*. New York: Columbia University Press.

Bergman, Peter M. 1969. *The Chronological History of the Negro in America*. New York: Harper and Row.

Blau, Peter M. 1964. *Exchange and Power in Social Life*. New York: John Wiley and Sons.

Breed, Warren. 1958. "Mass Communication and Sociocultural Integration." *Social Forces* 37: 109–16.

Breton, A., and R. Breton. 1969. "An Economic Theory of Social Movements." *American Economic Review Papers and Proceedings of the American Economic Association*, December 28–30, 1968: 59 (no. 2) (May).

Brink, William, and Louis Harris. 1963. *The Negro Revolution in America*. New York: Simon and Schuster.

———. 1967. *Black and White*. New York: Simon and Schuster.

Broderick, Francis L., and August Meier, eds. 1965. *Negro Protest Thought in the Twentieth Century*. Indianapolis: Bobbs-Merrill.

Brooks, Thomas R. 1974. *Walls Come Tumbling Down: A History of the Civil Rights Movement, 1940–1970*. Englewood Cliffs, N.J.: Prentice-Hall.

Broom, Leonard. 1959. "Social Differentiation and Stratification." In Robert K. Merton, Leonard Broom, and Leonard S. Cottrell, eds., *Sociology Today*. New York: Basic Books, 429–41.

Broom, Leonard, and Norval Glenn. 1970. "Occupation and Income." In Richard P. Young, ed. *Roots of Rebellion*. New York: Harper and Row, 71–85.

Brown, Lawrence A. 1981. *Innovation Diffusion*. London and New York: Methuen.

Buck, Paul H. 1937. *The Road to Reunion*. Boston: Little, Brown.

Bullock, Henry Allen. 1967. *A History of Negro Education in the South*. Cambridge: Harvard University Press.

———. 1970. "Education: Parallel Inequality." In Allen Weinstein and Frank Otto Gatell, eds., *The Segregation Era, 1863–1954*. New York: Oxford University Press, 262–79.

———. 1971. "Urbanism and race relations." In Rupert B. Vance and Nicholas J. Demerath, eds., *The Urban South*. Freeport, N.Y.: Books for Libraries Press, 207–29.

Burgess, M. Elaine. 1965. "Race Relations and Social Change." In John C. McKinney and Edgar T. Thompson, eds., *The South in Continuity and Change*. Durham, N.C.: Duke University Press, 337–58.

Burstein, Paul. 1978. "Public Opinion, Demonstrations, Media Coverage, and the Passage of Anti-discrimination Legislation." Unpublished paper. Yale University: Department of Sociology.

Button, James W. 1978. *Black Violence*. Princeton, N.J.: Princeton University Press.

Cameron, David R. 1974. "Toward a Theory of Political Mobilization." *Journal of Politics* 36 (February): 133–71.

Cantril, Hadley. 1965. *The Pattern of Human Concerns*. New Brunswick, N.J.: Rutgers University Press.

Caplan, Nathan S., and Jeffery M. Paige. 1968. "A Study of Ghetto Rioters." *Scientific American* 219 (August): 15–21

Carson, Clayborne, 1981. *In Struggle*. Cambridge: Harvard University Press.

Chalmers, David M. 1965. *Hooded Americanism*. Garden City, N.Y.: Doubleday.

Clark, Kenneth B. 1970. "The Civil Rights Movement: Momentum and Organization." In Richard P. Young, ed., *Roots of Rebellion*. New York: Harper and Row, 270–97.

Clayton, Edward, ed. 1964. *The SCLC Story*. Atlanta, Ga.: The Southern Christian Leadership Conference.

Cleghorn, Reese. 1963. "The Angels Are White." *The New Republic* (August): 12–14.

Clift, Virgil A. 1966. "Educating the American Negro." In John P. Davis, ed., *The American Negro Reference Book*. Englewood Cliffs, N.J.: Prentice-Hall, 360–95.

Cohn, Jules. 1970. "Is Business Meeting the Challenge of Urban Affairs?" *Fortune* 48 (March–April): 68–82.

Coleman, James Smoot. 1954. "Nationalism in Tropical Africa." *American Political Science Review* 48 (no. 2).

Collins, Charles Wallace. 1912. *The Fourteenth Amendment and the States*. Boston: Little, Brown.

Converse, Philip E., Jean D. Dotson, Wendy J. Hoag, and William H. McGee III. 1980. *American Social Attitudes Data Sourcebook, 1947–1978*. Cambridge: Harvard University Press.

Converse, Philip E., Warren E. Miller, Jerrold G. Rusk, Arthur C. Wolfe. 1969. "Continuity and Change in American Politics: Parties and Issues in the 1968 Election." *American Political Science Review* 63 (December): 1083–1105.

Crain, Robert, et al. 1969. *The Politics of Community Conflict*. New York: Bobbs-Merrill.

Currie, Elliott, and Jerome Skolnick. 1970. "A Critical Note on Conceptions of Collective Behavior." *Annals of the American Academy of Political and Social Science* 391 (September): 34–45.

Curtis, Russell L., and Louis A. Zurcher, Jr. 1973. "Stable Resources of Protest Movement: The Multi-organizational Field." *Social Forces* 52 (no. 1): 53–60.

Dahl, Robert A. 1967. *Pluralist Democracy in the United States*. Chicago: Rand McNally.

Dalfiume, Richard M. 1970. "Stirrings of Revolt." In Allen Weinstein and Frank Otto Gatell, eds., *The Segregation Era, 1863–1954*. New York: Oxford University Press, 235–47.

Danzger, M. Herbert. 1975. "Validating Conflict Data." *American Sociological Review* 40 (no. 5): 570–84.

Davies, James C. 1969. "The J-curve of Rising and Declining Satisfactions as a Cause of Some Great Revolutions and a Contained Rebellion." In Hugh Davis Graham and Ted Robert Gurr, eds., *Violence in America: Historical and Comparative Perspectives*. Washington, D.C.: U.S. Government Printing Office.

Davis, Allison, and John Dollard. 1940. *Children of Bondage*. Washington, D.C.: American Council on Education.

Dillingham, Harry C., and David F. Sly. 1966. "The Mechanical Cotton-picker, Negro Migration, and the Integration Movement." *Human Organization* 25 (no. 4): 344–51.

Dollard, John. 1957. *Caste and Class in a Southern Town*. Garden City, New York: Doubleday Anchor.

Domhoff, G. William. 1970. *The Higher Circles*. New York: Random House.

Donovan, John C. 1973. *The Politics of Poverty*. Indianapolis: Bobbs-Merrill.

Downes, Bryan T. 1970. "A Critical Reexamination of Social and Political Characteristics of Riot Cities." *Social Science Quarterly* 51 (no. 2): 349–60.

Drake, St. Claire, and Horace Cayton. 1963. *Black Metropolis*. New York: Harper Torchbook.

Du Bois, W. E. B. 1940. *Dusk of Dawn*. New York: Harcourt Brace.

Durkheim, Emile. 1965. *The Elementary Forms of Religious Life*. New York: The Free Press.

Edelman, Murray. 1971. *Politics as Symbolic Action*. Chicago: Markham.

Eisenstadt, S. N. 1965. *Essays on Comparative Institutions*. New York: John Wiley and Sons.

Eisinger, Peter K. 1973. "The Conditions of Protest Behavior in American Cities." *American Political Science Review* 67 (March): 11–28.

Erskine, Hazel. 1969. "The Polls: Negro Philosophies of Life." *Public Opinion Quarterly* 33 (no. 1): 147–58.

Eschen, Donald Von, Jerome Kirk, and Maurice Pinard. 1971. "The Organizational Substructure of Disorderly Politics." *Social Forces* 49 (no. 4): 529–44.

Esman, Milton J., and Hans C. Blaise. 1966. "Institution Building Research: The Guiding Concepts." Pittsburgh: University of Pittsburgh, Graduate School of Public and International Affairs.

Essien-Udom, E. U. 1962. *Black Nationalism: The Search for an Identity in America*. Chicago: University of Chicago Press.

Farley, Reynolds. 1968. "The Urbanization of Negroes in the United States." *Journal of Social History* 1 (no. 3): 241–58.

Farmer, James. 1965. *Freedom—When?* New York: Random House.

Feagin, Joe R., and Harlan Hahn. 1973. *Ghetto Revolts, The Politics of Violence in American Cities*. New York: MacMillan.

Ferree, Myra Marx, and Frederick D. Miller. 1977. "Winning Hearts and Minds: Some Social Psychological Contributions to the Resource Mobilization Perspective of Social Movements." Unpublished paper.

Fishel, Leslie H., Jr., and Benjamin Quarles. 1970. "In the New Deal's Wake." In Allen Weinstein and Frank F. Otto Gatell, eds., *The Segregation Era, 1863–1954*. New York: Oxford University Press, 218–32.

Fishman, Jacob R., and Frederic Solomon. 1970. "Youth and Social Action: Perspectives on the Student Sit-in Movement." In Ronald P. Young, ed., *Roots of Rebellion*. New York: Harper and Row.

Flacks, Richard W. 1967. "The Liberated Generation: An Exploration of the Roots of Student Protest." *Journal of Social Issues* 23 (July): 52–75.

Fligstein, Neil. 1980. "The Transformation of Southern Agriculture and the Migration of Blacks and Whites, 1930–50." Paper presented at the annual meetings of the American Sociological Association. New York City, August, 1980.

Fogelson, Robert M. 1971. *Violence as Protest*. Garden City, N.Y.: Doubleday.

Fogelson, Robert, and Robert Hill. 1968. "Who Riots? A Study of Participation in the 1967 Riots." In *Supplemental Studies for the National Advisory Commission on Civil Disorders*. Washington, D.C.: U.S. Government Printing Office.

Foner, Philip S. 1970. *The Black Panthers Speak*. Philadelphia-New York: J. B. Lippincott.

Franklin, John Hope. 1957. " 'Legal' Disfranchisement of the Negro." *Journal of Negro Education* 26: 241–48.

——. 1967. *From Slavery to Freedom*. 3d ed. New York: Knopf.

Frazier, E. Franklin. 1957. *Black Bourgeoisie*. New York: The Free Press.

——. 1974. *The Negro Church in America*. New York: Schocken Books.

Freeman, Jo. 1973. "The Origins of the Women's Liberation Movement." *American Journal of Sociology* 78 (no. 4): 792–811.

——. 1977a. "Crisis and Conflicts of Social Movement Organizations." Unpublished paper.

——. 1977b. "Networks and Strategy in the Women's Liberation Movement." Paper presented at a Frontiers of Sociology symposium held at Vanderbilt University, March 17–18, 1977.

Freidel, Frank. 1965. *F. D. R. and the South*. Baton Rouge: Louisiana State University Press.

Gallup, George H. 1972. *The Gallup Poll: Public Opinion, 1935–1971*. Vol. 3. New York: Random House.

Gamson, William A. 1966. "Rancorous Conflict in Community Politics." *American Sociological Review* 31: 71–81.

——. 1968. "Stable Unrepresentation in American Society." *American Behavioral Scientist* 12: 15–21.

——. 1975. *The Strategy of Social Protest*. Homewood, Ill.: The Dorsey Press.

Garfinkel, Herbert. 1959. *When Negroes March*. Glencoe, Ill.: The Free Press.

Garrow, David J. 1978. *Protest at Selma*. New Haven, Conn.: Yale University Press.

Gerber, Irwin. 1962. "The Effects of the Supreme Court's Desegregation Decision on the Group Cohesion of New York City's Negroes." *Journal of Social Psychology* 58 (December): 295–303.

Gerlach, Luther P., and Virginia H. Hine. 1970. *People, Power, Change: Movements of Social Transformation*. Indianapolis and New York: Bobbs-Merrill.

Gerth, Hans H., and C. Wright Mills. 1946. *From Max Weber: Essays in Sociology*. New York: Oxford University Press.

Geschwender, James A. 1964. "Social Structure and the Negro Revolt: An Examination of Some Hypotheses." *Social Forces* 43: 250–56.

———. 1967. "Continuities in Theories of Status Consistency and Cognitive Dissonance." *Social Forces* 46 (December): 165–67.

———. 1971a. "Civil Rights Protest and Riots: A Disappearing Distinction." In James A. Geschwender, ed., *The Black Revolt*. Englewood Cliffs, N.J.: Prentice-Hall, 300–311.

———. 1971b. "Explorations in the Theory of Social Movements and Revolutions." In James A. Geschwender, ed., *The Black Revolt*. Englewood Cliffs, N.J.: Prentice-Hall, 6–17.

———. 1971c. "Social Structure and the Negro Revolt: An Examination of Some Hypotheses." In James A. Geschwender, ed., *The Black Revolt*. Englewood Cliffs, N.J.: Prentice-Hall, 33–43.

Gillespie, David P. 1980. "Conservative Tactics in Social Movement Organizations." Paper presented at the annual meetings of the American Sociological Association, New York City, August, 1980.

Glantz, Oscar. 1960. "The Negro Voter in Northern Industrial Cities." *Western Political Quarterly* 13 (December): 999–1010.

Goldman, Peter. 1970. *Report from Black America*. New York: Simon and Schuster.

Goldstein, Robert. 1978. *Political Repression in Modern America*. Cambridge, Mass.: Schenkman Publishing.

Gouldner, Alvin W. 1960. "The Norm of Reciprocity: A Preliminary Statement." *American Sociological Review* 25 (no. 2): 161–78.

Gurr, Ted R. 1972. "The Calculus of Civil Conflict." *Journal of Social Issues* 28 (no. 1): 27–47.

———. 1973. "Psychological Factors in Civil Violence." In Ronald Ye-Lin Cheng, ed., *The Sociology of Revolution*. Chicago: Henry Regnery, 280–313.

Gusfield, Joseph R. 1970. *Protest, Reform, and Revolt*. New York: John Wiley and Sons.

Guzman, Jessie P., ed. 1952. *1952 Negro Yearbook*. New York: William H. Wise.

Handler, Joel F. 1978. *Social Movements and the Legal System*. New York: Academic Press.

Heath, G. Louis, ed. 1976. *Off the Pigs! The History and Literature of the Black Panther Party*. Metuchen, N.J.: The Scarecrow Press.

Helfgot, Joseph. 1974. "Professional Reform Organizations and the Symbolic Representation of the Poor." *American Sociological Review* 39 (no. 4): 475–91.

Helmreich, William B. 1973. *The Black Crusaders: A Case Study of a Black Militant Organization.* New York: Harper and Row.

Henri, Florette. 1975. *Black Migration.* Garden City, N.Y.: Doubleday Anchor.

Hicks, John D. 1961. *The Populist Revolt.* Lincoln, Nebr.: University of Nebraska Press.

Higgs, Robert. 1977. *Competition and Coercion.* Cambridge: Cambridge University Press.

Hirshson, Stanley. 1962. *Farewell to the Bloody Shirt.* Bloomington: Indiana University Press.

Hoffer, Eric. 1951. *The True Believer: Thoughts on the Nature of Mass Movements.* New York: Mentor Books, The New American Library.

Holmes, Dwight. 1969. *The Evolution of the Negro College.* New York: Arno Press and the New York Times.

Holt, Lee. 1965. *The Summer That Didn't End.* New York: William Morrow.

Holt, Rackham. 1964. *Mary McLeod Bethune.* Garden City, N.Y.: Doubleday.

Howard, John R. 1974. *The Cutting Edge. Social Movements and Social Change in America.* Philadelphia: J. B. Lippincott.

Hoyt, Edwin. 1967. *Paul Robeson: The American Othello.* Cleveland: World.

Hubbard, Howard. 1968. "Five Long Hot Summers and How They Grew." *Public Interest*, no. 12 (Summer): 3–24.

Hughes, Langston. 1962. *Fight for Freedom, The Story of the NAACP.* New York: W. W. Norton.

Jackson, Maurice, Eleanora Petersen, James Bull, Sverre Monsen, and Patricia Richmond. 1960. "The Failure of an Incipient Social Movement." *Pacific Sociological Review* 3 (no. 1): 35–40.

Jacobs, Paul, and Saul Landau. 1966. *The New Radicals.* New York: Vintage Books.

Jenkins, Joseph Craig. 1975. "Farm Workers and the Powers: Insurgency and Political Conflict (1946–1972)." Ph.D. diss., State University of New York at Stony Brook.

———. 1981. "Sociopolitical Movements." In Samuel Long, ed., *Handbook of Political Science.* Plenum Press, 81–153.

Jenkins, Joseph Craig, and Charles Perrow. 1977. "Insurgency of the Powerless: Farm Worker Movements (1946–1972)." *American Sociological Review* 42 (no. 2): 249–68.

Johnson, Charles S. 1930. *The Negro in American Civilization.* New York: Henry Holt.

———. 1941. *Growing Up in the Black Belt.* Washington, D.C.: American Council on Education.

Johnston, Ruby F. 1954. *The Development of Negro Religion.* New York: Philosophical Library.

———. 1956. *The Religion of Negro Protestants.* New York: Philosophical Library.

Katz, Irwin, and Patricia Gurin, eds. 1969. *Race and the Social Sciences.* New York: Basic Books.

Kellogg, Charles Flint. 1967. *NAACP: A History of the National Association for the Advancement of Colored People*, vol 1, *1909–1920.* Baltimore: John Hopkins Press.

Keniston, Kenneth. 1968. *Young Radicals*. New York: Harcourt, Brace and World.

Killian, Lewis M. 1975. *The Impossible Revolution, Phase II: Black Power and the American Dream*. New York: Random House.

Killian, Lewis M., and Charles Grigg. 1964. *Racial Crisis in America: Leadership in Conflict*. Englewood Cliffs, N.J.: Prentice-Hall.

Killingsworth, Charles C. 1969. "Jobs and Income for Negroes." In Irwin Katz and Patricia Gurin, eds., *Race and the Social Sciences*. New York: Basic Books, 194–273.

King, Martin Luther, Jr. 1958. *Stride Toward Freedom, The Montgomery Story*. New York: Harper and Brothers.

———. 1963. *Why We Can't Wait*. New York: Harper and Row.

Kornhauser, William. 1959. *The Politics of Mass Society*. Glencoe, Ill.: The Free Press.

Kriesberg, Louis. 1973. *The Sociology of Social Conflicts*. Englewood Cliffs, N.J.: Prentice-Hall.

Lane, Robert E. 1959. *Political Life: Why People Get Involved in Politics*. Glencoe, Ill.: The Free Press.

———. 1962. Political Ideology. New York: The Free Press.

Lang, Kurt, and Gladys Lang. 1961. *Collective Dynamics*. New York: Crowell.

Laue, James H. 1965. "The Changing Character of Negro Protest." *Annals of the American Academy of Political and Social Science* 357: 119–26.

———. 1971. "A Model for Civil Rights Change through Conflict." In Gary T. Marx, ed., *Racial Conflict*. Boston: Little, Brown, 256–62.

Lawson, Steven F. 1976. Black Ballots: Voting Rights in the South, 1944–1969. New York: Columbia University Press.

Le Bon, Gustave. 1960. *The Crowd: A Study of the Popular Mind*. New York: Compass Books, The Viking Press.

Lee, Everetts, Ann Ratner Miller, Carol P. Brainerd, and Richard A. Easterlin. 1957. *Population Redistribution and Economic Growth in the United States, 1870–1950*. Vol. 1, *Methodological Considerations and Reference Tables*. Philadelphia: American Philosophical Society.

Leites, Nathan, and Charles Wolf, Jr. 1970. *Rebellion and Authority*. Chicago: Markham.

Lenski, Gerhard. 1954. "Status Crystallization: A Non-vertical Dimension of Social Status." *American Sociological Review 19* (August): 405–13.

Leslie, Gerald R., Richard F. Larson, and Benjamin L. Gorman. 1980. *Introductory Sociology*. 3d ed. New York: Oxford University Press.

Levine, Sal, and Paul E. White. 1961. "Exchange as a Conceptual Framework for the Study of Interorganizational Relationships." *Administrative Science Quarterly* 5 (March): 555–601.

Lewinson, Paul. 1932. *Race, Class, and Party: A History of Negro Suffrage and White Politics in the South*. London: Oxford University Press.

Lewis, Hylan. 1954. "Innovations and Trends in the Contemporary Southern Negro Community." *Journal of Social Issues* 10 (January): 19–27.

Lewis, Michael. 1970. "The Negro Protest in Urban America." In Joseph R. Gusfield, ed., *Protest, Reform, and Revolt*. New York: John Wiley and Sons, 149–90.

Lionberger, H. F. 1960. *Adoption of New Ideas and Practices*. Ames: The Iowa State University Press.

Lipset, Seymour M. 1950. *Agrarian Socialism: The Cooperative Commonwealth Federation in Saskatchewan*. Berkeley: University of California Press.

Lipset, Seymour M., and Sheldon Wolin. 1965. *The Berkeley Student Revolt*. New York: Doubleday Anchor.

Lipsky, Michael. 1970. *Protest in City Politics*. Chicago: Rand McNally.

———. 1971. "Case Study of a Harlem Rent Strike." In Gary T. Marx, ed., *Racial Conflict*. Boston: Little, Brown, 326–35.

Lomax, Louis E. 1962. *The Negro Revolt*. New York: Harper and Row.

Lowi, Theodore J. 1971. *The Politics of Disorder*. New York: Basic Books.

Lubell, Samuel. 1964. *White and Black, Test of a Nation*. New York: Harper and Row.

McCarthy, John D., and Mayer N. Zald. 1973. *The Trend of Social Movements in America: Professionalization and Resource Mobilization*. Morristown, N.J.: General Learning Press.

———. 1977. "Resource Mobilization and Social Movements: A Partial Theory." *American Journal of Sociology* 82 (no. 6): 1212–41.

McConnell, Grant. 1966. *Private Power and American Democracy*. New York: Alfred A. Knopf.

McCormack, Thelma H. 1957. "The Motivation of Radicals." In R. H. Turner and L. M. Killian, eds., *Collective Behavior*. Englewood Cliffs, N.J.: Prentice-Hall, 433–40.

McMillen, Neil R. 1971. *The Citizens' Council, Organized Resistance to the Second Reconstruction, 1954–1964*. Urbana: University of Illinois Press.

Major, Reginald. 1971. *A Panther is a Black Cat*. New York: William Morrow.

Marx, Gary T. 1967. *Protest and Prejudice*. New York: Harper and Row.

———. 1971. "Religion: Opiate or Inspiration of Civil Rights Militancy among Negroes?" In Gary T. Marx, ed., *Racial Conflict*. Boston: Little, Brown, 161–71.

———. 1974. "Thoughts on a Neglected Category of Social Movement Participant: The Agent Provocateur and the Informant." *American Journal of Sociology* 80 (no. 2): 402–42.

———. 1976. "External Efforts to Damage or Facilitate Social Movements: Some Patterns, Explanations, Outcomes, and Complications." Paper prepared for Conference on The Dynamics of Social Movements: Resource Mobilization, Tactics, and Social Control. Vanderbilt University, March 1976.

Marx, Gary T., ed. 1971. *Racial Conflict*. Boston: Little, Brown.

Masotti, L., and J. Corsi. 1969. *Shootout in Cleveland*. Washington, D.C.: Government Printing Office.

Matthews, Donald R., and James W. Prothro. 1966. *Negroes and the New Southern Politics*. New York: Harcourt, Brace and World.

Mays, Benjamin, and Joseph W. Nicholson. 1969. *The Negro's Church*. New York: Arno Press and the New York Times.

Meier, August. 1956. "The Negro and the Democratic Party, 1875–1915." *Phylon* 17 (no. 2): 173–91.

———. 1961. "The Successful Sit-ins in a Border City: A Study in Social Causation." *Journal of Intergroup Relations* 2: 230–37.

———. 1971. "Negro Protest Movements and Organizations." In John H. Bracey, Jr., August Meier, and Elliott Rudwick, eds., *Conflict and Competition: Studies in the Recent Black Protest Movement*. Belmont, Calif.: Wadsworth, 20–33.

Meier, August, and Elliott Rudwick. 1973. *CORE, A Study in the Civil Rights Movement, 1942–1968*. New York: Oxford University Press.

Michels, Robert. 1959. *Political Parties*. New York: Dover Publications.

Miller, Loren. 1966. *The Petitioners—The Story of the Supreme Court of the United States and the Negro*. New York: Pantheon Books.

Mills, C. Wright. 1959. *The Power Elite*. New York: Oxford University Press.

Melder, Keith Eugene. 1964. "The Beginnings of the Woman's Rights Movement in the United States." Ph.D. diss., New Haven, Conn.: Yale Unversity.

Molotch, Harvey L., and Marilyn Lester. 1974. "News as Purposive Behavior: On the Strategic Use of Routine Events, Accidents and Scandals." *American Sociological Review* 38 (no. 1): 101–12.

Moore, Barrington, Jr. 1966. *Social Origins of Dictatorship and Democracy*. Boston: Beacon Press.

Morris, Aldon Douglas. 1979. "The Rise of the Civil Rights Movement and Its Movement Black Power Structure, 1953–1963." Ph.D. diss., State University of New York at Stony Brook.

Motley, Constance Baker. 1966. "The Legal Status of the Negro in the United States." In John P. Davis, ed., *The American Negro Reference Book*. Englewood Cliffs, N.J.: Prentice-Hall, 484–521.

Mueller, Carol McClurg. 1978. "The Problematic Outcomes of Elite-sponsored Movements." Unpublished paper.

Murray, Florence, ed. 1942. *The Negro Handbook*. New York: Wendell Malliet.

———. 1947. *The Negro Handbook, 1946–1947*. New York: Current Books, A. A. Wyn, Publisher.

Muse, Benjamin. 1964. Ten Years of Prelude: The Story of Integration Since the Supreme Court's 1954 Decision. New York: Viking Press.

———. 1968. *The American Negro Revolution*. Bloomington: Indiana University Press.

Myrdal, Gunner. 1944. *An American Dilemma*. New York: Harper and Row.

———. 1970. "America Again at the Crossroads." In Richard P. Young, ed., *Roots of Rebellion: The Evolution of Black Politics and Protest Since World War II*. New York: Harper and Row, 13–46.

Neal, Arthur G., and Melvin Seeman. 1964. "Organizations and Powerlessness: A Test of the Mediation Hypothesis." *American Sociological Review* 29 (no. 2): 216–26.

Neisser, W. 1967. *Cognitive Psychology*. New York: Appleton-Century-Crofts.

Nelsen, Hart M., and Anne Kusener Nelsen. 1975. *Black Church in the Sixties*. Lexington, Ky.: The University Press of Kentucky.

Oberschall, Anthony. 1971. "The Los Angeles Riot of August 1965." In James A. Geschwender, ed., *The Black Revolt*. Englewood Cliffs, N.J.: Prentice-Hall, 264–84.

———. 1973. *Social Conflict and Social Movements*. Englewood Cliffs, N.J.: Prentice-Hall.

———. 1978. "The Decline of the 1960's Social Movements." In Louis Kriesberg, ed., *Research in Social Movements, Conflicts, and Change*. Greenwich, Conn.: JAI Press.

Olson, Mancur, Jr. 1965. *The Logic of Collective Action*. Cambridge, Mass.: Harvard University Press.

Oppenheimer, Martin. 1963. "The Genesis of the Southern Negro Student Movement (Sit-In Movement): A Study in Contemporary Negro Protest." Ph.D. diss., University of Pennsylvania.

Orbell, John M. 1971. "Protest Participation among Southern Negro College Students." In James A. Geschwender, ed., *The Black Revolt*. Englewood Cliffs, N. J.: Prentice-Hall, 158–71.

Orum, Anthony M. 1966. "A Reappraisal of the Social and Political Participation of Negroes." *American Journal of Sociology* 72: (no. 1): 32–46.

———. 1972. *Black Students in Protest*. Washington, D.C.: American Sociological Association.

Parker, Thomas F., ed. 1974. *Violence in the U.S.*, Vol. 1, *1956–1967*. New York: Facts on File.

Payne, Raymond. 1953. "Organizational Activities of Rural Negroes in Mississippi." Mississippi State College Agricultural Experiment Station Circular no. 192, Starkville, Mississippi.

Peck, James. 1962. *Freedom Ride*. New York: Simon and Schuster.

Peck, James, ed. 1960. *Sit-ins: The Students Report*. New York: Congress of Racial Equality.

Perrow, Charles. 1968. "Members as Resources in Voluntary Organizations." Paper prepared for Symposium on Clients and Organizations. University of Rhode Island, June 27, 1968.

———. 1979. "The Sixties Observed." In Mayer N. Zald and John McCarthy, eds., *The Dynamics of Social Movements: Resource Mobilization, Social Control, and Tactics*. Cambridge, Mass.: Winthrop Publishers.

Pettigrew, Thomas F. 1964. *A Profile of the Negro American*. Princeton, N.J.: D. Van Nostrand.

Pinard, Maurice. 1971. *The Rise of a Third Party: A Study in Crisis Politics*. Englewood Cliffs, N.J.: Prentice-Hall.

Pinard, Maurice, Jerome Kirk, and Donald Von Eschen. 1971. "Process of Recruitment in the Sit-in Movement." In James A. Geschwender, ed., *The Black Revolt*. Englewood Cliffs, N.J.: Prentice-Hall, 184–97.

Piven, Frances Fox, and Richard A. Cloward. 1979. *Poor People's Movements*. New York: Vintage Books.

Ploski, Harry A., and Warren Marr II, eds. 1976. *The Afro American*. New York: The Bellwether Company.

Popenoe, David. 1980. *Sociology*. 4th ed. Englewood Cliffs, N.J.: Prentice-Hall.

Prewitt, Kenneth, and Alan Stone. 1973. *The Ruling Elites*. New York: Harper and Row.

Price, Daniel O. 1969. *Changing Characteristics of the Negro Population*. Washington, D.C.: U.S. Government Printing Office.

Proudfoot, Merrill. 1962. *Diary of a Sit-in*. New Haven, Conn.: College and University Press Publishers.

Quint, Howard H. 1958. *Profile in Black and White, A Frank Portrait of South Carolina*. Washington, D.C.: Public Affairs Press.

Raper, Howard H. 1969. *The Tragedy of Lynching*. New York: Arno Press and the New York Times.

Record, Jane Cassels, and Wilson Record. 1965. "Ideological Forces and the Negro Protest." *Annals of the American Academy of Political and Social Science* 357: 89–96.

Richardson, Harry V. 1947. *Dark Glory: A Picture of the Church among Negroes in the Rural South*. New York: Friendship Press.

Rogers, Everett M. 1962. *Diffusion of Innovations*. New York: The Free Press.

Rogers, Ray. 1971. "Intraminority Violence: US and the Panthers at UCLA." In Gary T. Marx, ed., *Racial Conflict*. Boston: Little, Brown, 387–90.

Rogin, Michael Paul. 1967. *The Intellectuals and McCarthy*. Cambridge, Mass.: M.I.T. Press.

Ross, J. Michael, Reeve D. Vanneman, and Thomas F. Pettigrew. 1976. "Patterns of Support for George Wallace: Implications for Racial Change." *Journal of Social Issues* 36 (no. 2): 69–91.

Rule, James, and Charles Tilly, eds. 1975. "Political Process in Revolutionary France: 1830–1832." In John M. Merriman, ed., *1830 in France*. New York: New Viewpoints, 41–85.

Rustin, Bayard. 1965. "From Protest to Politics: The Future of the Civil Rights Movement." *Commentary* 39 (no. 2): 25–31.

St. James, Warren D. 1958. *The National Association for the Advancement of Colored People: A Case Study in Pressure Groups*. New York: Exposition Press.

Sayre, Cynthia Woolever. 1980. "The Impact of Voluntary Association Involvement on Social-Psychological Attitudes." Paper presented at the Annual Meeting of the American Sociological Association, August 27–31, 1980, in New York City.

Scaff, Alvin H. 1952. "The Effect of Commuting on Participation in Voluntary Associations." *American Sociological Review* 17: 215–20.

Schattschneider, E. E. 1960. *The Semisovereign People*. Hinsdale, Ill.: The Dryden Press.

Schwartz, Michael. 1976. *Radical Protest and Social Structure*. New York: Academic Press.

Schwartz, Sandra Kenyon, and David C. Schwartz. 1976. "Convergence and Divergence in Political Orientations between Blacks and Whites: 1960–1973." *Journal of Social Issues* 32 (no. 2): 153–68.

Searles, Ruth, and J. Allen Williams, Jr. 1962. "College Students' Participation in Sit-ins." *Social Forces* 40: 215–20.

Seligmann, Herbert J. 1969. *The Negro Faces America*. New York: Harper and Row; first published in 1920.

Selznick, Phillip. 1960. *The Organizational Weapon*. New York: The Free Press.
————. 1970. "Institutional Vulnerability in Mass Society." In Joseph R. Gusfield, ed., *Protest, Reform, and Revolt*. New York: John Wiley and Sons, 258–74.
Shorter, Edward, and Charles Tilly. 1974. *Strikes in France, 1830–1968*. London: Cambridge University Press.
Simpson, Richard L., and David R. Norsworthy. 1965. "The Changing Occupational Structure of the South." In John C. McKinney and Edgar T. Thompson, eds., *The South in Continuity and Change*. Durham, N.C.: Duke University Press, 198–224.
Sitkoff, Harvard. 1978. *A New Deal for Blacks*. New York: Oxford University Press.
Skolnick, Jerome H. 1969. *The Politics of Protest*. New York: Simon and Schuster.
Smelser, Neil J. 1959. *Social Change in the Industrial Revolution*. Chicago: University of Chicago Press.
————. 1962. *Theory of Collective Behavior*. New York: The Free Press.
————. 1973. "Social and Psychological Dimensions of Collective Behavior." In Ronald Ye-Lin Cheng, ed., *The Sociology of Revolution*. Chicago: Henry Regnery, 314–18.
Smith, Charles V. 1961. "The Sit-ins and the New Negro Student." *Journal of Intergroup Relations* 2: 223–29.
Smith, Charles V., and Lewis M. Killian. 1958. *The Tallahassee Bus Protest*. New York: Anti-Defamation League of B'nai B'rith.
Smith, Tom W. 1980. "America's Most Important Problem—A Trend Analysis, 1946–1976." *Public Opinion Quarterly* 44 (no. 2): 164–80.
Snyder, David, and Charles Tilly. 1972. "Hardship and Collective Violence in France, 1830 to 1960." *American Sociological Review* 37 (October): 520–32.
Spengler, Joseph J. 1963. "Demographic and Economic Change in the South." In Allan P. Sindler, ed., *Change in the Contemporary South*. Durham, N.C.: Duke University Press, 26–63.
Storer, Norman W. 1980. *Focus on Society*. 2d ed. Reading, Mass.: Addison-Wesley.
Sugarmon, Russell, Jr. 1964. "Breaking the Color Line in Memphis, Tennessee." In Alan F. Westin, ed., *Freedom Now! The Civil Rights Struggle in America*. New York: Basic Books, 164–68.
Thompson, Charles H. 1960. "The Present Status of the Negro Private and Church-related College." *Journal of Negro Education* 29 (no. 3): 227–43.
Thompson, Lorin A. 1971. "Urbanization, Occupational Shift and Economic Progress." In Rupert B. Vance and Nicholas J. Demerath, eds., *The Urban South*. Freeport, N.Y.: Books for Libraries Press, 38–53.
Tilly, Charles. 1978. *From Mobilization to Revolution*. Reading, Mass.: Addison-Wesley.
Tilly, Charles, Louise Tilly, and Richard Tilly. 1975. *The Rebellious Century, 1830–1930*. Cambridge, Mass.: Harvard University Press.
Traugott, Mark. 1978. "Reconceiving Social Movements." *Social Problems* 26 (no. 1): 38–49.

Trent, William J., Jr. 1959. "Private Negro Colleges since the Gaines Decision." *Journal of Educational Sociology* 32 (February): 267–74.

———. 1960. "The Relative Adequacy of Sources of Income of Negro Church-related Schools." *Journal of Negro Education* 29 (no. 3): 356–67.

Tuchman, Gaye. 1973. "Making News by Doing Work: Routinizing the Unexpected." *American Journal of Sociology* 79: 110–31.

Tucker, David M. 1975. *Black Pastors and Leaders, Memphis, 1819–1972*. Memphis: Memphis University Press.

Turner, Ralph H., and Lewis Killian. 1957. *Collective Behavior*. Englewood Cliffs, N.J.: Prentice-Hall.

Von Eschen, Donald, Jerome Kirk, and Maurice Pinard. 1969. "The Disintegration of the Negro Non-violent Movement." *Journal of Peace Research* 3: 216–34.

———. 1971. "The Organizational Substructure of Disorderly Politics." *Social Forces* 49 (no. 4): 529–44.

Waite, E. F. 1946. "The Negro in the Supreme Court." *Minnesota Law Review* 30 (no. 4): 219–304.

Wakefield, Dan. 1960. *Revolt in the South*. New York: Grove Press.

Walker, Jack L. 1971. "The Functions of Disunity: Negro Leadership in a Southern City." In Gary T. Marx, ed., *Racial Conflict*. Boston: Little, Brown, 379–87.

Walton, Norman W. 1956. "The Walking City, a History of the Montgomery Boycott." *Negro History Bulletin* 20 (October–November): 17–20.

Washington, Joseph R., Jr. 1964. *Black Religion, The Negro and Christianity in the United States*. Boston: Beacon Press.

Watters, Pat. 1971. *Down to Now: Reflections on the Southern Civil Rights Movement*. New York: Pantheon Books.

Webb, Horace S. 1969. "Police Preparedness for Control of Civil Disorders." *Municipal Yearbook, 1969*. Washington, D.C.: International City Management Association.

Weiss, Nancy J. 1970. "The Negro and the New Freedom." In Allen Weinstein and Frank Otto Gatell, eds., *The Segregation Era, 1863–1954*. New York: Oxford University Press, 129–42.

Williams, Robin M. 1971. "Social Change and Social Conflict: Race Relations in the United States, 1944–1964." In James A. Geschwender, ed., *The Black Revolt*. Englewood Cliffs, N.J.: Prentice-Hall, 24–33.

Wills, Gary. 1968. *The Second Civil War*. New York: The New American Library.

Wilson, Kenneth L., and Anthony M. Orum. 1976. "Mobilizing People for Collective Political Action." *Journal of Political and Military Sociology* 4 (Fall): 187–202.

Wilson, James Q. 1961. "The Strategy of Protest: Problems of Negro Civil Action." *Journal of Conflict Resolution* 5 (no. 3): 291–303.

———. 1965. "The Negro in Politics." In Talcott Parsons and Kenneth B. Clark, eds., *The Negro American*. Boston: Houghton Mifflin, 423–47.

———. 1966. "The Negro in American Politics: The Present." In John P. Davis, ed., *The American Negro Reference Book*. Englewood Cliffs, N.J.: Prentice-Hall, 431–57.

———. 1973. *Political Organizations*. New York: Basic Books.
Wilson, John. 1973. *Introduction to Social Movements*. New York: Basic Books.
Wilson, William J. 1973. *Power, Racism, and Privilege*. New York: The Free Press.
Wolfinger, Raymond, et al. 1964. "America's Radical Right." In David Apter, ed., *Ideology and Discontent*. Glencoe, Ill.: The Free Press, 267–75.
Wolters, Raymond. 1970. *Negroes and the Great Depression*. Westport, Conn.: Greenwood.
Woodward, C. Van. 1966. *The Strange Career of Jim Crow*. London: Oxford University Press.
Wright, Stephen J. 1960. "The Negro College in America." *Harvard Educational Review* 30 (Summer): 280–97.
Zald, Mayer N. 1969. "The Power and Function of Boards of Directors: A Theoretical Synthesis." *American Journal of Sociology* 75 (no. 1): 97–111.
Zald, Mayer N., and Roberta Ash. 1970. "Social Movement Organizations: Growth, Decay and Change." In Joseph R. Gusfield, ed., *Protest, Reform, and Revolt*. New York: John Wiley and Sons.
Zinn, Howard. 1962. *Albany, a Study in National Responsibility*. Atlanta: Southern Regional Council.
———. 1965. *SNCC, The New Abolitionists*. Boston: Beacon Press.

GOVERNMENT DOCUMENTS

Commission on CIA Activities within the United States. 1975. *Report to the President*. Washington, D.C.: Government Printing Office.
Governor's Commission on the Los Angeles Riots. 1965. *Violence in the City — An End or a Beginning?* Los Angeles: College Book Store.
U.S. Bureau of Labor Statistics. 1966. *The Negroes in the United States*. Bulletin no. 1511. Washington, D.C.: U.S. Government Printing Office.
U.S. Bureau of the Census. 1932. *Fifteenth Census of the U.S., 1930. Population*, vol. 3, pts 1 and 2. Washington, D.C.: U.S. Government Printing Office.
———. 1935. *Negroes in the United States, 1920–1932*. Washington, D.C.: U.S. Government Printing Office.
———. 1952. *Census of the Population, 1950*. Vol. 2. Washington, D.C.: U.S. Government Printing Office.
———. 1961. *U.S. Census of the Population, 1960. General Population Characteristics, U.S. Summary*. Final Report PC (1)-1B. Washington, D.C.: U.S. Government Printing Office.
———. 1962a. *U.S. Census of the Agriculture, 1959*. "Color, Race and Tenure of Farm Operator." Vol. 2, chapter 10. Washington, D.C.: U.S. Government Printing Office.
———. 1962b. *Current Population Reports*, Series P-25, no. 247 (April). Washington, D.C.: U.S. Government Printing Office.
———. 1963. *Historical Statistics of the United States, Colonial Times to 1957*. Series C 25–75. Washington, D.C.: U.S. Government Printing Office.

———. 1972–77. *Statistical Abstract of the United States, 1972–1977*. 93d–98th eds. Washington, D.C.: U.S. Government Printing Office.

———. 1975. *Historical Statistics of the United States, Colonial Times to 1970. Bicentennial Edition, Parts 1 and 2*. Washington, D.C.: U.S. Government Printing Office.

U.S. Commission on Civil Rights. 1977. *Reviewing a Decade of School Desegregation, 1966–1975*. Washington, D.C.: U.S. Government Printing Office.

U.S. National Advisory Commission on Civil Disorders. 1968. *Report of the National Advisory Commission on Civil Disorders*. New York: Bantam Books.

U.S. Congress, Senate Select Committee to Study Governmental Operations with Respect to Intelligence Activities. 1976. *Final Report*. Hearings, vols. 1–7. Washington, D.C.: Government Printing Office.

MISCELLANEOUS SOURCES

Keesing's Research Reports. 1970. *Race Relations in the USA, 1954–1968*. New York: Charles Scribner's Sons.

Lemberg Center for the Study of Violence. 1968. "April Aftermath of the King Assassination." *Riot Data Review*, no. 2 (August). Waltham, Mass.: Lemberg Center for the Study of Violence, Brandeis University.

National Association for the Advancement of Colored People. 1930–70. *Annual Report of the National Association for the Advancement of Colored People*. New York: NAACP.

———. 1930–70. *Crisis*. New York: NAACP.

Southern Regional Council. 1960. *Intimidation, Reprisal, and Violence in the South's Racial Crisis*. Atlanta, Ga.: Southern Regional Council.

———. 1961. *The Student Protest Movement: A Recapitulation*. Atlanta, Ga.: Southern Regional Council.

———. 1966. *The Continuing Crisis: An Assessment of New Racial Tensions in the South*. Atlanta, Ga.: Southern Regional Council.

The New York Times. 1948–70. *The New York Times Index*.

Time. 1936. "Black Game." August 17, 1936.

Index

Abeles, Ronald P., 14
Ad Hoc Committee, 189. *See also*
Congress of Racial Equality
Albany movement, 150,152, 269n,
271n
Alford, Robert R., 28, 170
Allen, Michael Patrick, 27
Allen, Robert L., 223–24
Almond, Gabriel, 201
Anderson-Sherman, Arnold, 261n
Anglin, Robert A., 104, 110, 266n
Anniston, Ala., 176. *See also* Freedom
rides
Antiwar movement, the, 262n
Arab-Israeli conflict, 197
Arendt, Hannah, 10, 261n
Ash, Roberta, 264n
Atlanta, Ga.: 1954 NAACP conference in,
136; bus boycott in, 138; 1960 sit-in in,
139; early NAACP chapter located in,
265n; SCLC founding conference held
in, 268n
Atwood, Rufus, 101
Aveni, Adrian F., 20, 27, 169, 263n
Aya, Rod, 11, 32–33

Bachrach, Peter, 20
Badger, Henry G., 101
Bagdikian, Ben H., 235
Baron, Harold M., 67, 75, 88
Beach, Stephen W., 264n, 268n
Beale, Calvin L., 95
Bell, Inge Powell, 207–8
Bennett, Lerone, Jr., 107
Berger, Morroe, 72, 84–86
Bergman, Peter M., 237
Bethune, Mary McLeod, 110
Big Four, the: dominance of movement by,
154–55, 183; competition between, 154,

187; financial support for, 169;
disintegration of, 183–84, 213; growing
divisions between, 184. *See also*
Congress of Racial Equality; National
Association for the Advancement of
Colored People; Southern Christian
Leadership Conference; Student
Nonviolent Coordinating Committee
Birmingham, Ala.: 1963 SCLC-sponsored
campaign in, 129, 166, 171, 178, 200,
212, 269n; bus boycott in, 138; as
strategic choice of protest site, 178
Black church, the: generation of the
movement and, 87, 98, 105, 122, 125–26,
128–30, 132–33, 134, 136–38, 139, 141;
organizational weaknesses of the rural,
90–92; social control and, 91–92;
comparison between rural and urban, 91,
98–100; increased involvement in social
action by, 98–100; improved
organizational strength of, 99–100, 125,
230; as institutional base for movement
recruitment, 128–30, 132; role in the
Montgomery bus boycott, 129, 132,
137–38, 269n; as source of established
leadership, 132–33, 150, 254–55, 258–59;
as institution least vulnerable to white
control, 135, 266n; as established
communication network, 136–38, 139; as
meeting place, 141, 150. *See also* King,
Martin Luther, Jr.; Black ministers;
Montgomery bus boycott; Montgomery
Improvement Association; Southern
Christian Leadership Conference
Black colleges: generation of the
movement and, 87, 105, 125, 126–27,
128, 129–30, 131–32, 133, 136, 138–39;
organizational weaknesses of the early,
92–93; urban basis of, 92; data on

Montgomery bus boycott: accounts of,
129, 269n; role of black church in, 129,
132, 137–38, 269n; as stimulus to other
boycotts, 137–38; supremacist
mobilization and, 143–44; and
revitalization of established movement
organizations, 148. *See also* Black
church, the; Jemison, Theodore; King,
Martin Luther, Jr.; Montgomery
Improvement Association
Montgomery Improvement Association,
137–38
Moore, Barrington, 66
Morris, Aldon Douglas, 15, 127, 270n
Motley, Constance Baker, 85
Movement decline: in the political process
model, 51–52, 56, 58, 63, 181; in the
resource mobilization model, 63, 181,
208; absence of material on, 181, 272n;
late 1960s as period of, 181–82; and
black movement, 181–229
Movement goals: reformatory and
revolutionary, 58; and response of elite
groups, 58, 164; early consensus on,
152–53, 156, 186–87, 209, 227;
integration as focus of, 152–53, 164, 186;
limiting opposition during civil rights
phase, 164, 167, 169, 209, 231; growing
dissensus over, 183–84, 186–88, 206,
227; during black-power phase, 193, 208,
210–11, 213–14, 216–17, 228, 231;
growing radicalization of, 206–7, 214,
231. *See also* Federal government;
Social control
Movement organizations, formal: general
importance of, 23; replacement of
indigenous groups by, 54, 56, 147, 149,
156, 182; in black movement, 147–49,
156, 167, 270n; dominance of civil rights
phase by, 147, 153–56, 182; cooperation
between, 156, 187–88; conflict between,
154, 167, 187–89; decline of, 182–86,
227. *See also* Congress of Racial
Equality; National Association for the
Advancement of Colored People;
Southern Christian Leadership
Conference; Student Nonviolent
Coordinating Committee
Movement participants: in the classical
model, 6, 9, 10, 12–13, 15, 18, 22, 62,
127; rationality of, 1, 6, 17, 20, 22, 37,

261n, 262n, 263n; integration of, 7, 9–10,
13, 15–16, 17, 44–45, 62, 127, 128–29,
130, 131, 132, 263–64n; individual
characteristics of, 7, 8, 9, 10, 12–13, 15,
19, 22, 44, 62, 127–28, 129, 130,
263–64n; structural location of, 15–16,
44–45, 62–63, 127–28, 129, 130, 131, 132;
in the resource mobilization model, 22,
31, 62; in the political process model,
44, 62–63, 127–28; recruitment of,
44–45, 47, 129; black students as, 127,
128, 131, 132–33, 135, 150, 255, 257–58;
church members and ministers as, 128,
129–30, 132–33, 135, 137–38, 150,
254–55, 258–59; NAACP members as,
123, 130, 132–33
Movement tactics: and movement success,
30, 37, 58, 164, 166, 174–76, 177–79,
180, 221–22, 233; and social control of
movement, 57–58, 164, 208, 216–17,
222–24, 228–29, 231; institutionalized
and noninstitutionalized, 57, 184, 231;
black movement keyed by innovations
in, 164–66, 221, 227; effective counters
to, 166, 227; dissensus within movement
over, 183–84, 227; consensus within
movement over, 187; growing
radicalization of, 207–8, 216, 221–22,
231. *See also* Social control
Multi-organizational fields, 45
Murray, Florence, 101, 266n
Muse, Benjamin, 142, 144, 157, 169, 172,
201, 210, 237, 271n
Myrdal, Gunner, 73, 83, 265n

National Association for the Advancement
of Colored People: specific actions of,
80, 133, 136, 265n, 269n, 273n; federal
response to, 84, 110–11, 114–15, 266n;
and generation of movement, 87, 105,
125–27, 128–29, 130, 132, 133, 135,
136–37, 139, 141; in the pre-Depression
era, 93–94; membership figures for, 94,
103; in the post-Depression era, 98,
103–5; causes of growth in, 104–5,
110–11, 115–16; and movement
recruitment, 128–29, 130, 132, 268n; as
source of leadership, 132–33, 135,
254–55; legalistic bent of, 133–34, 136,
138, 141, 184–85; school desegregation
and, 135, 136–37; as communication